COVID-19 Pandemic and Global Inequality

Rajib Bhattacharyya · Ramesh Chandra Das ·
Achintya Ray
Editors

COVID-19 Pandemic and Global Inequality

Reflections in Labour Market, Business and Social Sectors

Springer

Editors
Rajib Bhattacharyya
Goenka College of Commerce
and Business
Kolkata, India

Ramesh Chandra Das
Department of Economics
Vidyasagar University
Midnapore, India

Achintya Ray
Department of Economics
Tennessee State University
Nashville, TN, USA

ISBN 978-981-99-4404-0 ISBN 978-981-99-4405-7 (eBook)
https://doi.org/10.1007/978-981-99-4405-7

This Springer imprint is published by the registered company Springer Nature Singapore Pte Ltd.
The registered company address is: 152 Beach Road, #21-01/04 Gateway East, Singapore 189721, Singapore

Dedicated to the memories of all those who lost their lives in the COVID-19 pandemic

Foreword

Economic and Financial Costs of the COVID-19 Pandemic: A Brief Assessment

The COVID-19 pandemic has unleashed major upheavals in the global economy. The spread of COVID-19 (novel coronavirus disease 2019) directly impacted economic conditions via lockdown, social distancing mandates and ongoing disruptions for most businesses and can, therefore, lead to a considerable decline in consumer and business confidence. Ashraf [2] notes that the stock markets in sixty-four (64) countries experienced negative shocks during the first phase of the pandemic as the stringency of measures adversely impacted economic conditions. Even for a developed economy like the US economy, the lockdown inflicted severe blows to its economy. The US lockdown—after the 20 March 2020 and before 20 May 2020—constituted the non-pharmaceutical interventions (NPI) to limit the spread of the pandemic. The NPI resulted in a 30% reduction in COVID-19 deaths in the US [1]. Yet, the economic impact of the NPI has been enormous as Arnon et al. [1] argued that the NPI had swelled US unemployment by 15%. In terms of numbers, during the first 3 months of the pandemic in the US, NPI resulted in about 3 million US job losses. Globally, the adverse impact of NPI on the labour market could have been better managed if the government responses were better coordinated across nations. For the US alone, the pandemic, NPI (lockdown) and social distancing pushed the economy into a deep recession.

Furthermore, the pandemic created *infodemic* that had dented business confidence and sent the stock markets into a tailspin across the globe. The World Health Organization (WHO) defines an infodemic as spread of "too much information including false or misleading information in digital and physical environments during a disease outbreak".[1] Infodemic tends to hurt mental health of people and has had secondary effects on the economy. The dip in confidence fuels a further slump in economic conditions. Thus, any "Bad News" about COVID-19 can engender a downward spiral,

[1] https://www.who.int/health-topics/infodemic#tab=tab_1.

or a vicious cycle, for an economy [7]—especially amid the rapid pace of infection and death rates of COVID-19. The ferocity of the pandemic has been unprecedented compared to other pandemic events in the past [13]. The emerging medical literature has highlighted the massive mental health crisis—ranging from anxiety, distress and depression to suicidal tendencies—that this current pandemic and infodemic have spawned [11, 12]. In the US, the proportion of adults with depression symptoms registered a threefold increase since the onset of the pandemic [5, 6]. The US Centre for Disease Control and Prevention argued that one of the main sources of this increase is the "heavy consumption of news stories" about the pandemic. This consumption of news stories is held responsible for increasing symptoms of depression [10]. The COVID-19 and infodemic—due to their influence on the mental health caused by the news/headline effects [8, 9]—did influence the US economy, and its stock markets, via what is called *market sentiments.* During the 2020, on the pandemic, Sacerdote et al. [10] identify that 91% of stories by U.S. major media outlets are negative in tone vis-à-vis 54% non-U.S. major sources and 65% for scientific journals. The pandemic, infodemic and market sentiments have also caused long-term damages as highlighted by Cheng [3, 4]. In financial markets the representative agent has responded to the pandemic-related risks with either under-reaction or over-reaction. In other words, the mispricing of risks can have long-run adverse consequences for the entire global economy.

The present book titled *COVID-19 Pandemic and Global Inequality: Reflections in Labour Market, Business and Social Sectors* edited by Rajib Bhattacharyya, Ramesh Chandra Das and Achintya Ray has well compiled the issues of inequality during the pandemic by relating labour market, business and social sectors of different countries and groups. With the club of 21 chapters the book arrives at good outcomes and policy recommendations. I hope the book will definitely reach to the potential readers in the fields like Economics, Sociology, Political Science and Business.

Partha Gangopadhyay, Ph.D.
Western Sydney University
Sydney, Australia

References

1. Arnon A, Ricco J, Smetters K (2020) Epidemiological and economic effects of lockdown. Brookings papers on economic activity conference drafts
2. Ashraf BN (2020a) Economic impact of government interventions during the COVID-19 pandemic: International evidence from financial markets. J Behav Experiment Finance 27:100371–100371. Doi: https://doi.org/10.1016/j.jbef.2020.100371
3. Cheng I-H (2020) Volatility markets underreacted to the early stages of the COVID-19 pandemic. Rev Asset Pricing Stud 10:635-668
4. Cheng I-H (2019) The VIX premium. Rev Finan Stud 32:180–227

5. Ettman CK, Abdalla SM, Cohen GH, Sampson L, Vivier PM, Galea S (2020) Prevalence of depression symptoms in US adults before and during the COVID-19 pandemic. JAMA Net Open 3(9):e2019686–e2019686. Doi: https://doi.org/10.1001/jamanetworkopen.2020.19686
6. Fetzer T, Hensel L, Hermle J, Roth C (2020) Coronavirus perceptions and economic anxiety. Rev. Econom Statist 1–36. Doi: https://doi.org/10.1162/rest_a_00946
7. He Z (2017) The contractionary effect of bad economic news. J Money Credit Banking 49(6):1339–1384. Doi: https://doi.org/10.1111/jmcb.12405
8. Jansen WJ, Nahuis NJ (2003) The stock market and consumer confidence: European evidence. Econom Let 79(1):89–98. Doi: https://doi.org/10.1016/S0165-1765(02)00292-6
9. Ludvigson SC (2004) Consumer confidence and consumer spending. J Econom Perspect 18(2):29–50. Doi: https://doi.org/10.1257/0895330041371222
10. Sacerdote B, Sehgal R, Cook M (2020) Why is all COVID-19 news bad news? NBER working paper 28110, national bureau of economic research, Inc. http://www.nber.org/papers/w28110
11. Su Z, McDonnell D, Wen J, Kozak M, Abbas J, Šegalo S, Li X, Ahmad J, Cheshmehzangi A, Cai Y, Yang L, Xiang Y-T (2021) Mental health consequences of COVID-19 media coverage: the need for effective crisis communication practices. Globalizat Health 17:1–8. Doi: https://doi.org/10.1186/s12992-020-00654-4
12. Wang Y, Pan B, Liu Y, Wilson A, Ou J, Chen R (2020) Health care and mental health challenges for transgender individuals during the COVID-19 pandemic. Lancet Diabet Endocrinol 8(7):564–565. Doi: https://doi.org/10.1016/S2213-8587(20)30182-0
13. Wilder-Smith, A, Chiew CJ, Lee VJ (2020) Can we contain the COVID-19 outbreak with the same measures as for SARS? Lancet Infect Dis 20(5):e102–e107. Doi: https://doi.org/10.1016/S1473-3099(20)30129-8

Partha Gangopadhyay Associate Professor Partha Gangopadhyay (equivalent to North American full professor) studied at Presidency College and JNU, India before undertaking his doctoral studies on game theory at University of Sydney, Australia under the supervision of Professor Yanis Varoufakis (former Finance Minister of Greece). Despite being a heterodox economist, Partha is formally rated among the top 1.2% of 64,800 economists of our globe & ranked 18 among all (1427) living Australian economists listed by RePEc. Since 2000 he published about 50 papers in top tier journals, seven research monographs and 80+ other papers and book chapters. He has advised several national governments and international agencies (e.g., Asian Development Bank) on inequality and working poverty in developing nations.

Preface

The global economy has been passing through one of its most challenging phases in its history after the largest disaster of the century in the form of COVID-19 pandemic since the beginning of 2020. It started with the health catastrophe in its first phase but gradually transformed into a severe socioeconomic shock. This was a devastating blow to the already fragile global economy. Though there were signs of recovery, it has been staggered with mounting debt levels, rising inflationary pressures, widening income inequality, geo-political instability, disruptions in global supply chains and disproportionate growth across regions and communities. Labour market has been the worst hit due to the pandemic in 2020. As per the latest report of the International Labour Organization (ILO), though the labour market is showing some signs of recovery, the pace is uneven and uncertain. It resulted in miseries, distress, impoverishment, deprivation particularly to lower income daily wage earners and informal sector workers. The aftershock of the pandemic has also brought about significant structural transformation in various segments of socioeconomic life-production, consumption, work pattern and social relations. The labour productivity and growth potential in the long run have been severely affected irrespective of whether the country is developed, developing or an emerging market economy. The uneven recovery rate amidst the global slowdown has given rise to the issue of whether convergence among nations is feasible or there will be an accentuation in global inequality.

The present edited volume titled *COVID-19 Pandemic and Global Inequality: Reflections in Labour Market, Business and Social Sectors* examines this fundamental question in light of the developments in the labour market, foreign trade and social sectors. Starting from the proposal to the final submission, the concerted efforts of all the editors as well as the contributors have finally led to the publication of the book. This volume will provide insights and tools to researchers, academicians, social and political thinkers, government officials, and policymakers to think about economic policies and management following a black swan-type global shock.

In the entire journey of this book project, the support and cooperation received from various institutions, organizations and expert opinions of academicians can never be ignored and forgotten. First, we extend our thanks to the entire team of

Springer Nature for their constant support and cooperation for making this project successfully completed. We remain indebted to all our respected eminent contributors who have made huge value additions in their respective chapters. Finally, we place on record our sincere gratitude for the unwavering support of our family members through the many months we worked hard to make this project a reality.

Although the editors have tried their best to make the entire project as flawless as possible, we humbly accept the genuine possibility of shortcomings in any parts of this volume. Needless to add, we remain responsible for any errors or omissions.

Kolkata, West Bengal, India — Rajib Bhattacharyya
Midnapore, West Bengal, India — Ramesh Chandra Das
Nashville, TN, USA — Achintya Ray

Introduction

Today's world confronts one of the biggest challenges humanity has ever faced in its untiring fight against the Coronavirus disease, the COVID-19. Various issues have tended to aggravate the problem of global inequality as an aftermath of the pandemic and macroeconomic shocks, which has severe repercussions for the labour market, manufacturing and trade, and social sector with varying degrees throughout the world. Though tangible signs of recovery have been observed in many advanced economies, many underdeveloped and poor nations have shown signs of sluggish recovery. Such stunted economic recoveries happened mainly due to mounting government debt burdens incurred while making considerable expenditures to fight the COVID war and rising inflationary pressure from supply bottlenecks. The countless casualties and fatalities have raised questions on the attainment and acceptability of "Sustainable Development Goals (SDGs)". In the long run, it has affected labour productivity and growth potential irrespective of developed, developing or emerging market economy. The crisis severely impacts nations heavily dependent on foreign trade, tourism and remittances from abroad. To survive the unprecedented exogenous shock of the global pandemic, Governments implemented support programmes to keep the economy alive. At the same time, businesses had to rely on debt and loans to continue their production process. The pandemic has also prominently demonstrated the divergence of the government's responses to increased spending on public health and social welfare in combination with the drastic fall in tax revenues, which has increased fiscal deficits and widened debt burdens.

Following the COVID-19 pandemic, the return to a "new normal" was uneven and suddenly disrupted by the outbreak of Russia's war on Ukraine. It created a situation of geo-political tension and generated a new series of crises in the food and energy markets, resulting in supply disruptions and high inflationary spiral. This was amplified by a further period of slow growth or stagflation, de-globalization, unsustainably high levels of government debt, deterioration in human development and swift climatic changes. This has resulted in a disproportionate shift of output, employment and trade—making the recovery path more divergent. Income, wealth and consumption inequality have increased significantly following the pandemic. The digital divide and gender discrimination have been a significant problem in the development of the social sector. The shift from the traditional "classroom teaching" method to online education has again created various challenges with the uneven spread of information and communication technology, infrastructure and digital education. Countries that could invest and afford new digital technologies (like Robotics, Artificial Intelligence, etc.) may be able to scale down their socioeconomic crisis to a manageable level. Still, it will be challenging for others to cope with the former set of nations. Hence, geo-political conflicts and segmentation, increase in multi-domain risk and vulnerability have raised doubts in the minds of social scientists and policymakers as to which set of policy actions may become the key to the economic revival of the world.

The present edited book titled *COVID-19 Pandemic and Global Inequality: Reflections in Labour Market, Business and Social Sectors* is a unique compilation of original essays on various economic issues that have assumed increased relevance in the aftermath of the COVID pandemic. It is also a blend of some scholarly contributions from multiple countries with a balanced, comprehensive mix of both theoretical modelling and empirical research.

This volume is divided into two separate but highly complementary strands: (a) Global Impact and (b) Trade, Employment, Health and Education Impacts. The first strand includes seven chapters covering issues ranging from the spillover effects of global economic uncertainty and economic shocks in Nigeria, the effect of COVID-19 on sustainable development in Europe, on U.S. payment protection and fiscal policy, financial stability, economic confidence, the incidence of poverty, economic growth and development on Ghana, to Turkey's energy crisis, etc. On the other hand, the second strand covers 14 more chapters focussing on some specific economic problems like the impact of the crisis on employment differential and health expenditure in African Countries; the effect on foreign trade in Sri Lanka and India; divergences of health expenditures and the role of the government, informal sector, online education, women employment, investment pattern, personal finance, digital movement, consumer choice, income inequality, and also psychological reactions of different socioeconomic groups.

In what follows, we provide succinctly summarized critical insights from each chapter. Our summaries are often heavily borrowed from the authors' own words. A quick review of the summaries informs busy readers of a high-level view of the entire spectrum of studies included in this volume. It helps them understand the multitudes of ways overlapping concerns can run through the policymaking challenges across countries and continents. In doing so, we expect to bring to the conversation the need to fine-tune and synchronize policies that help us create a resilient global economy while being mindful of the individualities of the participants and the uniqueness of their challenges and opportunities. Our shared future as humanity, especially in the face of black swan-type global disruptions like a pandemic, crucially depends on our ability to understand each other and design and implement policies suitable for the common good.

Chapter 1 deals with the impacts of inflation and consumption uncertainties at the domestic and international levels on industrial output and the real GDP of the Nigerian economy. The sources of uncertainties are global shocks like the COVID pandemic. The study finds that inflation uncertainty is suitable for industrial houses, while consumption uncertainty worsens it. On the other hand, international real output uncertainty reduces real domestic output and private consumption uncertainty and inflation uncertainty combinedly reduce real domestic output. The study thus recommends that policymakers should not worry much about inflation uncertainty under the domestic economy's intention of increasing industrial output; instead, private consumption should be managed appropriately. Also, the country should be closely monitored for real output, private consumption and inflation uncertainty at the international level.

Chapter 2 admits that the COVID-19 did not only lead to countless casualties and fatalities in the continents like Europe but it also led to the lack of attainment of sustainable development goals (SDGs) in the continent jeopardized. The study thus aims to analyse the impact of COVID-19 on the levels of sustainable development achieved by some countries of the European continent for 3 years, 2015, 2018 and 2020, through the construction of sustainable development indices (SDI) across the 17 indicators. The study finds that a general improvement in the levels of sustainable development is observed between 2015 and 2018 and a worsening result between 2018 and 2020. The presence of the declining values of the SDI from 2018 to 2020 demonstrates the adverse effects of the pandemic. The study recommends intervention by the European countries to mitigate the harmful effects of the pandemic.

Chapter 3 focusses on the impact of sizeable fiscal expansion during the COVID-19 shock in the United States as the government engaged itself in a massive spending programme to save small- and medium-sized businesses and jobs. The size of the programme, coupled with other measures of social safety net like the state-level unemployment benefits, contributed to a substantial increase in monetary savings and cash holdings, increasing the inflationary pressures on the economy and rising asset prices in many regions. This chapter provides a broad overview of the emerging research in this area while reviewing the impact of such significant government expansions on the labour market. Collating data from the money supply, interest rates, inflation and government finances, this chapter documents the fiscal and monetary disruptions that followed the large infusion of cash in the U.S. economy resulting in high inflation and escalating interest rates. The chapter also discusses policy implications for future macroeconomic shocks.

Chapter 4 shows how the pandemic has affected the economic confidence of both consumers and business houses. The study investigates whether COVID-19 incidences correlate and equilibrium relations with consumer and business confidence in the world's highly affected countries: the USA, the U.K., Italy, Spain, France, India, Brazil, China, Russia and South Africa. The study uses time series analysis for the monthly data from January 2020 to August 2022. In some countries, it finds positive correlations between COVID cases and death with business confidence (BCI) and negative with consumers' confidence (CCI). But, COVID death has maintained long-run relationships with CCI and BCI in many countries. The Granger causality test also reveals that COVID cases and death cause changes in consumers' and business sentiments in some countries.

Chapter 5 discusses the impact of COVID-19 incidences and deaths in Nigeria upon different financial indicators of the country using the daily data for the 2 years, 2020–2022, using time series analysis. The results show that confirmed COVID cases have a negative and significant impact on liquidity rate and a positive and significant impact on banks' loan-to-deposit ratio, government debt as a ratio of GDP and banks' credit to the economy in the long and short run. On the other hand, for the health crisis factor, the study observes that COVID-19-related deaths negatively and significantly impacted the liquidity ratio and significantly increased the bank loan-to-deposit ratio, government debt as a ratio of GDP and credit to the economy. The findings also showed that the liquidity rate fell as the health crisis increased due to COVID-19, while the bank loan-to-deposit ratio, government loan to GDP and credit to the economy improved as the health crisis increased due to an increase in COVID-19 cases. Thus, the study recommends more extensive government support for the financial sector players, including liquidity and other supports by the central bank, expansion of deposit insurance coverage, protection schemes and guarantees, and capital injections.

Chapter 6 looks at the impact of the COVID pandemic on the incidence of poverty, economic growth and development with evidence from Ghana. In particular, the chapter investigates the effects of the COVID-19 pandemic on the Ghanaian economy's top five key sectors (agriculture, tourism, building and construction, infrastructure and manufacturing). The chapter intends to model the effect of the COVID-19 pandemic on economic growth and development using the Discrete-time Markov Chain method and suggests policies for reducing poverty. This analysis is undertaken within the prism of the neoclassical economic model of long-run income equilibrium within the convergence theory. The chapter's primary goal is to contribute to formulating post-COVID-19 economic recovery policies and processes to reduce poverty and inequality within the sub-Saharan Africa region, with Ghana as a case study.

Chapter 7 describes the energy crisis issue in Turkey during the pandemic periods. It aims to see whether nuclear and renewable energy are good options over traditional fossil fuel-based energy sources. The study uses the Decision Making Trial and Evaluation Laboratory (DEMATEL) technique. It identifies that nuclear energy investments played a crucial role in effectively managing energy crises during the pandemic; renewable energy investments are also essential. The study prescribes that it would be appropriate for Turkey to focus on nuclear energy and renewable energy investments to fight the energy crisis more successfully during the pandemic and that the country's domestic sources should produce the energy.

Chapter 8 aims to justify the nexus among COVID-19 incidence, employment, health expenditure and productivity in 40 Sub-Saharan African (SSA) zone. It uses the Panel Vector Autoregressive (VAR) model with the quarterly data for 2020–2021. The results show that with rising cases of COVID-19, the employment gap has widened in SSA countries on average by about 50%, also leading to a significant increase in the out-of-pocket expenditure on health by approximately $0.42 billion and decreasing productivity in the countries by roughly $0.27 billion. Further, the panel VAR—impulse response function results show that when employment and productivity produce impulse, the COVID-19 pandemic responds by impacting significant gradual adverse effects on them but significant gradual positive effects on health expenditure. The study thus prescribes that the countries in the SSA zone should be alert in tackling the issues of such crises and their associated socioeconomic impacts.

Chapter 9 attempts to establish the impact of foreign trade and the COVID-19 pandemic on the Sri Lankan and Indian economies. It examines the export, import, unemployment rate, net foreign direct investment and links between economic growth for India and Sri Lanka from 1991 to 2022 collected from World Development Indicators published by the World Bank. Granger causality confirms unidirectional and bidirectional causal linkages between these variables. The finding of the cointegration test suggests a long-run link between export and GDP, as well as net foreign direct investment (NFDI) and GDP, for both nations.

Chapter 10 deals with the convergence or divergence in healthcare expenditures, both public and private, during the COVID-19 period for a selected list of low-income and high-income countries using the so-called beta and sigma convergence approaches. As the nations have variations in socioeconomic and cultural practices, the study contemplates that there should be variations in the healthcare expenditures to mitigate the COVID pandemic. The results show no convergence in health expenditures in the countries studied; instead, divergences are observed between these sets of countries. In addition, if the shock period (2020) is included, the spikes of deviations are even more significant. Hence, authorities like the WHO should take of the issues to minimize the differences in the per capita health expenses in low- and high-income earning countries using international policy packages.

Chapter 11 attempts to examine the relationship between COVID-19 and macroeconomic variables such as inflation, exchange rate and Nifty-Fifty of the Indian economy. The study used monthly data of selected variables from 2000 to 2022. Initially, the study conducted an Augmented Dickey-Fuller (ADF) unit root test to examine the stationary properties of the variables. After identifying the order of variables, the study employed Johansen & Juselius cointegration technique to find out the long-run association among the variables. The study's outcomes revealed that the variables used in this study are integrated of order one and have a statistically significant long-run relationship.

Chapter 12 compares the impacts on women's employment of two very different crises: the financial crisis of 2008 and the one generated by COVID-19. The aim is to show that, despite the other trends, with an increase in female employment in the first case and a fall in the second, we always have the same problem: the quality of female work. Using ELFS data, the study analyses the effects of explanatory variables on women's income levels in Italy over 3 years. The results confirm the robust segmentation of the Italian labour market, which penalize especially the weakest categories. Although it is impossible to assess the effects on female employment due to the pandemic, the 2020 data still allow us to highlight a downward trend. The results could provide several insights for policymakers. First, to get away from the idea of growth linked only to green transition and digital technology by marginalizing the other "essential" sectors. Second, to reschedule the investments planned in the post-pandemic recovery strategies, focussing on creating quality work in these sectors that would improve both employment conditions and the quality of services.

Chapter 13 shows the impact of COVID-19 on the education sector, particularly the shift from the traditional "classroom teaching" method to online education. This was inevitable to continue the teaching-learning process. But whether this shift was smooth enough or not, for both teachers and students, is a severe issue. Mentoring is one such thing that can take place throughout the day and beyond the regular teaching hours. It is essential to include teaching guidance for a more nuanced understanding. This paper looks to build a model to show how effective mentoring by teachers can help students overcome difficulties and attend classes regularly, even during the pandemic, through online mode. The study also shows that mentoring can increase the willingness to participate in classes, even in the areas that suffer from the digital divide. Policy-wise, influential mentor-mentee associations could overcome many problems, including mental health, and not only improve the dropout ratio but also bring students back to classes, whether the teaching mode is virtual or not.

Chapter 14 focusses on the role of government education spending in low and lower middle-income countries in a post-COVID world. This chapter investigates the impact of education spending in approximately 78 low and lower middle-income economies and 111 upper middle and high-income countries on education outcomes at primary, secondary and tertiary levels of schooling. The study finds that despite additional channels of external funding such as Official Development Assistance loans, government spending across all levels of educational enrolment, primary, secondary and tertiary, has had a more significant impact on education outcomes. The study finds that government spending on education as a share of GDP has contributed the most towards achieving global development goals. It also demonstrates that the divergence in educational outcomes between low and lower middle-income countries versus high-income countries will only persist if governments make a concentrated effort to implement policies geared towards secondary and tertiary levels of schooling.

Chapter 15 portrays that before 2010, the single-family rental market in the U.S. was primarily mom-and-pop investors, regional investment groups and house flippers. But after the 2009–2010 mortgage foreclosure crisis, a new type of landlord bought tens of thousands of single-family homes and converted them to single-family rental (SFR) homes. This change has had significant impacts on the U.S. housing situation. The companies were organized as Real Estate Investment Trusts (REITs) and are now traded on Wall Street. Private Equity investors mimicked the REIT model and have entered the market forcefully since 2015. This chapter explores how COVID-19 has impacted SFR institutional investors and the growth of their portfolios. The analysis concludes that institutional investors are well-capitalized and positively positioned to take advantage of further economic turmoil related to COVID.

Chapter 16 highlights the potential impact of the digital movement being noticeable in developing and less developed countries (with particular emphasis on India) recently. It provides a statistical illustration of how the ongoing revolution in India has created a condition of inequality, or a "Digital Divide", which has become a part of raging public debate post the pandemic outbreak. Besides, this paper developed a general equilibrium model to show the fallout of this digital revolution, which aligns well with the notion of the backwash effect (Myrdal, 1957). The study concludes that the inception of the digital revolution or movement as the big-shot technological transition is a significant threat to distributive justice for a developing or less developed country. This is especially true because there is a preponderance of semi-skilled or low-skilled labour force workers in these countries and they are most vulnerable regarding labour displacement.

Chapter 17 explores and analyses the changes in purchasing patterns, the prevalence of choice paradox and the decision-making process behind them, such as choice overload, nudges and unconscious bias. The study uses a primary survey conducted for 500 sample students residing in India over 2 months (August–October) in 2021. The questions include focal aspects of consumers' lives such as employment status, household income, local and online shopping, eating at a restaurant, real estate, automobiles, vocational and educational interests, investments and future planning. The study observes that the choice paradox in terms of choice overload, nudges and unconscious bias is very much dependent upon the demographic factors of the individuals, such as education, gender and the number of family members, and economic factors, such as the household's income. Further, the study finds that all three choice paradoxes are present if the individual is a student. Therefore, it recommends that government policies should tackle these choices paradoxes. Thus, controlling the choice paradox, the procedure must target the student group of society.

Chapter 18 analyses the impact of income inequality after COVID-19 in India. The paper analyses data from the CMIE's Consumer Pyramids Households Survey, corresponding to the first wave ranging from February 2020 to December 2020, the Delta wave period spanning from January 2021 to July 2021 and the OMICRON wave period running from November 2021 to February 2022. Interestingly, it shows that between January 2021 and July 2021, inequality had fallen relative to February 2020—December 2020, while it rose between November 2021 and February 2022 as compared to the January 2021—July 2021 period. The fall in income inequality is primarily due to the more considerable fall in income among upper income households and a smaller decline in the earnings observed among lower income families.

Chapter 19 analyses personal finance in the context of COVID-19 in the Mexican economy. In this context, the objective is to identify types of personal expenses in households in Culiacán, Sinaloa, Mexico, as of 15 July 2020, for which an exploratory study was carried out; 488 surveys with 48 items were applied electronically. The main results were that most of the respondents' budget, spending according to their income, had no problem paying their bank loans on time. Those who would also consider a fund for future contingencies have not purchased health insurance or a computer or cell phone, among other issues analysed. The main findings indicate that the studied population has not acquired additional medical insurance despite the pandemic. It is also concluded that the population under study has become aware of having savings for contingency funds and that digital life still resists making personal financial decisions.

Chapter 20 attempts a cross-sectional study on psychological reactions to COVID-19 across different socioeconomic groups in Assam, India. The study used a logistic regression model in addition to descriptive statistics. The DASS-21 depression and anxiety subscale scores are found to be correlated with gender and age. The study also revealed that depression, anxiety and stress were common among the Assamese community. Compared to the 2016 National Mental Health Survey of India results, it was significantly higher. Therefore, their study recommends that effective mental health experts' assistance is required to assist the public in coping with the COVID-19 epidemic and other similar crises.

A few central propositions arise from the diverse topics presented in this volume. Labour markets in various poor countries and developing nations are dominated by informal workers outside the purview of any social security norms. They are the most vulnerable component of the labour market and were the worst hit by the pandemic. The miseries and the disproportionate impact on gender (mainly women), school children, higher education, and informal and unskilled workers will likely exacerbate socioeconomic inequality and poverty. There is an immense need to re-think and re-construct policies both at the national and international levels to remove these disparities. The need for policy changes within nations and at the WTO, given threats to globalization arising due to the US-China trade war and re-emergence of trade protection amidst rising economic nationalism, needs consideration.

Changes in various dimensions of and segments within the labour market arising from the economic downturn and due to the impact of digital technologies also need further research. Policymakers must also reflect on policy priorities and options before governments in the post-COVID world, keeping in view that disruptive changes can happen at any point in time. Further research needs to be done to analyse how unanticipated mega shocks like this pandemic can reshape social policies concerning public health and education. With the financing needs of countries that need to catch up compared to the developed and advanced nations, there is a need to close the internal and external financing gap. International financial institutions must increase liquidity availability commensurate with the lagging economies' markets. For better cooperation and faster revival of countries more acutely affected, easy availability of liquidity and debt reduction measures can be considered an integral part of the financing for development strategy. The divergence in educational outcomes between low and lower middle-income countries versus high-income countries may be removed if governments make a concentrated effort to implement policies that are geared towards secondary and tertiary education and influential mentor-mentee association that could overcome many problems, including mental health. It will not only stem school dropouts but also bring students back to classes.

This title may open up new areas of research opportunities to the potential scholars around the world from the disciplines like economics, business, social sciences and natural sciences. Besides, it is palatable to the policymakers of the countries and groups to use it as a ready reckoner in mitigating economic and social crises that may arise further due to the COVID-19-type crises.

Rajib Bhattacharyya
Ramesh Chandra Das
Achintya Ray

Contents

Part II Sub-Theme—Trade, Employment, Health and Education

Editors and Contributors

About the Editors

Dr. Rajib Bhattacharyya is an Associate Professor in Economics, in Goenka College of Commerce and Business Administration, University of Calcutta, Kolkata, India. He graduated in Economics from St. Xavier's College; Masters, M.Phil. and Ph.D. in Economics—all from the University of Calcutta. He has 20 years of teaching experience. His fields of research interests are—International Trade, Finance, Indian Economic Development, and Women Empowerment. He has contributed a good number of articles and has also worked as a member of the Editorial Board in reputed national and international journals/books, viz., IGI Global (USA), Emerald (U.K.) and Springer. He has recently edited a book entitled "Gains and Pains of Financial Integration and Trade Liberalization—Lessons from Emerging Economies" (Emerald, U.K.); Comparative Advantage in the Knowledge Economy: A National and Organizational Resource—edited by Dr. Rajib Bhattacharyya [Emerald Publishing Limited, U.K.] and The Covid-19 Pandemic, India and the World- Economic and Social Policy Perspective- (Co-Editors Ananya Ghosh Dastidar and Soumyen Sikdar).

Ramesh Chandra Das Ph.D. is currently a Professor of Economics at Vidyasagar University, West Bengal, India. Prof. Das has the teaching and research experience of about 25 years. His main areas of research lie in Theoretical and Applied Macroeconomics, Environmental Economics and Political Economics. He has contributed several research papers to national and international journals of repute along with more than a dozen of edited volumes in different areas of the subject.

Dr. Achintya Ray is a Professor in the College of Business at Tennessee State University. He is a member of the Community Advisory Board at the Renasant Bank. He also serves on the Advisory Board of Audaz Capital, a boutique venture capital and private equity firm specializing in social mobility through the innovative application of advanced technology. Dr. Ray is a member of the Business Advisory Board of Nashville State Community College. In the past, Dr. Ray served as the President of the Faculty Senate and Chair of the Faculty Senate's Executive Committee at Tennessee State University. In addition, Dr. Ray serves on the Board of Directors of KCRCI, Inc., a renal care and research company with a presence in North America, Africa and Asia.

About the Contributors

Ebikabowei Biedomo Aduku is a researcher from the Department of Economics, University of Nigeria, Nsukka, Nigeria. He has attended several national and international conferences. He has publications in books and journals of reputation.

Leonardo Salvatore Alaimo is a Research Fellow of Social Statistics at the Department of Social Sciences and Economics of Sapienza University of Rome. He holds a Ph.D. in Social Statistics at the University of Rome La Sapienza. He was a researcher at the Italian National Institute of Statistics—Istat and an expert on statistics of the Italian Prime Minister Office—Italian Government (Conte's cabinet).

A. Eze Afamefuna is a Lecturer in the Department of Economics, University of Nigeria, Nsukka. He is a Ph.D. student and has published articles in both local and international journals, and attended quite a number of conferences. His research interests include financial economics and development economics.

Ogochukwu Christiana Anyanwu is a Lecturer in the Department of Economics, University of Nigeria, Nsukka. She is currently a Ph.D. student in the same department. She has attended several national and international conferences. She has publications in journals of reputation. Her area of interest includes development economics and environmental economics.

Haimanti Banerjee is from Marketing and Business Economics, Joseph M. Katz Graduate School of Business, University of Pittsburgh. She completed her Ph.D. from the University of Iowa in 2011. She joined the Katz Graduate School of Business, University of Pittsburgh in 2016. Prior to that, she has taught at The University of Akron and Cleveland State University. Her current research interests are global macroeconomic development topics.

Marianna Bartiromo holds an M.Sc. in Administration and Public Policies with honours and press dignity from the University of Genoa. She collaborates with the Channel & Retail Lab at SDA Bocconi School of Management in Milan. She works on data analysis from both quantitative and qualitative perspectives, and her research interests focus on sustainability, Corporate Social Responsibility, gender differences and political participation.

Deyanira Bernal-Domínguez Ph.D., is a Research Professor at the Autonomous University of Sinaloa, Faculty of Accounting and Management, Mexico. She also holds the position of the editorial director of a journal in administrative sciences.

Mainak Bhattacharjee is presently an Assistant Professor in Economics at Loreto College, Kolkata, India, and formerly, at The Heritage College, Kolkata, India. He has obtained M.Phil. and M.A. degrees in Economics from the Jadavpur University, Kolkata. He has been working in the areas of Macroeconomics and International Trade.

Rajib Bhattacharyya Ph.D., is an Associate Professor in Economics, at Goenka College of Commerce and B.A., Kolkata, India. He did his M.Phil. and Ph.D. in Economics from the University of Calcutta. He has 21 years of teaching and research experience. His fields of research interests are international trade, finance, Indian economic development, and women empowerment. He has contributed a good number of articles and has also worked as a member of the Editorial Board in reputed national and international journals/books, viz., Routledge, IGI Global (USA), Emerald (U.K.) and Springer.

Somdip Bhukta is presently a doctoral-level research scholar at the Department of Economics, Vidyasagar University, India. His research interest lies in the areas of agricultural economics, environmental economics and development economics.

Çağatay Çağlayan is currently pursuing an undergraduate degree in economics and finance at Istanbul Medipol University, where he is also a student with the Health Management Department. His research interests include sustainable energy economics, renewable energy and nuclear energy. He has some articles and international book chapters related to these topics and one of them is indexed in SSCI.

Ramesh Chandra Das Ph.D., is presently a Professor at the Department of Economics, Vidyasagar University, India. Dr. Das has a list of articles published in reputed journals and books with publishers such as Elsevier, Springer, Taylor & Francis, Sage, Emerald and IGI Global.

Nilendu Chatterjee Ph.D., is an Assistant Professor in the Department of Economics, Bankim Sardar College, India. He has research interests in resource economics, international economics, econometrics and development economics and has a list of publications with the internationally reputed journals and books.

Tonmoy Chatterjee Ph.D., is an Assistant Professor in the Department of Economics, Bhairab Ganguly College, India. He has research interests in international trade theory, general equilibrium, health economics and development economics and has a list of publications with the internationally reputed journals and books.

Kenneth Chilton is an Associate Professor of Public Administration at Tennessee State University in Nashville, TN. His research focuses on corporate single-family rental investors. Primarily, he analyzes ownership trends of single-family rental properties by Real Estate Investment Trusts and Private Equity investors. At present, Dr. Chilton is analyzing the relationship between single-family investors and neighborhood-level racial transition.

Antonio Corasaniti is a Ph.D. Candidate in Applied Social Sciences at the Department of Social Science and Economics, Sapienza University of Rome. He completed his B.A. in Sociology and M.A. in Applied Social Science at the same university. His main research interests encompass the labour regulation, the marketization of health and care systems and the transformations in the provision of care.

Maitree Dey is presently a doctoral-level research scholar at the Department of Economics, Vidyasagar University, India. Her research areas lie in public economics, applied macroeconomics and environmental economics.

Hasan Dinçer Ph.D., is a Professor of Finance at Istanbul Medipol University, Istanbul-Turkey. He has more than 100 scientific articles and some of them are indexed in SSCI. He is also editor of many different books published by Springer and IGI Global.

Ujjal Protim Dutta Ph.D., is presently an Assistant Professor in Economics at the Department of Economics of Rangia College, Assam, India. Dr. Dutta has research interests in the areas of international economics, development and environmental economics.

Ifeoma Augusta Eboh is a researcher from the Department of Economics, University of Nigeria, Nsukka, Nigeria. She has attended several national and international conferences. He has publications in books and journals of reputation.

Sucharita Ghosh is a Professor of Economics and Chair of the Department of Economics in the College of Business at The University of Akron. She has over 25 years of experience teaching undergraduate and graduate classes in macroeconomics, international trade and international monetary economics and was awarded the Buchtel College of Arts and Sciences Teaching Award in 2007. She has published articles in top journals such as the Journal of International Economics, Oxford Bulletin of Economics and Statistics, Regional Studies, and Research Policy.

Ananya Jyoti Gogoi is presently a Ph.D. Scholar at the Department of Anthropology at Gauhati University, India. She has research interests in the sociological aspects of human behaviour, man–nature interactions, etc.

Tanushree Gupta Ph.D., is currently working as an Assistant Professor at the School of Commerce and Management Sciences, Sandip University, Nashik Maharashtra. Finance, Microfinance, Stock Market, and International Business are some of her primary academic interests. Last but not least she has in her credit many research papers/publications of national and international repute and many of her book chapters have been published in international and Scopus-indexed journals.

Enrico Ivaldi Ph.D., Researcher in Social Statistics, is a member of the Editorial Board of "Revista de Estudios Andaluces" (REA). He is also a member of the Econometrics Research Center of the Universidad de Buenos Aires, Argentina, and of the Pontifical International Marian Academy, Department of Integral Welfare, Vatican City.

A. Mba Augustine is a Ph.D. student in Economics (bias in Public Finance) from the University of Nigeria, Nsukka. He is a Lecturer in the Department of Economics of the University. He has published widely in both local and international journals and attended many local and international conferences.

Dilan Kararoğlu is a graduate student in İstanbul Medipol University. She is currently working as a portfolio manager. The subjects she worked on were renewable energy, sustainable energy, nuclear energy.

Napoleon Kurantin is a Senior Research Fellow and Acting Vice Dean of the Academic Division at the Ghana Armed Forces Command and Staff College (GAFCSC) and former Head of the Department of Development Policy in the School of Public Service and Governance (SPSG) at the Ghana Institute of Management and Public Administration (GIMPA).

Susobhan Maiti Ph.D., is an Assistant Professor in the Department of Economics, School of Humanities and Social Sciences (SHSS), Jain (Deemed-to-be) University, Bangalore, India. He has published many research papers in the area of industry, efficiency and productivity in international and Scopus-indexed journals.

Debashis Mazumdar Ph.D., is now serving at The Heritage College, Kolkata, West Bengal, India as Professor & HOD in the Department of Economics. He has been teaching Economics both at Undergraduate and Post-Graduate levels for the last 42 years. He has authored/co-authored about 40 textbooks in Economics, contributed about 65 research articles in national and international journals and edited two conference volumes.

Chyanika Mitra has completed her Ph.D. from Indian Statistical Institute, Kolkata. She did her Bachelor's and Master's in Economics from Jadavpur University in 2011 and 2013, respectively. She was awarded the Young Researcher Award in 2020 by the Institute of Scholars (InSc) for the paper titled "Gender bias in household education expenditure: the case of West Bengal", Amita Majumder & Chayanika Mitra. Indian Growth and Development Review (2019).

Sovik Mukherjee is presently an Assistant Professor in Economics (Morning Section) under the Faculty of Commerce and Management at St. Xavier's University, Kolkata, India. He is a former Visiting Research Fellow (2019–2020) at NISPAcee, Bratislava, Slovak Republic. His current research interests are in applied econometrics, applied game theory, economics of climate change and public policy.

Johnson Nchege is a Lecturer in the Department of Economics, University of Nigeria, Nsukka. He has attended several national and international conferences. He has publications in journals of reputation. His area of interest includes energy and environmental economics.

Annesha Neogy is currently a student of Behavioural Economics at the London School of Economics and Political Science, and has a background in Economics. After graduating from Fergusson College, Pune, she pursued her Master's degree from St. Xavier's University, Kolkata. She aims to conduct enriching research and aid businesses and policymaking.

Ebele Stella Nwokoye is an Associate Professor, the Department of Economics, Nnamdi Azikiwe University, Awka Nigeria.

N. Obodoechi Divine is a Lecturer in the Department of Economics and a Research Fellow with the Health Policy Research Group, College of Medicine, University of Nigeria. He obtained his M.Sc. degree in Finance and Economics, at Manchester Business School, United Kingdom. He is a consultant with ThinkWell Global, United States of America.

N. Omeje Ambrose is a Lecturer and Doctoral student in the Department of Economics, University of Nigeria, Nsukka. He has published in both international and local peer-reviewed journals, and many conference papers. He has also researched and consulted for SAVI-DFID, and UNICEF and has facilitated research for the Central Bank of Nigeria–South-East Entrepreneurship Development Centre (SEEDC) Training on Entrepreneurship and Development, Nigeria.

Bertha Z. Osei-Hwedie is a Fellow of the Institute, Professor of International Relations, and former Coordinator of the Ph.D. Programme, School of Public Service and Governance, Ghana Institute of Management and Public Administration (GIMPA). She was the founding and Acting Dean of the School of Research and Graduate Studies, GIMPA. Her research interests include China. Japan, globalization, development, democracy, gender and development, African politics, and the environment.

Arindam Paul is presently serving as an Assistant Professor in Economics, at Jadavpur University, Kolkata. He also served as an Assistant Professor in Economics, at St. Xavier's University, Kolkata. He did his Ph.D. in Economics from ISI Kolkata.

Achintya Ray Ph.D., is a Professor in the College of Business at Tennessee State University, USA. He also serves on the Advisory Board of Audaz Capital, a boutique venture capital and private equity firm specializing in social mobility through the innovative application of advanced technology. Dr. Ray is a member of the Business Advisory Board of Nashville State Community College. In the past, Dr. Ray served as the President of the Faculty Senate, Chair of the Faculty Senate's Executive Committee, Chair of the Budget and Finance Committee, Chair of the Undergraduate Curriculum Committee, and Chair of the Faculty Handbook Committee at Tennessee State University.

Ruby Sarma Ph.D., is an Associate Professor at the Department of Economics, Rangia College, Assam, India with teaching and research experience of more than a decade. Her areas of research lie in development economics and applied economics.

Chandana Sarmah Ph.D., is presently a Professor at the Department of Anthropology of Gauhati University, India. She has done works on the biosocial aspect of ageing among the Assamese elderly in the urban context of Guwahati. Besides, she has undertaken research projects sponsored by ICSSR, New Delhi to understand the ageing experience and process among marginalized tribal communities.

R. Ukwueze Ezebuilo Ph.D., is a Senior Lecturer at the Department of Economics, University of Nigeria, Nsukka in Enugu State, Nigeria. He has published widely in both local and internationally recognized journals, and edited books. He teaches and supervises graduate students.

E. Urama Chinasa is a Lecturer at the Economics Department, University of Nigeria, Nsukka, where she obtained all her degrees. She has served as a Chief Planning Officer in the Academic Planning Unit before joining the Academia. She specializes in Health and Development Economics where she has published enormously.

José G. Vargas-Hernández is a Research Professor at Instituto Tecnológico Mario Molina Unidad Zapopan, Member of the National System of Researchers of Mexico. Professor Vargas-Hernández has a Ph.D. in Public Administration and a Ph.D. in Organizational Economics. He has been a visiting scholar at Carleton University Canada, the University of California Berkeley and Laurentian University, Canada.

Luisa De Vita is an Associate Professor in Economic Sociology, at the Department of Social Science and Economics of Sapienza University of Rome. She directs the Ph.D. program in Applied Social Sciences and joined several research projects at the national and international levels. Her current research concerns inequalities, gender policies, diversity management, labour market and working conditions, with a focus on self-employment, women's entrepreneurship, and career pathways.

Duygu Yavuz is studying at Istanbul Medipol University, Department of Health Management. She is working in the Department of Economics and Finance, where she has a double major. The subjects she worked on were renewable energy, sustainable energy, nuclear energy.

Serhat Yüksel Ph.D., is a Professor of Finance at Istanbul Medipol University, Istanbul-Turkey. He has more than 80 scientific articles and some of them are indexed in SSCI. He is also editor of many different books published by Springer and IGI Global.

List of Figures

Part I
Sub-Theme—Global Impact

Chapter 1
Spillover Effects of Global Economic Uncertainty Shocks in Nigeria

Ebele Stella Nwokoye, Ebikabowei Biedomo Aduku, and Ogochukwu Christiana Anyanwu

1.1 Introduction

Stronger economic, financial and political ties among nations are increasing fast in modern times. Economic uncertainty is also fast increasing in recent times in many parts of the world including advanced economies, emerging economies and low-income countries. Economic uncertainty is occasioned by global uncertainties or risks such as the outbreak of the COVID-19 global pandemic, the Russia-Ukraine War, the US housing bubble, the US-China trade tension, Brexit uncertainty, the aftermath of Lehman's collapse in September 2008, the North Atlantic subprime crisis by 2008–2009 and various geopolitical fragmentation or unrests across the globe. At least as significant as a sobering fact; global uncertainties or risks in recent times, the hardest-hit economies include large economies—US, China, Britain, Italy, Germany, France and Japan. Just the US, China, Britain, Italy, Germany, France and Japan, according to Baldwin and di Mauro [3] accounts for about 60% of the world GDP, 41% of world manufacturing exports and 65% of world manufacturing. These economies also make up the global value chains; therefore, economic uncertainties in their economies can produce 'supply-chain contagion' in almost every economy. An especially apt description is spillover (effects) to the rest of the world. What happens (a shock) in one country could easily be transmitted to other countries. Therefore, managers of the economy need to be vigilant not only of the domestic economy.

E. S. Nwokoye · E. B. Aduku (✉)
Department of Economics, Nnamdi Azikiwe University, Awka, Nigeria
e-mail: ebiopportunity@gmail.com

E. S. Nwokoye
e-mail: es.nwokoye@unizik.edu.ng

O. C. Anyanwu
Department of Economics, University of Nigeria, Nsukka, Nigeria
e-mail: ogochukwu.anyanwu@unn.edu.ng

R. Bhattacharyya et al. (eds.), *COVID-19 Pandemic and Global Inequality*,
https://doi.org/10.1007/978-981-99-4405-7_1

The global uncertainties in recent times have several unprecedented implications for the already slowly performing macroeconomic variables and have necessitated policy intervention coordination by policymakers at the global and regional levels. Because of interconnectedness and contagion effects across regions and the globe alike, global economic uncertainty shocks in a country spillover to other countries, capable of engendering economic growth brittleness and fragility in other macroeconomic variables [21, 22]. In Nigeria, the high-interest rate and inflationary pressure the country is facing could be associated with spillovers from global uncertainty shocks. Also, the frequent recessions the country has witnessed (first in 2016 and exited in 2017, and went back into recession in 2020) may be attributed to a spillover of global economic uncertainty shocks from other countries abroad. Empirical evidence is relevant for appropriate macroeconomic policy intervention coordination. In this chapter, we examine the spillover effects of global economic uncertainty shocks in Nigeria. The specific objective is to examine (1) the link between domestic (Nigeria's) inflation and private consumption uncertainties and real activity–industrial production and, (2) the spillover effects of real output uncertainty, inflation uncertainty and private consumption uncertainty from the US, China, and Europe to the domestic (Nigeria's) real output growth, the domestic price level and private consumption. Although, there are similar studies most of the studies are for developed economies. Given the increasing global risks in recent times studies like ours are crucial for policy formulation.

The chapter has policy relevance, particularly to the monetary policy authority. It would be difficult to determine appropriate policy coordination without empirical evidence to back up the policy formulation as global economic uncertainties shock spillover effects may not always be bad (good) to all key macroeconomic variables at the same time and in the same magnitude. Therefore, with empirical evidence, a better policy can be formulated in line with the nature of the effects and the macroeconomic variable to be given priority attention. The chapter is organized into five main sections. Following this introduction, the literature is reviewed in the second section. Within section two, the literature gap is identified. In section three, the theoretical framework, the dataset, and the model are considered. The methods used in the analysis are also explained in the third section. In section four, results are presented and discussed, while in section five, a conclusion is drawn and recommendations are proffered.

1.2 Review of the Extant Literature

Economic uncertainty has been broadly discussed and defined by several researchers. Çolak et al. [9], for example, described economic uncertainty as a situation such that the economy's future outlook is unpredictable. For Londono et al. [19], economic uncertainty is a risk that is a cross current or a headwind to the economic outlook of the domestic economy. The two definitions have a similar view of economic uncertainty, describing it as a situation or a risk that could cause the future economic outlook to be unpredictable. Describing from the perspective of economic agents, Bobasu et al. [6]

viewed economic uncertainty as the unforecastable conditional volatility of a disturbance, with a rise in economic uncertainty being linked generally with increasing difficulty of future economic outcomes. In differentiating uncertainty from economic policy uncertainty, An et al. [1] pointed out that uncertainty is a risk composed of several factors that may be difficult to analyze or foresee accurately. While economic policy uncertainty is a risk associated with the uncertainty of economic policies that the government formulates for future direction and intensity. The focus of this chapter is economic uncertainty. Economic uncertainty is occasioned by global uncertainties or risks such as the outbreak of the COVID-19 global pandemic, the Russia-Ukraine War, the US housing bubble, the US-China trade tension, Brexit uncertainty, the aftermath of Lehman's collapse in September 2008, the North Atlantic subprime crisis by 2008–2009 and various geopolitical unrests across the globe. Economic uncertainty brings about economic uncertainty shocks.

Economic uncertainty shocks are changes in economic uncertainty that have a consequential effect on core macroeconomic outcomes and economic performance measures like consumption, inflation and unemployment. Economic uncertainty shocks are mostly unpredictable and are usually the outcome of activities believed to be beyond the scope of normal economic activities. Economic uncertainty shocks could have widespread effects on an economy even in the long run. Following the real business cycle theory, economic uncertainty shocks are capable of causing economic recessions. Economic uncertainty shocks could affect an economy through either the demand side or the supply side. Economic uncertainty shocks may also be classified as either normal or real shocks, depending on whether the shock is on real economic activity or nominal values of economic variables. Demand side shocks are sudden changes in the pattern of spending in the form of consumer spending or investment spending and real income. Supply-side shocks occur in production in most industries in the economy more costly, difficult or impossible [17].

Economic uncertainty in a country could increase doubt about available information on economic fundamentals and influence decisions that could increase the likelihood of economic crises and spillover to other countries and affect macroeconomic variables and cause macroeconomic fluctuations. The structuralist theory is one of the theories that explain the effects of economic uncertainty shocks on macroeconomic variables. The theory is of the view that macroeconomic changes or fluctuations could be attributed to structural shocks like sudden large changes in macroeconomic variables such as prices and consumption and investment expenditures [23].

Based on the evidence in most developing countries and Latin America, a school of thought is of the view that structural shocks could be long-lasting and stem from bottlenecks in key sectors of the economy including agriculture and the oil sector. To this view, economic uncertainties such as the outbreak of the COVID-19 global pandemic, and the Russia-Ukraine War impede growth in agriculture, etc. causing prices to rise among others in the directly affected economies and later transmitted to other economies. A different strand of the theoretical literature builds on the theory of rational expectation to argue that the magnitude of the shock could be contingent on the behaviour of expectation. For example, the expectation that a given economic uncertainty is permanent will determine large and persistent shocks.

Similarly, when there is an expectation that the effect of the shocks is just temporary, then macroeconomic fundamentals will adjust quickly back to initial equilibrium. They are, therefore, of the opinion that empirical knowledge on the nature of the effect of the shock—whether permanent or transitory and the determinants of the magnitude of the effect will be necessary for relevant policy formulation [23].

Our point of argument, however, is that due to increasingly stronger economic, financial and political ties among nations, spillover (effects) to the rest of the world is very possible; What happens (a shock) in one country could easily be transmitted to other countries. Interconnectedness and contagion effects across regions and the globe alike, global economic uncertainty shocks in a country spillover to other countries, capable of engendering economic growth brittleness and fragility in other macroeconomic variables such as interest rate, inflation and consumption. Therefore, managers of the economy need to be vigilant not only of the domestic economy.

Several empirical studies have examined the spillover effect of global economic uncertainty shocks. Such literature has focused on macroeconomic activity and growth in real output, private consumption uncertainty, private investment uncertainty and the volatility of stock market indices implications. Ozili and Arun [21] examined the spillover impact of COVID-19 on the global economy, focusing specifically on the impact of social distancing policies on macroeconomic activity and stock market indices in Japan, the UK, the US and South Africa. The study used monthly frequency data that covered the periods from the 23rd of March to the 23rd of April, 2020. The authors employed a multivariate model that was estimated using a least square regression. The findings of the study showed that the macroeconomic activities were impacted by monetary policy decisions, several lockdown days and international travel restrictions. It was also found that restrictions on internal movement and higher fiscal policy spending positively impacted the level of economic activities. They, however, found no significant impact of the number of confirmed coronavirus cases on the level of economic activities. Using local projections, Biljanovska et al. [4] examined the spillover effects of economic policy uncertainty originating in the United States, Europe and China on other countries' economic activity using heterogeneous panel structural vector autoregressions. The study used unbalanced panel data starting from 1985 to 2017. It was found that economic policy uncertainty reduces growth in real output, private consumption, and private investment. It was also found that about two-thirds of the negative effect was accounted for, by spillovers from abroad accounts. Spillovers from China, the United States, and Europe were found to reduce economic activity in the rest of the world, especially in Europe and the Western Hemisphere.

Focusing on the G7 countries, Cuaresma et al. [10] employed a large-scale Bayesian VAR model with factor stochastic volatility to investigate the macroeconomic effects of international uncertainty shocks using quarterly data from 1979Q4 to 2013Q4. It was found that international uncertainty shocks had a significant effect on all G7 economies and variables that were studied. The impact of global uncertainty on the global economy and large developed and developing economies was examined by Kang et al. [18]. The study used monthly data covering the period from

January 1981 to December 2014. The VAR technique was employed to analyze the data. Global uncertainty was measured by the stock market volatility indexes for the largest 15 economies, constructed by the authors using principal component analysis. The study found that global uncertainty shocks bring about a sharp decline in global industrial production, global inflation and global interest rate. A maximum decline in industrial production and global inflation was recorded after 6 months of a global uncertainty shock, while the maximum decline period for the global interest rate was 16 months after a global uncertainty shock.

Based on the literature, it is understood that most of the studies focused on developed economies, especially Japan, the UK, and the US and few studies concentrated on developing economies. The studies also focused on macroeconomic activity and stock market indices. Even, the few that concentrated on the developing countries do not focus on Nigeria. Nigeria is the largest economy in Africa. Nigeria is a monolithic and commodity-dependent country and imports more than exports with oil being the major export commodity. Nigeria will present a case for the spillover effects of global economic uncertainty shocks in developing countries. The spillover effects of global economic uncertainty shocks could have severe economic implications. Nigeria just like most other African countries is highly dependent on imports than exports and the economy is not self-sustaining. Therefore, studies like this study that could broaden our understanding of the spillover effects of global economic uncertainty shocks would be vital for policy prescriptions that could be helpful in resilience in times of global economic uncertainties.

1.3 Methodology

1.3.1 Measurement of Economic Uncertainty

The literature on economic uncertainty has over the years adopted several methods to measure the economic uncertainty of time series variables. Rather, it is indisputable that most economic time series are typical of time-varying variance that is conditional upon volatility clustering. Volatility clustering implies periods of high variances and some other periods of low variances. Uncertainty shocks, beyond doubt, can impact macroeconomic variables and will make appropriate policy-making very difficult for any country if not well understood. The research agenda for this chapter, as noted earlier, is to determine the spillover effects of real output uncertainty, inflation uncertainty and private consumption uncertainty in the US, China and Europe, in particular, on real output growth, the domestic price level, and private consumption in Nigeria. A measure developed to model uncertainty is the Autoregressive Conditional Heteroscedasticity (ARCH) model developed by Engle [13]. There have been several modifications to the pioneer ARCH model. These include Engle et al. [14], the ARCH in Mean (ARCH-M) and Bollerslev's [7] Generalized ARCH (GARCH) model. There are different versions of the GARCH model, which are Engle and

Bollerslev's (1986) integrated GARCH (IGARCH) model, asymmetric GARCH models—exponential GARCH (EGARCH) developed by Nelson [20], the multivariate GARCH models (MGARCH) developed by Baba et al. [2] and later modified by Engle and Kroner [15], GJR-GARCH by Glosten et al. [16], asymmetric power GARCH (APGARCH) model by Ding et al. [12], etc.

For this chapter, the EGARCH model is used. This model is credited to Nelson [20] and it captures information asymmetries. Assuming that y_t follows an autoregressive process of order q, the general framework of the mean equation is specified as

$$y_t = \beta_0 + \sum_{i=1}^{q} \beta_i y_{t-i} + \varepsilon_t \tag{1.1}$$

The complete model will incorporate the following variance model:

$$\log \sigma_t^2 = \varphi + \sum_{i=1}^{q} \alpha_i \log \sigma_{t-i}^2 + \sum_{i=1}^{p} \beta_i \left| \frac{\varepsilon_{t-i}}{\sigma_{t-i}} \right| + \sum_{k=1}^{r} \gamma_k \left(\frac{\varepsilon_{t-k}}{\sigma_{t-k}} \right) \tag{1.2}$$

$\log \sigma_t^2$ is the logarithm of the conditional variance. The log form of the EGARCH (p, q) model certifies the non-negativity of the conditional variance. The asymmetric effect of positive or negative shocks (information) is captured by including $\varepsilon_{t-i}/\sigma_{t-i}$. If $\gamma_k > 0$ (<0) volatility seems to increase (decrease) when the lagged standardized shock, $\varepsilon_{t-i}/\sigma_{t-I}$ is positive (negative). The persistence of volatility to the conditional variance is given by $\sum_{i=1}^{q} \alpha_i$.

This method is considered better than some other measures like the rolling standard deviation because it has the advantage of disassociating the sources of uncertainty into anticipated and unanticipated changes far more than variability yield by the variance or standard deviation technique [8].

1.3.2 Data and Data Source

The dataset is a quarterly frequency time series and covers the 1981q1–2020q4 sample periods. The variables central to our study include consumer price index (for Nigeria only), inflation (for the US, China, and Europe), and real GDP and private consumption (for the US, China, Europe and Nigeria). The data will be sourced from the World Development Indicators (WDI). The real output uncertainty, inflation uncertainty and private consumption uncertainty as stated earlier will be generated from the conditional variances of real GDP, inflation and private consumption using the EGARCH technique.

1.3.3 Model Specification

Here, we first model the link between domestic (Nigeria's) inflation and private consumption uncertainties and real activity (measured by industrial production). Thereafter, we study the spillover effects of real output uncertainty, inflation uncertainty and private consumption uncertainty from the US, China, and Europe to the domestic (Nigeria's) real output growth, the domestic price level and private consumption.

1.3.3.1 Domestic Economic Effects

To determine the domestic (Nigeria's) inflation and private consumption uncertainties and real activity (measured by industrial production), we estimate a vector-autoregressive regression (VAR) model. The VAR technique enables us to control for possible endogeneity, which is now standard in the literature on the effects of uncertainty. We specify the following VAR

$$X_t = \sum_{t=1}^{k} X_{t-1} + e_t \tag{1.3}$$

where vector X_t contains the variables in the following order: PRICOUNC (private consumption uncertainty), INFUNC (inflation uncertainty) and INDP (industrial production—measured by industrial output). Employing Cholesky decomposition, the VAR residuals covariance matrix is orthogonalized with the variables ordered as stated above. We follow similar studies such as Bloom [5] and Londono et al. [19] and order the uncertainty before INDP based on the reason that shocks to uncertainty impact real economic activity contemporaneously but not the other way round. The posterior distribution of all the parameters of the VAR is estimated using Bayesian estimation with flat priors [19].

1.3.3.2 International Spillover Effects

In line with objective two, the international spillover effects of real output uncertainty, inflation uncertainty and private consumption uncertainty from the US, China, and Europe to the domestic (Nigeria's) real output growth, the domestic price level and private consumption are considered here. Following Diebold and Yilmaz [11], spillover effects could be measured based on forecast error variance decomposition from the generalized VAR framework such that the forecast error variance decompositions are invariable to variable ordering. Thus, we modify the vector in Eq. (1.3) to include foreign variables. We model real output growth, the domestic price level and private consumption in separate models. Thus, we have

$$X_t^{Ext1} = \sum_{t=1}^{k} X_{t-1}^{Ext1} + e_{t1} \quad (1.4a)$$

$$X_t^{Ext2} = \sum_{t=1}^{k} X_{t-1}^{Ext2} + e_{t2} \quad (1.4b)$$

$$X_t^{Ext3} = \sum_{t=1}^{k} X_{t-1}^{Ext3} + e_{t3} \quad (1.4c)$$

where vector X_t^{Ext1} in Eq. (1.4a) contains the variables in the following order: RGDPUN (real output uncertainty) for the US—$RGDPUN_{-US}$, China—$RGDPUN_{-Chi}$, and Europe—$RGDPUN_{-EUR}$ respectively, INFUN (inflation uncertainty) for the US—$INFUN_{-US}$, China—$INFUN_{-CHI}$, and Europe—$INFUN_{-EUR}$, respectively, and PRICUN (private consumption uncertainty) for the US—$PRICUN_{-US}$, China—$PRICUN_{-CHI}$, and Europe—$PRICUN_{-EUR}$, respectively, and $RGDPG_{-NIG}$ (real output growth) for Nigeria. Similarly, vector X_t^{Ext2} in Eq. (1.4b) contains the variables in the following order: RGDPUN (real output uncertainty) for the US—$RGDPUN_{-US}$, China—$RGDPUN_{-Chi}$, and Europe—$RGDPUN_{-EUR}$, respectively, INFUN (inflation uncertainty) for the US—$INFUN_{-US}$, China—$INFUN_{-CHI}$, and Europe—$INFUN_{-EUR}$, respectively, and PRICUN (private consumption uncertainty) for the US—$PRICUN_{-US}$, China—$PRICUN_{-CHI}$, and Europe—$PRICUN_{-EUR}$, respectively, and DPL_{-NIG} (domestic consumer price index) for Nigeria. In a like manner, for Eq. (1.4c), vector X_t^{Ext3} contains the variables in the following order: RGDPUN (real output uncertainty) for the US—$RGDPUN_{-US}$, China—$RGDPUN_{-Chi}$, and Europe—$RGDPUN_{-EUR}$ respectively, INFUN (inflation uncertainty) for the US—$INFUN_{-US}$, China—$INFUN_{-CHI}$, and Europe—$INFUN_{-EUR}$, respectively, and PRICUN (private consumption uncertainty) for the US—$PRICUN_{-US}$, China—$PRICUN_{-CHI}$, and Europe—$PRICUN_{-EUR}$, respectively, and $DPCON_{-NIG}$ (domestic private consumption) for Nigeria.

Equation (1.4a) will be estimated, respectively, for the US, China, and Europe to determine the spillover effect from the countries separately to the domestic (Nigeria's) real output growth. Also, Eq. (1.4b) will be estimated, respectively, for the US, China and Europe to determine the spillover effect from the countries separately to the domestic (Nigeria's) price level. Equation (1.4c) also will be estimated respectively for the US, China and Europe to examine the spillover effect from the countries separately to the domestic (Nigeria's) private consumption.

Similar to Eq. (1.3), the covariance matrix of VAR residuals of Eqs. (1.4a), (1.4b) and (1.4c), respectively, is orthogonalized using the Cholesky decomposition with the variables ordered as listed above for the respective equations. The ordering of the foreign variables coming before the domestic variables is necessary since, by construction, any shock to the foreign variables is contemporaneously uncorrelated with the domestic variables ($RGDPG_{-NIG}$, DPL_{-NIG} and $DPCON_{-NIG}$) and can only affect them with a lag. The posterior distributions of all the parameters in the VAR equations are estimated using the Bayesian estimation.

1.4 Results

1.4.1 Economic Uncertainties and the Asymmetric Uncertainties in Inflation and Private Consumption for Nigeria

To obtain the uncertainties of the variables and the asymmetric uncertainties of the variables for Nigeria, the EGARCH model was estimated with inflation and private consumption for Nigeria in the model. However, before the model was estimated, the level form series and the differenced series of inflation and private consumption for Nigeria were plotted. The graph is shown in the different parts of Fig. 1.1.

The level forms of the variables showed fluctuating trends. The differenced series, on the other hand, is characterized by random, rapid changes in inflation and domestic consumption movements, respectively, and can be described as volatile (uncertainty). The volatility change over time in addition to the evidence of inflation and domestic consumption volatility clustering enables us to quantify the impact of any shock on

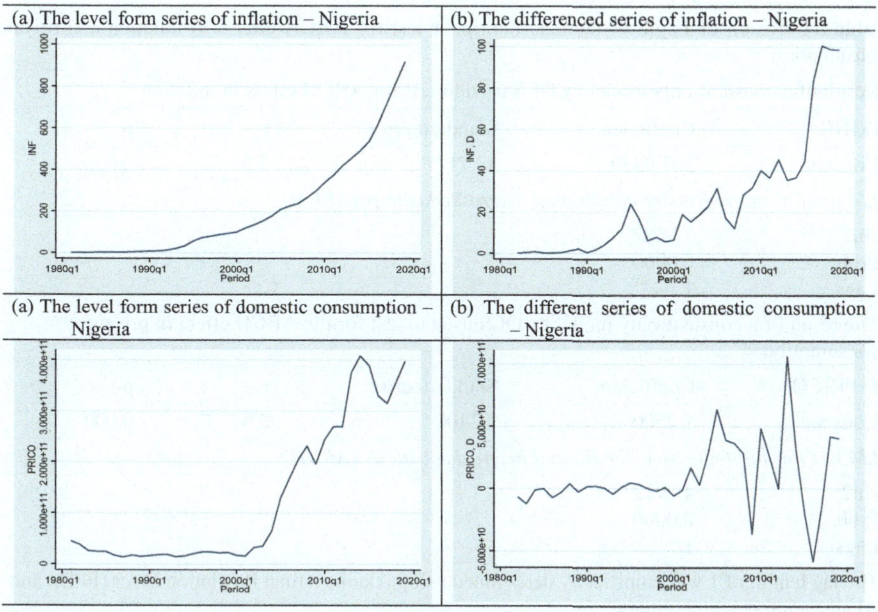

Fig. 1.1 Graph of inflation and private consumption for Nigeria. *Source* Plot by the authors

the variance, which transmits itself during adjacent time intervals—as a large shock is followed by a larger one and a small shock is followed by a smaller one. For example, from the last quarter of 1980 to the last quarter of 2008, private consumption was relatively sedate or calm (periods of relative tranquility). This was, however, followed by periods of high volatility (uncertainty), as indicated in the first quarter of 2010 until 2019. This is traced to the periods of the 2008/2009 financial crisis and COVID-19.

We fit a constant-only model by OLS and test ARCH effects in inflation and private consumption respectively by using Engle's Lagrange multiplier test. This is to ascertain the appropriateness of the EGARCH model in fitting the (inflation and private consumption) data. The result is reported in Table 1.1.

Engle's LM test showed a p-value (0.0000) both for inflation and domestic private consumption, which is below 0.05 in an absolute sense. Therefore, the null hypotheses of no ARCH effects at the 5% level are rejected for both inflation and private consumption. Since ARCH effects are confirmed, we went further to estimate the Exponential Generalized Autoregressive Conditional Heteroskedasticity (EGARCH) model respectively for inflation and private consumption. The result is shown in Table 1.2.

The result showed a strong indication of the leverage effect for inflation and a weak leverage effect for private consumption (leverage effect explains the shock that may strongly influence the variance as a result of a "negative shock" causing a greater loss in returns than the gains from a "positive shock") and strong indication for asymmetric effect for both inflation and private consumption (asymmetric

Table 1.1 Result of Engle's Lagrange multiplier test for ARCH effects in inflation and private consumption

Result of a constant-only model by OLS used to test for ARCH effect in inflation				
D.INF	Coefficient	Standard error	t	p
Constant	207.9339	39.7127	5.24	0.000
LM test for autoregressive conditional heteroskedasticity (ARCH)				
chi2	37.582			
Prob.	0.0000			
Lags	1			
The result of a constant-only model by OLS used to test for the ARCH effect in private consumption				
D.PRICO	Coefficient	Standard error	t	p
Constant	1.2500	2.2400	5.57	0.000
LM test for autoregressive conditional heteroskedasticity (ARCH)				
chi2	4.7912			
Prob.	0.0000			
Lags	1			
The lag length of 1 was empirically determined using Akaike's final Prediction Error (FPE), and Akaike's information criteria				

Source Author's computation

Table 1.2 Result of the EGARCH model

Inflation	Coefficient	OPG standard error	z-value	p-value
For inflation				
Inflation constant	2.7837	0.0106	261.0	0.000
ARCH				
earch (L1)	6.5314	2.2456	2.91	0.004
earch_a (L1)	−2.9687	2.4603	−1.21	0.228
egarch (L1)	0.7688	0.1925	3.99	0.000
Constant	−3.1493	1.5058	−2.09	0.036
For private consumption				
PRICO Constant	2.1500	1.0900	19.78	0.000
ARCH				
earch (L1)	0.5655	0.5784	0.98	0.328
earch_a (L1)	2.1186	1.1499	1.84	0.065
egarch (L1)	0.8168	0.1781	4.59	0.000
Constant	8.5370	8.3017	1.03	0.304

The lag length was empirically determined using Akaike's final Prediction Error (FPE), and Akaike's information criteria

Source Author's computation

effect concerns the significance and proportional contribution of negative shock that destabilizes variance). The positive e_arch (L1) coefficients both for inflation and private consumption mean that positive innovations (unanticipated increase in private consumption and decrease in inflation) are more profitable than negative innovations (unanticipated decrease in private consumption and increase in inflation). On the other hand, the asymmetric inflation uncertainty showed a negative coefficient of −2.9687 with a t-value of −1.21. Thus, the null hypothesis of no asymmetric inflation uncertainty in Nigeria is accepted. There is no significant asymmetric inflation uncertainty in Nigeria. In specific terms, the negative asymmetric coefficient (−2.9687) means that there is a tendency of inflation uncertainty to reduce by 2.97% when there is an unanticipated decline in inflation than an unanticipated increase in inflation. We generated the conditional variance of the series (inflation and private consumption) and are used as measures for inflation uncertainty and private consumption uncertainty.

1.4.2 International Economic Uncertainties and the Asymmetric of Uncertainties—Real Output, Inflation and Private Consumption for US, China and Europe

Before the measurement of real output uncertainty, and private consumption and inflation uncertainties of the US, China and Europe, we plot the level form and the differenced series of the variables, shown in Fig. 1.2.

The level form series shows fluctuating trends over the study periods. Also, the different series showed staggering movement. We tested for the ARCH effect of the variables for each of the countries respectively. Table 1.3 shows the test results.

In each column, the test accepts the null hypothesis of the presence of an arch effect. This means that the variables have an arch effect. Therefore, we estimated the EGARCH model for each of the variables for each of the countries selected for the study. The result is presented in Table 1.4.

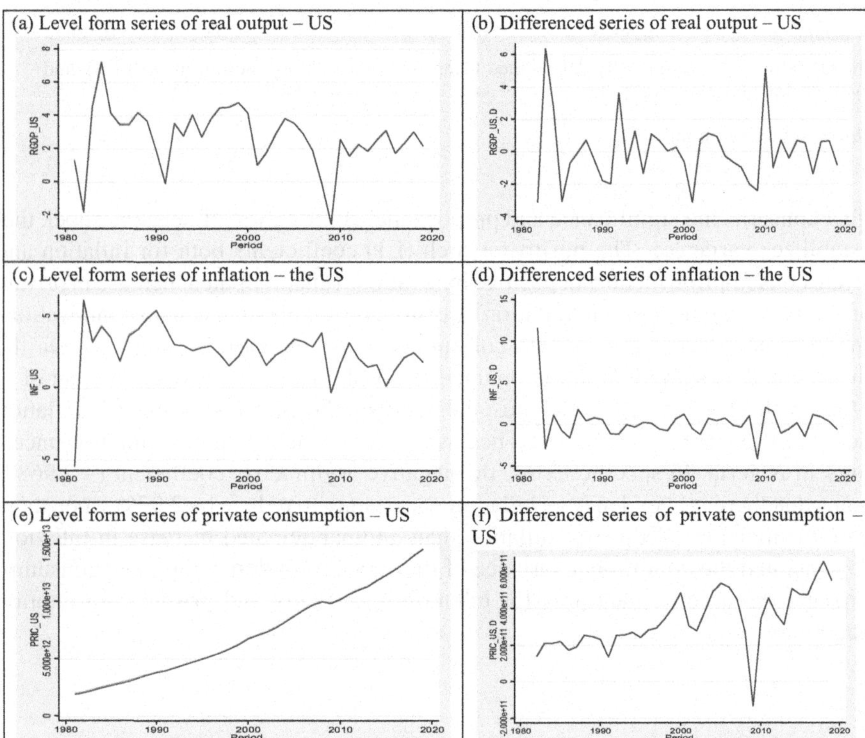

Fig. 1.2 Economic uncertainties and the asymmetric uncertainties in inflation and private consumption for Nigeria. *Source* Plot by the authors

Table 1.3 Estimates of test for ARCH effect

Result of a constant-only model by OLS used to test for ARCH effect—US variables			
Constant	(1) Real output	(2) Inflation	(1) Private consumption
	2.6817 (t = 9.30) (p = 0.000)	2.5551 (t = 8.69) (p = 0.000)	7.1800 (t = 11.88) (p = 0.000)
LM test for autoregressive conditional heteroskedasticity (ARCH)—US variables			
chi2	0.301	0.207	1.574
Prob > chi2	0.2032	0.1301	0.1420
df	1	1	1
Result of a constant-only model by OLS used to test for ARCH effect—China variables			
Constant	(1) Real output	(2) Inflation	(1) Private consumption
	9.481 (t = 21.47) (p = 0.000)	7.105 (t = 5.20) (p = 0.000)	8.6110 (t = 6.10) (p = 0.000)
LM test for autoregressive conditional heteroskedasticity (ARCH)—China variables			
chi2	1.494	0.193	1.191
Prob > chi2	0.7143	0.2213	0.6120
df	1	1	1
Result of a constant-only model by OLS used to test for ARCH effect—Europe variables			
Constant	(1) Real output	(2) Inflation	(1) Private consumption
	2.1877 (t = 4.30) (p = 0.000)	3.6115 (t = 6.30) (p = 0.000)	4.6817 (t = 7.40) (p = 0.000)
LM test for autoregressive conditional heteroskedasticity (ARCH)—European variables			
chi2	0.301	0.311	0.221
Prob > chi2	0.3032	0.1102	0.1711
df	1	1	1
The lag length of 1 was empirically determined using Akaike's final Prediction Error (FPE), and Akaike's information criterions			

Source Authors' computations

Table 1.4 EGARCH estimates respectively for real output, inflation and private consumption

	(1) Real output	(2) Inflation	(1) Private consumption
Result of the EGARCH—US variables			
Constant	4.6113 (t = 8.31) (p = 0.000)	7.1117 (t = 6.41) (p = 0.000)	5.1816 (t = 5.16) (p = 0.000)
ARCH			
earch (L1)	3.3314 (t = 3.59) (p = 0.000)	1.2364 (t = 3.79) (p = 0.000)	2.330 (t = 3.92) (p = 0.000)
earch_a (L1)	2.1982 (t = 2.08) (p = 0.046)	2.4312 (t = 2.18) (p = 0.046)	3.731 (t = 2.38) (p = 0.041)
egarch (L1)	1.9698 (t = 3.78) (p = 0.000)	5.3290 (t = 2.78) (p = 0.000)	3.910 (t = 2.69) (p = 0.000)
Constant	−3.3213 (t = −2.07) (p = 0.039)	2.121 (t = 2.17) (p = 0.036)	3.450 (t = 2.77) (p = 0.000)
Result of the EGARCH model—China variables			
Constant	2.9413 (t = 7.41) (p = 0.000)	6.1211 (t = 5.61) (p = 0.000)	4.121 (t = 4.26) (p = 0.000)
ARCH			
earch (L1)	2.8814 (t = 4.79) (p = 0.000)	1.2344 (t = 4.68) (p = 0.000)	2.133 (t = 3.97) (p = 0.000)
earch_a (L1)	2.1822 (t = 2.28) (p = 0.040)	2.5720 (t = 4.18) (p = 0.000)	2.790 (t = 2.98) (p = 0.000)
egarch (L1)	4.9008 (t = 5.08) (p = 0.000)	3.1294 (t = 3.78) (p = 0.000)	2.118 (t = 3.68) (p = 0.000)
Constant	5.0203 (t = 2.17) (p = 0.035)	2.220 (t = 2.57) (p = 0.000)	3.351 (t = 2.39) (p = 0.007)
Result of the EGARCH—Europe variables			
Constant	1.6210 (t = 5.21) (p = 0.000)	3.1267 (t = 4.61) (p = 0.000)	2.126 (t = 3.11) (p = 0.000)
ARCH			
earch (L1)	2.0114 (t = 2.52) (p = 0.000)	2.2364 (t = 2.61) (p = 0.001)	2.216 (t = 3.81) (p = 0.000)
earch_a (L1)	2.4081 (t = 2.68) (p = 0.000)	2.4013 (t = 2.38) (p = 0.026)	3.232 (t = 2.41) (p = 0.021)
egarch (L1)	2.9100 (t = 3.50) (p = 0.000)	3.3010 (t = 2.72) (p = 0.000)	2.622 (t = 2.55) (p = 0.000)
Constant	−3.0200 (t = −3.07) (p = 0.000)	2.229 (t = 2.66) (p = 0.000)	2.251 (t = 3.09) (p = 0.000)
The lag length of 1 was empirically determined using Akaike's final Prediction Error (FPE), and Akaike's information criterions			

Source Authors' computations

In columns (1), (2) and (3), the result showed a strong indication of leverage effect and a strong indication of asymmetric effect US, China and Europe. The positive arch (L1) coefficients in columns (1), (2) and (3) mean that positive innovations (unanticipated increase in real output, international private consumption and decrease in inflation) are more profitable than negative innovations (unanticipated decrease in real output, private consumption and increase in inflation). The asymmetric of real output, private consumption and inflation for the US, China and Europe respectively is positive and significant. Thus, the null hypothesis of no asymmetric real output, private consumption and inflation for the US, China and Europe respectively is rejected. The positive asymmetric coefficients of the variables mean that there is a tendency for the uncertainty of the variables to increase when there is an unanticipated global risk. We generated the conditional variance of the series (real output, inflation and private consumption) for the US, China and Europe respectively and the generated series are used as measures for, real output uncertainty, inflation uncertainty and private consumption uncertainty.

1.4.3 The Link Between Domestic (Nigeria's) Inflation and Private Consumption Uncertainties and Real Activity—Industrial Production

The model for the domestic economic effects of inflation and private consumption uncertainties (model 3) was estimated and the impulse response functions are shown in Fig. 1.3. In specific terms, the first panel in Fig. 1.3 shows the response of domestic industrial production (INDP) to domestic inflation uncertainty (INFUNC). The second panel, on the other hand, shows the response of domestic industrial production (INDP) to private consumption uncertainty (PRICOUNC).

The response of domestic industrial production to domestic inflation uncertainty is positive. Industrial production rises slowly with fluctuations until hitting a peak around the ma mark. It shows that the effect of inflation uncertainty is positive. The positive effect means that industrial production increases. Therefore, if the domestic economy is exposed to domestic risk in terms of uncertainty about the inflation level and then producers have more incentive to increase industrial production. However, the reverse is the case for private consumption uncertainty. The response of domestic industrial production to private consumption uncertainty is negative. The negative effect on industrial production reduces slowly until becomes 0 around the eight-quarter mark. The negative effect means that industrial production decreases. Therefore, if the domestic economy is exposed to domestic risk in terms of the uncertainty of private consumption and then producers have more incentive to decrease industrial production.

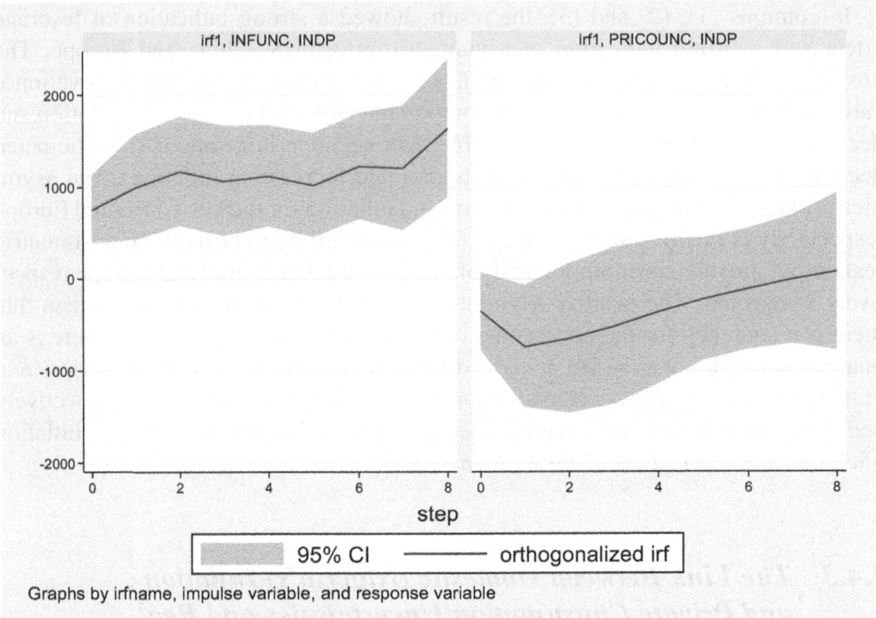

Fig. 1.3 IRFs to an inflation uncertainty and private consumption uncertainty shocks. *Source* Plot by the authors

1.4.4 Spillover Effects of Real Output Uncertainty, Inflation Uncertainty and Private Consumption Uncertainty from US, China, and Europe to the Domestic (Nigeria's) Real Output

The spillover effect of real output uncertainty, inflation uncertainty and private consumption uncertainty from the US, China, and Europe to the domestic (Nigeria's) real output is determined. Figure 1.4 shows the impulse response functions of the VAR estimates.

The response of domestic real output to US real output uncertainty was negative at the beginning of the uncertainty but the effect slowly reduces and returns to 0 at about the fifth-quarter mark. It shows that the effect of US real output uncertainty is negative but the negative effect becomes neutral after about the 5 quarter. The negative effect means that the domestic (Nigeria's) real output decreases. Therefore, if the domestic economy is exposed to global risk from the US in terms of real output uncertainty, then, the real output of the domestic economy decreases. The real output uncertainty spillover effect from China is similar to that of the US. The effect is negative. For Europe, the response of domestic real output to European real output uncertainty is 0 by construction. Thereafter, domestic real output dropped sharply at the first-quarter mark. The effect becomes neutral at about the second quarter. The spillover effects of

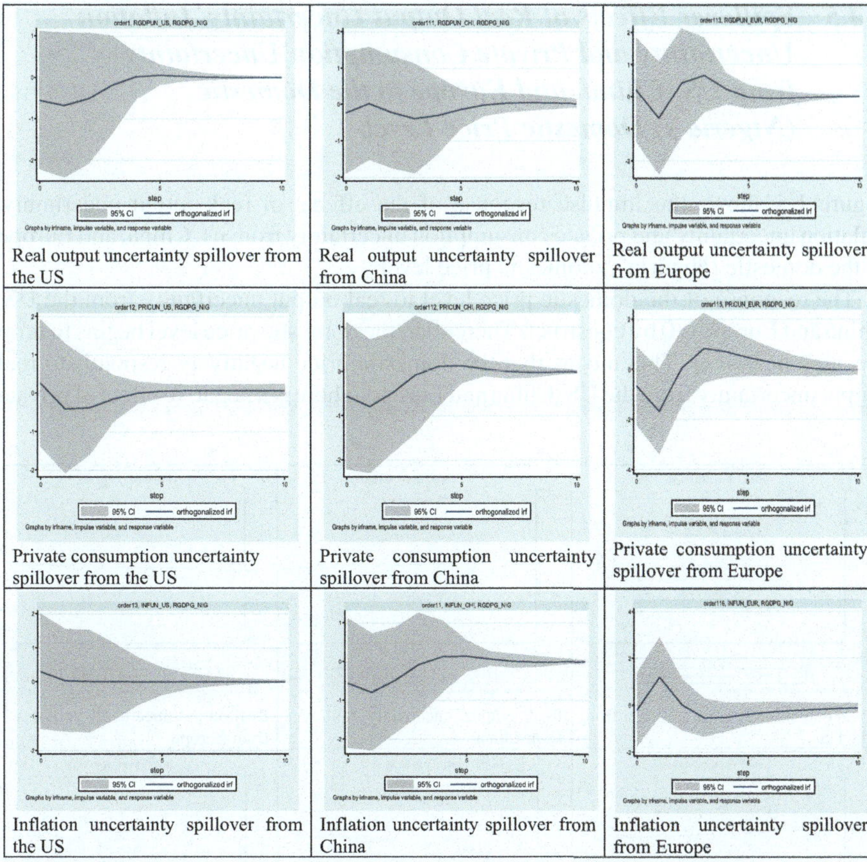

Fig. 1.4 International spillover effects of real output uncertainty, inflation uncertainty and private consumption uncertainty from the US, China, and Europe to the domestic (Nigeria's) real output growth. *Source* Plot by the authors

consumption uncertainty from the US, China and Europe are negative. The negative effect indicates that the domestic real output decreases if there is any uncertainty in private consumption from the US, China and Europe. For inflation, when there is global risk shock to which the domestic economy is largely exposed. Due to the connectedness of economies, inflation uncertainty from foreign economies brings about a reduction in domestic real output.

1.4.5 Spillover Effects of Real Output Uncertainty, Inflation Uncertainty and Private Consumption Uncertainty from US, China, and Europe to the Domestic (Nigeria's) Domestic Price Level

Figure 1.5 shows the impulse response of the effects of real output uncertainty, inflation uncertainty and private consumption uncertainty from us, China, and Europe to the domestic (Nigeria's) domestic price level.

The response of the domestic price level to real output uncertainty from the US, China and Europe is 0 by construct. Thereafter, the domestic price level begins to drop (became negative). This means that the domestic price negatively responds to real output uncertainty from the US, China and Europe. There is a negative effect of private

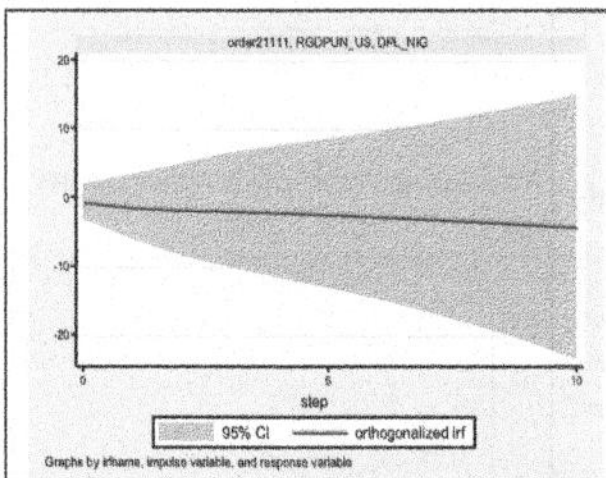 Real output uncertainty spillover from the US	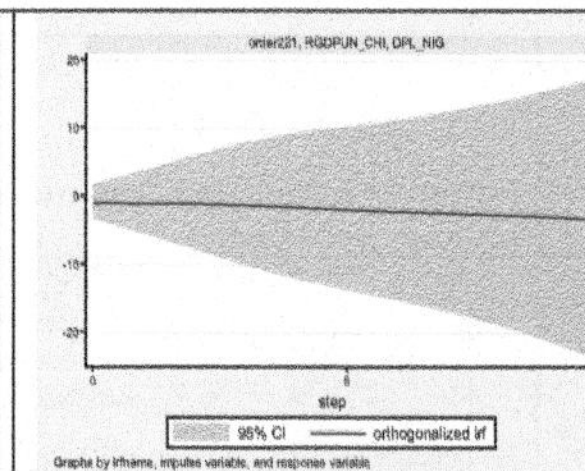 Real output uncertainty spillover from China	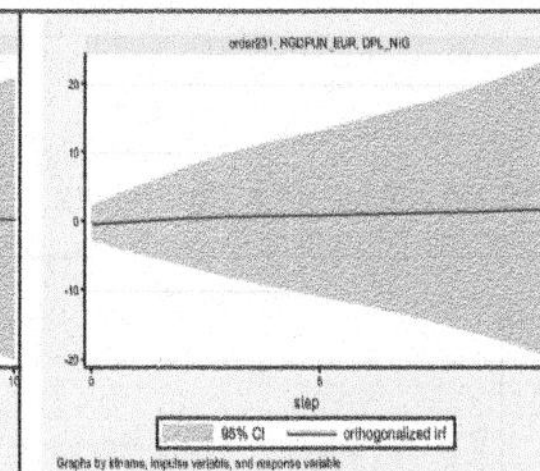 Real output uncertainty spillover from Europe
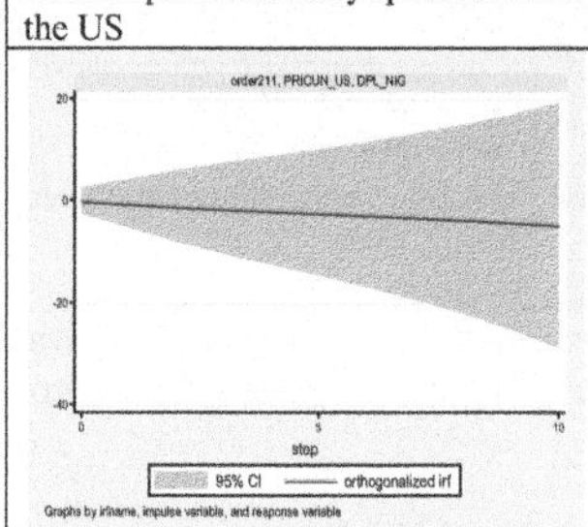 Private consumption uncertainty spillover from the US	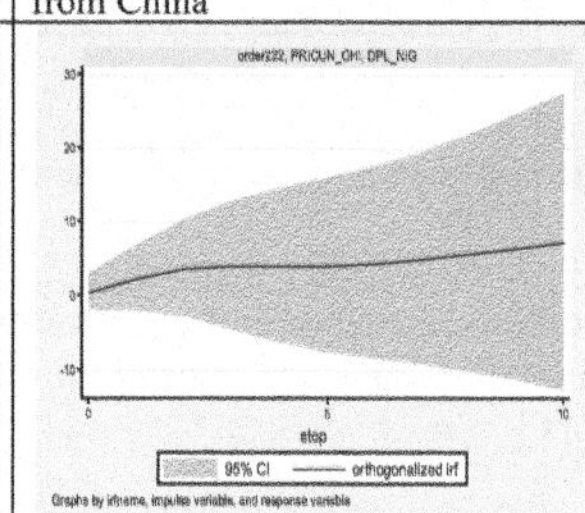 Private consumption uncertainty spillover from China	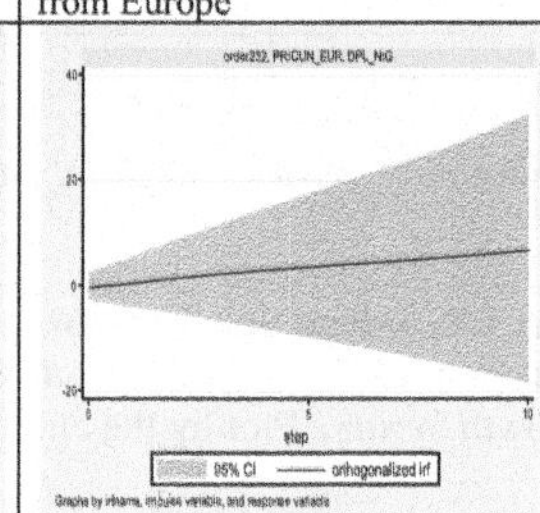 Private consumption uncertainty spillover from Europe
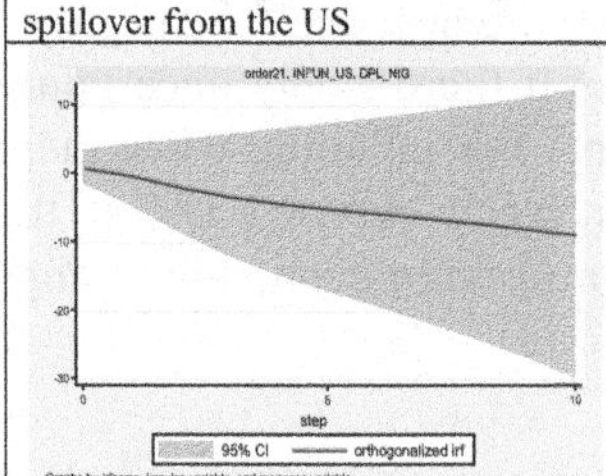 Inflation uncertainty spillover from the US	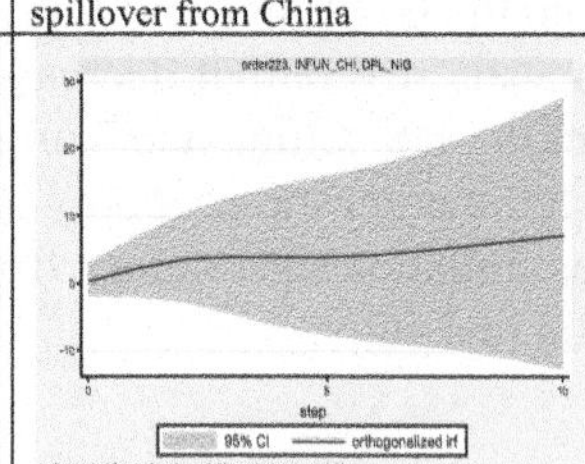 Inflation uncertainty spillover from China	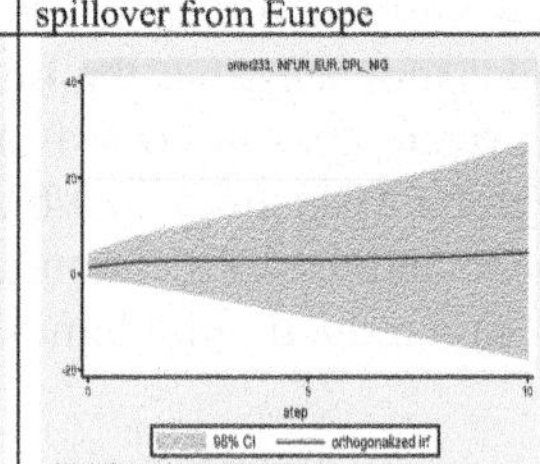 Inflation uncertainty spillover from Europe

Fig. 1.5 International spillover effects of real output uncertainty, inflation uncertainty and private consumption uncertainty from the US, China, and Europe to the domestic (Nigeria's) price level. *Source* Plot by the authors

consumption uncertainty on the domestic price level for both US, China and Europe. This means that if there is private consumption uncertainty in the US, China and Europe due to global risk, the domestic price responds negatively to the uncertainty. Concerning the response of the domestic price level to inflation uncertainty from the US, China and Europe, the result showed that from the US, the spillover effect of inflation uncertainty on the domestic price level is negative up to the tenth-quarter mark. The negative spillover effect means that inflation uncertainty in the US due to global risk results in a reduction in the domestic price level. However, in China and Europe, the inflation uncertainty spillover effect is positive. This means that inflation uncertainty in China and Europe due to global risk will bring about an increase in the level of the domestic price.

1.4.6 Spillover Effects of Real Output Uncertainty, Inflation Uncertainty and Private Consumption Uncertainty from US, China, and Europe to the Domestic (Nigeria's) Private Consumption

We also examined the spillover effects of real output uncertainty, inflation uncertainty and private consumption uncertainty from the US, China, and Europe to the domestic (Nigeria's) private consumption. The VAR impulse response function is shown in Fig. 1.6.

The response of domestic private consumption to real output uncertainty from the US, and Europe is positive. Real output uncertainty in the US and Europe due to global risks leads to an increase in domestic private consumption. But for China, real output uncertainty results in a decrease in private consumption in the domestic economy. It means that when there is real output uncertainty in China resulting from global risks, domestic private consumption decreases. It is similar to private consumption uncertainty. Its uncertainty in the US and Europe has a positive effect on domestic private consumption. But for China, private consumption uncertainty has a negative spillover effect on domestic private consumption. This means that uncertainty of private consumption in China causes a drop in private consumption in the domestic economy. For inflation, the US, China and Europe have a negative spillover effect on private consumption. It means that uncertainty of inflation from these countries due to global risk results in a drop in domestic private consumption.

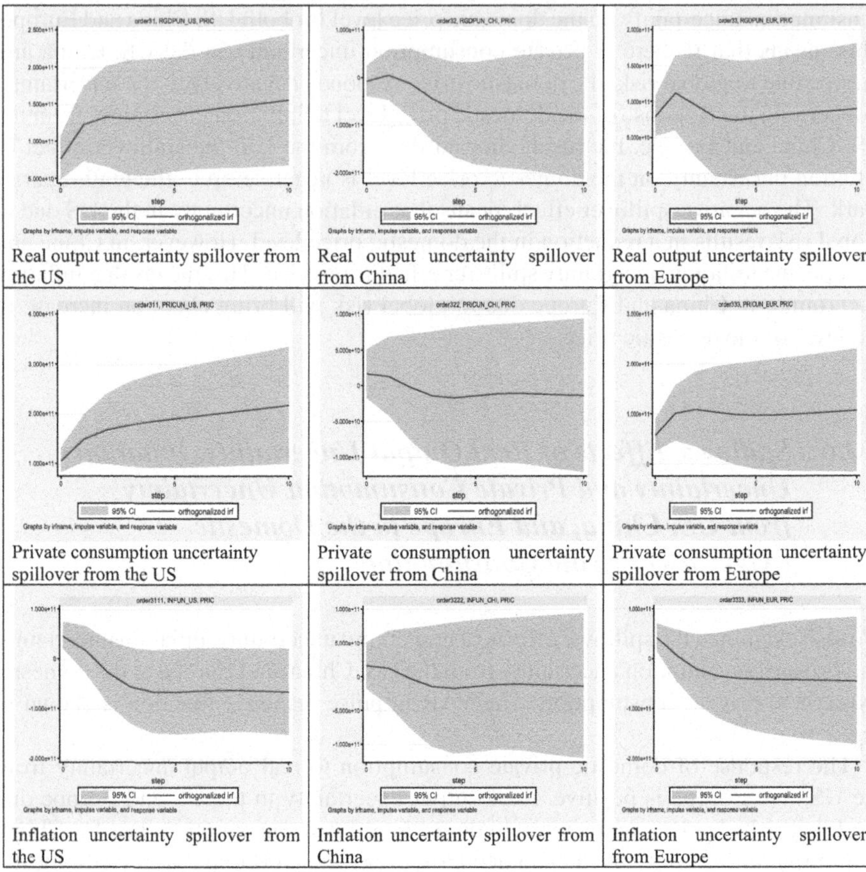

Fig. 1.6 International spillover effects of real output uncertainty, inflation uncertainty and private consumption uncertainty from the US, China, and Europe to the domestic (Nigeria's) private consumption. *Source* Plot by the authors

1.5 Conclusion and Policy Recommendations

The spillover effect of global economic uncertainty shocks in Nigeria has been examined in this chapter. We specifically examined the link between domestic (Nigeria's) inflation and private consumption uncertainties and real activity—industrial production and, the spillover effects of real output uncertainty, inflation uncertainty and private consumption uncertainty from the US, China, and Europe to the domestic (Nigeria's) real output growth, the domestic price level and private consumption. In the domestic economy, inflation uncertainty due to global economic shock brings about an increase in industrial production, especially between the 1st quarter and the eighth quarter. But private consumption uncertainty reduces industrial production, effective mostly up to the eight-quarter. For the international spillover, real output uncertainty reduces domestic real output to decrease. Private consumption uncertainty and inflation uncertainty also reduce domestic real output. Also, the price level of the domestic economy responds negatively to real output uncertainty and private consumption uncertainty from abroad (US, China and Europe) indicating the negative spillover effect. Inflation uncertain from foreign economies to the domestic price level is not the same. For example, the inflation spillover effect from the US is negative but China and Europe are positive, which is the domestic price level increases. Private consumption, also, responds differently to real output uncertainty and international private consumption uncertainty from different countries in the world. For the US and Europe, the private consumption response to real output uncertainty and international private consumption is positive, while that of China is negative, indicating private consumption reduction. US, China and Europe have negative inflation spillover uncertainty effects on domestic private consumption.

It is recommended that for the domestic economy if the intention is to increase industrial output, policymakers should not worry much about inflation uncertainty instead, private consumption should be closely followed up and managed appropriately, especially at times of global risks. Also, at the international level, every country that is closely connected to the domestic economy (Nigeria) in terms of trade and otherwise should be closely monitored for real output uncertainty, private consumption uncertainty and inflation uncertainty, mostly in periods of global risks such as COVID-19. Further studies could examine the optimum policy instrument for uncertainty management.

References

1. An X, Wu B, Dedahanov AT, Sun W (2022) Episodes of extreme international capital inflows in emerging and developing economies: the role of global economic policy uncertainty. PLoS One 17(9):e0275249
2. Baba Y, Engle RF, Kraft DF, Kroner KF (1990) Multivariate simultaneous generalized ARCH. MIMEO, Depart Econ Univ Calif San Diego
3. Baldwin R, di Mauro BW (2020) Economics in the time of COVID-19. Centre for Economic Policy Research Press, London. file:///C:/Users/user/Downloads/COVID-19.pdf
4. Biljanovska N, Grigoli F, Hengge M (2017) Fear Thy Neighbor: Spillovers from Economic Policy Uncertainty. IMF Working Paper No. 240. Available at: https://www.imf.org/en/Publications/WP/Issues/2017/11/15/Fear-Thy-Neighbor-Spillovers-from-Economic-Policy-Uncertainty-45346
5. Bloom N (2009) The impact of uncertainty shocks. Econometrica 77:623–685
6. Bobasu A, Geis A, Quaglietti L, Ricci M (2020) Tracking global economic uncertainty: implications for global investment and trade. European Central Bank Economic Bulletin, issue 1. https://www.ecb.europa.eu/pub/economic-bulletin/focus/2020/html/ecb.ebbox202001_01~b336806ed2.en.html
7. Bollerslev T (1986) Generalized autoregressive conditional heteroskedasticity. J Econometrics Elsevier 31(3):307–327
8. Central Bank of Nigeria–CBN (2015) Modelling the impact of macroeconomic uncertainty on the conduct of monetary policy. CBN Research Department Publication. https://www.cbn.gov.ng/out/2017/rsd/modeling%20the%20impact%20of.pdf

9. Çolak MS, Güney IE, Hacıhasanoğlu YS (2020) The relationship between economic uncertainty and firms' balance sheet strength. In: Haron R, Md Husin M, Murg M (eds) Banking and finance. https://www.intechopen.com/chapters/71646
10. Cuaresma JC, Huber F, Onorante L (2017) The macroeconomic effects of international uncertainty shocks. Vienna University of Economics and Business, Department of Economics Working Paper No. 245. http://pure.iiasa.ac.at/id/eprint/14558/1/wp245.pdf
11. Diebold FX, Yilmaz K (2012) Better to give than to receive: predictive directional measurement of volatility spillovers. Int J Forecast 28(1):57–66
12. Ding Z, Engle R, Granger C (1993) Long memory properties of stock market returns and a new model. J Empirical Finan 1:83–106
13. Engle RF (1982) Autoregressive conditional heteroscedasticity with estimates of the variance of UK inflation. Econometrica 50:987–1008
14. Engle R, Lilien D, Robins RP (1987) Estimating time-varying risk premia in the term structure: The Arch-M Model. Econometrica 55(2):391–407
15. Engle R, Kroner K (1995) Multivariate simultaneous GARCH. Econometric Theory 11:122–150
16. Glosten LR, Jagannathan R, Runkle DE (1993) On the relation between the expected value and the volatility of the nominal excess return on stocks. J Finan 48:1779–1801
17. Investopedia (2021) What is an economic shock and effects of Different Types. Available at: https://www.investopedia.com/terms/e/economic-shock.asp
18. Kang W, Ratti RA, Vespignani JL (2017) The impact of global uncertainty on the global economy, and largely developed and developing economies. Federal Reserve Bank of Dallas Globalization and Monetary Policy Institute Working Paper No. 303. https://www.dallasfed.org/-/media/documents/institute/wpapers/2017/0303.pdf
19. Londono JM, Ma S, Wilson BA (2021) The global transmission of real economic uncertainty. International Finance Discussion Papers No. 1317. Board of Governors of the Federal Reserve System, Washington. https://www.federalreserve.gov/econres/ifdp/files/ifdp1317.pdf
20. Nelson DB (1991) Conditional heteroskedasticity in asset returns: A new approach. Econometrica 59(2):347–370
21. Ozili P, Arun T (2020) Spillover of COVID-19: impact on the global economy. Munich Personal RePEc Archive Paper No. 99850
22. Shehzad K, Xiaoxing L, Bilgili F, Koçak E (2021) COVID-19 and the spillover effect of the global economic crisis on the United States financial stability. https://www.frontiersin.org/articles/. https://doi.org/10.3389/fpsyg.2021.632175/full
23. Sommer M (2002) Supply shocks and the persistence of inflation. The Johns Hopkins University, Department of Economics Working Papers No. 485

Chapter 2
The Impact of COVID-19 on Sustainable Development in Europe: A Temporal Analysis

Marianna Bartiromo and Enrico Ivaldi

2.1 Introduction

2.1.1 Sustainable Development: Definition and Historical Background

The recent COVID-19 pandemic is one of the greatest challenges of the century. In addition to having led to a deep economic and social crisis, it has shown the need to continue to implement both national and international policies for sustainable development. Sustainable development, in fact, is a type of economic and social development reconcilable with environmental protection, social equity and the rights of future generations. Therefore, to take up the definition proposed by the so-called Brundtland Report, we can define this phenomenon as "that development which allows the present generation to satisfy its needs without compromising the possibility of future generations to satisfy their own needs" [60].

Although sustainable development is an extremely important concept, it has only recently entered the public debate. In fact, it is only since the second half of the last century that there has been a gradual interest by scholars and institutions towards

This publication is supported by the Ministry of University and Research (MUR) as part of the FSE REACT-EU—PON 2014–2020 "Research and Innovation" resources—Green Action—DM MUR 1062/2021—Title of the Research: "Indicator systems for monitoring sustainable nautical tourism in ports of the upper Mediterranean Sea".

M. Bartiromo
Channel & Retail Lab, SDA Bocconi School of Management, Milan, Italy
e-mail: marianna.bartiromo@sdabocconi.it

E. Ivaldi (✉)
Department of Political and International Science, University of Genoa, Genoa, Italy
e-mail: enrico.ivaldi@unige.it

R. Bhattacharyya et al. (eds.), *COVID-19 Pandemic and Global Inequality*,
https://doi.org/10.1007/978-981-99-4405-7_2

issues of sustainability. Two books contributed to the birth of the concept of sustainable development: the book "Silent Spring" [7] and the book "The limits to growth" [33]. The first book—by the American biologist Rachel Carson—alerted the whole world about the environmental impact caused by the use of chemical pesticides and contributed to the birth of the first global environmentalist movements. As for the second book—"The limits to growth" [33]—it aimed to demonstrate the unsustainability of the economic development model used up to that moment. The Massachusetts Institute of Technology (MIT) scientists who worked on it concluded that industrialization can only go so far: sooner or later it will exceed the critical capacity and at that point, it will no longer be possible to intervene on the environmental consequences caused by it.

Between the release of these two volumes, there was an event that shocked American and world public opinion: the Santa Barbara oil spill (1969). This incident was one of the most serious environmental disasters in the United States: about 100,000 barrels of crude oil were spilled into the waters and beaches of Santa Barbara. This spill had a major impact on marine biodiversity: about 3,600 animals including seabirds, dolphins, seals, and sea lions died [11]. The extensive media coverage given to this disaster led to the creation of numerous regulations for environmental protection and the organization of many events dedicated to the environment. The most important of them was the famous World Earth Day held on April 22, 1970, in which 20 million people participated [41]. The following year, the president of the United Nations Maha Thray Sithu U Thant made the event official by putting World Earth Day on the calendar. This led to the organization of the Earth Summit in Rio de Janeiro in 1992. This conference, the largest in history in terms of the number of participants, resulted in the release of five documents: the United Nations Framework Convention on Climate Change (UNFCCC), the Convention on Biological Diversity, Agenda 21, the Rio Declaration on Environment and Development, and the Forest Principles [49].

The Framework Convention on Climate Change [54] is an international treaty with the objective of encouraging member states to promote action against the problems posed by the current climate change.

The Convention on Biological Diversity [55], on the other hand, entered into force on 29 December 1993 and has three objectives: the conservation of biological diversity, the sustainable use of its components, and the equidistribution of the benefits arising from the use of genetic resources.

From the point of view of sustainable development, however, the most important document is undoubtedly Agenda 21 [59]. The latter guided the governance choices of participating countries until 2015 when the 2030 Agenda for Sustainable Development was adopted. Through its 27 principles Agenda 21 outlined a global plan of action to be achieved during the twenty-first century. Within it, there are very detailed proposals for action that aim to: fight poverty, change the production model in favor of a more sustainable one, the preservation of terrestrial and marine ecosystems, the prevention of deforestation, and the promotion of sustainable agriculture. Moreover, already in the Preamble, it is understood that a collective effort is needed to arrive at an increasingly sustainable solution: "no nation can achieve these results alone, but together with a global partnership it will be possible". This effort, finally, must be implemented not only by States, but also and above all by civil society [50].

The Rio Declaration on Environment and Development [57], on the other hand, outlines the respective rights and responsibilities of member states regarding the goals set by the Earth Summit. As in the case of Agenda 21, it outlines 27 principles, among which the main ones are: (a) the anthropocentricity of actions for the promotion of sustainable development; (b) the importance of policy about the prevention of environmental degradation in a context of scientific uncertainty; (c) the concept that states, although they have full sovereignty in their territories, do not have the right to harm the environment and therefore harm global rights in these issues; (d) the eradication of poverty at the center of international policies as a fundamental factor in establishing sustainable development; (e) equal opportunities, equal rights and full participation of women; (f) the weight of developed countries on the implementation of sustainable policies.

Finally, with the Principles of Forests [58], the fundamental role of forests in the preservation of the environment is recognized for the first time in history, but above all from the point of view of world economic and social well-being.

Therefore, thanks to the "Earth Summit" for the first time the concept of sustainable development is adopted as a global concept shared by all member countries. However, 20 years later, during the United Nations Conference on Sustainable Development [56], dubbed Rio+20, it appeared that this concept had not been implemented [23] and that it is the only way for the development model to be defined as effective and efficient [56]. Due to this realization, the participating states decided to begin the process of defining a set of sustainable development goals (SDGs) through the creation of a network of scholars in the field specifically created for this purpose: the Sustainable Development Solutions Network (SDSN) [42]. The result of the SDGs will be the so-called 17 Sustainable Development Goals (SDGs contained within the 2030 Agenda. The 17 SDGs are as follows: 1. Defeat poverty, 2. Defeat world hunger; 3. Good health; 4. Quality education; 5. Gender equality; 6. Clean water and sanitation; 7. Renewable energy; 8. Good jobs and economic growth; 9. Innovation and infrastructure; 10. Reduce inequality; 11. Sustainable cities and communities; 12. Responsible consumption; 13. Combating climate change; 14. Aquatic flora and fauna; 15. Terrestrial flora and fauna; 16. Peace and justice; 17. Partnership for the goals. The 2030 Agenda is based on five critical dimensions—the so-called 5Ps-: People, Prosperity, Planet, Partnership and Peace. They are traditionally analyzed through the so-called 3Es of sustainable development: Economic, Environment and Equity. The intersection of these five dimensions constitutes true sustainability. Every State, before making any decision, must evaluate the impacts under these five different aspects. Therefore, economic, social, and environmental consequences must be considered for any state intervention, and governors must ensure that any decision has been carried out through comprehensive partnerships [51].

2.1.2 COVID-19 and Its Effects on Sustainable Development

Among the consequences of the current model of development, there is the loss of biodiversity of ecosystems. This is caused by the conversion of natural habitats into "agricultural and/or urban ecosystems, that have increased the contacts between humans and wildlife, and among its reservoirs of potential zones [37]. Reduced biodiversity coupled with the growth of urbanization and the resulting pollution [14] provides fertile ground for the spread of new pathogens such as COVID-19. On January 30, 2020, the World Health Organization declared coronavirus disease a health emergency of international concern [61]. COVID-19 is an infectious disease that originated in Wuhan in Hubei Province, China in December 2019 [31]. The virus is easily transmissible, and contagion occurs through droplets emitted from the mouth or nose of a sick individual. For most individuals, this virus has mild symptoms, however, weaker individuals may experience more severe symptoms such as pneumonia, pulmonary edema, organ failure, and in the worst cases the virus can even lead to death [9]. At first, the cases of COVID-19 remained confined to China, but in a short time the virus spread throughout the world because of globalization [9, 31]. After the January 30 declaration by the WHO, there was a surge in the number of cases worldwide: 100,000 cases were confirmed in 114 countries around the world [31]. For this reason, the WHO declared coronavirus disease a full-fledged pandemic on March 11 [62]. Also in March, the epicenter of the pandemic shifted from China to Europe (particularly Italy and the United Kingdom) and the USA [63]. As the pandemic spreads, countries, under the encouragement of the WHO, began to develop plans to manage the emergency [39]. The main strategies adopted by states include social distancing strategies (so-called "lockdowns") to reduce the spread of the disease, distance learning, travel restrictions, cancellation of cultural and sporting events, reduction of public transport and remote working (smart working) [39].

These strategies have had serious impacts on achieving the UN SDGs. In fact, the pandemic caused an economic crisis more devastating than the 2008 financial crisis [22], the effects of which had a greater impact on developing countries by dramatically worsening poverty rates [5, 29, 46]. This economic crisis also caused the unemployment rate to rise, which, even after gradual recovery, remained high throughout the 2020s. In fact, 20 million households reported not having enough to eat, and 10 million households reported difficulty paying rent [8]. One of the sectors most affected by the measures was mobility: COVID-19, in addition to causing large economic costs, had a strong impact on immigration leading to high human costs [45]. In addition to this, travel restrictions have affected all stages of the food supply chain and food distribution [38]. In fact, sourcing seeds, feed, and pesticides was particularly difficult during the period of the closures, and because of this, farmers had to store unsold products longer, which resulted in reduced food quality and increased production costs [19]. The second most affected sector is undoubtedly education: the school and university systems, in fact, had to be suddenly digitized. This forced digitization has affected as many as 1.2 billion students in more than 170 countries, a third of whom, due to lack of connectivity, have been excluded from learning [53].

This, in addition to the social effects, has led to numerous economic effects: in fact, education is one of the primary elements of economic well-being as it strengthens the economic and entrepreneurial fabric, produces innovation, development and makes areas more attractive for both domestic and international investment [10].

From an environmental perspective, however, the restrictive measures have had positive effects: there has been a general improvement in air quality, and a decrease in CO_2 leading to positive consequences in the short term [46]. One of the categories most affected by the effects of COVID-19 is undoubtedly women. In fact, the pandemic has had a greater impact on women's employment than on men's [24, 35] since they earn less than their male counterparts and are therefore more vulnerable to job loss [52]. The closure of third-sector activities has meant that many jobs have been lost in this female-dominated sector [24, 52]. Job loss has slowed and hindered the professional careers of many women [6]. In addition, men, unlike women, hold job positions that are more easily converted to smart working [2]. Finally, domestic confinement has only increased the likelihood of violence against women: in fact, 7 out of 10 women said that because of the pandemic, both physical and verbal violence from their partners has become more common [64]. The most visible effects of the pandemic involved health care: there has been a general overloading of healthcare facilities and a lack of use of medical care by many people due to the fear of infection [31]. In addition, the effort to fight this virus has shifted attention and many resources from other diseases interrupting a lot of disease prevention programs [31]. All these effects in addition to causing an increase in social inequalities have caused an increase in mental illness, self-harm, and suicidal behavior [4]. Finally, the economic and social crisis has increased the likelihood of conflict and fueled populism and nationalism [3, 26], phenomena that could undermine international peace [31].

The effects of COVID-19 on sustainable development can be summarized in Fig. 2.1.

2.1.3 Objectives of the Work

Sustainable development, therefore, is a complex and heterogeneous phenomenon, which in recent years has been strongly affected by the effects of the COVID-19 pandemic. The objective of this study is to analyze the levels of sustainable development in a number of countries of the European continent from 2015—the year in which the 2030 Agenda was promulgated—to 2020—the year in which the pandemic broke out. The case of Europe was chosen as the continent was undoubtedly one of the most affected by COVID-19 and at the same time the most committed to environmental policies.

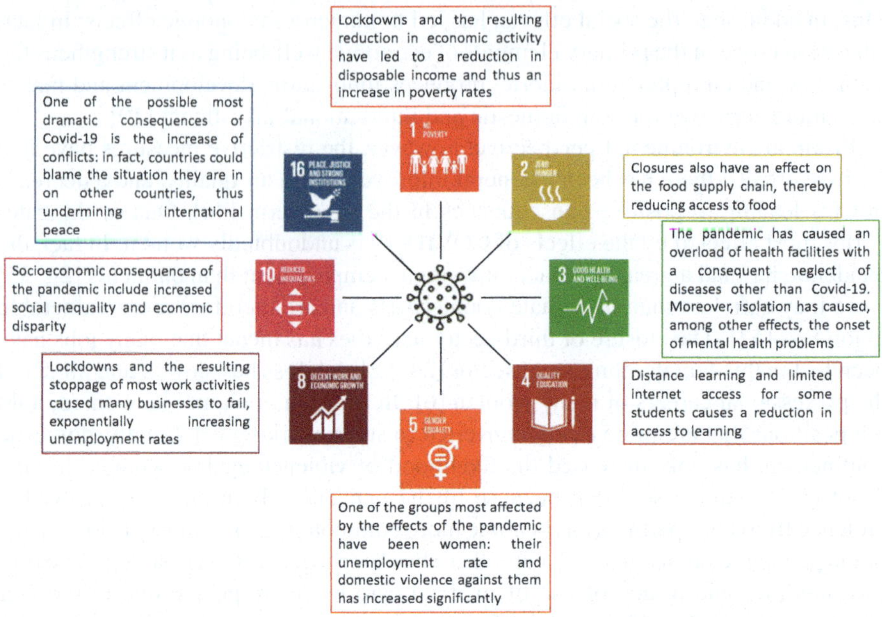

Fig. 2.1 Effects of Covid-19 on the SDGs. *Open source* Leal et al. [31], https://doi.org/10.3390/su12135343

2.2 Material and Methods

As sustainable development is a multidimensional and complex phenomenon, it is necessary to use indicators. In fact, the latter are tools that allow to analysis of all those aspects that would be left out of a first analysis [36]. In this study, it was decided to use 17 indicators from the free Eurostat database referring to three different years: 2015, 2018, 2020 (Table 2.1). The choice to use such a large number of indicators demonstrates how the phenomenon of sustainable development is complex and difficult to analyze using only limited conceptual frameworks [1].

These three different years were chosen with the aim of analyzing the improvements achieved in Europe in the three years following the promulgation of the 2030 Agenda and the effects of COVID-19 on the levels of sustainable development achieved by the various European countries. Based on the completeness of the 17 indicators chosen, in fact, 26 European countries were selected which presented complete data for all three years considered.

The European case was chosen because it is the continent that is most committed to environmental and sustainable policies and was one of the most affected by the COVID-19 pandemic. In addition, the European case is characterized by a strong gap between the Northern states (with lower levels of inequality, high rates of employment and income, etc.) and the Southern states (including Italy, Spain, Greece,

Table 2.1 Selected indicators and relative description

Indicator	Description
People at risk of poverty or social exclusion (sdg_01_10)	This indicator measures the sum of people who are at risk of poverty because of social transfers, with severe material deprivation, or living in households with very low work intensity. Even in the presence of more than one of these phenomena, people are counted only once. The risk of poverty is equivalent to an income below the threshold of 60% of the national median equivalent disposable income. Material deprivation, on the other hand, occurs when people have living conditions severely limited by a lack of resources and if they cannot afford at least 4 of the following amenities: (i) pay rent and utility bills; (ii) home heating; (iii) unexpected expenses; (iv) meat, fish or a protein equivalent every other day; (v) a week's vacation; (vi) a car; (vii) a washing machine; (viii) a color TV; (ix) a telephone. Finally, a household is very low work intensity if members between the ages of 18 and 59 worked 20% or less of their total work potential in the previous year
Area under organic farming (sdg_02_40)	This indicator analyzes the share of the total utilized agricultural area occupied by organic farming. Organic farming refers to all types of agriculture that comply with Council Regulation (EC) No. 834/2007
Share of people with good or very good perceived health by sex (sdg_03_20)	This is a subjectively measured indicator of how people rate their health. It is expressed as the proportion of the population aged 16 years or older who consider themselves to be in "good" or "very good" health". The data comes from the EU Survey on Income and Living Conditions (EU SILC)
Adult participation in learning by sex (sdg_04_60)	This is a subjective indicator that measures the share of persons who said they had received formal or non-formal education and training in the previous four weeks. The denominator is the total population in the same age group but excluding those who did not answer the question "participation in education and training." Data are from the EU Labour Force Survey (EU-LFS)
Positions held by women in senior management positions (source: EIGE) (sdg_05_60)	The indicator measures the share of women on the boards of directors of the largest publicly traded companies. Publicly traded companies mean that the shares of these companies are traded on the stock exchange. Instead, the largest companies are those companies whose members (maximum 50) are part of the primary blue-chip index, which is an index that covers the largest companies by market capitalization and/or market trading. The data comes from the database of the European Institute for Gender Equality (EIGE)
Population having neither a bath, nor a shower, nor indoor flushing toilet in their household by poverty status (sdg_06_10)	The indicator measures the share of the total population having neither a bath, nor a shower, nor an indoor flushing toilet in their household

(continued)

Table 2.1 (continued)

Indicator	Description
Primary energy consumption (sdg_07_10)	The indicator measures a country's total energy needs excluding all non-energy uses of energy carriers such as natural gas used to produce chemicals. Primary energy consumption covers energy consumption by end users for services such as industry, transportation, households, services, and agriculture added to the energy consumption of the energy sector itself for the production and transformation of energy and all losses caused by the transformation of energy
Real GDP per capita (sdg_08_10)	The indicator measures the ratio of real GDP to the average population for a specific year and is based on rounded figures
Gross domestic expenditure on R&D by sector (sdg_09_10)	The indicator measures gross domestic spending on research and experimental development (R&D)
Purchasing power adjusted GDP per capita (sdg_10_10)	The basic figures of this indicator are expressed in purchasing power standards (PPS). The PPS represents a common currency, which resets differences in price levels between countries to zero so that GDP can be compared in terms of volume. Values are calculated in relation to the EU average set at 100
Overcrowding rate by poverty status (sdg_11_10)	The indicator measures the percentage of people living in overcrowded conditions in the EU. Overcrowded conditions occur if the home does not have at least one room for the entire family and one room for a couple, for every single person over 18, for a same-sex teenage couple, for every different-sex teenager, and for a couple of children
Circular material use rate (sdg_12_41)	The indicator measures the share of materials recovered and returned to the economy. The circularity rate measures the ratio of circular use of materials to their overall use. The latter is the sum of the aggregate internal consumption of materials and the circular use of materials. The circular rate is approximated by subtracting major waste and exported waste destined for recovery from the amount of waste recycled at domestic recovery facilities
Population covered by the Covenant of Mayors for Climate & Energy signatories (sdg_13_60)	The indicator measures the share of the population covered Covenant of Mayors by member state
Surface of marine sites designated under Natura 2000 (sdg_14_10)	The indicator measures the area of marine sites designated under Natura 2000. The latter includes both marine protected areas and terrestrial areas and targets favorable conservation status for habitat types and species of EU interest
Surface of terrestrial sites designated under Natura 2000 (sdg_15_20)	The indicator measures the surface of terrestrial sites designated under Natura 2000. The latter includes both marine protected areas and terrestrial areas and targets favorable conservation status for habitat types and species of EU interest

(continued)

Table 2.1 (continued)

Indicator	Description
General government total expenditure on law courts (sdg_16_30)	The indicator measures total government spending on courts according to the government's function classification. The latter includes all those expenditures for the operation of government and justice (such as all those expenditures useful for the operation of civil, criminal, and judicial courts) except for prison administrations
EU imports from developing countries by country income groups (sdg_17_30)	The indicator measures the value at current prices of EU imports from developing countries. It is broken down by income groups of partner countries, but these may change groups over time

Source Eurostat

and Portugal) which have high public debt, high unemployment rates and strong economic and social inequalities.

The Stacking Method

Once the indicators have been identified, it is possible to proceed with the construction of the index. However, as can be seen from Table 2.1, the indicators chosen have different polarities. In fact, it is the sign of the relationship between the indicator and the phenomenon to be studied [32]. To correctly aggregate a set of indicators it is necessary that the totality of them have positive polarity. For this reason, a non-linear transformation was conducted through the following formula

$$x_{ij} = \frac{1}{\mathrm{x_{ij}}}$$

where x_{ij} is the value assumed by indicator j in unit i. This technique consists in calculating the reciprocal of the value of each unit.

Once the non-linear transformation of the indicators has been performed, the index can be calculated.

In this study, it was decided to use the stacking method [15, 34]. This method was chosen because it allows for an absolute temporal comparison and high replicability of results. To proceed with the index calculation, it was necessary to stack all 17 indicators for each reference year and calculate the index through the following formulas [30, 34]:

$$\mu_j = \frac{\sum_{i=1}^{n} x_{i,j,t_1} + \sum_{i=1}^{n} x_{i,j,t_2} + \sum_{i=1}^{n} x_{i,j,t_3}}{3n}$$

$$\sigma_j = \sqrt{\frac{\sum_{i=1}^{n}\left(x_{i,j,t1} - _j\right)^2 + \sum_{i=1}^{n}\left(x_{i,j,t2} - _j\right)^2 + \sum_{i=1}^{n}\left(x_{i,j,t3} - _j\right)^2}{3n}}$$

where $i = 1, 2, \ldots, n$ are the 26 countries considered, $j = 1, 2, \ldots, 17$ are the sustainable development indicators and t = 2015, 2018, 2020 are the three reference years. Therefore, in general terms, we obtain the following formulas [30]

$$\mu_j = \frac{\sum_{t=1}^{k} \sum_{i=1}^{n} x_{i.j.t}}{kn}$$

$$\sigma_j = \sqrt{\frac{\sum_{t=1}^{k} \sum_{i=1}^{n} (x_{i.j.t} - \mu_j)^2}{kn}}$$

where $i = 1, 2, \ldots, n$ are the number of countries considered, $j = 1, \ldots, m$ are the indicators used, and $t = 1, \ldots, k$ are the number of years considered.

2.3 Results

This section presents the analysis of the results obtained through the construction of the sustainable development indices. Table 2.2 shows the sustainable development indices (SDIs) obtained by applying the stacking method.

Overall, France is the country that has achieved a higher level of sustainable development in Europe. In fact, one can see how it has gone from a third position in 2015 (SDI_{2015} = 10.64) to a first position in both 2018 (SDI_{2018} = 15.87) and 2020 (SDI_{2020} = 12.04). Along with France in the Top 5 of selected European countries, there are the Netherlands (SDI_{2015} = 9.65; SDI_{2018} = 12.60; SDI_{2020}=), Sweden (SDI_{2015} = 11.76; SDI_{2018} = 14.68; SDI_{2020} = 11.51), Germany (SDI_{2015} = 10.77; SDI_{2018} = 13.05; SDI_{2020} = 9.51) and Finland (SDI_{2015} = 6.60; SDI_{2018} = 9.45; SDI_{2020} = 7.60). In the bottom five positions, however, there are Croatia (SDI_{2015} = −9.99; SDI_{2018} = −7.75; SDI_{2020} = −8.80), Greece (SDI_{2015} = −10.99; SDI_{2018} = −8.29; SDI_{2020} = −10.94), Bulgaria (SDI_{2015} = −11. 85; SDI_{2018} = −9.82; SDI_{2020} = −11.82), Lithuania (SDI_{2015} = −16.36; SDI_{2018} = −12.91; SDI_{2020} = −12.29), and Romania (SDI_{2015} = −18.70; SDI_{2018} = −13.63; SDI_{2020} = −13.65). The latter countries along with Latvia and Luxembourg have kept their ranks unchanged over the years. Furthermore, a general improvement in the levels of sustainable development can be observed between the years 2015 and 2018, while a decrease occurs between 2018 and 2020. (Fig. 2.2). Estonia, as can be seen from Fig. 2.2, is the state that shows the largest gap between the 2018 values and those of 2015 and 2018 (SDI_{2015} = −1.65; SDI_{2018} = 4.88; SDI_{2020} = −1.63). This is followed by Malta (SDI_{2015} = −7.62; SDI_{2018} = −3.42; SDI_{2020} = −7.37) and Cyprus (SDI_{2015} = −6.56; SDI_{2018} = −2.24; SDI_{2020} = −6.80).

Table 2.2 SDI 2015, SDI 2018, SDI 2020 and related ranks

	SDI 2015	Rank	SDI 2018	Rank	SDI 2020	Rank
France	10.64	3	15.87	1	12.04	1
The Netherlands	9.65	4	12.60	4	11.54	2
Sweden	11.76	1	14.68	2	11.51	3
Germany	10.77	2	13.05	3	9.51	4
Finland	6.60	6	9.45	6	7.60	5
Spain	8.14	5	11.17	5	6.65	6
Belgium	3.55	10	6.51	8	6.23	7
Italy	3.52	11	7.02	7	5.58	8
Luxembourg	4.12	9	6.21	9	5.12	9
Ireland	4.85	8	5.97	10	4.91	10
Denmark	5.19	7	5.62	11	3.54	11
Poland	−2.48	15	3.72	13	1.82	12
Czechia	−0.12	12	2.68	14	0.59	13
Slovenia	−0.65	13	2.44	15	−0.34	14
Estonia	−1.65	14	4.88	12	−1.63	15
Hungary	−8.39	20	−2.95	18	−3.97	16
Slovakia	−6.31	16	−3.66	20	−4.07	17
Portugal	−6.64	18	−2.83	17	−5.84	18
Cyprus	−6.56	17	−2.24	16	−6.80	19
Malta	−7.62	19	−3.46	19	−7.37	20
Latvia	−9.58	21	−5.93	21	−8.42	21
Croatia	−9.99	22	−7.75	22	−8.80	22
Greece	−10.99	23	−8.29	23	−10.94	23
Bulgaria	−11.85	24	−9.82	24	−11.82	24
Lithuania	−16.36	25	−12.91	25	−12.29	25
Romania	−18.70	26	−13.63	26	−13.65	26

Source Authors' elaborations

2.4 Discussion and Conclusion

The European continent cares about sustainable issues. For this reason, it has set up an observatory to promote sustainable development in Europe: the so-called Sustainable Development Observatory (SDO). The main mission of the SDO "is to promote sustainability in the EU by advancing economic prosperity, social inclusiveness and environmental responsibility in an integrated and balanced way" [47]. It is the only organization in Europe that deals with the promotion of sustainable development in all sectors. The SDO also facilitates cooperation between civil society and institutions through the organization of events such as public hearings and conferences and

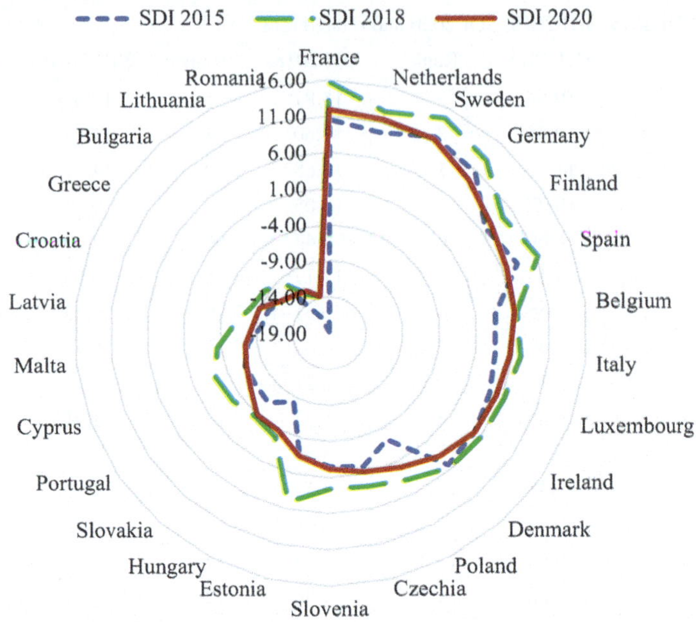

Fig. 2.2 SDI 2015, SDI 2018, and SDI 2020 radar chart. *Source* Authors' elaborations

through sector studies and dedicated workshops [47]. However, as can be seen from Table 2.2, the levels of sustainable development achieved by different European countries from 2015 to 2018 differ from country to country. There are, in fact, some virtuous countries such as France, Netherlands, Sweden, Germany and Finland that, between 2015 and 2020, have maintained high levels of sustainable development; other countries such as Croatia, Greece, Bulgaria, Lithuania and Romania were less virtuous instead, holding the last 5 places in the ranking in all 3 years considered.

The first country in the ranking following the promulgation of the 2030 Agenda—France—has designated a special inter-ministerial representative in order to better achieve and attain high levels of sustainable development: the Inter-ministerial Delegate for Sustainable Development (DIDD). The latter coordinates all sustainable development issues within the different ministries [21]. It also led to the drafting of France's first report on the SDGs [40]. Financially, France allocated €4 billions, of which €2 billions were assigned to climate [21]. In addition, it decided to allocate 400 million euros in the form of bilateral grants to help developing countries achieve the goals set by the UN. Finally, France is making a strong commitment to make decision-making processes increasingly inclusive. This is why two forums, the National Council for Development and International Solidarity (CNDSI) and the National Council for Ecological Transition (CNTE), have been created and are open to civil society [21].

As in the case of France, the Netherlands is also making significant efforts to increase the level of sustainable development. Unlike the French case, there is no specific delegate, but coordination of sustainable development activities is entrusted to the Ministry of Foreign Affairs. On the other hand, the analysis of the progress achieved is entrusted to one of the most renowned statistics offices in the Netherlands [44]. The peculiarity of the Dutch case is the strong participation of civil society in the process: a special team "Build the Change: Global Goals at Home and Abroad" was created, through which civil society can express its feedback about the progress of the SDGs. In 2019, the Building Change team launched the so-called "SDG Test" project, which consists of a request to Dutch policymakers to include in new policy and legislative proposals an analysis of their effects on the achievement of the SDGs [44]. Finally, regarding the environmental perspective, the Netherlands has among its national priorities the ecological transition, targeted action to reduce climate change, and strengthening environmental protection and biodiversity [27].

One example to follow in terms of environmental protection is undoubtedly Sweden. In fact, it was the first state in the world to pass an environmental protection law in 1967 [48]. Moreover, in Sweden more than half of the energy produced comes from renewable energy sources and, as if that were not enough, it is a national objective to further reduce greenhouse gas emissions [48]. In fact, the Swedish government has set ambitious goals such as eliminating fossil fuels by 2045 and producing 100% renewable energy [48]. In 2015, the Swedish government established an ad hoc body for sustainable issues: the Scientific Council for Sustainable Development [28]. It is tasked with facilitating dialogue between the government and the scientific community [18, 28]. Finally, the goals of the 2030 Agenda have been included in the budget, demonstrating Sweden's strong focus on sustainable issues [18, 28].

The fourth country in the ranking—Germany—reduced its greenhouse gas emissions by 27.7% from 1990 to 2014 [20]. Since the promulgation of the 2030 Agenda, it has decided to further reduce these emissions by setting ambitious goals such as achieving 1/5 of organic agricultural production and more than half of its energy produced through renewable sources by 2050 [20]. In addition, in 2016, the Ministry of Economic Cooperation and Development promulgated an action plan for marine biodiversity conservation and sustainable fisheries. For this, it allocated resources of more than 180 million euros [17]. The German Government periodically communicates its progress in achieving Sustainable Development Goals [20]. Every 4 years, in fact, reports are published on the progress of the SDGs and every 2 years reports are published on indicators and key areas of policies pursued by the German State [20].

Like the previous states, Finland is also working hard towards achieving the UN goals [43]. Much attention is given to civil society and reducing social inequalities. In fact, there are both informal groups and networks formed by youth, women, trade unions, and environmentalists that meet every 1–2 months to share information and plan advocacy [43]. Finally, policy dialogues are regularly organized by the National Commission for Sustainable Development, an ad hoc body for these issues [43].

COVID-19 has posed new challenges for the European continent. As can be seen from Table 2.2, the pandemic has caused a general reduction in the levels of sustainable development achieved by European countries, in almost all cases wiping out the progress achieved between 2015 and 2018. In order to face this new challenge, the various countries have, therefore, promulgated national recovery plans. The latter is part of a more ambitious project: the famous Next Generation EU (NGEU). This is a temporary recovery instrument with an appropriation value of over 800 billion euros that aims to create a post-COVID-19 Europe that is greener, more digital, resilient, and adapted to present and future challenges [16]. It contains several measures at its core. At the heart of it is the Recovery and Resilience Facility, which through €732.8 billion in loans and grants will support reforms and investments by European states aimed at halting the economic and social effects caused by the pandemic. The pandemic has also profoundly undermined European territorial cohesion. This is why the second measure of the NGEU is the so-called Recovery Assistance for Cohesion and Territories of Europe (REACT-EU). REACT-EU is thus a parallel measure to the NGEU with a long-term budget for the period 2021–2027 of 1074.3 billion euros. Other areas supported by the REACT-EU include green and digital transition [12]. In addition, temporary support to mitigate the risks of unemployment in an emergency (SURE) was established to try to combat the increase in unemployment rates caused by the pandemic [12]. The largest beneficiary of these funds is Italy (with financial support of 27.4 billion euros), one of the European countries most affected by the pandemic and its effects [12].

In fact, in Italy, due to the pandemic, there was a collapse of −3.9 billion hours worked in the first quarters of 2020 (−12% compared to the first three quarters of 2019) [25]. In addition, more than 6 million Italian workers were beneficiaries of the Cassa Integrazione Guadagni (CIG) during the first lockdown [25]. The decline in employment resulted in a 13% drop in Italian consumption and a decline in household disposable income [25]. Therefore, there has been a gradual impoverishment of Italian families, and this has provoked the establishment of a climate of distrust, which has had the effect of paralyzing demand in many sectors [25].

Italy, furthermore, on February 17, 2022, instituted the so-called "Bonus Psychologist" to combat the mental health problems caused by closures. This is a contribution towards the cost of psychotherapy sessions available to Italians stressed by closures, changes in everyday life caused by health regulations, and, above all, the economic and social consequences of the crisis [13].

This work has demonstrated the devastating effects of COVID-19 in some European countries. In fact, in addition to the disastrous economic effects, the pandemic has caused numerous social consequences such as increased inequality, increased mental illnesses, and a large digital divide. This has posed a threat to the achievement of the goals set by the UN in the 2030 Agenda. For this reason, many European countries have responded through national plans to try to curb the negative consequences of the pandemic. The strength of this work lies in having created 3 different indices of sustainable development useful for measuring the progress achieved from 2015 to 2020 in 26 countries of the European continent. Another strength lies in the method chosen—the stacking method—which ensures both an absolute temporal comparison and high replicability of results. As regards the critical aspects of this work, a major limitation was the lack of complete data for all countries of the European continent, which made it impossible to analyze Europe in its entirety.

The results have shown an almost unchanged trend over the years: the first and last 5 positions were taken by the same countries. This demonstrates the need for a common effort to try to raise the last countries and then guide them towards efficient and effective sustainable development policies, because only by working together will it be possible to arrive at an efficient sustainable development model.

References

1. Alaimo L, Ciacci A, Ivaldi E (2021) Measuring sustainable development by non-aggregative approach. Soc Indic Res 157:101–122. https://doi.org/10.1007/s11205-020-02357-0
2. Alon T, Doepke M, Olmstead-Rumsey J, Tertilt M (2020) The impact of COVID-19 on gender equality. Working paper [26947]. National Bureau of Economic Research, Cambridge, MA. www.nber.org/papers/w26947
3. Audi R (2009) Nationalism, patriotism, and cosmopolitanism in an age of globalization. J Ethics 13:365–381
4. Bar H (2021) COVID-19 lockdown: animal life, ecosystem and atmospheric environment. Environ Dev Sustain 23(6):8161–8178
5. Barbier EB, Burgess JC (2020) Sustainability and development after COVID-19. World Dev 135:105082. https://doi.org/10.1016/j.worlddev.2020.105082
6. Carli LL (2020) Women, gender equality and COVID-19. Gend Manag Int J 35(7/8):647–655. https://doi.org/10.1108/gm-07-2020-0236
7. Carson R (1962) Silent spring, 1st edn. Fawcett World Library
8. Center on Budget and Policy Priorities (2022) Tracking the COVID-19 economy's effects on food, housing, and employment hardships. https://www.cbpp.org/research/poverty-and-inequality/tracking-the-covid-19-economys-effects-on-food-housing-and
9. Chen N, Zhou M, Dong X, Qu J, Gong F, Han Y, Qiu Y, Wang J, Liu Y, Wei Y, Xia J, Yu T, Zhang X, Zhang L (2020) Epidemiological and clinical characteristics of 99 cases of 2019 novel coronavirus pneumonia in Wuhan, China: a descriptive study. Lancet 395(10223):507–513. https://doi.org/10.1016/s0140-6736(20)30211-7
10. Ciacci A, Ivaldi E, Gonzales R (2021) A partially non-compensatory method to measure the smart and sustainable level of Italian municipality. Sustainability 13:435. https://doi.org/10.3390/su13010435
11. Clarke KC, Hemphill JJ (2002) The Santa Barbara oil spill: a retrospective. Yearb Assoc Pac Coast Geogr 64:157–162
12. Consilium Europa (2022) COVID-19: la risposta dell'UE alle ricadute economiche. https://www.consilium.europa.eu/it/policies/coronavirus/covid-19-economy/. Last Accessed 30 Mar 2022
13. Cottone N (2022) Bonus psicologo: l'aiuto fino a 600 euro in dieci domande e risposte. Il Sole 24 ORE. https://www.ilsole24ore.com/art/bonus-psicologo-perimetro-dell-aiuto-fino-600-euro-dieci-domande-e-risposte-AEVxbpEB?refresh_ce=1. Last Accessed 30 Mar 2022
14. Das RC, Chatterjee T, Ivaldi E (2021) Sustainability of urbanization, non-agricultural output and air pollution in the world's top 20 polluting countries. Data 6:65. https://doi.org/10.3390/data6060065
15. Exeter DJ, Boyle PJ, Norman P (2011) Deprivation (im)mobility and cause-specific premature mortality in Scotland. Soc Sci Med 72:389–397
16. European Commission (2022) Recovery plan for Europe. https://ec.europa.eu/info/strategy/recovery-plan-europe_it

17. European Enviroment Agency (2020a) Germany country profile-SDGs and the environment. https://www.eea.europa.eu/themes/sustainability-transitions/sustainable-development-goals-and-the/country-profiles/germany-country-profile-sdgs-and. Last Accessed 29 Mar 2022
18. European Environment Agency (2020b) Sweden country profile-SDGs and the environment. https://www.eea.europa.eu/themes/sustainability-transitions/sustainable-development-goals-and-the/country-profiles/sweden-country-profile-sdgs-and. Last Accessed 29 Mar 2022
19. FAO (2020) How is COVID-19 affecting the fisheries and aquaculture food systems
20. Federal Government (2022) Germany's national sustainable development strategy. https://www.bundesregierung.de/breg-en/issues/sustainability/germany-s-national-sustainable-development-strategy-354566. Last Accessed 29 Mar 2022
21. France Diplomacy-Ministry for Europe and Foreign Affairs (2017) 2030 Agenda for sustainable development: how is france doing? https://www.diplomatie.gouv.fr/en/french-foreign-policy/development-assistance/the-international-development-agenda/article/2030-agenda-for-sustainable-development-how-is-france-doing-may-2017
22. Grasso M, Klicperová-Baker M, Koos S, Kosyakova Y, Petrillo A, Vlase I (2021) The impact of the coronavirus crisis on European societies. What have we learnt and where do we go from here?—introduction to the COVID volume. Eur Soc 23:S2-32
23. Haines A, Alleyne G, Kickbusch I, Dora C (2012) From the earth summit to Rio+20: integration of health and sustainable development. Lancet 379(9832):2189–2197. https://doi.org/10.1016/S0140-6736(12)60779-X
24. ILO (2020) ILO monitor: COVID-19 and the world of work, 3rd edn. Geneva. www.ilo.org/global/topics/coronavirus/impacts-and-responses/WCMS_743146/lang-zh/index.htm
25. Istat (2021) Rapporto Annuale 2021. La situazione del Paese
26. Keller S (2005) Patriotism as bad faith. Ethics 115:563–592
27. Kingdom of the Netherlands (2017) Report on the implementation of the sustainable development goals. Ministry of Foreign Affairs of the Netherlands, the Netherlands. Last Accessed 29 Mar 2022
28. Kingdom of Sweden (2017) Agenda 2030. Kingdom of Sweden. Last Accessed 29 Mar 2022
29. Ju J (2020) What will COVID-19 do to the sustainable development goals? UN dispatch. https://www.undispatch.com/what-will-COVID-19-do-to-the-sustainable-development-goals/. Last Accessed 28 Mar 2022
30. Landi S, Ivaldi E, Testi A (2017) Measuring change over time in socio-economic deprivation and health in an urban context: the case study of Genoa. Soc Indic Res 139(2):745–785. https://doi.org/10.1007/s11205-017-1720-3
31. Leal Filho W, Brandli LL, Lange Salvia A, Rayman-Bacchus L, Platje J (2020) COVID-19 and the UN sustainable development goals: threat to solidarity or an opportunity? Sustainability 12(13):5343. https://doi.org/10.3390/su12135343
32. Mazziotta M, Pareto A (2015) On a generalized non-compensatory composite index for measuring socio-economic phenomena. Soc Indic Res 127(3):983–1003. https://doi.org/10.1007/s11205-015-0998-2
33. Meadows DH, Meadows DL, Behrens RJ, William W III (1972) The limits to growth. Universe Books, New York
34. Norman P (2010) Identifying change over time in small area socio-economic deprivation. Appl Spat Anal Policy 3(2–3):107–138
35. OECD (2020) Women at the core of the fight against COVID-19 crisis. OECD Publishing, Paris. https://www.oecd.org/coronavirus/policy-responses/women-at-the-core-of-the-fight-against-covid-19-crisis-553a8269/
36. Parra Saiani P (2009) Gli indicatori sociali. In: Metodologia delle scienze sociali/18. Franco Angeli
37. Platto S, Wang Y, Zhou J, Carafoli E (2021) History of the COVID-19 pandemic: origin, explosion, worldwide spreading. Biochem Biophys Res Commun 538:14–23. https://doi.org/10.1016/j.bbrc.2020.10.087
38. Poudel PB, Poudel MR, Gautam A, Phuyal S, Tiwari CK, Bashyal N, Bashyal S (2020) COVID-19 and its global impact on food and agriculture. J Biol Today's World 9(5):221–225

39. Primc K, Slabe-Erker R (2020) The success of public health measures in Europe during the COVID-19 pandemic. Sustainability 12(10):4321. https://doi.org/10.3390/su12104321
40. Republic of France (2016) Report on the implementation by France of the sustainable development goals. France. https://sustainabledevelopment.un.org/content/documents/10726Report%20SDGs%20France.pdf. Last Accessed 29 Mar 2022
41. Rome A (2010) The genius of earth day. Environ Hist 15(2):194–205. https://doi.org/10.1093/envhis/emq036
42. Sachs JD (2014) The age of sustainable development. Columbia University Press
43. SDG WATCH EUROPE (2019a) Finland. https://www.sdgwatcheurope.org/finland/. Last Accessed 29 Mar 2022
44. SDG WATCH EUROPE (2019b) The Netherlands. https://www.sdgwatcheurope.org/the-netherlands/. Last Accessed 29 Mar 2022
45. Sirkeci I, Murat Y (2020) Coronavirus and migration: analysis of human mobility and the spread of COVID-19. Migr Lett 17(2):379–98. https://doi.org/10.33182/ml.v17i2.935
46. Shulla K, Voigt BF, Cibian S, Scandone G, Martinez E, Nelkovski F, Salehi P (2021) Effects of COVID-19 on the sustainable development goals (SDGs). Discov Sustain 2(1). https://doi.org/10.1007/s43621-021-00026-x
47. Sustainable Development Observatory (2022) European Economic and Social Committee. https://www.eesc.europa.eu/en/sections-other-bodies/observatories/sustainable-development-observatory
48. SWEDEN.SE (2021) Sweden and sustainability. Sweden.Se. https://sweden.se/climate/sustainability/sweden-and-sustainability. Last Accessed 30 Mar 2022
49. Tokuç A (2013) Earth summit. In: Idowu SO, Capaldi N, Zu L, Gupta AD (eds) Encyclopedia of corporate social responsibility. Springer, Berlin. https://doi.org/10.1007/978-3-642-28036-8_17
50. Toprak Z (2013) Agenda 21 (UN). In: Idowu SO, Capaldi N, Zu L, Gupta AD (eds) Encyclopedia of corporate social responsibility. Springer, Berlin. https://doi.org/10.1007/978-3-642-28036-8_246
51. UN (2016) Transforming our world: the 2030 agenda for sustainable development. https://sustainabledevelopment.un.org/content/documents/21252030%20Agenda%20for%20Sustainable%20Development%20web.pdf. Last Accessed 24 Mar 2022
52. UN (2020) Policy brief: the impact of COVID-19 on women. New York. www.un.org/sites/un2.un.org/files/policy_brief_on_covid_impact_on_women_9_april_2020.pdf
53. UNESCO (2022) Education: from disruption to recovery. UNESCO. https://en.unesco.org/covid19/educationresponse
54. United Nations (1992a) United Nations framework convention on climate change
55. United Nations (1992b) Convention on biological diversity
56. United Nations (2012) The future we want. Outcome document on sustainable development. Rio de Janeiro, Brazil, 20–22 June 2012
57. United Nations General Assembly (1992a) Report of the United Nations conference on environment and development (Rio de Janeiro, 3–14 June 1992). Rio Declaration on Environment and Development
58. United Nations General Assembly (1992b) Report of the United Nations conference on environment and development (Rio de Janeiro, 3–14 June 1992) A/CONF.151/26 (vol. III) forest principles
59. United Nations Sustainable Development (1992). AGENDA 21. In: United Nations conference on environment & development Rio de Janerio, Brazil, 3–14 June 1992
60. WCED (1987) Our common future. Oxford University Press, London
61. WHO (2020a) Coronavirus disease 2019 (COVID-19) situation report-51. https://www.who.int/docs/default-source/coronaviruse/situation-reports/20200311-sitrep-51-covid-19.pdf?sfvrsn=1ba62e57_10. Last Accessed 11 Mar 2022
62. WHO (2020b) Coronavirus disease 2019 (COVID-19) situation report-135. https://www.who.int/docs/default-source/coronaviruse/situation-reports/20200603-covid-19-sitrep-135.pdf?sfvrsn=39972feb_2. Last Accessed 11 Mar 2022

63. WHO (2020c) Coronavirus disease 2019 (COVID-19) situation report-60. https://www.who.int/docs/default-source/coronaviruse/situation-reports/20200320-sitrep-60-covid-19.pdf?sfvrsn=d2bb4f1f_2. Last Accessed 11 Mar 2022
64. Women UN, Count W (2021) Measuring the shadow pandemic: violence against women during COVID-19. UN Women Data Hub

Chapter 3
Impact of Large Fiscal Expansion During Catastrophic Macroeconomic Shocks: Lessons from U.S. Paycheck Protection Program

Achintya Ray

3.1 Background

The global spread of the COVID-19 pandemic and associated pressure on the government to contain the spread of the virus compelled the American government to order an economy-wide shutdown in March 2020 [3, 4]. However, that drastic public health intervention came at a heavy price. Businesses were suddenly looking at an economic abyss with no definite end. Unemployment was widespread, and many companies faced an imminent and irreversible collapse. To stem the catastrophic market decline and help businesses keep paying their employees, the Paycheck Protection Program (PPP) was passed into law by the U.S. Congress as a part of the Coronavirus Aid, Relief, and Economic Security Act (CARES Act) [31].

PPP is a loan program that covers incorporated businesses, self-employed individuals, sole proprietors, many nonprofit organizations, and tribal industries [33]. It allows the affected entities to access cash quickly to make their payrolls. The loan proceeds were permitted to cover other necessary expenses like rent, interest, utilities, and payrolls. Furthermore, although designed as a loan program, proceeds from PPP were intended to be partially or fully forgiven if the receiving entities followed the program's requirements and tried to keep employment stable. This feature made PPP essentially an employment subsidy program to avoid mass layoffs and fend off an unsustainable spike in unemployment. In addition, since the loan was primarily designed to be forgiven, PPP was a massive uncollateralized loan program that became a giant direct untargeted transfer of taxpayers' money to the business owners [3, 4, 8, 10].

A. Ray (✉)
College of Business, Tennessee State University, Suite J-401, 330 10th Ave. N., Avon Williams Campus, Nashville, TN 37203, USA
e-mail: aray4@tnstate.edu

R. Bhattacharyya et al. (eds.), *COVID-19 Pandemic and Global Inequality*,
https://doi.org/10.1007/978-981-99-4405-7_3

The PPP program provided up to $10 million in forgivable loans to small businesses and nonprofits with fewer than 500 employees. To apply for a PPP loan, businesses and nonprofits were required to work with a participating lender, such as a bank or credit union, who processed their loans. The application process required the applicants to provide documentation of their previous payroll costs, a list of other eligible expenses like rent, utilities, etc., their number of employees, and any additional relevant financial information that would help the lender process the loans.

The first round of the PPP provided $349 billion in funding and ran from April 2020 to August 2020. The program was immensely popular and attracted a massive number of applicants. It ran out of money just two weeks since it was implemented. The swelling demand for PPP loans prompted Congress to provide an additional $310 billion in funding in a new law named Paycheck Protection Program and Health Care Enhancement Act. The second round of the PPP through The Paycheck Protection Program Flexibility Act of 2020 provided $284 billion in funding from January 2021 to May 2021 [26, 35, 36].

Given the enormous size and reach of the PPP, immense academic attention has been devoted to the measurement of the success of the program and its overall impact on the American economy. The number of jobs it saved, and the associated costs of PPP remain highly debated [3, 4, 23, 31]. Furthermore, the effect of PPP in stemming the spread of the pandemic remains hotly discussed too. Intense attention has also been focused on the integrity of the program and its presumed susceptibility to fraudulent and inappropriate exploitation. Researchers have asked if PPP helped the workers as intended and if it worsened economic inequality by being highly regressive [3, 4, 5, 15, 17].

The PPP has been a very controversial program right from the beginning. Some critics argued that it could have been better designed and needed to be more targeted. Another major criticism of the program is that it primarily benefited larger businesses and organizations that had existing solid and ongoing relationships with banks and were, therefore, able to access the program benefits more quickly. Small businesses often need help properly documenting their expenses in real-time, working with lawyers, accountants, and bankers to access public benefits, etc. As a result, smaller businesses might have suffered disproportionately due to their inability to take quick and decisive action to access the benefits of PPP. Additionally, some companies that did receive PPP loans were criticized for using the funds for non-essential expenses or for not maintaining their payroll levels as required by the program. Some other critics also point to the failure of the PPP to stem the spread of the pandemic [15, 16, 17, 22, 29, 32].

In this chapter, we seek answers to the following questions:

1. Did PPP control the spread of the pandemic in the USA?
2. Was PPP successful in efficiently saving jobs?
3. To what extent was PPP suffering from fraud and abuse?
4. Did PPP worsen economic inequality and squander precious public resources?
5. What impact did PPP have and continue to have on American fiscal and monetary policies?

3.2 Stemming the Spread of the COVID-19 Pandemic

PPP was not explicitly intended to address the spread of the virus itself. Still, one of the rationales of the program was to stem the spread of the COVID-19 pandemic by allowing workers to keep earning while (potentially) staying at home by converting their jobs to work-from-home. At the same time, the program also covered businesses with on-site operations irrespective of the spread of the pandemic in their local region. It was envisioned that reducing workplace interactions and limiting direct consumer-to-business interactions would reduce the transmission of the SARS-Cov-2 virus and hence, help stem the spread of the pandemic [3, 4, 6, 8, 9, 16, 21].

Under PPP, businesses that used the funds for eligible expenses, such as payroll and rent, could have their loans forgiven. This may have incentivized firms to keep their employees on the payroll even if they could not work due to quarantine or other COVID-19-related reasons. There were also some serious concerns that the PPP may have negatively impacted the spread of the virus, especially for the industries where work-from-option does not exist. The only way those businesses could operate was to continue their everyday business operations. Some critics argued that the program may have incentivized companies to stay open even if they could not implement adequate safety measures to prevent the spread of the virus. This could have led to increased virus transmission in workplaces that could not move their workflow online, which would have been detrimental to public health. One of the weakest aspects of PPP was that the nature of the industry or the jobs therein did not guide it. This aspect makes measuring the impact of PPP on pandemic progression even more difficult [12, 13, 28, 30, 31].

There is no substantial evidence to prove that the PPP did anything significant to slow down the spread of the pandemic. While the program's economic impact remains hotly debated, the impact of the program on the actual spread of the pandemic remains surprisingly thinly documented. However, indirect evidence does not support the hypothesis that the PPP itself had any impressionable impact on the spread of the virus. There are several reasons for that. First, the PPP was not targeted based on the prevalence of the disease. Instead, it was an equal opportunity tool rolled out nationwide without considering the ferocity of the pandemic in different regions of the country. Eligible businesses, irrespective of the prevalence region they were from, were qualified for the support. Therefore, the correlation between the spread of the pandemic and eligibility was essentially non-existent and did not even form eligibility guideposts according to the law itself. Since the program was not well-targeted, the hardest-hit states regarding disease prevalence did not necessarily receive the most significant loans [8, 10, 12, 13, 19, 30].

There is some modest evidence, however, that the areas receiving the most significant amount of PPP support could afford to remain closed for longer terms, and that might have helped them to tame the spread of the pandemic [20, 21, 23]. However, this is, at best, an unintended gain from the program. For example, think about two states, A and B, experiencing the different spread of the virus. Assume that A is facing a raging pandemic while B is yet to be significantly affected by the pandemic.

Furthermore, assume that loans are available to A and B equally as the spread of the pandemic is not a criterion for loan disbursement. Even if an equal amount of loan is disbursed to both A and B, it would likely have minimal impact on the spread of the pandemic as far as A is concerned. However, the injection of loans in B might help the business owners of B to manage contact between their employees, undertake preventive measures, migrate their workflow online, remain closed for a longer time, etc., which might help B to register lower numbers for the pandemic. This is a Pareto improvement-type example, where A did not do any better, but B got to log in with better results. But this could also be a difficult to prove assertion as the spread of the virus and the onset of disease and death from the infection also got affected by the continuous evolution of the virus itself, availability of vaccinations and treatments, and other mitigating factors like remoteness, travel restrictions, etc. In other words, attenuated virus strength and the availability of advanced treatments could have helped B to achieve a lower impact from the disease. It may be difficult to fully identify the net impact of PPP with all these confounding factors [6, 10, 13, 15, 18].

It is easy to see that the impact of the PPP on the spread of the COVID-19 pandemic is complex and multifaceted. While the program may have had some positive effects on the spread of the virus by incentivizing businesses to keep their employees on payroll and preventing widespread closures of small businesses, it also had potential negative impacts by incentivizing companies to stay open, often without adequate safety measures and potentially diverting resources away from other pandemic response efforts. As policymakers respond to the ongoing pandemic or prepare for any future widespread health crisis, it will be essential to consider the potential impacts of the PPP and other relief efforts on the spread of the virus and other aspects of the economic and social implications of the pandemic.

3.3 The Cost of Saving Jobs and the Impact on Savings

The PPP was a hugely costly program that saved "*2 and 3 million job-years of employment over 14 months at a cost of $169 K to $258 K per job-year retained.*" Furthermore, "*23–34% of PPP dollars went directly to workers who would otherwise have lost jobs; the balance flowed to business owners and shareholders, including creditors and suppliers of PPP-receiving firms.*" In other words, the "*majority of PPP loan dollars issued in 2020–66 to 77%—did not go to paychecks, however, but instead accrued to business owners and shareholders.*" These are stunning and uncomfortable results and perhaps the most biting inditement of the program's efficacy. However, the conclusions are relatively nuanced and must be understood with the proper context in mind [3, 4].

There is no doubt that the PPP saved jobs and saved businesses. That is an undisputed result that has been echoed in numerous studies. By helping companies to keep workers on the payroll, the PPP might have provided support for a higher demand than what would have resulted had the economy-wide shutdown forced companies to lay off millions of workers. In doing so, the PPP might have helped the American economy to avoid a worrisome contagion that could have disturbed an already fragile economic situation and potentially landed the country in depression-like troubles. The controversy is not about those outcomes. It is about the resources it took the nation to achieve those outcomes and whether the same results could have been achieved with a smaller outlay. With this context, concluding that the entire PPP was a colossal waste of public money may be easy but incorrect [14, 21, 23].

It may be noted that the PPP was implemented not as an isolated program but as a part of a package that also involved significant resource infusion in terms of generous unemployment benefits far exceeding the benefits usually available before the pandemic. For example, the CARES Act also provided benefits, including an additional $600 per week in federal unemployment insurance and extended eligibility for unemployment benefits. By providing this assistance, the program helped to prevent widespread financial distress. It increased the ability of unemployed individuals to save money and, in doing so, gave elevated support to the overall demand in the economy. It is an interesting question as to how many jobs would have been lost without this enhanced support. Furthermore, it is still being determined how many businesses would have continued to operate if this accompanying support was not available to the unemployed. Some critics argue that the combined impact of state and federal unemployment benefits offered many people significantly more income than they would have earned by working in a minimum wage job. This could have exacerbated the labor availability challenge for many companies as it took considerably more wages to lure individuals away from higher income guaranteed by the combined state and federal unemployment benefits [1, 2, 7, 8, 11, 24, 25].

Given the contextual elements above, it is likely that the effect of PPP on employment protection was considerably limited compared to the program's size. In addition, $169,000 to $258,000 per job-year saved is a huge sum considering the median real household income was $70,784 in 2021 and $71,186 in 2020. The per capita income was $37,683 in 2021 dollars. Because 66–77% of the outlay was not directed to the paychecks, the cost of the saving jobs was astronomically high. For example, if $200,000 was used to save a job year, as much as $154,000 of that sum went to other places, not to the paychecks, and only $46,000 reached the intended beneficiaries in terms of paychecks [3, 4, 13, 14].

Another troubling aspect of the lack of targeting resulted in a highly regressive nature of the program. It may be noted that most of the spending did not go to paychecks and instead enriched the shareholders, owners, and other vendors of companies that received support under PPP. The owners and shareholders are often considerably wealthier than the average company worker. As a result, more affluent sections of society who owned lucrative company shares received a disproportionately high amount of money even when that was not the program's intended purpose [14, 16, 25, 28].

By transferring valuable taxpayer resources to affluent capital owners, PPP became one of the most controversial government intervention programs and a poster case for government inefficiency. The controversy is predominantly fueled by the fact that this distribution asymmetry might have robustly contributed to increasing inequality in American society. Furthermore, since business ownership is highly skewed against the members of minority communities, the PPP money might have disproportionately helped the whites at the expense of the minority-owned businesses, as many of them lacked resources to apply for the PPP support quickly and take advantage of the public resources that were available to them [1, 3, 4, 6].

The PPP was not targeted toward any particular industry. Every business, from small to medium-sized businesses, physician practices, agricultural sector, etc. got benefitted from the forgivable PPP loans. Clearly, the needs of various sectors are not the same and their needs did not get addressed in any thoughtful manner. There is a persistent worry that small businesses and businesses that are not usually very plugged in with the banking and financial sector might have fallen behind in terms of both putting in their applications and the rate at which their applications were met with success. Businesses with "concierge" type relationships with the banks were disproportionately more successful, potentially adversely affecting the members of the marginalized societies, including the minorities [29, 30, 31, 33, 34].

3.4 Fraud, Abuse, and the Impact on Fiscal and Monetary Policies

PPP is essentially a giant employer subsidy program implemented as a "loan" designed to be forgiven. The "loan" aspect of the PPP is a compliance tool to ensure that businesses use the proceeds for legitimate purposes only. Furthermore, the entire program was not backed by government surplus or tax revenues. It was an extensive deficit finance program poorly designed, haphazardly implemented, and hardly monitored. Therefore, it is unsurprising that the program suffered from large amounts of fraud and abuse. New emerging evidence suggests that many employers misrepresented their company records, employment history, overall costs, etc., and received significant sums of money through the program. In many circumstances, the owners of the companies engaged in lavish purchases of luxury goods and services with the money that was supposed to help workers and their families. In many instances, unscrupulous individuals created shell corporations and engaged in outright fraud to siphon precious public money for private use [16, 17, 22, 26, 27].

To a large extent, the investigation of fraud and abuse of the PPP is being facilitated by a tremendous amount of transparency that allows public discovery of every entity that received support and the financial institutions that worked to channel the money to them. ProPublica maintains one such prominent website, and data from them is easily accessible from https://projects.propublica.org/coronavirus/bailouts/. This massive database reports 11.5 million approved loans, with nearly a million organizations receiving loans between $150 million and $10 million. As of January 11, 2023, this resource lists the details of recipients that received about $793 billion in support, of which $742 billion has already been forgiven [31, 33, 34].

The fraud from PPP is sometimes described as the "Biggest fraud of a generation." News reports suggest that $80 billion of the PPP money was stolen outright. This is

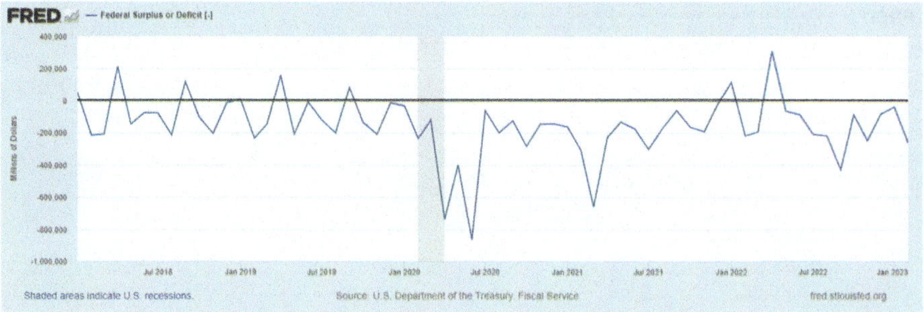

Fig. 3.1 Federal surplus and deficit (monthly data) before and after the onset of Covid pandemic. *Source* U.S. Department of the Treasury. Fiscal Service, Federal Surplus or Deficit [-] [MTSDS133FMS], retrieved from FRED, Federal Reserve Bank of St. Louis; https://fred.stlouisfed.org/series/MTSDS133FMS, April 23, 2023

on top of $90 billion to $400 billion stolen from the $900 billion Covid unemployment support programs, with at least half taken by international fraudsters. It might have been the most prominent cyber fraud experienced by the U.S. Government, where con artists, crime syndicates, organized crime, foreign fraudsters, etc., stole precious public money. The auditors in Nebraska found that over two-thirds of the unemployment funds were misspent. Auditors in Kentucky found that the program's internal controls were so weak that they violated federal laws [16, 17, 22, 27, 32].

PPP was a significant component of the overall CARES Act; almost all the spending for PPP might have been financed by massive government borrowing. Data from the Federal Reserve System exhibits a large and persistent impact on the federal deficit created by the gigantic pandemic-related contraction and the size of the programs rolled out [26–28] (Fig. 3.1).

The deficit financing aspect is particularly troubling as massive public debt drives interest rates through the crowding-out effect. Significant demand for loanable funds from the government creates a higher demand in the debt market and upward pressure on the interest rates. Furthermore, such a massive injection of cash in the economy also acted as a significant expansionary activity pushing up the inflation risk in the economy. Subsequent Federal Reserve data exhibited persistent inflation shock to the economy following the height of the pandemic when most government money was injected into the economy. It is well known that higher interest rates are the primary tools central bankers use to tame raging inflation [10, 15, 19, 22] (Fig. 3.2).

However, as might be expected under a traditional expansionary monetary policy regime, a significant cash injection helped the interest rate plunge, initially creating an unsustainable upward pressure on the asset prices, and fueling further inflationary pressures. Poor monetary management might have exacerbated the problem by tightening monetary policies to contain inflation, further creating unsustainable pressure on the interest rates [10, 25, 26, 28, 36] (Fig. 3.3).

Another indirect impact of the significant federal expansion was a massive expansion in the checkable deposits in banking institutions. There are several reasons for

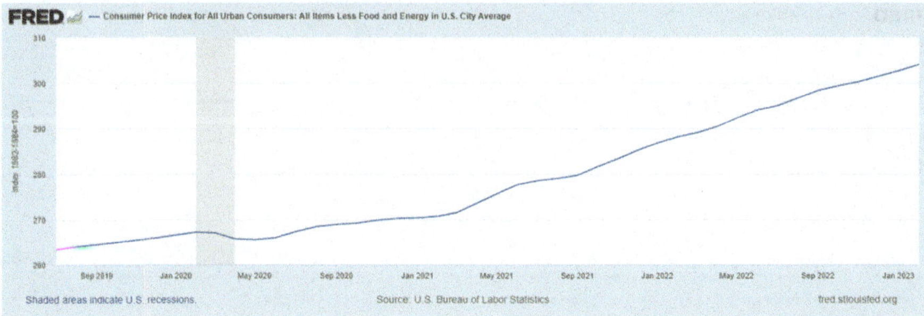

Fig. 3.2 Consumer price index for all urban consumers: all items less food and energy in the U.S. City average. *Source* U.S. Bureau of Labor Statistics, Consumer Price Index for All Urban Consumers: All Items Less Food and Energy in the U.S. City Average [CPILFESL], retrieved from FRED, Federal Reserve Bank of St. Louis; https://fred.stlouisfed.org/series/CPILFESL, April 23, 2023

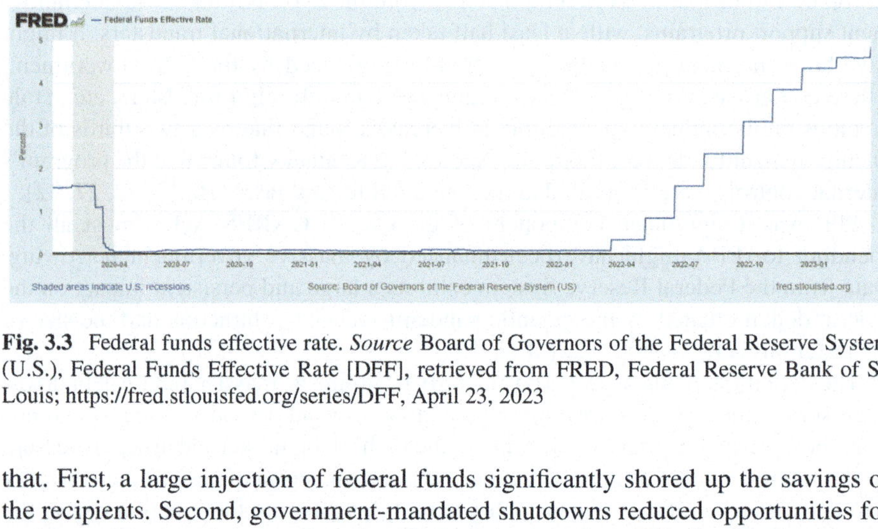

Fig. 3.3 Federal funds effective rate. *Source* Board of Governors of the Federal Reserve System (U.S.), Federal Funds Effective Rate [DFF], retrieved from FRED, Federal Reserve Bank of St. Louis; https://fred.stlouisfed.org/series/DFF, April 23, 2023

that. First, a large injection of federal funds significantly shored up the savings of the recipients. Second, government-mandated shutdowns reduced opportunities for consumers to travel, eat out, and embark on a vacation. Travel-related costs are a significant component of workers' expenditure, and by keeping the travel to a minimum, shutdowns might have increased the workers' savings. As a result, checkable deposits increased from $1.13 trillion in the first quarter of 2020 to over $3 trillion in the 4th quarter of 2020, almost at a two hundred percent increase during the calendar year [7, 8, 10, 13, 24, 28, 31] (Fig. 3.4).

The four figures above tell a complete story whose impact may be felt on the U.S. economy for years and decades. Massive deficit-financed government programs like the PPP massively increased the government deficit. They shored up the overall money supply in the U.S. economy leading to significant inflationary pressures and rapidly escalating interest rates precipitated by a crowding-out and regulatory response towards managing the inflationary conditions.

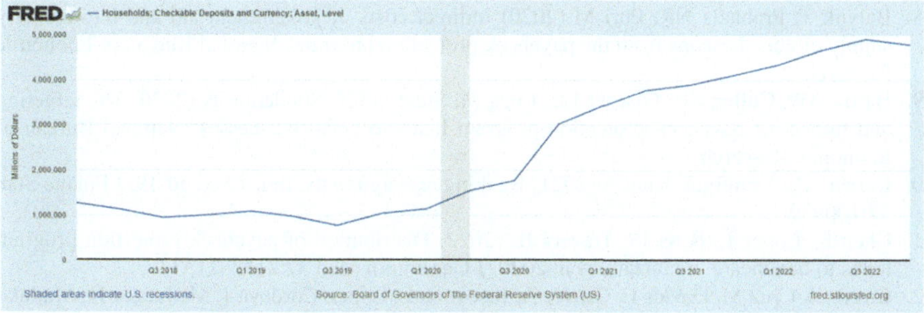

Fig. 3.4 Checkable deposits and currency; asset, level. *Source* Board of Governors of the Federal Reserve System (US), Households; Checkable Deposits and Currency; Asset, Level [BOGZ1FL193020005Q], retrieved from FRED, Federal Reserve Bank of St. Louis; https://fred.stlouisfed.org/series/BOGZ1FL193020005Q, April 23, 2023

3.5 Conclusion

PPP is one of U.S. history's most significant direct injection subsidy programs. Although the program might have saved many jobs during the critical months of the COVID-19 pandemic, the program came at a significant cost to the treasury. The program's efficacy remains hotly debated as emerging evidence suggests that most resources failed to reach the intended beneficiaries. Furthermore, there is significant evidence that the program was poorly implemented and fell victim to fraud and abuse. As a mainly deficit-financed program, the PPP contributed to trillions of dollars in the fiscal deficit that increased inflation, tightened monetary policy, and raised interest rates in subsequent months and years.

References

1. Allen KD, Whitledge MD (2022) Further evidence on the effectiveness of community banks in the paycheck protection program. Financ Res Lett 47:102583
2. Atkins R, Cook L, Seamans R (2022) Discrimination in lending? Evidence from the paycheck protection program. Small Bus Econ 58:843–865
3. Autor D, Cho D, Crane LD, Goldar M, Lutz B, Montes J, Peterman WB, Ratner D, Villar D, Yildirmaz A (2022) The $800 billion paycheck protection program: where did the money go and why did it go there? J Econ Perspect 36:55–80
4. Autor D, Cho D, Crane LD, Goldar M, Lutz B, Montes J, Peterman WB, Ratner D, Villar D, Yildirmaz A (2022) An evaluation of the paycheck protection program using administrative payroll microdata. J Public Econ 211:104664
5. Bailey C, Brody R, Sokolowski M (2022) Fraudulent loans and the united states paycheck protection program. J Financ Crime 29:519–532
6. Bailey C, Sokolowski M (2022) Lender financial reporting incentives and loan prioritization during the paycheck protection program. Manag Financ 48:1707–1725
7. Ballew HB, Nicoletti A, Stuber SB (2022) The effect of the paycheck protection program and financial reporting standards on bank risk-taking. Manage Sci 68:2363–2371

8. Balyuk T, Prabhala NR, Puri M (2020) Indirect costs of government aid and intermediary supply effects: Lessons from the paycheck protection program. National Bureau of Economic Research
9. Bartik AW, Cullen ZB, Glaeser EL, Luca M, Stanton CT, Sunderam A (2020) The targeting and impact of paycheck protection program loans to small businesses. National Bureau of Economic Research
10. Berger AN, Demirgüç-Kunt A (2021) Banking research in the time of covid-19. J Financ Stab 57:100939
11. Chen K, Lopez L, Ross JS, Travers JL (2022) Distribution of paycheck protection program loans to healthcare organizations in 2020. J Gen Intern Med 37:2132–2133
12. Cirera X, Cruz M, Davies E, Grover A, Iacovone L, López-Córdova J, Medvedev D, Maduko F, Nayyar G, Ortega S, Torres J (2021) Policies to support businesses through the covid-19 shock: a firm level perspective. The World Bank Res Obs 36
13. Cororaton A, Rosen S (2021) Public firm borrowers of the u.S. Paycheck protection program. Rev Corp Finance Stud 10:641–693
14. Dahl D, Emmons W (2022) Was the paycheck protection program effective? Reg Econ
15. Deming K, Weiler S (2023) Banking deserts and the paycheck protection program. Econ Dev Quart 0:1–18
16. Dilanian K, Ramgopal K, Atkins C (2021) Easy money: how international scam artists pulled off an epic theft of covid benefits. NBC News. https://www.nbcnews.com/news/us-news/easy-money-how-international-scam-artists-pulled-epic-theft-covid-n1276789. Accessed 29 June 2023
17. Dilanian K, Strickler L (2022) 'Biggest fraud in a generation': the looting of the covid relief plan known as ppp. NBC News. https://www.nbcnews.com/politics/justice-department/biggest-fraud-generation-looting-covid-relief-program-known-ppp-n1279664. Accessed 29 June 2023
18. Duchin R, Martin X, Michaely R, Wang H (2022) Concierge treatment from banks: evidence from the paycheck protection program. J Corp Finan 72:102124
19. Erel I, Liebersohn J (2020) Does fintech substitute for banks? evidence from the paycheck protection program National Bureau of Economic Research
20. Fairlie R, Fossen FM (2022) Did the paycheck protection program and economic injury disaster loan program get disbursed to minority communities in the early stages of covid-19? Small Bus Econ 58:829–842
21. Granja J, Makridis C, Yannelis C, Zwick E (2022) Did the paycheck protection program hit the target? J Financ Econ 145:725–761
22. Griffin JM, Kruger S, Mahajan P (2022) Did fintech lenders facilitate ppp fraud? J Finance (forthcoming)
23. Hubbard RG, Strain MR (2020) Has the paycheck protection program succeeded? National Bureau of Economic Research
24. Humphries JE, Neilson CA, Ulyssea G (2020) Information frictions and access to the paycheck protection program. J Public Econ 190:104244
25. Kapinos P (2021) Did the paycheck protection program have negative side effects on small-business activity? Econ Lett 208:110045
26. Karakaplan MU (2021) This time is really different: the multiplier effect of the paycheck protection program (ppp) on small business bank loans. J Bank Finance 133:106223
27. Kickul J, Griffiths MD, Robb CC, Gundry L (2021) All for one? the paycheck protection program distribution disparity. J Entrep Public Policy 10:323–335
28. Lee S (2023) Banking infrastructure and the paycheck protection program during the covid-19 pandemic. Reg Stud 57:84–96
29. Lester, TW, Wilson MD (2023) The racial and spatial impacts of the paycheck protection program. Econ Dev Quart 08912424231157693
30. Lopez JA, Spiegel MM (2023) Small business lending under the ppp and ppplf programs. J Financ Intermed 53:101017

31. Pfeiffer S, Fast A (2023) How the paycheck protection program went from good intentions to a huge free-for-all. National Public Radio. https://www.knkx.org/2023-01-09/how-the-paycheck-protection-program-went-from-good-intentions-to-a-huge-free-for-all
32. Ramgopal K, Blankstein A, Winter T (2021) How billions in pandemic aid was swindled by con artists and crime syndicates. (NBC News). https://www.nbcnews.com/news/us-news/how-billions-pandemic-aid-was-swindled-con-artists-crime-syndicates-n1257766
33. Sabasteanski N, Brooks J, Chandler T (2021) Saving lives and livelihoods: the paycheck protection program and its efficacy. Economia 22:278–290
34. Şahin A, Tasci M (2022) The great resignation and the paycheck protection program. Econ Comment
35. Sivadasan P, Soileau JS, Zhang R-Z (2023) The auditors' role in the u.S. Paycheck protection program (ppp). AUDITING: A J Pract Theory 1–16
36. Staples AJ, Krumel TP (2022) The paycheck protection program and small business performance: evidence from craft breweries. Small Bus Econ

Chapter 4
COVID-19 Incidence and Economic Confidence: Any Relationships So Far for the world's Highly Affected Countries?

Somdip Bhukta, Maitree Dey, and Ramesh Chandra Das

4.1 Introduction

All the people of the world have recently endured huge setbacks in their development in different heads due to the eruption of the novel coronavirus, COVID-19. The disease has not been over; its ramifications are still continuing. It has swept away a sizable amount of gross domestic product (GDP) of the countries, making lay off a huge labour force, creating mental distress, and raising income inequality, among others, in the affected countries. Moreover, there are also the occurrences that the disease has affected the economic confidence of both the consumers and business houses during the entire phase of the pandemic. It is obvious that the COVID-19 pandemic is not only a major economic emergency but also a major economic downturn. Most of the countries like the USA, UK, India, Russia, China, etc. and the groups like EU, have reacted to the COVID-19 shock by adopting the lockdown survival strategy. Pandemic has affected both supply side and demand side factors. Supplier and demander both faced uncertainty about the future, as a result, supply and demand both had decreased. Mitigation measures of lockdowns (closure of business, travel, restriction etc.) led to decrease in the consumption and investment levels while production and employment had shrunk to unforeseen levels. Financial and commodity markets, global trade and supply chains, and tourism were also disrupted. Job loss, unemployment benefit claims that the impact of the COVID-19 is likely to be exceptionally high in the EU. However, the global job loss is difficult to measure because the decline of the working hours thus for already exceeds 195 million jobs. Because of the adverse effects of COVID-19, different countries faced negative sectoral growth. Recovery is different for the different countries, for Russia,

S. Bhukta · M. Dey · R. C. Das (✉)
Department of Economics, Vidyasagar University, Midnapore, India
e-mail: ramesh051073@gmail.com

R. Bhattacharyya et al. (eds.), *COVID-19 Pandemic and Global Inequality*,
https://doi.org/10.1007/978-981-99-4405-7_4

it is W-shaped recovery of economic growth, according to the International Monetary Fund. On the other hand, India faced V-shaped recovery of economic growth, according to the Reserve Bank of India. The pandemic creates challenges for the policymakers as they seek to cope with the devastating effects of the pandemic on health services, the economy and society in general. Effective crises management is important to promote appropriate measures during the pandemic. In this context, most of the governments take preventive measures to stem the pressure on the health system and launched economic support programs to compensate the households and the firms for the income losses they incurred. Policies are different across the countries. Recovery will greatly depend on vaccination progress, easing of containment measure and continued policy supports. The various elements (reaction to the case report, deaths attitude toward the vaccination, lockdown compliance, and government measures to support the business) combined to create different outlooks of in the mind of the investor, that strongly influenced their investment strategies. Besides all these, the countries faced vacillations in the confidence levels of the consumers and business houses during the pandemic. It has been shown by many studies such as of Das and Das [6] that consumers' and business sentiments have close connections with consumption and investment decision-making and thereby influencing the overall GDP and trade linkages of the countries and groups in the world. Under the backdrop, the present study aims to investigate whether COVID-19 incidences do have any correlation and long-run relationships with both the consumer and business confidence in the world's highly affected countries, namely, the USA, the UK, Italy, Spain, France, India, Brazil, China, Russia and South Africa for the monthly data of the period January 2020-August 2022.

4.2 Literature Review

Consumer and business sentiment during the pandemic are influenced by a number of factors, including the country's economic standing, information on COVID-19 cases and deaths, adherence to lockdowns, vaccination programmes, and government initiatives to stop the spread of COVID cases. According to a recent study, immunisation often reduced fear and increased the efficiency of governmental involvement in lowering pessimism [19]. Bui et al. [4] found that both in Thailand and Vietnam following the phase of lockdown in May 2020 consumer perception was impacted by the COVID-19 situation. Sun et al. [21] discovered that COVID-related news generally has a positive and significant impact on medical stock portfolios, and that announcements about the economy during COVID-19 also generally have a significant positive impact on investor sentiment in the United States, Japan, China, Korea, and Hong Kong. In a new research, Hsu and Tang [11] demonstrated that a rise in investor mood during COVID-19 will cause the stock market to experience unexpectedly greater volatility.

The relationship of GDP growth and economic sentiment in Russia during the COVID-19 crisis was examined by Kitrar and Lipkind [14]. The study demonstrates a nearly synchronous cyclic congruence between TESI dynamics and GDP growth for the years 1998–2020. Simionescu et al. [20] discovered that between March 2020 and May 2021, Google searches for COVID-19 had a detrimental effect on job expectations in the EU's new member states. Both unemployment and inflation rates had a negative impact, but the employment anticipation has climbed as the economic confidence index has improved. Liu et al. [16] found that the COVID-19 epidemic has had a profoundly detrimental effect on public perception, which has led to fear and some illogical purchasing behaviour, which in turn has had a complicated effect on agricultural commodity prices. Buckman et al. [3] have attempted to evaluate how news sentiment influenced US consumer sentiment during the COVID pandemic. Using daily data, researchers have seen a dramatic fall in news sentiment with rising pandemic news coverage. Also, they find that a drop in news sentiment indicates a massive drop in consumer spending, revealing a positive relationship between consumer sentiment and news sentiment.

Increased pandemic concern results in unfavourable investors' attitude, according to Dash and Maitra [7]. They also examined a correlation between pandemic uncertainty and stock market activity globally. The effect of COVID-19 on European financial markets and economic sentiment was examined by Kanapickiene et al. [13]. By lowering stock market indices and future prices, as well as by boosting volatility and hazards, COVID-19 has a detrimental impact on the financial market. They found that in May 2020 some countries had positive strong consumer confidence and some other countries had negative strong consumer confidence. While in that month 25 countries had positive economic sentiment. Abosedra et al. [1] discovered that a shock to consumer sentiment has a big impact on how much money consumers spend. They also found that fluctuations in consumer attitude had a considerable detrimental influence on the COVID-19 period's volatility of consumer spending. Leduc et al. [15] termed this as the uncertainty of the Pandemic in their literature. Zhang et al. [26] discovered that the epidemic has raised the risks associated with the global financial market. The pandemic's high level of uncertainty and the resulting economic losses have made markets very volatile and unpredictable.

Boitan et al. [2] studied the impact of COVID-19 on the economic sentiment pattern in European Union countries by hierarchic agglomerative clustering and panel regression. They found that in both the first and second waves of COVID-19, the number of clusters increased which implies that heterogeneity increases between countries in terms of people's expectations of economic performance of the country. With the aid of an online poll, Verma and Naveen [24] investigated how the COVID-19 affected consumers' purchasing habits. People now understand the value of local, eco-friendly, and hygienic products in leading healthy and secure lives as a result of COVID-19. They discovered that people are more likely to purchase Indian goods because of their negative attitudes toward foreign goods. Wielen and Barrios [23] studied the economic sentiment during COVID-19 in the EU. Compared to the Great Depression, people's fears about unemployment have increased significantly during the COVID crisis. They noticed a considerable decline in the labour market and durable consumption. Das and Das [6] found that there are causal relationships between consumer sentiment and household spending in a number of nations. In contrast to the main growing nations, like China and India, where consumption is directly responsible for confidence levels during the course of the study, most developed and some developing countries yield results from bidirectional causalities between the two.

Zervoyianni et al. [25] found that European economic agents' emotions have fallen dramatically as a result of the slowdown in the economy brought on by the implementation of travel restrictions and other laws. Certain structural aspects of economies, such as exposure to poverty, a substantial informal sector, a high percentage of susceptible jobs, and a lack of financial and informational openness, may exacerbate the detrimental economic impacts of a pandemic. The COVID-19 pandemic has a negative significant influence on economic mood, but it has a good impact on consumer sentiment and a negative impact on industry confidence, according to Zhang et al. [27].

4.3 Theoretical Underpinning

Economic sentiment has close links with the micro and macroeconomic systems; it influences the decision-making processes of the individual economic agents and thereby motivates the macroeconomic indicators such as income, employment, capital movements, etc. According to Makridis [17, 18], economic sentiment is a measuring rod of economic confidence and it signifies the credence in current and future national economic growth. The concept is similar to the Keynesian popular concept, "animal spirit" which is the natural instinctive expectation of economic agents. According to Keynes, the sudden change of mood due to many unknown factors such as climate change, terrorism, pandemic, etc. explain the fluctuations in the business cycle. Therefore, the Covid pandemic has close associations with consumers and business confidences as measured, respectively, by the consumers' confidence index (CCI) and business confidence index (BCI). CCI affects the GDP of the country by means of aggregate consumption (C), savings (S) and labour supply (NS) and BCI affects GDP by means of investment (I), capital formation (K) and labour absorption (ND). Thus,

GDP = f(C, S, I, K, NS, ND)

C, S & NS = f(CCI(Covid Cases & Death))

and

I, K & ND = f(BCI(Covid Cases & Death))

where dGDP/dC, dGDP/dS, dGDP/dI, dGDP/dK, dGDP/dNS and dGDP/dND > 0 and consumers and business behaviours are negatively related to Covid cases and death.

The present study captures the theoretical linkages of the CCI and BCI with the Covid cases and death to verify empirical findings.

4.4 Data and Methodology

The study has four key variables, covid-19 cases, covid-19 death, consumers' sentiments measured in the consumer confidence index (CCI), and business sentiments measured in the business confidence index (BCI). The data on covid cases and covid death across the countries are taken from the World Health Organization database (https://covid19.who.int/data) and the data on CCI and BCI are supplied by different central banks and statistical institutes of the countries and compiled by OECD.org (visit https://data.oecd.org/leadind/consumer-confidence-index-cci.htm). There are ten countries on the list that are considered as most affected countries during the pandemic period. Data are taken on a monthly basis for the period, January 2020 to August 2022. BCI and CCI data for India are taken from rbi.org (www.rbi.org.in).

In the methodology section, the study first presents the data in figures then it goes for computing correlations in the pairs of Covid Death—BCI, Covid Death—CCI, Covid Case—CCI, and Covid Case—BCI. After having the correlation results the study goes for testing the unit root of all four series following ADF [8] technique to find any long-run and short-run linkages in the two pairs across the countries. For testing long-run relation, the Engel-Granger [9] cointegration technique is used followed by the error correction mechanisms, and for the causality test, the Granger [10] test is followed.

4.5 Results and Discussion

Before attempting the quantitative exercise on the relationships between Covid indicators and the indicators for economic sentiments the study goes for presenting the data over time to have a brief idea of their movements. Figure 4.1 presents the same for the Covid cases, Fig. 4.2, Covid death and Fig. 4.3, the BCI and CCI. With respect to the Covid cases, the USA tops the list followed by India, France, etc. USA's first wave takes the peak in July 2020, the second peak in May 2021 and the third peak in January 2022. On the other hand, India's first peak is in September 2020, the second peak in May 2021 and the third peak, though in mild magnitudes, in January 2022. China is at the lowest level throughout. January 2022 is the month in which all countries' trends take the peak where USA is at the highest number of attacks.

On the other hand, with respect to the number of covid death, the same ranking of the countries are there except that Brazil stays in rank third but the highest number of deaths is observed in India in May 2021. The trends are rising over time.

The trends of business sentiment as evidenced from Fig. 4.3 are upward rising and that of consumers' sentiment is downward sloping for all the countries. There is a common break in the developed countries in the BCI during April–May 2020 and the trends for all move down since November 2021. Russia and the UK dominate the list in BCI through the entire period and China stays at the bottom maximum times. On the other hand, out of all countries' falling trends in CCI, India stays at the top

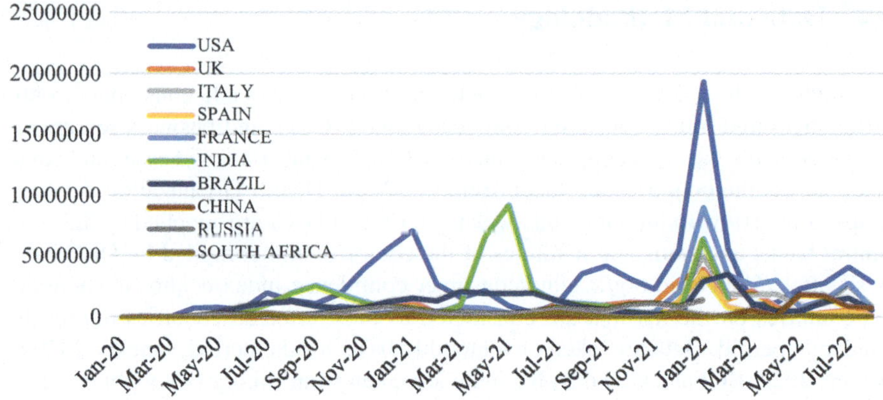

Fig. 4.1 Trends of Covid cases of the countries. *Source* Drawn by the authors

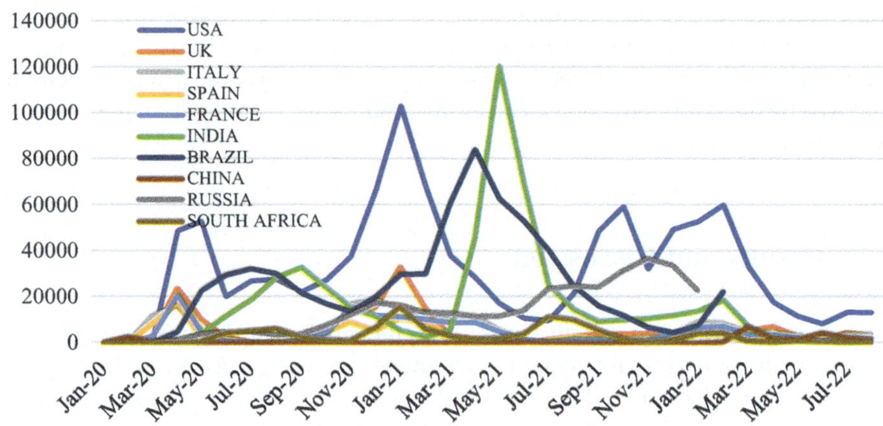

Fig. 4.2 Trends of Covid deaths of the countries. *Source* Drawn by the authors

in maximum number of months while South Africa stays at the bottom. The major countries faced a downturn in CCI during the first wave and in the last wave.

4.5.1 Correlation Analysis

Based upon the above sketches on the indicators on covid 19 and economic sentiments it is now required to compute the degrees of associations among these two sets of indicators. Increases in the number of covid deaths and covid cases adversely affect consumers' and investors' expectations and as a result, both investment and demand for consumer goods have decreased. This adversely affects consumers and

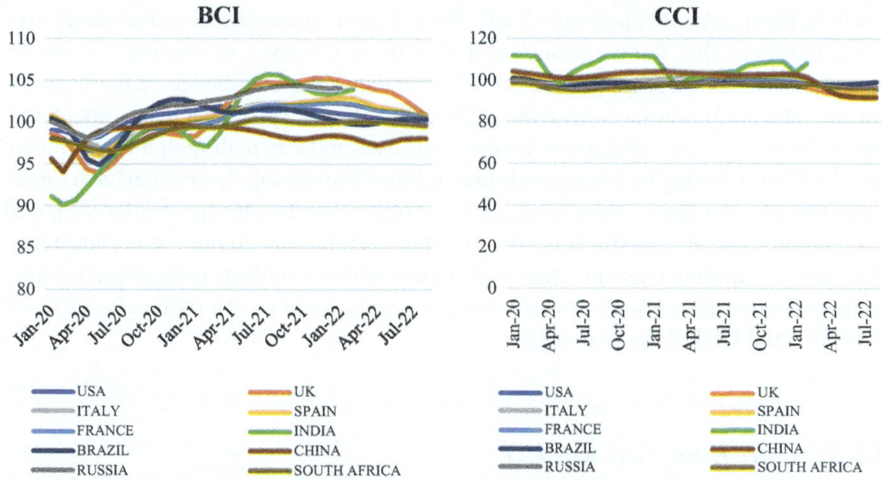

Fig. 4.3 Trends of BCI and CCI of the countries. *Source* Drawn by the authors

business sentiments of the country. Only the signs and values of the correlation coefficient of covid cases with BCI & CCI and Covid death with BCI & CCI do not imply the significance of the values, so the Student t test is required and study goes with it. Table 4.1 represents the values of the estimates t statistic and corresponding correlation coefficient.

It is observed from the table that positive associations are there between BCI and Covid cases and death, and significant results are found for the UK, Italy, Spain, France, India and Russia. The upward trends in BCI are associated with the rising

Table 4.1 Correlation results

Countries	Covid cases & BCI (t values)	Covid cases & CCI (t values)	Covid death & BCI (t values)	Covid death & CCI (t values)
USA	0.30(1.8)	−0.3(−1.7)	**0.35(2.1)**	0.06(−0.3)
UK	**0.56(3.7)**	0.05(0.3)	−0.32(−1.9)	−0.15(−0.8)
Italy	**0.38(2.3)**	−0.24(−1.3)	0.19(−1.0)	−0.16(−0.9)
Spain	**0.40(2.4)**	0.11(0.6)	**0.36(−2.1)**	−0.20(−1.1)
France	**0.42(2.5)**	−0.15(−0.8)	**0.38(−2.2)**	−0.21(−1.1)
India	**0.41(2.2)**	−0.35(−1.8)	**0.45(2.4)**	−0.29(−1.5)
Brazil	0.26(1.5)	−0.11(−0.6)	0.22(1.2)	−0.21(−1.2)
China	−0.19(−1.1)	**0.85(−9.0)**	**−0.40(−2.4)**	**−0.58(−3.9)**
Russia	**0.73(5.1)**	−24(−1.2)	**0.86(8.0)**	−0.05(−0.2)
South Africa	0.25(1.4)	0.09(0.5)	0.16(0.9)	0.12(0.7)

Notes The bold marks indicate significant results
Source Computed by the authors

trends in the number of cases and death. Though the results are somewhat unrealistic, it has the basis that the countries' spending upon restoring the business activities in terms of stimulus packages would help in raising the confidence of the business houses. The observations go with the study of Teresiene et al. [22]. On the other hand, the CCI has negative correlations with Covid cases and death, though it is significant only for China. Rising health expenditure and shock in the supply channel have forced consumers to stay away from consumption habits. The results are similar to that of Chronopoulos et al. [5]. But it is also true that correlations do not mean causations. Hence, it is required to go for a time series econometric analysis to examine whether there are long-run relationships and causal interplays between Covid cases & death with BCI and CCI of the countries.

4.5.2 *Unit Root Test Results*

Since it is necessary to have all the series to be of I (1) for the prevalence of long-run association, it is required to test whether the first difference of the three series is stationary. The results are calculated by using ADF. Table 4.2 presents the results for Covid Death, Covid Cases, BCI & CCI. It is observed that seven countries have the variables integrated of order one, and the three are with integration of order two.

So, the next step will be to test for cointegration and error correction for the differenced series of (Covid case & BCI), (Covid Case & CCI), (Covid death & BCI) and (Covid death & CCI).

Table 4.2 Unit root test results for the countries

Countries	ADF				Remarks
	BCI	Cc	CCI	Cd	
USA	−6.42(0.00)	−6.39(0.00)	−4.69(0.00)	−4.60(0.00)	Stationary at 1st diff
UK	4.14(0.00)	6.29(0.00)	−4.06(0.01)	−5.66(0.00)	Stationary at 1st diff
Italy	−5.50(0.00)	−7.7(0.00)	−3.19(0.00)	−5.97(0.00)	Stationary at 1st diff
Spain	−6.41(0.0)	−6.38(0.0)	−1.91(0.0)	−5.51(0.00)	Stationary at 1st diff
France	−4.68(0.00)	−7.1(0.00)	−3.72(0.00)	−6.47(0.00)	Stationary at 1st diff
India	−5.06(0.00)	−5.48(0.00)	−5.27(0.00)	−6.16(0.00)	Stationary at 2nd diff
Brazil	−6.98(0.00)	−5.77(0.00)	−7.59(0.00)	−2.97(0.00)	Stationary at 1st diff
China	−8.44(0.00)	−3.4(0.00)	−2.05(0.04)	−7.26(0.00)	Stationary at 1st diff
Russia	−3.16(0.00)	−4.22(0.00)	−8.07(0.00)	−3.28(0.00)	Stationary at 2nd diff
South Africa	−4.98(0.00)	−6.46(0.00)	−5.91(0.00)	−5.73(0.00)	Stationary at 2nd diff

Source Computed by the authors

4.5.3 Engle–Granger Cointegration and Error Correction Test Results

As mentioned, the EG method of cointegration is done by testing whether the estimated residuals of the relation of BCI, CCI upon covid cases and covid death are stationary. Table 4.3 presents the regression results where the estimated regression coefficients are depicted in column '2' and '3' and the ADF values of the estimated residuals are respectively in column '4' and '5'. Column '6' and '7' presents the respective error correction terms. It is observed that the series for BCI and Covid Cases are cointegrated for Brazil and China, but the errors are not corrected for them around the long-run path. There is a weak cointegration of BCI and Covid cases in the UK, Spain, France and India. On the other hand, the series of CCI and covid cases are cointegrated for the majority of the countries which are, the UK, Spain, France, India, Brazil, China, Russia, and South Africa but the errors are corrected for Brazil and Russia only. Hence, for the majority of the highly affected countries of the world, Covid incidence maintains a long-run or equilibrium relationship with the business and consumers' confidence; the business houses and consumers' expectations about the future were based upon the movements of the Covid spread.

On the other hand, from the lower panel of the table, it is observed that BCI and Covid death are congregated for the USA, Italy, Brazil, China, Russia and South Africa but the errors are corrected for the USA, Brazil and China. The short-run dynamics around the long-run relation ensure that the deviation is converging or temporary for these three countries. On the other hand, CCI and Covid Death are congregated for the majority of the listed countries which are, the USA, Italy, Spain, India, Brazil, China, Russia, South Africa but the errors are corrected only for Brazil, Russia and India. Therefore, the Covid death, the indicator for Covid fatality, has relatively better long-run relationships with BCI and CCI compared to the Covid cases, the indicator of Covid fear. Again, the consumers are highly scared of both the Covid cases and death, although the latter is relatively stronger than the former. Hence, Covid 19 has affected the decision-making processes of both the business houses and consumers in the world's highly affected ten countries.

4.5.4 Granger Causality Test Results

The absence or presence of long-run equilibrium relation does not mean that there will be no interplays in the short run. So, it is required to focus on the interplays in the short run for the four pairs of series (Covid cases & BCI) and (Covid cases & CCI), (Covid death & BCI), (Covid death & CCI), in the 1st differenced and 2nd differenced forms as applicable. The results are given in Table 4.4. The two sets of null hypotheses for the causality test are given below:

Table 4.3 Engle–Granger Cointegration test and error correction results

Countries	Regr. Coeff (Prob) Covid cases on BCI	Regr. Coeff (Prob) Covid Cases on CCI	Residual ADF (Prob) Covid cases on BCI	Residual ADF (Prob) Covid cases on CCI	EC term (prob) Covid cases on BCI	EC term (prob) CCI on covid cases	Remarks whether cointegration is present
Covid cases							
USA	9.67E–08(0.09)	−1.17E–07(0.09)	−1.44(0.13)	−1.58(0.10)	–	–	NO FOR BOTH
UK	2.26E–06(0.00)	1.52E–07(0.79)	−1.71(0.08)	−2.43(0.01)	–	−0.02(0.67)	Yes, for CCI on covid cases
Italy	6.44E–07(0.03)	−4.32E–07(0.18)	−1.39(0.15)	−0.32(0.56)	–	–	NO FOR BOTH
Spain	1.10E–06(0.02)	3.65E–07(0.55)	−1.70(0.08)	−2.98(0.05)	–	−1.52(0.14)	Yes, for CCI on covid cases
France	3.89E–07(0.01)	−1.26E–07(0.42)	−1.68(0.08)	−2.99(0.05)	–	−0.44(0.66)	Yes, for CCI on covid cases
India	8.69E–07(0.03)	−180,734.1(0.08)	−1.58(0.10)	−3.86(0.00)	–	2.02E–07(0.63)	Yes, for CCI on covid cases
Brazil	5.98E–07(0.00)	−1.02E–07(0.56)	−3.98(0.00)	−9.27(0.00)	−0.14(0.09)	−0.30(0.01)	Yes for both
China	−4.98E–07(0.29)	−7.05E–06(0.00)	−3.61(0.01)	−3.41(0.01)	−0.08(0.07)	−1.02(0.09)	Yes, for both
Russia	3.99E–06(0.00)	−6.92E–07(0.24)	−1.48(0.13)	−4.19(0.00)	–	−0.22(0.02)	Yes, for CCI on covid cases

(continued)

Table 4.3 (continued)

Countries	Regr. Coeff (Prob) Covid cases on BCI	Regr. Coeff (Prob) Covid Cases on CCI	Residual ADF (Prob) Covid cases on BCI	Residual ADF (Prob) Covid cases on CCI	EC term (prob) Covid cases on BCI	EC term (prob) CCI on covid cases	Remarks whether cointegration is present
South Africa	2.09E–06(0.18)	6.92E–07(0.61)	−0.98(0.28)	−4.97(0.00)	–	−0.1006(0.18)	Yes, for CCI on covid cases
Covid death							
	Regr. Coeff (Prob) Covid death on BCI	Regr. Coeff (Prob) Covid death on CCI	Residual ADF(Prob) Covid death on BCI	Residual ADF(Prob) Covid death on CCI	EC term (prob) Covid death on BCI	EC term (prob) Covid death on CCI	Remarks whether cointegration is present
USA	1.65E–05(0.05)	−3.58E–06(0.73)	−3.12(0.03)	−3.42(0.01)	−0.09(0.05)	−0.05(0.21)	Yes, for both
UK	−0.000159(0.07)	−6.05E–05(0.40)	−1.11(0.23)	−1.01(0.27)	–	–	No for both
Italy	−5.79E–05(0.30)	−5.25E–05(0.39)	−2.98(0.05)	−2.99(0.05)	−0.03(0.47)	0.02(0.66)	Yes, for both
Spain	−0.000171(0.04)	−0.000115(0.27)	−1.31(0.17)	−2.70(0.06)	–	−0.02(0.69)	No for both
France	−0.000123(0.03)	−6.09E–05(0.25)	−1.12(0.23)	−1.20(0.20)	–	–	No for both
India	8.49E–05(0.02)	−4.95E–05(0.15)	−1.37(0.15)	−3.74(0.00)	–	−0.33(0.06)	Yes, for CCI
Brazil	2.16E–05(0.28)	−8.42E–06(0.30)	−4.57(0.00)	−9.73(0.00)	−0.16(0.06)	−0.40(0.01)	Yes, for both
China	−0.000330(0.02)	−0.001496(0.00)	−3.64(0.00)	−3.04(0.05)	−0.25(0.00)	−0.08(0.22)	Yes, for both
Russia	0.000158(0.0000)	−4.99E–06(0.80)	−3.34(0.00)	−3.63(0.00)	0.003(0.97)	−0.25(0.01)	Yes, for both
South Africa	5.39E–05(0.36)	3.57E–05(0.49)	−1.75(0.07)	−4.839(0.00)	−0.03(0.35)	−0.11(0.13)	Yes, for CCI

Source Computed by the authors

Table 4.4 Granger causality test results

Countries	Lags	BCI		CCI		Directions of causality
		F values	Prob	F values	Prob	No
Covid cases						
USA	3.3	0.52(0.01)	0.48(0.93)	1.45(0.10)	0.25(0.95)	No causality
UK	3.3	0.43(0.52)	0.73(0.67)	0.44(0.34)	0.72(0.79)	No causality
Italy	3.3	0.04(0.05)	0.83(0.81)	2.94(0.44)	0.07(0.64)	No causality
Spain	3.3	0.04(0.16)	0.83(0.68)	0.27(0.01)	0.60(0.92)	No causality
France	3.3	0.00(0.14)	0.98(0.70)	0.00(0.03)	0.95(0.85)	No causality
India	3.3	0.61(4.47)	0.55(0.02)	0.42 (1.34)	0.73(0.29)	ΔΔBCI → ΔΔCovid cases
Brazil	1.3	0.29(0.25)	0.83(0.85)	0.03(0.93)	0.98(0.44)	No causality
China	3.3	0.81(0.49)	0.50(0.69)	0.10(9.86)	0.74(0.00)	ΔCCI → ΔCovid cases
Russia	3.3	0.26(0.27)	0.85(0.84)	0.87(1.72)	0.36(0.20)	No causality
South Africa	3.3	0.21(0.55)	0.88(0.65)	0.41(0.54)	0.74(0.65)	No causality
Covid death						
USA	3.3	3.23(0.26)	0.04(0.85)	1.12(1.76)	0.29(0.19)	ΔCovid Death → ΔBCI
UK	3.2	2.71(3.08)	0.07(0.04)	4.09(0.16)	0.01(0.92)	ΔCovid Death → ΔCCI
ITALY	3.3	1.11(1.49)	0.36(0.24)	0.14(1.57)	0.93(0.22)	No causality
SPAIN	1.2	0.53(4.26)	0.66(0.01)	0.11(0.36)	0.95(0.77)	ΔBCI → ΔCovid Death
FRANCE	3.3	3.25(2.20)	0.04(0.12)	2.10(4.16)	0.14(0.02)	ΔCCI → ΔCovid Death
INDIA	3.3	0.93(4.15)	0.45(0.02)	0.04(6.00)	0.96(0.01)	ΔΔBCI → ΔΔCovid Death ΔΔCCI → ΔΔCovid Death
BRAZIL	3.3	0.43(0.94)	0.73(0.44)	0.78(2.01)	0.47(0.16)	No casuality
CHINA	2.1	3.72(1.21)	0.03(0.31)	7.48(0.26)	0.01(0.61)	ΔCovid Death → ΔBCI ΔCovid Death → ΔCCI
RUSSIA	3.3	0.11(0.27)	0.95(0.84)	0.63(0.60)	0.60(0.62)	No causality
SOUTH AFRICA	3.3	1.27(0.34)	0.31(0.79)	0.29(0.82)	0.83(0.49)	No causality

Source Computed by authors

For Covid cases—

H (0): ΔCovid cases do not Granger cause ΔBCI & ΔCCI

H (0): ΔBCI & ΔCCI do not Granger cause Covid cases

For Covid death—

H (0): ΔCovid death does not Granger cause ΔBCI & ΔCCI

H (0): ΔBCI & ΔCCI do not Granger cause Covid death

It is observed from the table that Covid cases do not have causal interplays with BCI and CCI in almost all countries. But there is much such causal interplay of both BCI and CCI in case of Covid death. For the USA, Covid death is a cause of BCI while for the UK; it is a cause of CCI. In China, there are causal interplays from Covid death to both BCI and CCI. The case of fatality has influenced much to both consumers and business houses compared to the number of incidences. Covid death is a direct shock to the consumers and investors in making their immediate future decisions. However, there is some reverse causation from BCI and CCI to Covid death such as in case of Spain, France and India. The advanced countries having stimulus packages have experienced higher levels of BCI and CCI which led to a larger number of Covid tests and as a result, the number of cases increased. Besides, due to fear about the future, the sentiment levels changed and the workers engaged in the informal sectors outside their own geographical territories started to migrate to their homelands (which is called reverse migration), gathered in railway stations, airports, bust stoppages, etc. leading to further spread and death. In addition, the Covid testing also identified comorbidity results which led to rising number of deaths. Therefore, the both-way causal interplay is possible during the outbreak.

The overall results go with the study of Chronopoulos et al. [5], Teresiene et al. [22], Zhang et al. [27], among others, although the present study bears special attention to its attempts to examine the prevalence of long run and short run linkages of Covid indicators with the indicators of economic sentiments for the monthly data of the pandemic.

4.6 Conclusion

The study aimed to examine whether business and consumer sentiment are associated and maintain long-term relationships with Covid cases and death in the world's highly affected countries. It observes that business confidence is positively correlated to both Covid cases and death in many countries unlike that of the consumers' confidence. The econometric analysis shows that the series of CCI and covid cases are cointegrated for the majority of the countries which are, the UK, Spain, France, India, Brazil, China, Russia, South Africa but for BCI, the number is a few. Hence, for the majority of the highly affected countries of the world, Covid incidence maintains a long-run or equilibrium relationship with the business and consumers' confidence;

the business houses and consumers' expectations about the future were based upon the movements of the Covid spread. On the other hand, there are relatively larger numbers of countries where Covid deaths maintain long-run relations with BCI and CCI. Besides, there are mixed results in the Granger causality exercise. Therefore, the pandemic has affected both the consumers' and business sentiments in the highly affected countries of the world.

References

1. Abosedra S, Laopodis NT, Fakih A (2021) Dynamics and asymmetries between consumer sentiment and consumption in pre- and during-COVID-19 time: Evidence from the US. J Econ Asymmetries 24:1703–4949
2. Boitan IA, Câmpeanu EM, Mališ SS (2021) Economic sentiment perceptions during COVID-19 pandemic—A European cross-country impact assessment. Amfiteatru Econ 23(15):982–1002
3. Buckman SR, Shapiro AH, Sudhof M, Wilson DJ (2020) News sentiment in the time of COVID-19. FRBSF Econ Lett 08:1–05
4. Bui D, Dräger L, Hayo B, Nghiem G (2021) Consumer sentiment during the Covid19 pandemic: the role of others' beliefs. CESifo. Retrieved from CESifo website: https://EconPapers.repec.org/RePEc:ces:ceswps:_9010
5. Chronopoulos DK, Marcel L, John OSW (2020) Consumer spending responses to the COVID-19 pandemic: an assessment of GreatBritain. In: Working papers in responsible banking & finance WP N 20–012. University of St Andrews Scotland's First University, St Andrews, KY, USA, pp 1–41
6. Das RC, Das A (2015) Does consumers' confidence cause consumption spending?—an analysis of selected countries under the purview of global financial crisis. In: Das RC (ed) Handbook of research on globalization, investment, and growth-implications of confidence and governance. IGI Global, Hershey, PA
7. Dash SR, Maitra D (2022) The COVID19 pandemic uncertainty, investor sentiment, and global equity markets: evidence from the time frequency co movements. The North Am J Econ Finance 62:101712. https://doi.org/10.1016/j.najef.2022.101712
8. Dickey DA, Fuller WA (1979). Distribution of the estimators for autore gressive time series with a unit root. J Am Stat Assoc 74(366a):427–431
9. Engel RF, Granger CW (1987) Co-integration and error correction: Representation, estimation and testing. Econometrica: J Econom Society 55:251–276
10. Granger CWJ (1969) Investigating causal relations by econometric models and cross spectral methods. Econometrica: J Econom Society 37(3):424–438
11. Hsu Y, Tang L (2022) Effects of investor sentiment and country governance on unexpected conditional volatility during the COVID19 pandemic: evidence from global stock markets. Int Rev Financ Anal 82(C), S1057521922001478. Retrieved from https://EconPapers.repec.org/RePEc:eee:finana:v:82:y:2022:i:c:s1057521922001478
12. Iustina B, Campeanu E, Malis S (2021) Economic sentiment perceptions during COVID-19 pandemic—a European cross-country impact assessment 23(15):982. www.amfiteatrueconomic.ro.https://doi.org/10.24818/EA/2021/S15/982
13. Kanapickienė R, Teresienė D, Budriene D, Keliuotytė-Staniulėnienė G, Kartasova J (2020). The Impact of COVID-19 on European financial markets and economic sentiment. Econ Bus J 14(1):144–163
14. Kitrar L, Lipkind T (2021) The relationship of economic sentiment and GDP growth in Russia in light of the Covid19 crisis. Entrep Bus Econ Rev 9(1):7–29. https://doi.org/10.15678/EBER.2021.090101

15. Leduc S, Liu Z (2020) The uncertainty channel of the coronavirus. FRBSF Econ Lett 2020(issue 07, 05). Retrieved from https://EconPapers.repec.org/RePEc:fip:fedfel:87701
16. Liu Y, Liu S, Ye D, Tang H, Wang F (2022) Dynamic impact of negative public sentiment on agricultural product prices during COVID19. J Retail Consum Serv 64:102790
17. Makridis CA (2018) Can you feel the heat? extreme temperatures, stock returns, and economic sentiment. SSRN Electron J. https://doi.org/10.2139/ssrn.3095422
18. Makridis CA, Hartley JS (2020) The cost of COVID-19: a rough estimate of the 2020 US GDP impact. SSRN Electron J. https://doi.org/10.2139/ssrn.3570731
19. Reis N (2022) Determinants of qualified investor sentiment during the COVID19 pandemic in North America, Asia, and Europe. Economies 10(6):143. https://doi.org/10.3390/economies 10060143
20. Simionescu M, Raišienė AG (2021) A bridge between sentiment indicators: what does Google Trends tell us about COVID19 pandemic and employment expectations in the EU new member states? Technol Forecast Soc Change 173:121170. https://doi.org/10.1016/j.techfore.2021.121170
21. Sun Y, Bao Q, Lu Z (2021) Coronavirus (Covid19) outbreak, investor sentiment, and medical portfolio: evidence from China, Hong Kong, Korea, Japan, and U.S. Pac Basin Finance J 65:101463
22. Teresiene D, Keliuotyte-Staniuleniene G, Liao Y, Kanapickiene R, Pu R, Hu S, Yue X-G (2021) The impact of the COVID-19 pandemic on consumer and business confidence indicators. J Risk Financ Manage 14(4):159
23. Van der Wielen W, Barrios S (2021) Economic sentiment during the COVID pandemic: Evidence from search behaviour in the EU. J Econ Bus 115:105970. https://doi.org/10.1016/j.jeconbus.2020.105970
24. Verma M, Naveen BR (2021) COVID-19 impact on buying behavior. Vikalpa 46(1):27–40. https://doi.org/10.1177/02560909211018885
25. Zervoyianni A, Dimelis S, Livada A (2022) Economic sentiment and the covid19 crisis: evidence from European countries. Appl Econ 55(1):1–18. https://doi.org/10.1080/00036846.2022.2061903
26. Zhang D, Hu M, Ji Q (2020) Financial markets under the global pandemic of COVID-19. Finance Res Lett 36:101528–101528. https://doi.org/10.1016/j.frl.2020.101528
27. Zhang H, Ding Y, Li J (2021) Impact of the COVID19 pandemic on economic sentiment: a cross country study. Emerg Markets Finance Trade 57(6):1603–1612. Retrieved from https://EconPapers.repec.org/RePEc:mes:emfitr:v:57:y:2021:i:6:p:16031612

Chapter 5
COVID-19 Pandemic, Health Crisis and Financial Stability

Ebikabowei Biedomo Aduku, Ifeoma Augusta Eboh, and Johnson Nchege

5.1 Introduction

The outbreak and escalation of several viral infections that ravaged economic, financial and health infrastructures among others remind us of the variance of John Donne's poem, "No Man is an Island". In the context of this chapter, we could say that "No Country is an Island", demonstrating the interconnectedness of the global economy, irrespective of region or country. In the past, there have been several epidemics and pandemics that spread between and across countries and affected several communities. The most prominent pandemics include the influenza outbreak in 1918, the outbreak of Several Acute Respiratory Syndrome (SARS) pandemics in 2002, the Ebola outbreak in 2013, and the novel coronavirus 2019 (COVID-19) [1]. The influenza outbreak, for example, led to a stupendous rate of infection for about one-third of the world's population. SARS originated in Guangdong–China and spread rapidly all over Asia and its environment and infected over 8,000 people and was responsible for over 900 deaths. The Ebola pandemic disease was viral and caused over 11,300 deaths. COVID-19, which is the focus of this chapter emerged in Wuhan–China, in December 2019 and rapidly spread to other parts of the world [2–5].

In mid-March 2020, the COVID-19 infection spread to Europe, beginning in Italy to other European countries. By April, the United States became the new epicentre of COVID-19 where infections accelerated. By April 2021, Brazil, India, and some parts of Africa and Asia became viral hot sports with high daily records of infections and deaths. The World Health Organization (WHO) in [1] reported that as of November

E. B. Aduku (✉) · I. A. Eboh
Department of Economics, Nnamdi Azikwe University, Awka, Nigeria
e-mail: ebiopportunity@gmail.com

J. Nchege
Department of Economics, University of Nigeria, Nsukka, Nigeria
e-mail: johnson.nchege@unn.edu.ng

R. Bhattacharyya et al. (eds.), *COVID-19 Pandemic and Global Inequality*,
https://doi.org/10.1007/978-981-99-4405-7_5

1, 2021, the virus had globally afflicted more than 246.6 million people with over 5.0 million fatalities worldwide. As of 23 January 2023, the global confirmed cases were 664 097 132, while the number of confirmed deaths globally was 6 716 108 [6]. As reported by the Africa Center for Disease Control and Prevention [7], as of 1 January 2023, out of a total of 125,168,543 tests conducted, a total of 12,216,748 confirmed cases were reported, of which the total number of deaths was 256,542, and the recoveries were 11,517,411 in total.

In Nigeria, the first case was reported on 27th February 2020. As of 9th May 2020, about 4,151 COVID-19 cases were confirmed with 128 deaths representing a case fatality rate of about 3.1% [8]. As of 2nd December 2022, about 266,283 confirmed cases of COVID-19 with 3,155 deaths were reported for Nigeria [9]. Some of the issues that could have aided the spread of COVID-19 include a lack of thrust for the government management of COVID-19, religious beliefs, ignorance on sharing of face masks, poverty, misconception, poor health facilities, stigmatization of infected people, shortage of health workers among others [8].

Healthcare services such as mental, substance use disorder, neurological and immunization services were disrupted as a result of COVID-19. Other requisite health services for maternal, child and adolescent health and nutrition, services for productive health, and communicable and non-communicable diseases were also disrupted [10]. From a neuropsychiatric point of view, following [11] there were fears of illness, fears of life under lockdowns, death, and other uncertainties concerning the future. For most patients in the early series of COVID-19, there were neurological signs such as headache, ataxia, anosmia, seizures, ageusia, paresthesia, ataxia, and several encephalopathies [11]. Pressure mounted in the hospitals in addition to the challenges of caring for a large number of infected people needing intensive care and shortage of mechanical ventilators and personal protective equipment. In Africa, countries such as Nigeria, even before COVID-19 had inequality in the provision of health services, the disparity in access to vital primary health care and qualified protective healthcare providers. With COVID-19, the healthcare system became worsened with an increase in inequality in access to primary healthcare. Sustaining primarily donor-funded healthcare programs like those concerning the prevention of treatment of tuberculosis, malaria, etc. became an issue [12].

The COVID-19 pandemic challenge and the associated health issues led to economic lockdowns and closures globally resulting in a reduction in the demand for oil and a fall in oil prices. This affected Nigeria's revenue, given that the country relies heavily on oil. While income was reduced, there was more pressure for the government to intervene to prevent the spread of the virus and reduce its impacts on the people and the economy. To cope with the situation, the government amended the 2020 budget in May 2020 with an inclusion of a fiscal stimulus of $1.3bn (representing 4.7% of the total expenditure in the 2020 amended budget) appropriated as an intervention fund for COVID-19 [13]. Three social intervention funds were also used by the government in response to the pandemic. As reported by Ejiogu, Okechukwu and Ejiogu [14], a 3-month moratorium was given to about 2 million micro and small-scale enterprises on government intervention loans. Also, the national cash transfer scheme was expanded from about 2.6 million households to about 3.6 million households with an increase in payout from $13 to $52 monthly due to COVID-19—which was an advance payment and not an increase in monthly payout. In addition, food palliatives were provided to vulnerable households to cushion the effect of the lockdown and other measures [15, 16].

To finance the budget and fund the intervention measures, the government increased domestic and foreign borrowing—with a pandemic-related debt of about $6.9 billion [12, 17]. Also, the COVID-19 basket fund was launched in partnership with the United Nations in Nigeria—UNAIDS and UNDP to serve as a platform for international donors to support the country [14]. In addition, the private sector in partnership with the Central Bank of Nigeria established the Coalition Against COVID-19 (CACOVID) fund in March 2020 to fund the COVID-19 government interventions [18]. Over $72 million was raised through CACOVID, it was however, far below the $310 million that was the target [14].

There was pressure on the government and the financial system of the country, which was worsened by a drastic fall in government revenue due to the pandemic that resulted in a worsening deficit-to-revenue ratio. It was 26% before the pandemic (according to the initial 2020 budget) and increased to 89% based on the revised budget [14]. By this, the country's ability to repay is abating rapidly. The debt profile of the country is increasing and the credit rating of the country is reducing drastically. Funding COVID-19 through borrowing intensified the pressure on government finances and the financial stability of the country. This raises a concern about the financial stability of the country resulting from the pandemic and the pandemic-related health crisis. This chapter, therefore, examines the impact of the COVID-19 and COVID-19-related health crises on the financial stability of Nigeria. This is important because the financial system plays a key role in any economy. It is a condition through which the economic mechanisms that determine funds allocation, prices and risk management function efficiently. It also plays a significant role in the economic growth trajectory of a country through efficient funds allocation [19]. Efforts to reduce the risk of financial instability in a country's financial system are paramount, especially to evade huge economic losses.

5.2 Review of Extant Literature

Novel coronavirus 2019 was the name given by the World Health Organization (WHO) to the coronavirus that affects the lower respiratory tract of individuals with a disease likened to pneumonia, which was first detected and documented in December 2019 in Wuhan–Hubei Province in China [10, 20, 8, 21]. The reference name for the virus is severe acute respiratory syndrome coronavirus 2—SARS-CoV-2 [22]. While the official (therefore, the well-known and broadly used) name that was given to the illness resulting from the SARS-CoV-2 by the WHO is COVID-19—where 'CO' stands for corona, 'VI' represents virus and 'D' for disease [8, 20, 23]. Therefore, it is called 'coronavirus disease 2019'—COVID-19. The name COVID-19 was given in order not to stigmatize the virus origin concerning animal associations, population or geography—for example, it would have been discriminatory to name the virus Wuhan coronavirus.

Coronaviruses are a collection of viruses that cause illnesses like SARS, Middle East Respiratory Syndrome (MERS), common cold among others. It is, therefore, part of the coronavirus family. In Latin, the term corona translates to the crown and, therefore, the virus was named corona because it has spikes proteins that look like or take a crown-like shape sticking out of them using electron microscopy [24]. The spike protein is part of the virus that sticks to the cell of a human to infect it, enabling it to reproduce or duplicate inside of the cell it attaches and disseminates to other cells. Over time, genetic changes to the virus occur and genetic lineage is then formed by the SARS-CoV-2 virus. The viruses with these changes are known as "variants", as described by scientists. The variants of the virus may act differently, but they are still SARS-CoV-2 [15]. Similar to most other respiratory viruses, coronaviruses spread fast via droplets of an infected person that fall from the mouth or nose through coughing, breathing, speaking, sneezing, or touching virus-contaminated surfaces [15]. On surfaces, the virus could survive for a couple of hours except if a disinfectant is applied to it. In less severe cases, the symptoms may include cough and shortness of breath and fever. But in more severe cases, the infection of COVID-19 may lead to pneumonia or difficulty in breathing and, can sometimes be very fatal [23]. One of the crises associated with or caused by the outbreak of the COVID-19 pandemic is the global public health crisis.

A global health crisis is a complex health situation that faces or affects humans in wide geographic areas, from a particular country to encompass several countries—impacting community health, deaths and the economy. It is an acute situation such that the health status is affected adversely. It includes health situations associated with an outbreak of a disease or a virus such as the COVID-19 pandemic and the Ebola outbreak that pose a threat to the health conditions of people. Nelson, Lurie and Wasserman [25] viewed health crises from the perspective of health consequences, causes and precipitating events. According to them, it is a health situation in which its scale, unpredictability or timing pose a threat to overwhelm a routine capability. This definition is consistent with the all-hazards perspective to preparedness rather than concentrating on a "disaster du jour" and, therefore, enables optimal capabilities development across scenarios and appropriately prepares health systems for the broad spectrum of likely risks. The [26] categorizes public health crises as an impending threat of a health condition or an illness that is brought by a pandemic, epidemic or an infectious agent among others that puts humans a major risk either by leading to a high rate of human fatalities or long-term or permanent disability.

One of the most typical health crises among others during the COVID-19 pandemic is the COVID-19 related deaths, defined by [26] as anyone whose death certificate listed COVID-19 as a cause of death, and anyone who had a COVID-19 diagnosis within 30 days, however, their death certificate did not list COVID-19 as a cause of death. This metric offers a better indicator of the severity of the impact on the health system. Therefore, it is an appropriate indicator of the health crisis. [27] explains further that those deaths 'involved' COVID-19 means that anywhere in the death certificate COVID-19 is mentioned, perhaps along with other health issues that may not be the cause of death. However, deaths 'due to' COVID-19 imply that COVID-19 is the root cause of death—either the cause of death listed in the death certificate or it was the one that brought about other issues that resulted in death. The health crisis brought about by COVID-19 put pressure on governments to intervene, which in turn, is said to pose a threat to the financial stability of countries.

Financial stability does not have a generally accepted useful definition. Most authors defined financial instability in place of financial stability, while some other authors defined it as financial system risk instead of maintaining the stability of the financial system. A more general definition is that financial stability is a condition such that there is a well-functioning mechanism for allocating, pricing, and managing financial risks (credit and liquidity, etc.) that could contribute to economic performance [28], 19]. An encompassing definition of financial stability is a definition that could cover the functions of a financial system, which are to facilitate and improve economic processes—to allocate risks, price and manage, and to enable the economy to absorb and dispel internal and external shocks. Two concepts are important here. These are "financial system" and "system risk".

Three broad components make up the financial system. These are: (i) the financial intermediaries that pool funds and risk and allocate the funds to competing users; (ii) financial markets that directly coordinate investors and savers, for instance, in the form of initial issuance and sale of equities and bonds directly to investors; (iii) financial infrastructure, made up of owned and operated private and public institutions like settlement systems for financial transactions, payments, clearance, regulatory, supervision, monetary, and surveillance infrastructures among others. Public and private individuals especially own and invest in financial institutions; take part in financial markets; and either own or manage and operate in important components of the financial infrastructure. The government borrows in financial markets, hedges risks and operates via markets to carry out, especially monetary policy and ensure monetary stability, and owns and runs settlement and payment systems. Therefore, the financial system comprises the monetary system alongside its official agreements, institutions and processes, and conventions of private financial activities [29].

Financial system risk, on the other hand, is the risk or likelihood that an event could instigate a loss of confidence in the system or economic value and a resultant rise in uncertainty concerning a large part of the financial system that is solemn enough to quite likely have an adverse impact on the economy. Events that could cause system risk can be unexpected and sudden such as the sudden outbreak of the COVID-19 pandemic. Payment system disruption, asset values and credit flow are among the adverse economic effects of systemic problems [29].

Based on the above, financial stability could be described as a condition whereby the financial system is competent simultaneously carrying out its three key functions satisfactorily. First, there is an efficient financial system well facilitates intertemporal resource allocation between investors to savers as well as the general allocation of economic resources. Second, the assessment of forward-looking financial risks is relatively well managed. Third, the financial system is in good condition, such that it can properly and comfortably absorb sudden shocks, surprises or uncertainties [29], without these, there is financial instability. A financial system is in the scope of stability as long as it is efficient (rather than hindering) the economy's performance, and dispelling financial imbalances that emerge endogenously or due to a severe adverse or unexpected event. As a result of COVID-19 and the associated health crisis, countries could face financial stability due to higher credit and default risk because of cash management and insolvency challenges to debt servicing associated with the closure of businesses, lockdowns and fall in demand for goods and services during and after the pandemic. Also, the rate of bank lending could reduce because of a decline in private-sector consumption and investment. Most lending and investment decisions were pending, while the cost of financing rose because of savings decay or the lower availability of money due to COVID-19 and the health crisis.

There is empirical evidence. Some of the related studies include [1] which examined the effect of the economic and health crisis due to COVID-19 on its financial stability using the autoregressive distributed lag (ARDL) technique. It was found that the economic and health crisis due to COVID-19 had a spillover effect on the financial stability of the United States. The effect of the spread of the COVID-19 pandemic on banking sector risk, lending growth, credit risk and financial soundness indicators in the Euro area was examined by [30]. The study found that the spread of COVID-19 had a negative and significant effect on the banking sector's financial distress, credit risk, profitability and solvency. A similar study conducted by [31] examined the impact of the Covid-19 pandemic on global banking stability. Financial stability was measured by default risk and asset risk. It was found that the COVID-19 pandemic harmed global financial stability. Maria, Yudaruddin and Yudaruddin (2022) examined the impact of COVID-19 on banking stability by differentiating bank core capital size and ownership. 108 commercial banks in Indonesia were used as a case study. The data covers the periods from the period March 2020 and March 2021. The fixed effects regression was employed to analyze the data. The findings showed that COVID-19 had a negative and significant effect on bank stability. Irrespective of the size and ownership of a bank's core capital, the findings revealed that no bank was immune for a year to the severe COVID-19 implications. Nguyena, Nguyena, Nguyena, Nguyena, Chu and Nguyena [32] examined if cash holding enhanced the financial stability of firms under the influence of the COVID-19 pandemic. Quarterly data of 285 Vietnamese listed firms from quarter 1–2011 to 3–2020 was used for the study. It found that cash holding had a positive impact on financial stability under the impact of the COVID-19 pandemic. It was also found that cash holding was especially vital for firms that were more vulnerable to the COVID-19 pandemic.

There are a lot of studies on COVID-19, but studies on COVID-19, health crisis and financial stability are lacking especially in developing countries. Given the increasing rate of global uncertainties that mostly cause health crises and put financial sectors under pressure, a study such as this is crucial. The financial stability of developing countries is the most threatened compared to the developed countries because of the weak financial system and low government revenue. Appropriate measures and policies to put in place to hedge the financial sector and the system in case of a pandemic or other global uncertainties will require empirical backup. Lessons learnt on the COVID-19 pandemic and the health crisis and its impact on financial stability should be backed up with empirical evidence for more efficient measures for financial stability. These among other reasons justify the appropriateness and the timeliness of this chapter. The chapter will have policy relevance to the managers of the economy, particularly to the monetary policy authority in charge of financial stability management.

5.3 Data and Research Methods

The data is daily frequency data for Nigeria drawn from the Nigerian Center for Disease Control (NCDC), and the Central Bank of Nigeria (CBN) statistical bulletin various issues. The period covered 23/03/2020 to 23/03/2022. Therefore, a total of 731 data observations are used for the analysis. The data points are considered enough for analysis, covering the most crucial periods during the COVID-19 pandemic. The start period marked when the first COVID-19-related death was recorded, while the end period marked the period before the drastic fall in COVID-19-confirmed cases and deaths. The COVID-19 pandemic is captured by the COVID-19 confirmed cases, while the health crisis is measured by the number of COVID-19-related confirmed deaths. Financial stability, on the other hand, is measured by banking system indicators and macroeconomic indicators. The banking system indicators used for this study are liquidity (measured by the liquidity ratio) and banks' loan-to-deposit ratio. The macroeconomic indicators, on the other hand, are government debt as a ratio of GDP and banks' credit to the economy. Other variables include economic growth measured by GDP growth. The data for the COVID-19 confirmed cases and deaths are sourced from the NCDC database, while the data for the rest of the variables are sourced from the CBN statistical bulletin. The data for the COVID-19 confirmed cases and deaths were sourced in daily frequency, while the rest of the variables were in annual frequency but were converted to daily frequency data by the authors.

The Autoregressive Distributed Lag (ARDL) model is employed to analyze the data. The dependent variable in the ARDL model is assumed to be a function of the past values of itself and the current and past values of other explanatory variables. The functional relationship is stated as

$$FINSTAB = f(CO19\_CONF, CO19\_DEATH, RGDPG) \quad (5.1)$$

where FINSTAB stands for financial stability—to be measured by liquidity ratio, banks loan to deposit ratio (banking system indicators); government debt as a ratio of GDP and banks' credit to the economy (macroeconomic indicators). CO19_CONF is COVID-19 confirmed cases (indicator for COVID-19 pandemic), CO19_DEATH is the number of recorded COVID-19 deaths (a proxy for health crisis), and RGDPG is real GDP growth. We interact the CO19_CONF and CO19_DEATH to enable us to determine the interaction effect that would explain the effect associated with high confirmed COVID-19 cases with a high number of COVID-19 deaths, and the effect if there are high confirmed COVID-19 cases but a low number of COVID-19 deaths.

Equation (5.1) is presented in an ARDL model specification with the inclusion of the interacted variable:

$$\begin{aligned} FINSTAB_t &= a_0 + a_1 lnFINSTAB_{t-1} + a_2 lnCO19\_CONF_{t-1} \\ &+ a_3 lnCO19\_DEATH_{t-1} \\ &+ a_4 lnCO19\_CONF_{t-1} * lnCO19\_DEATH_{t-1} \\ &+ a_5 RGDPG_{t-1} \sum_{k=1}^{p} \varphi_k \Delta lnFINSTAB_{t-k} \\ &+ \sum_{j=1}^{p} \phi_j \Delta lnCO19_CONF_{t-k} + \sum_{j=1}^{p} \beta_j lnCO19\_DEATH_{t-k} \\ &+ \sum_{j=1}^{p} \vartheta_j \Delta lnCO19\_CONF * lnCO19\_DEATH_{t-k} + \sum_{j=1}^{p} \gamma_j \Delta RGDPG_{t-k} \\ &+ u_{1t} \end{aligned}$$

The differenced terms in Eq. (2) are the short-run variables whereas the lagged terms are the long-run process. RGDPG, RIR and the financial stability variables except for banks' credit to the economy are not logged because the variables are in rate, while the rest of the variables in the model are logged. μ 1t is the error term, and ai (i = 1,2, 3,..., 5), and φ, Ø, β, ϑ and γ are the long and short-run parameters of the variables respectively. The optimal lag length is determined using the Akaike information lag length selection method.

For the interaction term, if the COVID-19 coefficient is positive and the interaction term coefficient is negative, then, it means that financial stability weakens as the health crisis increases due to an increase in COVID-19 cases. On the contrary, if the COVID-19 coefficient is negative and the interaction term is positive or if both are positive, then it means a rise in the financial stability indicator as a result of an increase in the health crisis due to an increase in COVID-19 cases.

A major advantage of the ARDL model is that it has a small sample property. It provides unbiased estimates and t-values for the long and short run even for endogenous regressors. The model can be applied even if the regressors are stationary at I(0) or I(1) or a mix of I(0) and I(1). If cointegration is found among the variables, then it implies that the variables adjust to equilibrium in the long run, captured by an error correction model, specified as

$$\begin{aligned} & lnFINSTAB_t \\ &= a_0 \sum_{k=1}^{p} \varphi_k \Delta lnFINSTAB_{t-k} + \sum_{j=1}^{p} \phi_j \Delta lnCO19_CONF_{t-k} \\ &+ \sum_{j=1}^{p} \beta_j \Delta lnCO19\_DEATH_{t-k} \end{aligned}$$

$$+ \sum_{j=1}^{p} \vartheta_j \Delta lnCO19\_CONF * lnCO19\_DEATH_{t-k}$$
$$+ \sum_{j=1}^{p} \gamma_j \Delta RGDPG_{t-k} + \vartheta ECM1_{t-1} + u_{1t}$$

where ECM1t-1 is the error correction term. In estimating Eq. (3), the liquidity ratio is used first as the dependent variable. After that, the liquidity ratio was substituted with the bank's loan-to-deposit ratio and the model was estimated again. After the estimation using the bank's loan-to-deposit ratio as the dependent variable, the government debt as a ratio to GDP was used as the dependent variable. Thereafter, the government debt as a ratio to GDP was replaced with banks' credit to the economy and used as the dependent variable. Therefore, four models were estimated using each of the four proxies of financial stability as the dependent variable.

Once the order of the ARDL is known, the model can be estimated using the Ordinary Least Square Technique (OLS). The OLS technique is the Best Linear and Unbiased Estimator (BLUE). The estimation started with a test for the appropriate lag order using the Akaike information criteria. Also, macroeconomic time series are usually trended and, therefore, in most cases are non-stationary. Thus, Augmented Dickey–Fuller (ADF) and Philips–Perron unit root tests were carried out to test the stationarity of the variables. Thereafter, a test for the long-run relationship among the variables was carried out using the Bounds test for cointegration to test the level form relationship among the variables in the model.

5.4 Results and Discussion

5.4.1 Unit Root

Unit root test was conducted using the Augmented Dickey–Fuller and the Phillips–Perron tests. Also, the cointegration of the variables was tested to determine the level relationship using the Pesaran, Shin, and Smith (2001) bounds test. The results are presented in Table 5.1. As shown in panel A, real GDP growth is stationary at the level, while the rest of the variables are nonstationary at the level. The at-level nonstationary variables were differenced once and tested at their 1st difference. After the 1st difference, the variables became stationary. A similar result was found in the Phillips-Perron test. Based on the test results, real GDP growth is stationary at order 0, I(0), while the rest of the variables are stationary at order 1, I(1).

At the 5 per cent level, the F-value and the t-value are above the critical values for both the I(0) variable and the I(1) variables with significant p-values. Since the test is significant, the null hypothesis of no level relationship is rejected for both Panel B (a) and (b). Therefore, based on the bounds test, there is a level relationship among the variables under study. The ARDL error correction estimates are reported

Table 5.1 Unit root and cointegration tests results

Panel A: Augmented Dickey–Fuller and Phillips–Perron unit root tests

Augmented Dickey–Fuller unit root test					**Phillips–Perron unit root test**				
Variable	**ADF—Statistic**		**Lag**	**~ I(d)**	**Variable**	**ADF—Statistic**		**Lag**	**~ I(d)**
	Level	**1st Diff.**				**Level**	**1st Diff**		
lnCO19_CONF	−0.318	−36.500*	2	I(1)	lnCO19_CONF	−0.776	−106.672*	2	I(1)
lnCO19_ DEATH	−0.428	−38.193*	2	I(1)	lnCO19_DEATH	−1.343	−117.310*	2	I(1)
lnCRED_ECO	−0.192	−26.239*	2	I(1)	lnCRED_ECO	−0.133	−63.446*	2	I(1)
DEBT_GDP	−0.193	−26.526*	2	I(1)	DEBT_GDP	−0.373	−65.865*	2	I(1)
LOAN_DEP	−0.611	−31.649*	2	I(1)	LOAN_DEP	−0.862	−80.112*	2	I(1)
LR	−0.896	−30.179*	2	I(1)	LR	−1.388	−76.775*	2	I(1)
RGDPG	−4.495*	–	2	I(0)	RGDPG	−10.615	–	2	I(1)

Where * denotes significance at 5% and the rejection of the null hypothesis of the presence of unit root. The optimal lag lengths were chosen according to Akaike's final Prediction Error (FPE) criterion. The estimated unit root models do not include constant. The ADF 5% Critical value at the level and 1st difference is −1.950. The Phillips-Perron Critical value at the level and 1st difference is −1.950

Panel B: Results of Bounds Test for Cointegration

(a) Test result when banking system indicator is used to measure financial stability

Critical Values (0.1–0.01), F-statistic, Case 3

	10%		5%		1%		p-value	
	I(0)	I(1)	I(0)	I(1)	I(0)	I(1)	I(0)	I(1)
F	2.449	3.518	2.868	4.012	3.765	5.049	0.000	0.000
t	−2.562	−3.646	−2.860	−3.971	−3.436	−4.578	0.000	0.006

F = 92.855; t = −19.257

(continued)

Table 5.1 (continued)

(b) Test result when the macroeconomic indicator is used to measure financial stability

Critical Values (0.1–0.01), F-statistic, Case 3	10%		5%		1%		p-value	
	I(0)	I(1)	I(0)	I(1)	I(0)	I(1)	I(0)	I(1)
F	2.726	3.753	3.226	4.331	4.306	5.557	0.000	0.000
t	−2.564	−3.422	−2.861	−3.743	−3.436	−4.346	0.000	0.006

F = 44.206; t = −13.239

Source Computed by the Authors

in Table 5.2. Column (1) shows the result when the liquidity ratio is used to measure financial stability—the dependent variable. Column (2) presents the result when the liquidity ratio is changed to a bank loan-to-deposit ratio to measure financial stability. In column (3), government debt as a ratio to GDP was used to proxy financial stability, while column (4) reports the result using banks' credit to the economy as the proxy for financial stability. Columns (1) and (2) capture financial stability in the banking system. Columns (3) and (4), on the other hand, capture macroeconomic financial stability.

The adjustment speed coefficient in the columns respectively is negative and significant. For any disequilibrium, the liquidity ratio and the explanatory variables adjust to equilibrium at an adjustment speed of 64.72% daily, while the bank loan-to-deposit ratio and the explanatory variables adjust to equilibrium at a speed of 64.72% per day. Government debt as a ratio of GDP and the explanatory variable adjusts to equilibrium at a daily speed of 64.72%, while credit to the economy and the explanatory variables adjust at a speed of 64.89% per day.

In the long run, COVID-19 confirmed cases had a negative and significant impact on liquidity rate and a positive and significant impact on banks loan to deposit ratio of about 20.17% and 9.30% respectively in columns (1) and (2). The implication is that COVID-19 is responsible for a significant reduction in liquidity rate, and a significant increase in banks loan to deposit ratio. Also, in the short run, an increase in COVID-19-confirmed cases results in a significant decrease in liquidity rate, and a significant increase in banks loan to deposit ratio of about 14.51 and 2.67% in columns (1) and (2). This means that COVID-19 cause a significant reduction in liquidity rate, and a significant increase in banks loan to deposit ratio in the short run. In essence, both in the long and short run, the COVID-19 pandemic significantly reduces the liquidity rate and increases the bank's loan-to-deposit ratio. A rise in COVID-19 cases leads to weakening financial stability. Therefore, the COVID-19 pandemic is negatively and significantly associated with the banking sector's financial stability.

Both in the long and short run, the coefficient for the COVID-19 confirmed cases is positive and significant in columns (3) and (4). This means that an increase in COVID-19 confirmed cases leads to an increase in government debt as a ratio of GDP and banks' credit to the economy. This conforms with empirical reality; during the peak of COVID-19, for example, (especially developing) countries with a high rate of confirmed cases source more government loans than countries with a low number of confirmed cases. The credit to the economy was increased in the highly affected countries to ease off the effect of the pandemic on the economy. Therefore, the pandemic significantly poses a threat to macroeconomic financial stability.

The coefficient for COVID-19 death is negative and significant in columns (1), and positive and significant in columns (2), (3) and (4) both in the long and short run. This implies that the COVID-19 death significantly reduces the liquidity ratio, and increases the bank loan-to-deposit ratio, government debt as a ratio of GDP, and the credit to the economy. The COVID-19 death limits financial transactions and business activities, which decreases the purchasing power of people. The amount of savings held or deposits was reduced, while government debt and the credit provision to the economy increased. Thus, weakening the financial stability.

Table 5.2 Regression estimates of the effect of COVID-19 and the health crisis on financial stability

	Banking system financial stability indicators		Macroeconomic financial stability indicators	
	(1) Liquidity Ratio (LR)	(2) Bank Loan to Deposit Ratio	(3) Government Debt as a Ratio of GDP	(4) Banks' Credit to the Economy
Adjustment	−0.6472 (t = −13.24) (p = 0.000)	−0.6474 (t = −13.25) (p = 0.000)	−0.6473 (t = −13.24) (p = 0.000)	−0.6489 (t = −13.25) (p = 0.000)
Long run				
lnCO19_CONF	−20.1759 (t = −10.46) (p = 0.000)	9.2995 (t = 10.46) (p = 0.000)	0.0705 (t = 10.46) (p = 0.000)	0.1115 (t = 10.45) (p = 0.000)
lnCO19_DEATH	−14.5102 (t = −6.43) (p = 0.000)	6.6880 (t = 6.43) (p = 0.000)	0.0507 (t = 6.43) (p = 0.000)	0.0796 (t = 6.38) (p = 0.000)
lnCO19_CONF* lnCO19_ DEATH	−4.1200 (t = −16.15) (p = 0.000)	1.9000 (t = 16.15) (p = 0.000)	0.0507 (t = 6.43) (p = 0.000)	2.2700 (t = 16.00) (p = 0.000)
RGDPG	1.5785 (t = 5.87) (p = 0.000)	−0.0287 (t = −0.23) (p = 0.817)	−0.0168 (t = −17.91) (p = 0.000)	0.0285 (t = 19.18) (p = 0.000)
Short run				
LR	−0.2770 (t = −7.62) (p = 0.000)	−0.2770 (t = −7.62) (p = 0.000)	−0.2770 (t = −7.62) (p = 0.000)	−0.2781 (t = −7.66) (p = 0.000)
lnCO19_CONF	−17.9302 (t = −24.00) (p = 0.000)	2.6759 (t = 5.87) (p = 0.000)	0.0626 (t = 24.00) (p = 0.000)	0.0993 (t = 23.98) (p = 0.000)
lnCO19_DEATH	−13.0010 (t = −15.52) (p = 0.000)	1.9945 (t = 4.59) (p = 0.000)	0.0454 (t = 15.52) (p = 0.000)	0.0716 (t = 15.40) (p = 0.000)
lnCO19_CONF* lnCO19_ DEATH	−3.6800 (t = −37.82) (p = 0.000)	1.7000 (t = 37.82) (p = 0.000)	1.2900 (t = 37.82) (p = 0.000)	2.0300 (t = 37.18) (p = 0.000)

(continued)

Table 5.2 (continued)

	Banking system financial stability indicators		Macroeconomic financial stability indicators	
	(1) Liquidity Ratio (LR)	(2) Bank Loan to Deposit Ratio	(3) Government Debt as a Ratio of GDP	(4) Banks' Credit to the Economy
RGDPG	0.4051 (t = 1.44) (p = 0.151)	−0.8855 (t = −6.82) (p = 0.000)	−0.0098 (t = −10.06) (p = 0.000)	0.0175 (t = 11.21) (p = 0.000)
Constant	129.3397 (t = 12.57) (p = 0.000)	79.3100 (t = 12.91) (p = 0.000)	−0.0233 (t = −1.68) (p = 0.093)	6.1349 (t = 13.19) (p = 0.000)
R-squared	0.8755	0.8930	0.8311	0.8289
Adj R-squared	0.8736	0.8914	0.8286	0.8263
Durbin–Watson	1.9119	1.9635	1.9435	1.9674

Source Computed by the authors

In column (1) the C0VID-19 coefficient is negative and the interaction term is also negative. Meaning that the liquidity rate falls as the health crisis increases due to COVID-19. In columns (2), (3) and (4) respectively, the COVID-19 coefficient and the interaction term coefficient are both positive. The implication is that the bank loan-to-deposit ratio, government loan to GDP, and the credit to the economy increase as the health crisis increases due to increase in the COVID-19 cases.

An increase in real GDP led to an increase in liquidity ratio and credit to the economy in columns (1) and (4), and a decrease in loan-to-deposit ratio and government debt to GDP in columns (2) and (3) in the long and short run. This implies that economic growth increases the liquidity ratio and credit to the economy and reduces loan to deposit ratio and government debt to GDP which can bring about financial stability in the long and short run.

5.5 Conclusion

The impact of the COVID-19 pandemic and health crisis on financial stability has been examined empirically in this chapter using daily frequency data. The evidence showed that the effect of the COVID-19 pandemic and the health crisis is significantly felt in the short run and also in the long run. The COVID-19 pandemic and the health crisis significantly weaken the financial stability in the banking sector and the macroeconomy. Liquidity ratio, loan-to-deposit ratio, government debt-to-GDP ratio and credit to the economy are particularly significantly affected by the COVID-19 pandemic and the health crisis. The COVID-19 pandemic and the health crisis limit financial transactions and business activities, which decreases the purchasing power of people. The liquidity and the amount of savings held or deposits were reduced, while government debt and the credit provision to the economy increased. Therefore, weakened the financial stability.

Reforms to make the financial sector more stable can be expected to hedge the financial sector against pandemics and health crises in the future. There should be a provision for larger government support for the players of the financial sector including liquidity and other supports by the central bank, expansion of deposit insurance coverage, protection schemes and guarantees, and capital injections. Capital requirements should be more flexible and adjust financial stability management policy measures and actions to mitigate the negative (weakening) impact of the COVID-19 pandemic and the health crisis. Also, diversification of public revenue sources could reduce government borrowing, especially during pandemics and health crises.

References

1. Shehzad K, Xiaoxing L, Bilgili F, Koçak E (2021) COVID-19 and spillover effects of global economic crises on the United State's financial stability. Front Psychol 12:1–13
2. Albulescu, C. (2020). Coronavirus and oil price crash. Available at: https://hal.archives-ouvertes.fr/hal-02507184/document
3. Ashraf BN (2020) Stock markets' reaction to COVID-19: Cases or fatalities? Res Int Bus Finance 54:101–249
4. Béland LP, Brodeur A, Wright T (2020) The Short-term economic consequences of Covid-19: exposure to disease, remote work and government response. PLoS One 18(3):e0270341. Available at: https://journals.plos.org/plosone/article?id=https://doi.org/10.1371/journal.pone.0270341
5. Fernandes N (2020) Economic effects of coronavirus outbreak (COVID-19) on the world economy. Available at: https://foroparalapazenelmediterraneo.es/wp-content/uploads/2020/03/SSRN-id3557504.pdf.pdf
6. World Health Organization—WHO (2023) Coronavirus disease (COVID-19) pandemic. Available at: https://www.who.int/emergencies/diseases/novel-coronavirus-2019
7. Africa Center for Disease Control & Prevention (2023) Coronavirus disease 2019 (COVID-19): Latest updates on the COVID-19 crisis from Africa CDC. *African Union*. Available at: https://africacdc.org/covid-19/
8. Akinyemi KO, Fakorede CO, Anjorin AAA, Abegunrin RO, Adunmo O, Ajoseh SO, Akinkunmi FM (2020) Intrigues and challenges associated with the COVID-19 pandemic in Nigeria. Health 12:954–971
9. WHO (2022) Covid-19. Available at: https://covid19.who.int/region/afro/country/ng
10. Etienne CF (2021) The health crisis: future scenarios and strategies from the health sector to control the covid-19 pandemic. Pan American Health Organization. Available at: https://www.paho.org/en/documents/health-crisis-future-scenarios-and-strategies-health-sector-control-covid-19-pandemic
11. Wiebers DO, Feigin VL (2020) What the COVID-19 crisis is telling humanity. Neuroepidemiology, pp 1–4
12. Assefa N, Sie A, Wang D et al (2021) Reported Barriers to healthcare access and Service disruptions caused by COVID-19 in Burkina Faso, Ethiopia, and Nigeria: a telephone survey. Am J Trop Med Hyg 105(2):323–330
13. Budget Office of the Federation (2020) *Addendum to the 2020–2022 Medium Term Expenditure Framework & Fiscal Strategy Paper [MTEF/FSP]*. Budget Office of the Federation & Federal Ministry of Finance, Budget and National Planning, Abuja, Nigeria
14. Ejiogu A, Okechukwu O, Ejiogu C (2020) Nigerian budgetary response to the COVID-19 pandemic and its shrinking fiscal space: Financial sustainability, employment, social inequality and business implications. J Public Budg Account Financ Manag 32(5):919–928
15. Centers for Disease Control and Prevention (2021) Basics of COVID-19. Available at: https://www.cdc.gov/coronavirus/2019-ncov/your-health/about-covid-19/basics-covid-19.html
16. Sanni K (2020) Buhari orders three-month moratorium on TraderMoni, MarketMoni and FarmerMoni loans. Premium Times, 30 March. Available at: https://www.premiumtimesng.com/news/top-news/384807-buhari-orders-three-month-moratorium-on-tradermoni-marketmoniand-farmermoni-loans.html
17. Osae-Brown A, Soto A (2020) Nigeria to borrow $6.9 billion to counter coronavirus spread. Bloomberg, 6 April. Available at: https://www.bloomberg.com/news/articles/2020-04-06/nigeriato-borrow-6-9-billion-to-offset-virus-impact-on-economy
18. GBCHealth (2020) Nigerian private sector supporting government efforts to fight COVID-19. GBCHealth, March. Available at: http://gbchealth.org/wp-content/uploads/2020/03/cacovidpress-release_full_reduced.pdf
19. Viphindrartin S, Ardhanari M, Wilantari RN, Somaji RP, Arianti S (2021) Effects of bank macroeconomic indicators on the Stability of the financial system in Indonesia. J Asian Fin Eco Busin 8(1):647–654

20. WHO (2020) Novel Coronavirus—China. Available at https://www.who.int/csr/don/12-january-2020-novel-coronavirus-china/en/
21. Mcleod V (2020) COVID-19: A history of coronavirus. Lab health and safety. Available at: https://www.labmanager.com/lab-health-and-safety/covid-19-ahistory-of-coronavirus-22021
22. Adhikari SP, Meng S, Wu Y-J, Mao Y-P, Ye R-X, Wang Q-Z, Sun C, Sylvia S, Rozelle S, Raat H, Zhou H (2020) Epidemiology, causes, clinical manifestation and diagnosis, prevention and control of coronavirus disease (COVID-19) during the early outbreak period: a scoping review. Infect Dis Poverty 9(29):48–67
23. UNICEF (2020) Coronavirus disease 2019 (COVID-19): What is it really? Available at: https://www.unicef.org/wca/what-is-coronavirus
24. Pan X, Chen D, Xia Y, Wu X, Li T, Ou X, Zhou L, Liu J (2020) Asymptomatic cases in a family cluster with SARS-CoV-2 infection. Lancet Infect Dis 20:410–411
25. Nelson C, Lurie N, Wasserman J, Zakowski S (2007) Conceptualizing and defining public health emergency preparedness. Am J Public Health 97(1):9–11
26. Massachusetts Emergency Management Agency (2023) Public health emergencies. Commonwealth of Massachusetts Publications. Available at: https://www.mass.gov/info-details/public-health-emergencies
27. UK office for National Statistics (2021) Definition of deaths involving COVID-19. Available at: https://www.ons.gov.uk/aboutus/transparencyandgovernance/freedomofinformationfoi/definitionofdeathsinvolvingcovid19
28. Central Bank of Malaysia (2023) Financial stability. Available at: https://www.bnm.gov.my/the-importance-of-financial-stability
29. International Monetary Fund—IMF (2007) Defining financial stability. Available at: file:///C:/Users/OPPORTUNITY/Downloads/9781589064409-ch005.pdf
30. Teresiene D, Keliuotyte-Staniuleniene G, Kanapickiene R (2021) Sustainable economic growth support through credit transmission channel and financial stability: In the context of the COVID-19 pandemic. Sustainability 13(5):2692. Available at: https://www.mdpi.com/2071-1050/13/5/2692
31. Elnahass M, Trinh V, Li T (2021) Global banking stability in the shadow of the Covid-19 outbreak. J Int Finan Markets Inst Money 72:101–122
32. Nguyena CK, Nguyena AQ, Nguyena NQ, Nguyena TT, Chu AN, Nguyena LTM (2021) Cash holding and financial stability during a crisis: a case study of Vietnamese firms in COVID-19 pandemic. Available at: https://www.tandfonline.com/doi/abs/https://doi.org/10.1080/07360932.2021.1944260
33. Centre for Disease Control—CDC (2020) 2019 Novel Coronavirus, Wuhan, China. Available at: https://www.cdc.gov/coronavirus/2019-nCoV/summary.html
34. Dixit S, Ogundeji YK, Onwujekwe O (2020) How well has Nigeria responded to COVID-19? Brookings: future development, 2 July. Available at: https://www.brookings.edu/blog/futuredevelopment/2020/07/02/how-well-has-nigeria-responded-to-covid-19/
35. Maria S, Yudaruddin R, Yudaruddin YA (2022) The impact of COVID-19 on bank stability: do bank size and ownership matter? Banks Bank Syst 17(2):124–137
36. Opejobi S (2020) COVID-19: Buhari govt begins cash transfer to poor Nigerians. Daily Post, 31 March. Available at: https://dailypost.ng/2020/03/31/covid-19-buhari-govt-begins-cash-transferto-poor-nigerians/

Chapter 6
The Impact of COVID-19 Pandemic on the Incidence of Poverty, Economic Growth and Development: Evidence from Ghana

Napoleon Kurantin and Bertha Z. Osei-Hwedie

6.1 Introduction

Despite the difficulty to present the exact economic impact of the COVID-19 coronavirus pandemic, it has resulted in adverse impacts on the global economy. According to the [1], the emergence of COVID-19 sent shock waves through the world economy with heightened concerns about the high levels of private and public sector debts. As expected, the initial impacts of the pandemic were felt most directly by households and firms; thus, there was a sharp decline in household income and business revenue. Taken as a whole and/or aggregately, such a decline had repercussions for the macro economy through several integrated re-enforcing means and pipe channels that connect the financial status of households, firms, financial institutions, and the government at large. The financial status of households is connected to the wider economy through the household-financial sector nexus and household-government nexus. The ability of banks to issue new loans to creditworthy borrowers is reduced when the financial health of households deteriorates, through a rise in loan defaults and an increase in loan provisioning requirements [1]. Moreover, economic activity is depressed when the financial status of banks deteriorates as banks supply households with less credit and charge higher interest rates. Similarly, Governments' reliance on households as a source of tax revenue declines when incomes are low, unemployment is high, and household incomes are under stressed [1].

N. Kurantin (✉)
Ghana Armed Forces Command and Staff College (GAFCSC), Academic Division, Accra, Ghana
e-mail: nkurantin@gafcsc.mil.gh.edu

B. Z. Osei-Hwedie
Ghana Institute of Management and Public Administration, School of Public Service and Governance, Accra, Ghana

R. Bhattacharyya et al. (eds.), *COVID-19 Pandemic and Global Inequality*,
https://doi.org/10.1007/978-981-99-4405-7_6

The corporate-financial sector nexus and corporate-government nexus equally, exhibited stress and ill-health during the COVID-19 pandemic. The financial status of the corporate sector affects banks and non-bank financial institutions directly through insolvency and loan defaults. When there is stress on the financial sector, bank's ability to extend credit is reduced and instead, charge more for such services [2]. The government-financial sector nexus is directly connected when banks are exposed to government's default risk if they hold government securities; deterioration in government's financial position negatively affects financial institutions balance sheets, increasing borrowing costs and reducing the ability to supply credit.

On the other hand, banks are an important source of funding for the government through the purchase of government bonds; when the financial sector is stressed, funding costs increases, thus, making it difficult and expensive for governments to refinance existing short-term debt and to finance new expenditure's __ rollover risk [2]. In developing economies, the interconnected risks of households, firms, and the financial sector and that of government are worsened by exogenous variables within the global economy. The depression of local currencies due to the worsening global economic situation relative to the COVID-19 pandemic, results in more expensive and often unsustainable debt servicing. Furthermore, global shocks such as the COVID-19 crisis often coincide with a decline in commodity prices within the world economy resulting in the deterioration of government revenue and henceforth, adversely impacting the government ability to counteract the crisis through expansionary fiscal policy (higher government spending and/or tax reduction) [2]. As experienced in Ghana, the result is a decline in household incomes, increase in poverty, increase in the rate of inequality and reduced growth of the wider economy and real Gross Domestic Product. It was in the face of such debt challenges that the government of Ghana, reached a staff-level agreement of Special Drawing Rights (SDR) of 2.242 billion or 3 billion United States dollars as part of economic policies and reforms to be supported by a three-year arrangement under the Extended Credit Facility (ECF) by the International Monetary Fund (IMF) [3]. At the end of the IMF mission to evaluate Ghana's economy as part of the processes of securing the bailout, it was agreed that "the Ghanaian authorities have committed to a wide-ranging economic reform programme, which builds on the government's Pos-COVID-19 Programme for Economic Growth (PC–PEG) and tackles the deep challenges facing the country" [3]. The bedrock of the reforms is to ensure the sustainability of public finances while protecting the vulnerable as a result of the adverse impact of COVID-19. Therefore, the fiscal strategic programme depends on frontloaded measures intended to increase domestic resource mobilization and hence, streamline expenditure. Furthermore, the programme is intended to strengthen already existing social safety nets, including a re-enforcement of existing targeted cash-transfer programmes for vulnerable households and thus, improve the coverage of and efficiency of social spending as part of the Post-COVID-19 economic recovery policies [3].

The presented chapter involves six integrated sections and/or headings. Apart from the abstract, section one of the chapter introduces the study and lays the foundation for subsequent sections. Section two thus, brings forth, the relevant literature reviewed and the theoretical framework underpinning the chapter. This is followed by section three which details the adopted research design and data requirements in meeting the goal and objectives of the chapter. Section four, on the other hand, presents well-integrated results and analysis of the chapter, and section five focuses on the noted limitations of the chapter. The last part of the study, which is section six, provides the conclusions and policy implications of the chapter.

6.2 Literature Review and Theoretical Framework

The World Health Organization (WHO) first announced a global health emergency in January 2020 and on March 11, 2020, it declared the viral COVID-19 outbreak an official pandemic which is the highest level of health emergence. This brought to the fore, the highly interconnected nature of the global economy, and in consonance with John Donne's poem: "No Man is an Island" [4]. Since its inception, the global public health and economic crisis affected about 90 trillion dollars of the global economy [5].

The *World Economic Outlook* report in October 2021, presented a sober reflection of the global economic growth that had fallen to an annualized rate of around -3.2% in 2020, with a recovery of 5.9% progression for 2021 and 4.9% for the subsequent year of 2022 respectively [6]. By the close of 2020, the total number of confirmed COVID-19 cases had surpassed more than 40 million worldwide. Although many countries were relatively unaffected during the first wave, the situation was different as subsequently, they experienced dramatic increases in fatalities [7].

Apart from its impact on public health, COVID-19 has led to major economic shock within world economies including that of Ghana. In accord with this, the United Nations framework for the immediate socio-economic response to the COVID-19 crisis warned: "the COVID-19 pandemic is far more than a health issue as it is affecting societies and economies at their core. Whilst the impact of the pandemic will vary from country to country, it will most likely increase poverty and inequalities at a global scale, making achievements of the Sustainable Development Goals even more urgent" [8].

The African continent's openness to international trade is thus, not immune from the adverse effects of COVID-19. The internal effects are because of the rapid spread of the virus in many African countries. They are associated with and linked to morbidity and mortality which lead to a disruption of economic activities. It resulted in a decline in domestic demand in tax revenue due to the loss to commodity prices in the face of increased public expenditure to safeguard human health and support economic activities relative to growth and development [9]. On the other hand, the exogenous effects result from direct trade links between the continents of Europe, Asia, and the Americans. Decrease in Foreign Direct Investment (FDI) and Official Development Assistance, decline in remittances from African Diaspora, and illicit financing flows and domestic financial market tightening have contributed to the negative growth rates in African economies [7].

After adjusting for the effects of gender, employment status, marital status, religion, level of education and occupation. Multivariable Analysis of Factors of the impact of COVID-19, revealed that the location and region of residence was the main factor associated with any impact of the virus sampled respondents [10]. Thus, those from the Eastern part of the African continent (Adjusted Odds Ration [AOR] with 95% Confidence Interval [CI] and 1.95 Z value: 1.42–2.69; Southern African (AOR 1.46 M 95%, CI: 1.09 -1.1.96) and Central Africa (AOR 1.47, 95% CI: 1.06–2.03) had much higher odds of any adverse impact of COVID -19 than the West African sub-region [10]. Furthermore, the study reported that older adults thus (> 49), were more likely to have closed down their respective businesses at the height of the COVID-19 pandemic [10].

It's reported that out of the over 30, 000 firms that closed at the height of the COVID-19 pandemic, nearly half (15,179) are fully open; close to half (14,162) are still closed suggesting more support is needed in helping such businesses to fully recover and hence, economic growth and development [11].

As of January 2023, Ghana had recorded 171, 070 COVID-19 cases with 1456 Coronavirus deaths. The number of Coronavirus recovered cases stood at 932, 69. The country administered a total of 21,400,939 vaccine doses [12].

There was a large drop in Ghana's non-residential electricity consumption after the lockdown as commercial activities froze up; compared to 2019, non-residential electricity consumption fell by 3.9% in April and 12.7% in May 2021. By contrast, there was a notable increase in the rate of electricity consumption by residential consumers [13]. Despite budget constraints, the Government of Ghana, in April 2020, announced an electricity subsidy programme; providing free electricity for three months to lifeline consumers: those who consumed less than 50 kWh in the month of March. Those who consumed more than the threshold of 50 kWh were presented with a 50% reduction in their cost of electricity consumption under Ghana's Coronavirus Alleviation and Revitalisation of Enterprises Support (CARES) Obaatanpa Programme. Although the Government removed the 50% absorption of the cost of electricity, it extended the programme for those with a threshold of 50 kWh [13].

In a study conducted in South Africa, it revealed that male farmers were in the majority as opposed to female counterparts. The low rate of female participation in agriculture was attributed to inequalities experienced by women within the sub-Sahara Africa. Women in agriculture face difficulties with access to land, land rights, inputs, credit facilities, and extension services [14]. COVID-19 lockdown and restrictions further exacerbated agricultural inputs limitations. These resulted in reduced crop yields such as cereal maize and legumes that constitute staple foods in the region.

Although governments as part of national policies to mitigate the adverse effects of COVID-19 in their respective countries, containment measures including stay-at-home and travel restrictions meant that farmers and traders were logistically challenged, leading to supply delays and post-harvest losses. Furthermore, the requirements for COVID-19 tests for long-distance truckers, for instance, resulted in a shortage of food truck drivers and delays in the delivery services across international borders in Eastern Africa (Rossi, 2020) in [15].

Although African indigenous vegetables (AIVs) are a very important source of food security and nutrition as well as the income of the poor farm households, COVID-19 negatively, impacts the production and distribution of AIVs. Farmers within this sub-sector recorded a 75% drop in production resulting from reduced access to input, farm labour and output market. During the first phase of the pendemic, farmers' production and sales volumes declined by 39 and 65% [16].

Moreover, in the East African region, COVID-19 lockdown measures including reduced access to markets resulted in the loss and reduction of employment opportunities and thus, adversely affecting those within the lower income bracket earning opportunities and hence, reduced purchasing power. The concomitant effect was to resort to negative coping strategies and widening of the poverty gap. The negative effect and impact were equally felt within the non-farming labour-supporting sector including transport operators, petty traders, market vendor and rural-based loan and credit operator [15].

Ironically, recent data shows that agriculture continues to be the main source of livelihoods for smallholder households in sub-Saharan Africa. The share of households involved in and/or moving into the agricultural sector has increased since the start of the pandemic. Before the outbreak of the COVID-19 pandemic, 76% of households were directly involved in the agricultural sector either as crop or livestock farmers. However, this figure has increased to 84%. Similar observations have been made in Malawi and Uganda, respectively. The former recorded 91% and the latter, recorded 79% of households are involved in the agricultural sector as compared to the pre-pandemic levels of 84 and 76% respectively [15].

The negative impact of COVID-19 on Ghana's economy is felt in the country's agricultural sector which happens to be the backbone of the economy contributing tremendously to its Gross Domestic Product (GDP) year on year. It employs over 60% of the country's population [17]. Sub-Saharan African countries including Ghana, the majority of farmlands practice rainfed agriculture. Lockdown and restricting people's movement adversely affected the availability of farm inputs as well as other farm-related services. For instance, farmers couldn't access tractor service centers and this adversely affected food production, resulting in reduced farm income and thus, increased spatial inequalities within the agricultural sector. The poultry industry suffered as a result of disruption in international shipping; feed ingredients mostly imported weren't available. There was an increase in prices of the few available feed ingredients [18]. Gender inequality increased during the period under review relative to COVID-19 and its impact on the agriculture sector. Patrilineal inheritance in Ghana, limits women's accessibility to land acquisition and therefore, being able to expand farm acreage and production. COVID-19 negatively, affected women farmers and traders as they were restricted from accessing farm implements and bringing their farm produce to locked-down city centers [19].

It's well noted that an estimated number of agribusiness employment fell from 51.111 at the height of the COVID-19 lockdown to 78.412 in the post-lockdown period. Furthermore, reduced wages of workers within the agribusiness sector increased from 175,255 to 267.211 in the post-lockdown period [20]. In addition, an estimated 124,364 workers had their working hours reduced within the agribusiness.

In a nutshell, more than 55.2% of the total workforce in the agribusiness and the agricultural sector lost their respective employment. About 44.7% of the total workforce across the agribusiness sector were laid off because of the COVID-19 lockdown. This translated into an estimated 22,873 workers and a wage reduction for 63,167 workers [20].

The imposition of a lockdown by the Government during the COVID-19 pandemic led to labour migrant crisis for the first time in Ghana's history. There was a reverse migration from the southern part of the country to the northern part of the country. The labour crisis affected fish processing activities, infrastructure development, manufacturing, construction activities adversely affected the country's economic growth and development [21].

By July 2020, over 400,000 businessmen and women had lost their businesses; 42,000 small traders, daily workers and wage-laborers lost their jobs [21]. The slowdown in the manufacturing sector has led to a downward trend in Ghana's economic growth from 5.8 to 1.5%. The impact of the COVID-19 pandemic led to a wide gap in the official fiscal deficit to 11.7% of GDP thus, driving up the public debt to 76% of GDP; interest expenditure further increased to 44.6% of total revenue. Henceforth, at the end of the 2020 fiscal year, the government embarked on an urgent fiscal consolidation agenda from 2021 onwards [22].

The Markov processes and in particular Markov chains have been applied to study different phenomena in different disciplines and/or fields [23]. In the discipline of economics, Hamilton developed the Markov process as a tool to study and analyse the switches of observable variables between different regimes [24]. Therefore, memoryless stochastic processes could be applied in such models in which the future is thus, conditioned only on the current state of the system [20, 23]. Applied the model for analyzing the switches of observables between different regimes and/or time periods, between high and low levels of time series as the Markov switching model allows for an analysis of how a non-stationary series transitions thus, drawing the probability distribution of the switches between regimes. Nevertheless, the applied method has been criticized on the grounds that few of the real-world growth rates are non-stationary, it has relevant implications for the understanding of this phenomenon. To overcome the perceived weakness of the Markov model, the application of the Hidden Markov Model (HMM) and in addition, of the stayer model are refined versions of the basic Markov model to enhance its robustness and application [20].

The applied Markov model thus, led to the conclusion that national policy to address inequalities relating to the spread of unemployment should not only depend on the efficiency of local initiatives but rather complemented with extended partnership. This should exceed the traditional forms and institutions of cooperation. Rather, the partnership should include local, national institutions with ties to national or regional administrative institutions, the private sector, civil society organizations and/or chambers. To reduce regional inequalities, especially in the developing world, it is the development of infrastructure that has a dominant role as increases demand side of employment based on Keynesianism [25].

The application of the Markov model provided relevant information relating to growth-path forecasts of the cycles of the American economy. Indeed, the model provided good predictions of the duration of cycles in the economy of the United States of America [26]. As a statistical system modelling technique, the Hidden Markov Chain allowed for the study and analysis from one state in this case, confirmed cases, recovered, and active or death of COVID-19 pandemic in Morocco. The application of the Hidden Markov Chain model enabled the forecast for a cumulative number of cases that helped the Moroccan authorities to set up adequate protocols for managing the post-confinement due to COVID-19 [27].

To achieve the goal of this chapter, a basic discrete Markov chain model is presented; time and space are discrete. This construction demonstrates how to simulate a discrete-time Markov chain model in the study and analysis of the intent of the chapter which is a focus on the ramifications of the Coronavirus disease (COVID-19) pandemic on Ghana's Gross Domestic Product (GDP) since its inception in 2019.

Let $\boldsymbol{X_n}$, $\boldsymbol{n} = 0, 1, 2 \ldots$ which is discrete-time stochastic process with a discrete state with space $\boldsymbol{S}$.

$\boldsymbol{S}$ = a discrete variable that is either finite or countably infinite; always assume that S is either {1, …, N} or {0, …, N-1} relative to a finite case/state, and could either be {0,1, …} or {1, 2, …} in the infinite case/state [28, 29].

To comprehend the process, it is valuable to know and understand the values of:

$$P\{X_0 = i_0, X_1 = i_1, \ldots, X_n = i_n\} \tag{6.1}$$

Note that for each n and finite sequence of states i_0, …, i_n Ɛ S. Therefore, finite-dimensional distribution enables the calculation of a path probability. Henceforth, the axioms of probability could be applied [29, 30]:

$$PX_0 = i_0, X_3 = i_3 = PX_0 = i_0, X_1 \varepsilon S, X_2 \varepsilon S, X_3 = i_3 \tag{6.2}$$

$$= \sum_{j1 \in S} \sum_{J1 \in S} P\{X_0 = i_0, X_1 = j_1, X_2 = j_2, X_3 = i_3\} \tag{6.3}$$

From Eq. 6.3, the rule of second equality holds when the related events are mutually exclusive [29]. Accordingly, the Markov chain to a degree, describes a sequence of the probability of events of a given case/state resulting from the preceding event. Thus, depending on the nature of the inquiry being undertaken, the stochastic model could either be presented in a discrete-time model or as a continuous-time model [31]. Consequently, for the purposes of this chapter, it is assumed that the Markov Chain is a countable case/state space of a discrete-time model.

Similar to the modelling of the impact of COVID-19 on the economy of Kenya, this chapter applies Markov Chain model, and henceforth, simplifies the socio-economic statutes of the Ghanaian economy relative to the most relevant five sectors that contributes to the processes of economic growth and development. These noted sectors include agriculture, tourism, building and construction, infrastructure development and manufacturing sectors, respectively [32]. Relatively, the applied probability transition matrix, $p_{x,t}^{ij}$ is presented as:

$$PC_{x,t}^{ij} = \begin{matrix} p_{11} & p_{12} & p_{13} & p_{14} & p_{15} \\ p_{21} & p_{22} & p_{23} & p_{24} & p_{25} \\ p_{31} & p_{32} & p_{33} & p_{34} & p_{35} \\ p_{41} & p_{42} & p_{43} & p_{44} & p_{45} \\ p_{51} & p_{52} & p_{53} & p_{54} & p_{55} \end{matrix} \tag{6.4}$$

$$P_{x,t}^{ij} = \begin{matrix} & s_1 & s_2 & s_3 & s_4 & s_5 \\ s_1 & p_{11} & p_{12} & p_{13} & p_{14} & p_{15} \\ s_2 & p_{21} & p_{22} & p_{23} & p_{24} & p_{25} \\ s_3 & p_{31} & p_{32} & p_{33} & p_{34} & p_{35} \\ s_4 & p_{41} & p_{42} & p_{43} & p_{44} & p_{45} \\ s_5 & p_{51} & p_{52} & p_{53} & p_{54} & p_{55} \end{matrix}$$

where

S_1 = Poor

S_2 = Lower class

S_3 = Middle class

S_4 = Upper class

S_5 = Wealthy class

Source: [33].

From the applied probability transition matrix, five simultaneous equations are presented:

$$\pi_1 = \pi_1 P_{11} + \pi_2 P_{21} + \pi_2 P_{31} + \pi_2 P_{41} + \pi_2 P_{51} \tag{6.5}$$

$$\pi_2 = \pi_1 P_{21} + \pi_2 P_{22} + \pi_2 P_{23} + \pi_2 P_{24} + \pi_2 P_{25} \tag{6.6}$$

$$\pi_3 = \pi_1 P_{31} + \pi_2 P_{32} + \pi_2 P_{33} + \pi_2 P_{34} + \pi_2 P_{35} \tag{6.7}$$

$$\pi_4 = \pi_1 \, p_{41} + \pi_2 \, p_{42} + \pi_2 \, p_{43} + \pi_2 \, p_{44} + \pi_2 \, p_{45} \tag{6.8}$$

$$\pi_5 = \pi_1 \, p_{51} + \pi_2 \, p_{52} + \pi_2 \, p_{53} + \pi_2 \, p_{54} + \pi_2 \, p_{55} \tag{6.9}$$

Source: [33].

The noted values of π_1, π_2, π_3, π_4, π_5, are assumed to be proportional to GDP contributions of these five economic variables/sectors at a given equilibrium in the long run. This is intended to present relevant information on how COVID-19 has impact Ghana's processes of economic growth and development relative to the incidence of poverty and inequality during the time period under review.

Empirical estimates of the effect of epidemics and thus, pandemics for instance, on income inequality and the spread of poverty are investigated, calculated, and analyzed via:

$Gini_{it} = \alpha + \beta EpiPan_{it\text{-}1} + X_{it\text{-}1}\gamma + \delta_i + \mathcal{E}_t + \mu_{it}.$

where

$Gini_{it}$ = Gini coefficient in country *i* in year *t*.

$\beta EpiPan_{it\text{-}1}$ = an indicator for epidemics and/or pandemics in country *i in year t -1.*

$X_{it\text{-}1}$ = vector of control variables of income inequality in country *i in year t -1.*

δ_i = denotes country dummies

$\mathcal{E}_t$ = represents the full set of time effects

μ_{it} = error term for all omitted factors/variables

$E\ (\mu_{it}) = 0$ for *i* and *t*

Source: [34].

Related to the statistical model of the Gini coefficient is the Neoclassical economy model of long-run equilibrium of income within the theory of convergence. As more nations formulate and implement principles underpinning the free market system of economic growth and development, in the long run, incomes will increase and converge. Thus, with shocks like the COVID-19 pandemic, which results in a disequilibrium, there are natural forces that will return the economy back to its equilibrium as humans are rational beings [9, 35]. The neoclassical theory of convergence henceforth implies that in the very long term, the incidence of poverty as experienced under COVID-19, will demise if not eliminated. Among others, the theory assumes that people have full access to information; process information; are rational; people are price takers; capital exhibits a diminishing return; intend to maximize profit and/

or utility (satisfaction); and moreover, technology thus, exhibits constant returns to scale [36–38].

6.3 Research Design and Data Requirements

This section of the chapter presents the research design involving the methodology, method and/or data requirements in attaining the goal of the study. Research design involves the overarching plan for connecting the research problem statement, conceptual framework to the achievable empirical research; it thus, provides the specific direction for observed procedures in the research [39]. In a nutshell, research design advance the type of analysis to be carried out in arriving at a conclusion. It therefore, espouses what data is required, the methodology and methods to be applied in the collection and analysis of the data in meeting and answering the research goal, questions and objectives [40]. Research is considered a careful and thus, a systematic means of solving noted problems and therefore, gaining new knowledge [41]. In addition, the discipline of research is said to be a systematic process of discovering the advancement of human knowledge [42–44].

The chapter adopts and applies a quantitative research methodology/approach with the Discrete-Time Marko Chain model as the main statistical technique or method in the analysis of the COVID-19 pandemic on Ghana's Gross Domestic Product (GDP). Quantitative approach/methodology/strategy involves the collection and analysis of statistical/numerical data in the description, explanation, prediction or control of variables and phenomena of interest (Daniel, 2016). A cardinal philosophy of quantitative methodology is the underlying belief that the world is relatively stable and hence, could be measured as well as infer broad generalizations of sample data [45].

Within the methodology of quantitative research, the chapter adopted and applied Discrete-Time Marko Chain statistical technique in modelling the ramifications of the Coronavirus disease (COVID-19) pandemic on Ghana's Gross Domestic Product (GDP). The discrete-time Marko chain (DTMC) involves the sequence of random variables, known as a stochastic process. The value of the next variable, therefore, depends on the value of the current variable and not variables in the past [46].

The required datasets are obtained from the Ghana Ministry of Finance (https://mofep.gov.gh), Ghana Statistical Service (https://www.statsghana.gov.gh), Ghana Ministry of Health (https://ghs.gov.gh), World Health Organization (https://www.who.int), the World development indicators from the World Bank (https://databank.worldbank.org/source/world-development-indicators), and Statista (https://statistia.com) respectively.

The chapter employed Excel Xlstat version 2023 via the application of the Discreet-Time Make Chain model relative to the five variables/sectors and their impact on the Ghanaian economy.

6.4 Results and Analysis

The purpose of this section of the chapter is to present and analyze the data relative to an investigation of the impact of the COVID-19 pandemic on the incidence of poverty, economic growth, and development. Specifically, the chapter investigates the impact of the COVID-19 pandemic on the top five key sectors (agriculture, tourism, building and construction, infrastructure, and manufacturing) of the Ghanaian economy: research into the proportion of their contributions to GDP at a steady state. The implications of the COVID-19 pandemic have had an adverse impact on the incidence of poverty, in all economic sectors of Ghana as a case study of the processes of economic growth and development. The economic sectors contribution to GDP in Ghana is summarized and presented in Table 6.1.

Table 6.1 confirms the observation in other studies that agriculture continues to play a major role in Ghana's economy. It's the most single employer in the country. The share of households involved in and/or moving into the agricultural sector has increased since the start of the pandemic. Before the outbreak of the COVID-19 pandemic, 76% of households were directly involved in the agricultural sector either as crop or livestock farmers. However, this figure has increased to 84%. Similar observations have been made in Malawi and Uganda respectively. The former recorded 91% and the latter, recorded 79% of households are involved in the agricultural sector as compared to the pre-pandemic levels of 84 and 76% respectively [15].

The weighted index per GDP contribution of each of the noted five sectors based on the equation:

$\sum_{i=1}^{n} \pi_i$ is presented in Table 6.2.

Henceforth, the vector of the economy under review is written and presented as a vector:

$$\Pi = (\pi_1, \pi_2, \pi_3, \pi_4, \pi_5)$$

$$= (0.33, 0.01, 0.24, 0.24, 0.17)$$

Table 6.1 Economic sector variable proportion to GDP in Ghana

Economic sector	Percentage (%) contribution to GDP
Agriculture = X_1	22.1
Tourism = X_2	6.2
Building and Construction = X_3	15
Infrastructure Development = X_4	15
Manufacturing = X_5	10.7

Source Author's construction, (2022)

Table 6.2 Weight index per GDP contribution

Economic sector	Weighted index
Agriculture = X_1	0.33
Tourism = X_2	0.01
Building and Construction = X_3	0.24
Infrastructure Development = X_4	0.24
Manufacturing = X_5	0.17

Source Author's construction, (2022)

The model and analysis indicators that the proportion of tourism (X_2) to GDP has reduced remarkably as compared to the other sectors of the economy as a result of the COVID-19 pandemic. Spatially, this is observed in Ghana's major cities and, along the country's coastlines where ancient and historical forts are located. As the cities serve as magnets for immigration from the hinterlands and overseas, the lockdown reversed in-bond travel as airport and transport terminals were restricted. As the number of tourists visiting the country dwindled, the number of restaurants and associated workers drastically reduced. Similarly, the manufacturing sector suffered as imports from overseas serving as inputs reduced due to distortion in global shipping lines. The average Gini index for sub-Saharan Africa is one of the highest in the world. However, economic reforms and high commodity prices before COVID-19 led to a significant reduction in inequalities in education and health [47]. Between 1991 and 2011, the region recorded a Gini index in the range of 0.40 to 0.529 [48]. Due to the pandemic, poverty level increased to 54.3% and living standards fell by 61.4% respectively [8].

As noted in the preceding pages, by July 2020, over 400,000 businessmen and women had lost their businesses; 42,000 small traders, daily workers and wage-laborers lost their jobs [21]. Furthermore, the slowdown in the manufacturing sector has led to a downward trend in Ghana's economic growth from 5.8 to 1.5%. The impact of the COVID-19 pandemic led to a wide gap in the official fiscal deficit to 11.7% of GDP thus, driving up the public debt to 76% of GDP; interest expenditure further increased to 44.6% of total revenue. Henceforth, at the end of the 2020 fiscal year, the government embarked on an urgent fiscal consolidation agenda from 2021 onwards [22].

6.5 Conclusions and Policy Implications

It is important to note that COVID-19 had an adverse effect on the Gross Domestic Product of Ghana. It negatively affected all noted sectors of the economy and thus, increased the incidence of poverty particularly, within the southern urban centers of the country. Apart from a reduced growth rate in tourism including the arts and entertainment, the manufacturing sector suffered a reduced contribution to the country's

GDP. As income levels fell among the general population, those in the urban centers recorded a sharp decline in their respective incomes and as such, increased the levels of poverty and inequality due to the COVID-19 pandemic. Policies including free water supply and reduced rate of the price of electricity consumed by individual households, instituted during the lockdown period mitigated against the adverse effect of the COVID-19 pandemic. However, the economy as a whole suffered high levels of debt due to reduced productivity as the government continued to pay workers who had to stay home during the period of lockdown and labour restrictions across the length and breadth of the country.

The research in this chapter has shown that there is a need for the government to reduce its fiscal and monetary expansionary policies under the IMF programme in order to reverse the slowdown in the economy. Notwithstanding the short-comings of the theory of convergence, the intention is to put the economy back on a path of sustained growth and development as espoused by the neoclassical economists. Henceforth, in the long-run, it is hoped the economic policies and reforms to be supported by the three-year arrangement under the Extended Credit Facility (ECF) by the International Monetary Fund as part of the Post-COVID-19 recovery measures, will reduce the incidence of poverty and income inequality.

6.6 Limitations of the Study

The novel coronavirus is noted to be part of a general series of infectious diseases worldwide that includes i. Avian influenza ii. Ebola iii. Middle East respiratory syndrome coronavirus and iv. Influenza A [34]. However, this chapter focused on COVID-19 and its impact on the economy of Ghana especially, as it relates to the incidence of poverty and inequality during the period under review. As such, there are two basic limitations of the study that are noteworthy. The first is due to data constraints [11]; obtaining data for testing the intensity of the relationship between COVID-19 and its impact on the economy is very difficult. The data is spread in many domains and the chapter therefore, had to collate such data with its many different forms of measurement into one standard format to enable modelling and thus, statistical analysis. The second most important constraint stems from the short—time span to undertake such an investigation and analysis. The standard decade of panel data sets wasn't available henceforth, this could have affected the power and intensity of generalizations as is expected of such a study.

References

1. World Bank (2022) Emerging risks to the recovery. World Bank. Retrieved from chrome-extension://efaidnbmnnnibpcajpcglclefindmkaj/https://openknowledge.worldbank.org/bitstream/handle/10986/36883/9781464817304_Ch01.pdf
2. World Development Report (2022) Emerging risks to the recovery: policy priorities. World Bank, Washington
3. International Monetary Fund (2022) IMF reaches staff-level agreement on a $3 billion, three years Extended Credit Facility with Ghana. Washington: International Monetary Fund. Retrieved from https://www.imf.org/en/News/Articles/2022/12/12/pr22427-imf-reaches-staff-level-agreement-on-a-3-billion-three-years-ecf-with-ghana
4. Donne J (2007) John Donne's Poetry. (D. Dickson, Ed.) London: W.W. Norton & Company
5. Congressional Research Service (2021) Global economic effects of COVID-19. Retrieved from Congressional Research Service : chrome-extension://efaidnbmnnnibpcajpcglclefindmkaj/https://sgp.fas.org/crs/row/R46270.pdf
6. International Monetary Fund (2021) IMF/World Economic Outlook October 2021 Forcast. Retrieved from IMF: Politics & Economics https://www.thenewsmarket.com/news/imf---world-economic-outlook-october-2021-forecast/s/b81600f3-cb01-47c0-8751-7a10690341af?utm_term=&utm_campaign=TNM+consideration+-+Q4+(UK%26US)&utm_source=adwords&utm_medium=ppc&hsa_acc=4023792588&hsa_cam=11451195049&h
7. World Bank (2021) Somalia economic update: Impact of COVID-19 policies to manage the crisis and strengthen economic recover. Retrieved from World Bank: https://openknowledge.worldbank.org/bitstream/handle/10986/34239/Somalia-Economic-Update-Impact-of-COVID-19-Policies-to-Manage-the-Crisis-and-Strengthen-Economic-Recovery.pdf?sequence=6&isAllowed=y
8. Bukari C, Essilfie G, Aning-Agyei M, Otoo I, Kyeremeh C, Owusu A, … Bukari K (2021) Impact of COVID-19 on poverty and living standards in Ghana: a micro- perspective. Cogent Eco Fin 9(1):1-23. https://doi.org/10.1080/23322039.2021.1879716
9. Xiang L, Tang M, Yin Z, Zheng M, Lu S (2021) The COVID-19 pandemic and economic growth: theory and simulation. Front Public Health 9:1–14. https://doi.org/10.3389/fpubh.2021.741525
10. Mashige K, Osuagwu L, Uagathan S, Ekpenycrg B, Abu E, Goson P, … Agho K (2021) Econoomic, health and physical impacts of COVID-19 pandemic in sub-Saharan African regions: a cross sectional survey. Risk Manag Healthcare Policy 14:4799-4807. https://doi.org/10.2147/RMHP.S324554
11. Su D, Alshehri K, Pagan J (2022) Income inequality and the disease burden of COVID-19: survival analysis of data from 74 countries. Elsevier 27:1–9. www.elsevier.com/locate/pmedr
12. Trading Economics (2023) Ghana Coronavirus COVID-19 Cases. Retrieved from Trading Economics https://tradingeconomics.com/ghana/coronavirus-cases
13. Dzansi J, Kim M, Lagakos D, Telli H (2021) Real-time economic impacts of COVID-19 in Ghana. Retrieved from International Growth Centre: chrome-extension://efaidnbmnnnibpcajpcglclefindmkaj/https://www.theigc.org/wp-content/uploads/2021/04/Dzansi-et-al-March-2021-Policy-brief.pdf
14. Mthembu B, Mkhize X, Arthur G (2022) Effects of COVID-19 pandemic on agricultural food production among smallholder farmers in northern Drakensberg areas of Bergville, South Africa. Agronomy 12(2):531–537. https://doi.org/10.3390/agronomy12020531
15. Food and Agricultural Organization (2020) Impact of COVID-19 on agriculture, food systems and rural livelihoods in Eastern Africa: policy and programmatic options. Rome: FAO. Retrieved from chrome-extension://efaidnbmnnnibpcajpcglclefindmkaj/https://www.fao.org/3/cb0552en/CB0552EN.pdf
16. Ogada M, Justus O, Paul M, Omondi S, Juma A, Taracha E, Ahmed H (2021) Impact of COVID-19 pandemic on African indigenous vegetables value chain in Kenya. Agricul Food Sec 10(52):2–10. https://doi.org/10.1186/s40066-021-00328-3

17. Ghana Statistical Service (2020) Mobility analysis to support the Government of Ghana in responding to the COVID-19 outbreak. Retrieved from Ghana Statistical Service https://statsghana.gov.gh/gsspublications.php?category=MTkwMDE4MjI2Ny4xMDg=/webstats/90r897632o
18. Abroquah S (2020) Impact of COVID-19 on Ghana's agriculture - In the eyes of a youth farmer. Retrieved from IMPAKTER https://impakter.com/covid-19-ghana-agriculture/
19. Ojoko B, Makinde O, Fayeun L, Babalola O, Salako K, Adzitey F (2022) Impact of COVID-19 and lockdown policies on farming, food security, and agribusiness in West Africa. Elsevier Public Health Emergence Collection, pp 209 - 223. https://doi.org/10.1016/B978-0-323-90769-9.00014-1
20. Privault N (2018) Discrete-time markov chains: In understanding Markov Chains. *Springer*, pp 89–113
21. Aduhene D, Ose-Assiby E (2021) Socio-economic impact of COVID-19 on Ghana's economy: challenges and prospects. Int J Soc Econ 48(4):543–556. https://doi.org/10.1108/IJSE-08-2020-0582
22. Institute for Fiscal Studies (2023) The institute for fiscal studies assessment of the 2022 budget. Retrieved from IFS: chrome-extension://efaidnbmnnnibpcajpcglclefindmkaj/https://www.ifsghana.org/wp-content/uploads/2022/01/IFS_Assessment_of_2022_Budget.pdf
23. Hamilton J (1989) A new approach to the economic analysis of non-stationary time series and the business cycle. Econ J Econ Soc 357–384
24. Gagnine P (2017) Markov chains: from theory to implementation and experimentation. John Wiley & Sons, Washington
25. Liptak K (2011) The application of Markov chain model to the description of Hungarian labour market process. Zarzadzanie Publiczne 4(16):133–149. https://doi.org/10.4467/20843968ZP.12.033.0500
26. Filardo A, Gordon S (1998) Business cycle durations. J Econ 85(1):99–123
27. Marfak A, Achak D, Azizi A, Nejjari C, Aboudi K, Saad E, ... Youlyouz-Marfak I (2020) The hidden Markov chain modelling of the COVID-19 spreading using Moroccan dataset. Elseview, 1-4. doi:https://doi.org/10.1016/j.dib.2020.106067
28. Doob J (1953) Stochastic processes. John Wiley and Sons, New York
29. Paris Descartes University (2023) Discrete time Markov chains. Paris: Paris Descartes University. https://helios2.mi.parisdescartes.fr
30. Meyn S, Tweedie R (1993) Makov chains and stochastic stability. London: Springer=Verlag
31. Norris J, Norris J (1998) Markov chains. Cambridge University Press, Cambridge
32. Wolde-Rufael Y (2009) Re-examining the financial development and economic growth nexus in Kenya. Econ Model 26(6):1140–1146
33. Odhiambo J, Weke P, Ngare P (2020) Modeling Kenyan economic impact of Corona Virus in Kenya using discrete-time Markov Chains. J Fin Econ 2:80–85. http://pubs.sciepub.com/jfe/8/2/5
34. Esseau-Thomas C, Galarraga O, Khalifa S (2022) Epidemics, pandemics and income inequality. Health Econ Rev 12(7):1-15. https//doi.org/https://doi.org/10.1186/s13561-022-00355-1
35. Quiroga P (2007) Theory, history and evidence of economic convergence in Lation America. La Paz, Bolivia: Instituto de Estudios Avanzados en Desarrollo. http://www.jstor.com/stable/resrep00574.4
36. Acemoglu D (2009) The Solow growth model. Princeton University Press, Princeton
37. Robert S (1956) A contribution to the theory of economic growth. Quart J Econ 70(1):65–94. https://doi.org/10.2307/1884513
38. Trevor S (1956) Economic growth and capital accumulation. Econ Record 2:334–361. https://doi.org/10.1111/j.1475-4932.1956.tb00434.x
39. Creswell J (2014) Research design: qualitative, quantitative and mixed methods approaches. Sage Publications, Inc., Thousand Oaks, California
40. Asenahabi B (2019) Basics of research design: a guide to selecting appropriate research design. Int J Contemp Appl Res 6(5):76–89. http://www.ijcar.net/assets/pdf/Vol6-No5-May2019/07.-Basics-of-Research-Design-A-Guide-to-selecting-appropriate-research-design.pdf

41. Bhattacharyya D (2006) Research methodology. Excel Books, New Delhi
42. Gratton C, Jones I (2010) Research methods for sports studies. Abingdon: Roultedge.
43. Kothari C (2007) Research methodology: methods and techniques. New Delhi: New Age International (P) Limited, Publishers
44. Kumar C (2008) Research methodology. APH Publishing Corporation, New Delhi
45. Gay L, Mills G, Airasian P (2009) Educational research: competencies for analysis and applications. Pearson Education, London
46. Gagniuc P (2017) Markov chains: from theory to implementation and experimentation. John Wiley & Sons, New Jersey
47. Adesina J (2016) World social science report 2016: inequality in sub-Saharan Afica: dimensions and drivers. Retrieved from United Nations Educational, Scientific and Cultural Organisation: chrome-extension://efaidnbmnnnibpcajpcglclefindmkaj/https://en.unesco.org/inclusivepolicylab/sites/default/files/analytics/document/2019/7/Adesina_wssr_2016_chap_18.pdf
48. Odusanya I, Akinlo A (2021) Income inequality and population health in Sub-Saharan Africa: a test of income inequality health hypothesis. J Popul Soc Stud 26:235–254. http://doi.org/https://doi.org/10.25133/JPSSv292021.015
49. Colander D (2000) The death of neoclassical economics. J Hist Eco 22(2):127–147
50. Daniel E (n.d.) The usefulness of qualitative and quantitative approaches and methods in researching problem-solving ability in science education curriculum. J Edu Pract 7(15):91–100. http://www.iiste.org
51. GIZ, Ghana Statistical Service , & United Nations Development Programme (2021) Summary report on impact of COVID-19 on agribusinesses in Ghana. Accra: United Nations Development Programme. Retrieved from chrome-extension://efaidnbmnnnibpcajpcglclefindmkaj/https://www.undp.org/sites/g/files/zskgke326/files/migration/gh/AGRIBUSINESS_TRACKER_GH_COVID-19_PPT_SUMMARY_REPORT_FINDINGS_GSS_GIZ_UNDP.pdf
52. United Nations Development Programme (2022) Business in Ghana are recovering from COVID-19 shocks, albeit variations in response across different types of firms. Retrieved from Ghana https://www.undp.org/ghana/press-releases/businesses-ghana-are-recovering-covid-19-shocks-albeit-variations-response-across-different-types-firms?utm_source=EN&utm_medium=GSR&utm_content=US_UNDP_PaidSearch_Brand_English&utm_campaign=CENTRAL&c_src=CENTRAL&
53. United Nations Development Programme (2022) COVID-19 socio-economic impact. Retrieved from United Nations Development Programme https://www.undp.org/coronavirus/socio-economic-impact-covid-19?utm_source=EN&utm_medium=GSR&utm_content=US_UNDP_PaidSearch_Brand_English&utm_campaign=CENTRAL&c_src=CENTRAL&c_src2=GSR&gclid=CjwKCAiAwomeBhBWEiwAM43YIEhZZ1UCDnNXnRK-QcJDAwv42CbIcSxqNnH85Xz30

Chapter 7
Determining the Right Strategies for Turkey to Avoid an Energy Crisis During the Pandemic Process

Serhat Yüksel, Hasan Dinçer, Çağatay Çağlayan, Dilan Kararoğlu, and Duygu Yavuz

7.1 Introduction

The COVID-19 pandemic is one of the crises with the most comprehensive health, economic and social effects after the 2008 financial crisis [40]. In the last months of 2019, a new infectious respiratory disease emerged in the city of Wuhan, China. This disease has been named as COVID-19 by the World Health Organization. The disease spread rapidly in a short time and affected the whole world. Since there is no vaccine or medicine for the disease, it has had serious consequences for all people [7]. People have had to face many economic, social and psychological problems brought about by this disease. States have taken various measures to stop the spread of the disease in question. Comprehensive curfews, countries closing their borders to each other, stopping many international and national flights, and quarantining infected patients and people in contact with these patients are examples of restrictions frequently applied by states [3]. The reasons such as the closing of the borders of the countries, the fact that the tourist activities came to a standstill, and the fact that various sectors, mostly the service sector, had to stop production, greatly aggravated the economic bill of the COVID-19 pandemic.

The economic consequences of the pandemic can be summarized as follows. With the pandemic, health systems and commercial activities of various sectors have come to a standstill. The unemployment rate increased significantly with the inhibition of economic activity [31]. As supply chains have come to the breaking point, price increases have been experienced in various basic needs products. The financial sector suffered as a result of the slowdown in global money circulation. These problems in the financial sector had a serious negative impact on the real sector as well. With the

S. Yüksel (✉) · H. Dinçer · Ç. Çağlayan · D. Kararoğlu · D. Yavuz
The School of Business, İstanbul Medipol University, İstanbul, Turkey
e-mail: serhatyuksel@medipol.edu.tr

R. Bhattacharyya et al. (eds.), *COVID-19 Pandemic and Global Inequality*,
https://doi.org/10.1007/978-981-99-4405-7_7

restrictions of international and national flights, there was a contraction in the tourism sector due to the COVID-19 measures [34]. The difficulties experienced by all sectors within the scope of COVID-19 measures and the health concerns of individuals have significantly increased global uncertainty. Unemployment and inflation increase and problems in the supply chain caused households to lose income and have difficulties in meeting their basic needs. States have implemented various financial support packages to protect sectors and households from the negative economic effects caused by the pandemic measures. This step increased the fragility of the national economies by increasing public expenditures [9].

The measures taken by the states to prevent the spread of the pandemic caused the country's economies to decline by stopping commercial activities and production. Thus, the effects of the pandemic on energy demand, energy supply and energy prices can be mentioned. The COVID-19 pandemic has had a negative impact on many industries, including agriculture, manufacturing, finance, education, health, sports, tourism and food. Therefore, the energy industry was also directly affected by the negativities experienced by other sectors [38]. The decline in economic activity in many sectors because of the measures taken across the country also reduced the global energy demand. The global decline in energy demand has done vital damage to energy companies. For example, at least 19 companies went bankrupt in the US during the COVID-19 pandemic [23]. In addition, while energy consumption in industries decreased, the amount of energy used in households increased [60]. However, in parallel with the falling energy demand in total, energy companies reduced their energy production. Energy companies faced a serious energy demand due to increasing economic activity with the removal of restrictions in parallel with increasing vaccination efforts [44, 46, 49]. In a possible new pandemic, some measures can be taken to avoid an energy crisis or to better manage the crisis that will occur.

7.2 Some Measures to Manage Energy Crisis in the Pandemic Period

This section includes some significant precautions with the following subtitles.

7.3 Incentives and Application of Free Market Conditions

The energy crisis has a serious negative impact on energy companies in countries. Because, with increasing energy costs, energy companies need to react as quickly as possible to excessive energy demand. But all energy companies must reflect the increased costs on energy users' bills. Otherwise, energy companies will not be able to continue their activities by not being able to cover their costs. Parallel to this, some wrong measures taken by the states in order not to reflect the cost of the energy crisis to the public may deepen the energy crisis even more. For example, governments may tend to limit energy companies at the point of billing energy users to prevent the increase in energy prices from being passed on to the public. Thus, they prevent energy companies from reflecting the increased costs on users' bills. Therefore, energy companies that fail to reflect the price rise on their consumer bills may suffer significant losses and must declare bankruptcy. Transforming energy companies into public institutions to manage the energy crisis will have negative consequences both in the short term and in the long term. Transforming energy companies into public institutions will reduce possible private enterprise investments in the energy field in the future. This situation will make countries more vulnerable to energy crises in the future. Therefore, states should use their regulatory authority in accordance with free market conditions. States should try to minimize the effects of the current crisis in the short term by subsidizing the rising costs of energy companies with tax cuts, credit supports and incentives [30]. With the new private enterprise investments to be made in the energy field, it should be aimed to increase the competition in the energy sector. New investments in various energy sources will increase competition in the energy sector and will make countries more sheltered against energy crisis in the long run. Therefore, each country must establish the right balance between competition, regulation, and cooperation in energy markets [17].

7.4 Smart Meters and Flexible Billing

Smart meters are electronic measuring devices used by distribution companies to exchange information bi-directionally with consumers and operate their electrical systems. Smart meters are actively used by some distribution companies to provide accurate billing data for at least some of their customers [5]. With smart meters, distribution companies can easily access historical and instant data of customers such as energy consumption and power quality [10, 43]. With the data received from smart meters, the ideal levels of energy consumption used by consumers can be determined according to the needs of the consumer. If the consumer consumes more energy than he needs, the unit price of the supplied energy should be higher than the normal price. Thus, the consumer will try to minimize the energy cost by avoiding excessive energy consumption. In certain periods of the year, the increase in general energy demand will increase or decrease at a more predictable rate. Thus, the probability of an energy crisis based on demand–supply imbalance at the national level will decrease.

7.5 Nuclear Energy Investments

Nuclear energy is generally produced using the heat released by the splitting of uranium atoms to obtain water vapor, and the resulting water vapor rotates the turbines. Energy is obtained by the rotation of the turbines. Plutonium and thorium can also be used instead of uranium [22, 53]. Nuclear energy has many advantages. No matter what time of year it is, nuclear energy can be produced at the same level. Nuclear energy is more cost-effective as a raw material than fossil fuels. Nuclear power plants where accidents can happen, should be equipped with good safety precautions. Using nuclear power, which emits very little carbon dioxide, could help the world economy transition to a more sustainable form of energy. Since most of today's society is dependent on fossil fuels, nuclear energy is important in avoiding the use of fossil fuels [14]. It is widely accepted that nuclear energy can be used to reduce greenhouse gas emissions, as it releases much less carbon dioxide than other forms of energy such as fossil fuels. Additionally, nuclear power has been associated with job creation and economic expansion. New nuclear power plant construction is hard without an energy policy that seeks to encourage long-term, capital-intensive investments.

7.6 Investments in Energy Storage Techniques

The world population is increasing, the need for energy is also increasing and it is increasing the price of traditional fuels. On the other hand, the world's conventional fuel reserves are finite and are decreasing over time because of increasing global energy consumption. This jeopardizes the future balance between production and consumption. The use of conventional fuels also causes a great increase in greenhouse gas emissions, and due to these emissions, it has serious effects on the whole world, such as global warming. As a result, alternative and renewable energy systems, such as solar and wind-based systems, are seen as crucial for the future because of their environmental friendliness and sustainable functioning [18].

In contrast, several alternative energy sources listed are heavily dependent on the weather. As a result, the energy produced by these sources can be subject to large periodic, daily, and even sudden imbalances. The amount of energy produced may not be enough to meet the general demand. Energy storage devices are critical to ensure that energy requirements are always met. In case the primary energy sources are not available or insufficient, the extra energy produced from the alternative sources mentioned above is stored in various energy storage devices. Research and evaluation of energy storage systems for off-grid applications are particularly important [58]. For energy to be useful, it must be available when and where it is needed. The term "storage" refers to the act of separating energy for later consumption [21, 26]. Different storage systems are available today, from capacitors/supercapacitors, batteries, pumped hydro to compressed air and flywheels, as well as superconducting magnetic energy storage. There are several interesting candidates for energy storage, including hydrogen, which is expected to lead to a new hydrogen economy [59]. The development of storage techniques will be an important tool in preventing possible energy crises in the future and minimizing their effects.

7.7 Making Short-Term Projections

Projection is a statistical and planning technique for predicting the future based on past data. If we have regular historical data about a given variable and there are no significant changes in the long run, the future can be reasonably predicted. Projections are the name given to such estimates. Energy is a critical strategic issue for all nations, developing and developed alike [37]. Political decisions are taken, economic policies are determined according to the projections made about the macroeconomic data of the countries, and all sectors continue their economic activities according to these projections. Expectations about data such as predicted economic growth, unemployment rate, and exchange rate are one of the basic elements in the formation of policies for sectors. However, unexpected, and sudden economic crises affect the consistency of long-term projections negatively. Therefore, instead of determining long-term projections such as one year, especially for energy markets, it will be useful to determine monthly shorter projections to obtain more consistent results. In this way, extraordinary developments in the markets will be noticed in a shorter time and actions will be taken in a shorter time.

Many evaluations of economic, energy, and environmental issues need a forecast of future energy demand. For example, future energy investment decisions need an understanding of how much energy will be used in the future [8]. Among energy planners and politicians, efficient use of energy resources has become a must. The focus has recently switched to energy forecasts, since climate circumstances are heading for significant reversals [41, 50]. Many evaluations of economic, energy, and environmental policy need projections of future energy demand. Many variables influence future energy growth, but the most important are economic growth, population expansion, energy pricing and fuel availability, efficiency-improving technology, and the development of new renewable energy sources, environmental and emissions rules and standards [45]. To achieve better results, forecasts must consider various factors such as energy price shocks, economic recession, and structural changes [4].

7.8 Renewable Energy Investments

Due to the COVID-19 epidemic, which affected the whole world, the demand for energy decreased. Due to this falling demand, there has been a decrease in energy supply. Energy production has been curtailed. There was a contraction in the sectors. After the discovery of the vaccine, the demand for energy increased excessively as the normalization processes were taken. Energy prices increased significantly as energy supply could not meet energy demand. The reason why the energy production was not enough was that the countries were in great economic difficulties. However, if investments were made in renewable energy and production was made from renewable energy sources in terms of energy production, countries would not have had problems in energy production during the epidemic period. This situation had a positive effect on the economy of the countries. Because renewable energies are inexhaustible energies. Renewable energy is energy produced in nature from self-renewing sources. Renewable energies are energies that do not harm human health. It is safe for humans as they do not emit carbon gas when burned. They are also environmentally friendly energies. In this sense, investments in renewable energy need to be increased. The implementation of renewable energy projects is of great importance. For this, it is necessary to determine the best sources of financing. Correct financing decisions need to be made. Project financing is of great importance for renewable energy projects. Government grants and subsidies play an important role in financing the renewable energy project. In summary, the government needs to take measures to increase renewable energy projects. Green investors need to be funded with government support [13, 53]. The biggest disadvantage of renewable energy sources is their cost. The installation costs of renewable energy sources and power plants are very high. In this sense, the government should provide tax deductions to renewable energy investors. On the other hand, credit support should be provided to renewable energy investors. In parallel with these, it can be said that the use of green bank loans is another way. Organizational support also mediates the development of renewable energy projects. Countries that support renewable energy infrastructure are countries that are on the way to continuously develop their economies. This provides great advantages for countries in the long run [12].

7.9 Ensuring High Efficiency in Energy Production

First, if it is necessary to define energy efficiency, it can be explained as the use of energy without disrupting the quality of production. Energy efficiency provides a significant reduction in carbon dioxide emissions [2]. Transition to a green economy can be counted among the factors that increase energy efficiency. The green economy is an economy that aims at sustainable development without harming the environment. It is possible to see the green economy as a great opportunity for countries. So, what can be done to ensure high efficiency in energy production? First, it is possible to say about the transition to renewable energy. Because renewable energy sources also significantly affect carbon dioxide emissions. In other words, it reduces carbon dioxide emissions. In addition, energy projects need to be increased. At the same time, it is important to increase R&D investments. Investments in technology should also be increased. Another important point is to increase the use of domestic resources. The increase in the use of domestic resources reduces the foreign dependency ratio and countries invest in their own economies by consuming the energy they produce. In this way, it can be said that the current account deficit of countries will also decrease. In this sense, countries should give priority to establishing power plants working with renewable energy. The use of renewable energy can be said to be a factor that also prevents climate change. Climate change is the change of the world's climate due to the increase in temperatures as carbon dioxide and similar gases in the air accumulate in the atmosphere. Climate change is an element that threatens the environment and living things. Therefore, as the use of renewable energy increases, the efficiency of energy production increases. As the efficiency in energy production increases, carbon gas emissions to the environment decrease, this situation also prevents climate change [20, 42, 52]. As a result, it is possible to say that efficiency in energy production will largely prevent the energy crisis from being experienced again in a new epidemic.

7.10 An Evaluation for Turkey

In this study, an evaluation is conducted for Turkey with the aim of understanding key issues to cope with the energy crisis in the pandemic period effectively. For this purpose, seven different criteria are identified by making a comprehensive literature evaluation. The details of these items are given in Table 7.1.

While evaluating these factors, DEMATEL methodology is taken into consideration. This approach aims to find the significant items [25, 48]. In other words, it is quite helpful to identify more critical factors among many different alternatives [24, 28, 47]. This methodology is considered in the literature for various purposes [1, 6, 11, 19].

In the process of the DEMATEL methodology, firstly, expert evaluations are obtained. After that, these evaluations are converted into linguistic variables. In the next process, a direct relation matrix is created by taking the average of these values. In the following step, this matrix is normalized. Later, the defuzzification process is applied to this matrix. In the next step, the total relation matrix is generated. While making evaluations of the values in the total relation matrix, the sums of the rows and

Table 7.1 List of criteria

Factors	References
Incentives and application of free market conditions	[39, 51]
Smart meters and flexible billing	[6, 61]
Nuclear energy investments	[39, 54–55]
Investments on energy storage techniques	[15, 62–63]
Making Short-Term projections	[35, 36]
Renewable energy investments	[16, 29, 33]
Ensuring high efficiency in energy production	[27, 32]

Source Authors' calculations

Table 7.2 Weights of criteria

Factors	Weights
Incentives and application of free market conditions	0.1119
Smart meters and flexible billing	0.1132
Nuclear energy investments	0.1834
Investments on energy storage techniques	0.1460
Making Short-Term projections	0.1004
Renewable energy investments	0.1832
Ensuring high efficiency in energy production	0.1621

Source Authors' calculations

columns are computed. These values are taken into consideration for the calculation of the weights of the determinants.

The steps of DEMATEL have been implemented to these items. As a result, the weights of them can be calculated. Table 7.2 gives information about the weights of the criteria.

It is identified that nuclear energy investments play a crucial role in the effective management of energy crisis in the pandemic period. Similarly, renewable energy investments are also essential for this purpose. On the other side, ensuring high efficiency in energy production has the third highest weight.

7.11 Conclusion

The measures taken by the states to prevent the spread of the pandemic caused the country's economies to decline by stopping commercial activities and production. Thus, the effects of the pandemic on energy demand, energy supply and energy prices can be mentioned. Therefore, the energy industry was also directly affected by the negativities experienced by other sectors. The decline in economic activity in many sectors because of the measures taken across the country also reduced the global energy demand. The global decline in energy demand has done vital damage to energy companies. Energy companies faced a serious energy demand due to increasing economic activity with the removal of restrictions in parallel with increasing vaccination efforts.

In this study, an evaluation is conducted for Turkey with the aim of understanding key issues to cope with the energy crisis in the pandemic period effectively. For this purpose, seven different criteria are identified by making a comprehensive literature evaluation. While evaluating these factors, DEMATEL methodology is taken into consideration. This approach aims to find the significant items. In other words, it is quite helpful to identify more critical factors among many different alternatives. The steps of DEMATEL have been implemented to these items. As a result, the weights of them can be calculated. It is identified that nuclear energy investments play a crucial role in the effective management of energy crisis in pandemic period. Similarly, renewable energy investments are also essential for this purpose. On the other side, ensuring high efficiency in energy production has the third highest weight.

It would be appropriate for Turkey to focus on nuclear energy and renewable energy investments to fight the energy crisis more successfully during the pandemic period. As can be understood from these results, it is vital for Turkey to produce its own energy. In this way, Turkey will not be dependent on other countries for energy. Currently, Turkey imports most of its energy needs from abroad. This situation affects Turkey's current account balance very negatively. The constant current account deficit makes the country's economy quite fragile. The biggest reason for the current account deficit is energy imports. Nuclear energy and renewable energy investments will also contribute significantly to the solution of this problem.

It is understood that the most correct solution proposal for Turkey in an international energy crisis is national energy policies. Therefore, nuclear energy investments need to be increased urgently. In this context, it would be appropriate to carry out joint projects with countries that have serious experience in nuclear energy, especially Russia, France and China. This situation will both help Turkey to produce its own energy and contribute to the learning of nuclear energy technology. On the other hand, it is very important to take necessary measures to increase renewable energy investments in the country. In this context, necessary incentives should be given to renewable energy investors by the government. Renewable energy investments should become attractive thanks to some advantages such as tax reductions.

References

1. Adalı Z, Dinçer H, Eti S, Mikhaylov A, Yüksel S (2022) Identifying new perspectives on geothermal energy investments. Emerald Publishing Limited, In Multidimensional Strategic Outlook on Global Competitive Energy Economics and Finance
2. Akram R, Chen F, Khalid F, Ye Z, Majeed MT (2020) Heterogeneous effects of energy efficiency and renewable energy on carbon emissions: evidence from developing countries. J Clean Prod 247:119122
3. Atalan A (2020) Is the lockdown important to prevent the COVID-19 pandemic? Effects on psychology, environment and economy-perspective. Annals of medicine and surgery 56:38–42
4. Aydin G (2014) Modeling of energy consumption based on economic and demographic factors: The case of Turkey with projections. Renew Sustain Energy Rev 35:382–389
5. Benzi F, Anglani N, Bassi E, Frosini L (2011) Electricity smart meters interfacing the households. IEEE Trans Industr Electron 58(10):4487–4494
6. Bhuiyan MA, Dinçer H, Yüksel S, Mikhaylov A, Danish MSS, Pinter G, Stepanova D (2022) Economic indicators and bioenergy supply in developed economies: QROF-DEMATEL and random forest models. Energy Rep 8:561–570
7. Chakraborty I, Maity P (2020) COVID-19 outbreak: Migration, effects on society, global environment and prevention. Sci Total Environ 728:138882
8. Chang Y, Lee J, Yoon H (2012) Alternative projection of the world energy consumption-in comparison with the 2010 international energy outlook. Energy Policy 50:154–160
9. Das RC (2021). Management of COVID-19 through strategic roles of governments: a study on highly affected countries, in Dincer and Yuksel (eds) management strategies to survive in

a competitive environment-how to improve company performance, Springer, Singapore, May, pp 175–190
10. Depuru SSSR, Wang L, Devabhaktuni V, Gudi N (2011) Smart meters for power grid—Challenges, issues, advantages and status. In: 2011 IEEE/PES Power Systems Conference and Exposition (pp. 1–7). IEEE.
11. Dinçer H, Yüksel S, Martínez L (2022) Collaboration enhanced hybrid fuzzy decision-making approach to analyze the renewable energy investment projects. Energy Rep 8:377–389
12. Dinçer H, Lisin A, Ubay GG, Çağlayan Ç (2021). Identifying the best financing sources for renewable energy companies in latin american countries. In Strategic Approaches to Energy Management (pp 1–12). Springer, Cham.
13. Dinçer H, Yüksel S, Çağlayan Ç, Uluer GS (2020) The contribution of nuclear energy investment on sustainable financial and economic development. J Financ Econ Bank 1(1):39–51
14. Don MacElroy JM (2016) Closing the carbon cycle through rational use of carbon-based fuels. Ambio 45(1):5–14
15. Dong W, Zhao G, Yüksel S, Dinçer H, Ubay GG (2022) A novel hybrid decision making approach for the strategic selection of wind energy projects. Renew Energy 185:321–337
16. Du L, Dinçer H, Ersin İ, Yüksel S (2020) IT2 Fuzzy-Based multidimensional evaluation of coal energy for sustainable economic development. Energies 13(10):1–21
17. González DML, Rendon JG (2022) Opportunities and challenges of mainstreaming distributed energy resources towards the transition to more efficient and resilient energy markets. Renew Sustain Energy Rev 157:112018
18. Hadjipaschalis I, Poullikkas A, Efthimiou V (2009) Overview of current and future energy storage technologies for electric power applications. Renew Sustain Energy Rev 13(6–7):1513–1522
19. Haiyun C, Zhixiong H, Yüksel S, Dinçer H (2021) Analysis of the innovation strategies for green supply chain management in the energy industry using the QFD-based hybrid interval valued intuitionistic fuzzy decision approach. Renew Sustain Energy Rev 143:110844
20. Herring H (2006) Energy efficiency—a critical view. Energy 31(1):10–20
21. Ibrahim H, Ilinca A, Perron J (2008) Energy storage systems—Characteristics and comparisons. Renew Sustain Energy Rev 12(5):1221–1250
22. Wang J, Li Y, Wu J, Gu J, Xu S (2020) Environmental beliefs and public acceptance of nuclear energy in China: A moderated mediation analysis, Energy Policy, 137(111141)
23. Jiang P, Van Fan Y, Klemeš JJ (2021) Impacts of COVID-19 on energy demand and consumption: Challenges, lessons and emerging opportunities. Appl Energy 285:116441
24. Jun Q, Dinçer H, Yüksel S (2021) Stochastic hybrid decision-making based on interval type 2 fuzzy sets for measuring the innovation capacities of financial institutions. Int J Financ Econ 26(1):573–593
25. Kalkavan H, Baş H, Ersin İ, Eti S, Yüksel S (2021). Defining appropriate government strategies to reduce unemployment during COVID-19 pandemics. In Management Strategies to Survive in a Competitive Environment (pp 155–172). Springer, Cham
26. Karami H, Sanjari MJ, Gooi HB, Gharehpetian GB, Guerrero JM (2017) Stochastic analysis of residential micro combined heat and power system. Energy Convers Manag 138:190–198
27. Kostis P, Dinçer H, Yüksel S (2022) Knowledge-Based energy investments of european economies and policy recommendations for sustainable development. J Knowl Econ, 1–33
28. Kou G, Olgu Akdeniz Ö, Dinçer H, Yüksel S (2021) Fintech investments in European banks: a hybrid IT2 fuzzy multidimensional decision-making approach. Financ Innov 7(1):1–28
29. Kou G, Yüksel S, Dinçer H (2022) Inventive problem-solving map of innovative carbon emission strategies for solar energy-based transportation investment projects. Appl Energy 311:118680
30. Kuzemko C, Bradshaw M, Bridge G, Goldthau A, Jewell J, Overland I, Westphal K (2020) Covid-19 and the politics of sustainable energy transitions. Energy Res Soc Sci 68:101685
31. Lai H, Khan YA, Thaljaoui A, Chammam W, Abbas SZ (2021) COVID-19 pandemic and unemployment rate: A hybrid unemployment rate prediction approach for developed and developing countries of Asia. Soft Computing, 1–16

32. Li X, Zhu S, Yüksel S, Dinçer H, Ubay GG (2020) Kano-based mapping of innovation strategies for renewable energy alternatives using hybrid interval type-2 fuzzy decision-making approach. Energy 211:1–16
33. Li YX, Wu ZX, Dinçer H, Kalkavan H, Yüksel S (2021) Analyzing TRIZ-based strategic priorities of customer expectations for renewable energy investments with interval type-2 fuzzy modeling. Energy Rep 7:95–108
34. Liu A, Kim YR, O'Connell JF (2021) COVID-19 and the aviation industry: The interrelationship between the spread of the COVID-19 pandemic and the frequency of flights on the EU market. Ann Tour Res 91:103298
35. Liu J, Lv J, Dinçer H, Yüksel S, Karakuş H (2021) Selection of renewable energy alternatives for green blockchain investments: A Hybrid IT2-based Fuzzy Modelling. Arch Comput Methods Eng 28:3687–3701
36. Meng Y, Zhou R, Dinçer H, Yüksel S, Wang C (2021) Analysis of inventive problem-solving capacities for renewable energy storage investments. Energy Rep 7:4779–4791
37. Meunier F (2007) The greenhouse effect: A new source of energy. Appl Therm Eng 27(2–3):658–664
38. Mofijur M, Fattah IR, Alam MA, Islam AS, Ong HC, Rahman SA, Mahlia TMI (2021) Impact of COVID-19 on the social, economic, environmental and energy domains: Lessons learnt from a global pandemic. Sustain Prod Consum 26:343–359
39. Mukhtarov, S., Yüksel, S., & Dinçer, H. (2022). The impact of financial development on renewable energy consumption: Evidence from Turkey. *Renewable Energy*.
40. Notteboom T, Pallis T, Rodrigue JP (2021) Disruptions and resilience in global container shipping and ports: the COVID-19 pandemic versus the 2008–2009 financial crisis. MaritE Econ & Logist 23(2):179–210
41. O'Neill BC, Desai M (2005) Accuracy of past projections of US energy consumption. Energy Policy 33(8):979–993
42. Oikonomou V, Becchis F, Steg L, Russolillo D (2009) Energy saving and energy efficiency concepts for policy making. Energy Policy 37(11):4787–4796
43. Pepermans G (2014) Valuing smart meters. Energy Econ 45:280–294
44. Poudyal R, Loskot P, Nepal R, Parajuli R, Khadka SK (2019) Mitigating the current energy crisis in Nepal with renewable energy sources. Renew Sustain Energy Rev 116:109388
45. Santamouris M, Kapsis K, Korres D, Livada I, Pavlou C, Assimakopoulos MN (2007) On the relation between the energy and social characteristics of the residential sector. Energy Build 39(8):893–905
46. Shaikh I (2022) Impact of COVID-19 pandemic on the energy markets. Econ Chang Restruct 55(1):433–484
47. Shang H, Su F, Yüksel S, Dinçer H (2021) Identifying the strategic priorities of the technical factors for the sustainable low carbon industry based on macroeconomic conditions. SAGE Open 11(2):21582440211016344
48. Silahtaroğlu G, Dinçer H, Yüksel S (2021) Identifying indicators of global financial crisis with fuzzy logic and data science: a comparative analysis between developing and developed economies. In Data Sci Mult Criteria Decis Mak Approaches Financ (pp 17–53). Springer, Cham
49. Singh S, Ru J (2022) Accessibility, affordability, and efficiency of clean energy: a review and research agenda. Environ Sci Pollut Res, 1–15
50. Suganthi L, Samuel AA (2012) Energy models for demand forecasting—A review. Renew Sustain Energy Rev 16(2):1223–1240
51. Wan Q, Zhao X, Liu H, Dinçer H, Yüksel S (2022) Assessing the new product development process for the industrial decarbonization of sustainable economies. SAGE Open 12(1):21582440211067230
52. Wilkinson P, Smith KR, Beevers S, Tonne C, Oreszczyn T (2007) Energy, energy efficiency, and the built environment. The lancet 370(9593):1175–1187
53. Xie Y, Peng Y, Yüksel S, Dınçer H, Uluer GS, Çağlayan Ç, Li Y (2020) Consensus-based public acceptance and mapping of nuclear energy investments using spherical and pythagorean fuzzy group decision making approaches. IEEE Access 8:206248–206263

54. Yuan G, Xie F, Dinçer H, Yüksel S (2021) The theory of inventive problem solving (TRIZ)-based strategic mapping of green nuclear energy investments with spherical fuzzy group decision-making approach. Int J Energy Res 45(8):12284–12300
55. Yüksel S, Dinçer H (2022) Identifying the strategic priorities of nuclear energy investments using hesitant 2-tuple interval-valued Pythagorean fuzzy DEMATEL. Prog Nucl Energy 145:104103
56. Yüksel S, Dinçer H, Çağlayan Ç, Uluer GS, Lisin A (2022b). Bitcoin mining with nuclear energy. In *Multidimensional Strategic Outlook on Global Competitive Energy Economics and Finance*. Emerald Publishing Limited
57. Yüksel S, Dinçer H, Mikhaylov A, Adalı Z, Eti S (2022a). Key issues for the improvements of shallow geothermal investments. In Sustainability in Energy Business and Finance (pp. 183–194). Springer, Cham
58. Zhang F, Zhao P, Niu M, Maddy J (2016) The survey of key technologies in hydrogen energy storage. Int J Hydrogen Energy 41(33):14535–14552
59. Zhang H, Baeyens J, Cáceres G, Degreve J, Lv Y (2016) Thermal energy storage: Recent developments and practical aspects. Prog Energy Combust Sci 53:1–40
60. Zhang X, Pellegrino F, Shen J, Copertaro B, Huang P, Saini PK, Lovati M (2020) A preliminary simulation study about the impact of COVID-19 crisis on energy demand of a building mix at a district in Sweden. Appl Energy 280:115954
61. Zhang Y, Zhang Y, Gong C, Dinçer H, Yüksel S (2022) An integrated hesitant 2-tuple Pythagorean fuzzy analysis of QFD-based innovation cost and duration for renewable energy projects. Energy, 123561
62. Zhao Y, Xu Y, Yüksel S, Dinçer H, Ubay GG (2021) Hybrid IT2 fuzzy modelling with alpha cuts for hydrogen energy investments. Int J Hydrogen Energy 46(13):8835–8851
63. Zhe L, Yüksel S, Dinçer H, Mukhtarov S, Azizov M (2021) The positive influences of renewable energy consumption on financial development and economic growth. SAGE Open 11(3):1–9

Part II
Sub-Theme—Trade, Employment, Health and Education

Chapter 8
COVID-19 Pandemic, Employment Differential and Health Expenditure Nexus in Sub-Saharan African Countries: Evidence from Vector Autorfegressive (VAR) Model

N. Omeje Ambrose, N. Obodoechi Divine, E. Urama Chinasa, A. Eze Afamefuna, A. Mba Augustine, and R. Ukwueze Ezebuilo

8.1 Introduction

Africa and the entire world have witnessed tough times due to COVID–19 pandemic. This pandemic has ravaged a lot of economies and killed millions of people, the world over, leading to worldwide economic catastrophe. The GDP in Africa reduced by 2.1% in 2020 and it was projected that if adequate assistance was not provided, about 39 million people in Africa especially women would fall into severe poverty [3]. In 2020, the world experienced the most horrible economic downturn ever since the Second World War [34] resulting in many businesses closing down in order to restrain COVID-19 spread. This gave rise to a great fall (collapse) in human economic activities and the first recession for the past 25 years in Africa [35], which also had consequences for international trade.

One of the biggest health problems in recent times has emerged, the COVID-19 pandemic [31]. According to studies, it broke out in the Republic of China and within a few months it spread across all world continents with millions of recorded infections and deaths [14]. African continent surprisingly had a lesser infection and death rate contrary to what was predicted. Among sub-Saharan African (SSA) countries, the first country to record a positive test was Nigeria even though South Africa later became the worst hit [27]. According to Lucero-Prisno et al. [20], the WHO found SSA region is among the least worldwide in terms of ability and readiness to provide urgent and demanding services to COVID-19 patients (Table 8.1).

N. O. Ambrose · N. O. Divine · E. U. Chinasa · A. E. Afamefuna · A. M. Augustine · R. U. Ezebuilo (✉)
Department of Economics, University of Nigeria, Nsukka, Enugu State, Nigeria
e-mail: ezebuilo.ukwueze@unn.edu.ng

R. Bhattacharyya et al. (eds.), *COVID-19 Pandemic and Global Inequality*,
https://doi.org/10.1007/978-981-99-4405-7_8

Table 8.1 Regional statistics of COVID-19 in SSA by April 30, 2021

African region	Infections	Deaths	Recoveries
Central Africa	1,60,873	2,774	142,817
Eastern Africa	6,02,893	11,279	465,438
Northern Africa	1,437,645	397,521	1,297,325
Southern Africa	2,013,589	62,731	1,948,234
Western Africa	458,271	6,467	428,391

Source Africa Centre for Disease Control and Prevention COVID-19 Daily Updates [1]

The emergence of COVID-19 in Africa became a drawback from the great expectations of the region. The region had expected to gain a growth rate of 3.2% against 2.9% in 2019 and a giant stride to 3.5% in 2021 [30] were all cut short. Also, the promised gain by the African Continental Free Trade Area (AfCFTA) it joined in 2019 with the intention to improve trade up to 25% were all lost [29].

Analysis of lockdown as a COVID-19 mitigation and containment measure indicated that reducing public movement, closing schools and places of work and staying at home were effective in reducing COVID-19 spread rate. The impact of this measure on African countries where the majority belong to the informal sector—about 77% of all employments (excluding those in agriculture) were not able to work from their homes [17], which implies either losing their jobs and means of livelihood or risking COVID-19 infection by going out to work. It was reported that African countries that have stricter lockdown measures experienced more contractions in economic activities. Many children already lost many months of schooling/learning. There were also noticeable interference/hindrances in regular vital health care services including malaria treatment, other vaccinations and child and maternal health care services due to such severe restrictions. These likely gave rise to more severe health disasters, especially among children whose nutritional needs were jeopardized and all progress made in developing human capital in recent times was also lost (https://en.unesco.org/covid19/educationresponse).

The COVID-19 pandemic interrupted the workings of the healthcare system worldwide causing some minor ailments to degenerate and become a secondary health challenge worldwide. This affected the demand and supply of healthcare facilities as the available facilities were mobilized for the rapid response to COVID-19 management, thus upsetting services to outpatients—family planning and contraception, HIV therapy, mental health care and immunization services in many counties [33].

The pandemic also affected some places where a great percentage of women are engaged in employment, like hotels and restaurants, leading to complete loss of earnings or reduced wage earnings for those who are self-employed. It was estimated that about 103 million people who are working full-time, out of which about 54% are women, lost their employment during the pandemic globally. This resulted in malnutrition in children and generally poor health conditions in households. Our study is therefore poised to investigate the nexus among the COVID-19 pandemic, employment differential and government health expenditure in SSA.

8.2 Literature Review

As already known, the COVID-19 epidemic engulfed the world in a public health emergency in December 2019. The highly contagious virus began in China's Wuhan city, according to Du Toit [12] and Johnson and Roberto [19], and quickly spread all over the world, and subsequently reached Africa in February 2020 [2, 12, 19]. The pandemic, which has been dubbed the "biggest global disaster since World War II" ([16]: 2), has produced enormous economic and health consequences for countries, leaving governments rushing to respond [19].

When a person comes in close contact with an infected person increases the rate of infection or transmission of the virus [28]. Following H1N1 (2009), polio (2014), Ebola in West Africa (2014), Zika (2016), and Ebola in the Democratic Republic of the Congo (2019), the WHO declared the COVID-19 pandemic to be the sixth global public health emergency on January 30, 2020. This is an indication that the connection between human health and disease is not a recent idea or problem, but that of COVID-19 appears to have led to just as much or even worse human suffering globally than other transmissible diseases. In addition to its catastrophic consequences on human life, the COVID-19 Pandemic has the capacity to significantly overturn nations' economies [7]. As an illustration, Fernandes [13] claims that given the immense economic risk, the disease involves and the economic channels via which global economic activity is controlled, the disease's prevalence has created an imminent world economic recession.

Specifically, the COVID-19 epidemic presents two problems: a healthcare crisis and a global economic collapse. The Pandemic has had a significant impact on health care. Based on Johns Hopkins Hospital (2020)'s report, as of July 17, 2020, 14 million people had tested positive for the COVID-19 pandemic. By November 17, 2020, there were 54 million documented cases of diseases including 1.3 million deaths [32]. The enormous number of infections quickly overloaded health institutions in Italy, Spain, China, and the United Kingdom [19], forcing hospital staff and resources to their breaking points. While these numbers seem harrowing, it is necessary to note that the COVID-19 pandemic is a rapidly evolving pandemic, so they could get worse over time.

The outbreak of COVID-19 has had significant economic repercussions as well. Governments all over the world quickly enacted policies of lockdowns, preventing people from leaving their homes, restricting mass gatherings, closing schools and businesses, and grounding public transportation systems in an effort to slow the virus's spread [10, 14, 19]. This was done in response to the virus's ease and speed of transmission. On the other side, restrictions on people's freedom of movement and lockdowns have generally had two negative effects: slowed economic growth and, consequently, high unemployment [25]. Due to businesses filing for bankruptcy because of sluggish economic activity, millions of individuals were displaced and lost their jobs or were receiving reduced pay [19]. For example, the ILO [16] estimates that the COVID-19 virus has harmed 2.7 billion workers, resulting in decreased pay. Out of this total, lockdown regimes have had a disproportionately negative impact on 1.6 billion workers in the unorganised sector [16].

The Pandemic (COVID-19) has had less impact on the SSA region's health than it has on nations in the Global North. Public health professionals and virologists are baffled by the fact that in SSA, fewer people than expected have contracted the virus or passed away due to the COVID-19 outbreak than other nations in the Global North [22]. As an example, according to Chitungo et al. [8], while 10 million persons in America and 3 million in Europe were infected as of August 9, 2020, Africa had 1 million cases. By November 24, 2020, there were six times as many diseases and fatalities in the US as there were in Africa, despite the latter's population of about 320 million compared to Africa's over 1 billion. In America, 12 million people had contracted COVID-19 in November 2020, which led to 255,000 fatalities [33], as opposed to 2 million infections and 50,000 fatalities in Africa [33]. COVID-19 has, therefore, not had as much of an impact on health in SSA.

COVID-19, on the other hand, has had significant economic consequences. Africa's economic growth rates are expected to drop to between −2 and −5% in 2020, compared to a 2.4% average growth rate in 2019. Job losses are an unavoidable consequence of negative growth rates. Nearly 20 million people were expected to lose their jobs as a result of the sharp decline in growth rates of African economies [4]. For a reason, the adoption of severe lockdown regimes and the resulting business closures has disproportionately impacted Africans, being predominantly characterized by a sizable informal economy. Over 86% of employees in Africa reportedly have jobs in the informal sector [17]. As street vendors, day labourers and domestic workers who "live on the edge," and people engaged in the informal sector, frequently face the threat of starvation if their employment is interrupted for even a day ([10]: 254). Lockdowns and social separation orders have significant effects on Africa's informal sector employees' lives and livelihoods [30].

If lockdowns were adopted in SSA, many "household earners would be forced to choose between the virus and putting food on the table" ([30]: 14). To make matters even worse, about 90% of African women labor in the informal economy [30]. Women-headed households are particularly vulnerable in this situation, with possible consequences for children. Therefore, a lockdown regime will only create a disproportionately larger number of poor and vulnerable Africans suffering more.

While the pandemic's economic effects have been particularly severe in sub-Saharan Africa (SSA), SSA governments' monetary and fiscal measures have been less comprehensive than those in the Global North in terms of coverage. The region has the lowest COVID-1919-related stimulus investment compared to other regions, despite evidence of the magnitude of the pandemic's economic and social repercussions [26]. While developed capitalist countries have spent an average of 8% of their GDP on stimulus packages, the region (SSA) has spent only 0.8 percent of its GDP [9]. Additionally, low-income and SSA countries received just 0.06% out of the $10.6 trillion spent on fiscal and monetary measures to tackle the COVID-19 epidemic by September 3 2020 [15].

The ILO and other international organisations have pushed for the creation of safety nets and new social protection programmes or the expansion of current social protection programmes to include individuals who had previously been left out as a key policy option to cushion the harsh economic effects of the COVID-19 Pandemic. As a result, governments devised various social protection programmes and stimulus packages, mainly social assistance programmes to help cushion enterprises, individuals, and homes against the economic hardships posed by the epidemic while enforcing draconian lockdown regimes.

Social security benefits and cash transfers, for Chowdhury and Sundaram [9], are the most common types of social assistance programs that have been implemented. While the Irish government approved a cash payment of €350 per week for the Unemployment Payment programme, the US government approved a $2 trillion stimulus package for individuals and businesses to cushion the biting effects of the COVID-19 Pandemic [19]. In general, social assistance programmes as non-contributory social protection programmes have been crucial in assisting people in the Global North to deal with the financial effects of the COVID-19 pandemic.

All the examples from the Global North showcase the fact that nations with strong and efficient social protection systems and safety nets before the crisis are better equipped to respond to the effects of COVID-19, either by expanding social protection coverage or increasing the size of benefits [18]. On the contrary, countries with poor social protection systems are less likely to react swiftly and successfully to a pandemic. The majority of Africans must rely on their families and other non-state networks and participants during shock and disaster because these are unusual in Africa [11]. Government investment in social programmes (COVID-19 related crises) in Africa is quite low, which is a reflection of the fragmented and narrowly focused nature of the continent's social security system.

According to [21], the COVID-19 outbreak is a reminder for African nations to (re)invest in their social safety nets and health systems in order to assist prevent or lessen crises and shocks. The argument that there aren't enough resources to respond to calls for bigger social protection programs is no longer valid. African governments must not put up with severe suffering and hunger as a result of their inadequate response to the epidemic, given the size of the COVID-19 pandemic's economic impact in SSA. COVID-19's human and social costs are far too high to be reversed. Although many have argued that expanding special protection programmes in SSA is unaffordable, various simulations and models have shown that expanding social protection coverage, even in low-income countries, is possible if there is political will and commitment to look into alternative funding options, including preventing illicit money flows and corruption or reallocating public expenditure, among others.

In order to determine the one-year direct medical cost of COVID-19 in Turkey, Oksuz et al. [24] examined the healthcare resource usage (HCRU) and costs of hospitalised COVID-19 patients. A retrospective cohort research (n = 1056) was done at an Istanbul tertiary hospital between March and July 2020. COVID-19 is predicted to cost PPP$ 2.1 billion in direct medical costs each year. The COVID-19 pandemic's direct medical expenses made up 2.0% of government health spending and 0.8% of Turkey's GDP.

The study by Henry et al. [5] across the selected Sub-Saharan African countries found that life expectancy, domestic private health expenditure, and health expenditure are among the top opportunities for improving public health in SSA countries. The study used the panel data estimation technique and the World Bank Indicators (WBI) from 2000 to 2019. The findings also revealed that considerable improvements in health care in most SSA nations are largely funded by external aid and domestic private investment.

A well-resourced public healthcare infrastructure, according to Nyakubaya [23], is essential for lowering mortality and disease burden, retaining advancements made in other health programmes including HIV/AIDS and tuberculosis (TB) and enhancing global health security. The Ebola virus, which struck Africa in 2014–2016, put the continent's healthcare infrastructure to the test. Prior to the outbreak of Ebola, public health organisations in Guinea, Liberia, and Sierra Leone lacked enough physical facilities and resources. Three years later, during the COVID-19 epidemic, public healthcare infrastructure shortages still remain in SSA. Controlling a highly contagious viral disease like COVID-19 demands critical care and laboratory capabilities, as well as readily accessible medical supplies and healthcare personnel. The SSA still has a deficient public health infrastructure, which slows down efforts to control the COVID-19 outbreak. Reliable and sustainable health funding enables long-term planning, enabling healthcare systems to develop and provide the public with better and more timely responses.

From the empirical evidence above, no study has been done on the nexus between COVID-19OVID-19 pandemic, employment differentials and health spending in SSA, thus the motivation of this study.

8.3 Methodology

8.3.1 Data Source

We sourced our data from the World Development Indicators WDI [36], and this is the latest version of the data so far. The data comprises quarterly data for 40 countries in the Sub-Sahara African region. The data were transformed from annual to quarterly series in order to increase the sample size of the study. Variables in the model include; COVID-19 pandemic which is proxied by the number of inflicted persons, out-of-pocket expenditure on health (proxy for health expenditure), employment, and productivity. While other variables were sourced from World Banks' WDI [36] data set, COVID-19 pandemic data was generated from Worldometer's COVID-19 data set (2022). The variable definitions and their sources are shown in Table 8.2 given below.

Table 8.2 Definition of variables

Variables	Definition	Source
covid-19	Number of infected persons	Worldometer's COVID-19 data [37]
emp	Number of employed persons	WDI [36]
oophexp	Out-of-pocket expenditure on health (proxy for health expenditure)	WDI [36]
produ	Productivity variable	WDI [36]

Source Author's compilation

8.3.2 Model Specification

We used the panel vector autoregressive (PVAR) model and the panel VAR-impulse response function (PVAR-IRF) to accurately represent the goal of this paper. The model is expressed in its functional form as follows.

$$\text{covid19} = f(\text{emp}, \text{oophexp}, \text{produ}) \tag{8.1}$$

The model is further specified mathematically as follows:

$$\text{covid19}_t = \beta_0 + \beta_1\text{emp}_t + \beta_2\text{oophexp}_t + \beta_3\text{produ}_t \tag{8.2}$$

The model is further specified econometrically as:

$$\text{covid19}_t = \beta_0 + \beta_1\text{emp}_t + \beta_2\text{oophexp}_t + \beta_3\text{produ}_t + u_t \tag{8.3}$$

where

covid19 = Number of infected persons

emp = Number of employed persons

oophexp = Out-of-pocket expenditure on health

produ = productivity level

$\beta_{i's}$ = parameter estimates

u_t = innovations/shocks

Representing the above equation in a general panel VAR model form yields the specification seen in Eq. 8.4 given below.

$$y_{it} = \mu_i + By_{it-1} + \varepsilon_{it} \tag{8.4}$$

where $y_{it} = (\Delta D_{it}, \Delta Y_{it})'$, μ_{it} is a 3 × 1 country specific term. B is a 3 × 3 coefficient matrix of the independent variables, while ε_{it} is a 3 × 1 error term. The subscripts, i and t, denote the country and time of the year, respectively.

The study also computed the panel VAR impulse response functions and the panel forecast variance error decompositions from an estimated panel VAR (PVAR) model in order to support the panel VAR model's findings. The essence of this is to measure how much shock and/or effect that is being transmitted to one variable, say, employment (emp), health expenditure (oophexp), and productivity (produ) by covid-19 pandemic (covid19) in SSA economies.

8.4 Results and Discussion

8.4.1 The Variables Descriptive Statistics

Descriptive statistics was applied to inspect the nature of, and data characteristics of model variables. Hence, the variables' mean, standard deviation, minimum and maximum values of the data are examined. This is, therefore, presented in Table 8.3 given here under.

Table 8.3 reveals that all the model variables exhibited sufficient variations with respect to their mean, standard deviation, minimum, and maximum values. They show that the overall observation of the data (N) is 320 (i.e., from 2020Q1–2021Q4 for each of the 40 Sub-Saharan Africa (SSA) economies). For between-group panels, its observation (n) is 40, which matches exactly with the number of sampled SSA

Table 8.3 Results of the variables' descriptive statistics

Variable	Mean	Std. Dev.	Min	Max	Observations
covid19 overall	105,200.5	401,498.2	275	3,458,286	N = 320
between		354,575.5	373	2,260,917	n = 40
within		195,539.8	−1,092,169	1,302,570	T = 8
emp overall	60.07313	12.70868	36.69	82.73	N = 320
between		12.80167	38.405	81.575	n = 40
within		1.106323	57.36312	62.78313	T = 8
oophexp overall	35.37089	19.1856	2.993242	77.2248	N = 320
between		19.33215	3.154122	76.91296	n = 40
within		1.598898	27.99931	42.74248	T = 8
produ overall	2368.512	2981.762	261.2453	16,213.48	N = 320
between		2969.244	267.6274	13,488.95	n = 40
within		517.646	−356.0175	5093.042	T = 8

Source Author's computation from available data using STATA 13

Table 8.4 Panel unit root test results

Variables	Inverse chi-squared P	Inverse normal Z	Inverse logit L*	Modified inv. chi-squared Pm	p-values	Order of integration
covid19	121.7530	−4.9203	−4.4590	3.3009	0.0018	I(0)
emp	121.7530	−4.9203	−4.4590	3.3009	0.0000	I(0)
oophexp	121.7530	−4.9203	−4.4590	3.3009	0.0000	I(0)
produ	121.7530	−4.9203	−4.4590	3.3009	0.0000	I(0)

Source Author's computation from available data using STATA 13

economies in the study. For within-panel group, its observation (T) is 8, which corresponds with the time period (2020Q1–2021Q4) in each sampled SSA country. The mean score of covid19 cases is about 105,200.5 people, employment differential (emp) in SSA has a mean of about 60.07313 billion, that of out-of-pocket expenditure on health (oophexp) is about USD 35.37089 billion, while that of productivity (produ) is about USD 2368.512 billion.

In an effort to confirm the stationarity of the variables chosen for the model, the panel unit root test was also examined. The Augmented Dickey–Fuller (ADF) unit root test based Fisher-type panel unit-root test was used. Thus, the results of the panel unit root test can be seen as presented in Table 8.4.

The panel unit root test based on Fisher ADF strongly rejects the null hypothesis that all panels have unit roots, as shown by the results in Table 8.4. In all the variables under consideration, the inverse logit L∗ test and the inverse normal Z test are perfectly complementary in this regard. In addition to the aforementioned, the modified inverse $\neg\neg\chi^2$ Pm test and the inverse $\neg\chi^2$ P test both agree. Once more, given the 5% threshold of significance, the p-values for all the variables (covid19, emp, oophexp, and produ) show that they are all integrated of order zero, or I(0).

8.4.2 Presentation of the Panel Vector Autoregressive (PVAR) Model

The study adopted the Panel Vector Autoregressive (PVAR) model based on the Generalized Method of Moments (GMM) estimation technique to examine the nexus that exists among covid19, employment differential (emp), and health expenditure measured by out of pocket expenditure on health (oophexp), while controlling for productivity (produ) in SSA economies. The panel VAR model's summary results are displayed in Table 8.5.

This study investigated the nexus among the COVID-19 pandemic, employment differential and government health expenditure in SSA. In line with this, the study relied on each of the equations for COVID-19 pandemic, employment differential, health expenditure, and that of productivity for the interpretation of the results with

Table 8.5 Summary results of the panel VAR model

Variables	Coef	Std. Err	z	P > |z|
covid19				
covid19 L1.	0.8800614	0.3610935	2.44	0.015
emp L1.	−0.6312212	0.152737	−4.13	0.000
oophexp L1.	−0.5712123	0.2195059	−2.60	0.004
produ L1.	−0.8413143	0.3253340	−2.59	0.007
emp				
covid19 L1.	−0.5042391	0.1340755	−3.76	0.000
emp L1.	0.8800614	0.0892304	9.86	0.000
oophexp L1.	0.6341621	0.1948457	3.25	0.000
produ L1.	0.2012099	0.0901059	2.23	0.028
oophexp				
covid19 L1.	0.4202275	0.1660721	2.53	0.009
emp L1.	0.2916298	0.1046537	2.79	0.003
oophexp L1.	0.8800614	0.2847376	3.09	0.002
produ L1.	0.3012033	0.1001278	3.01	0.002
produ				
covid19 L1.	−0.2720265	0.1015064	−2.68	0.004
emp L1.	0.9063152	0.1316141	6.89	0.000
oophexp L1.	0.5314384	0.0954469	5.57	0.000
produ L1.	0.8800614	0.2266418	3.88	0.000

Source Authors

regard to ascertaining the nexus among COVID-19 pandemic, employment differential, health expenditure, and that of productivity as a control variable in SSA. This requires studying the single association between the covid-19 epidemic (covid19) and the study objective's relevant variables in each of the panel equations.

As a result, the analysis and interpretations of the variables of interest in the PVAR model for the study objective show that in Table 8.5, the COVID-19 pandemic (covid19) equation shows that the past uncontrolled influence of the COVID-19 pandemic (covid-19 L1.) in SSA countries has a positive significant effect on the current COVID-19 pandemic (covid19). The implication of this finding is that an unchecked increase in COVID-19 pandemic cases (covid-19 L1) in SSA economies would, on average, result in an increase in current COVID-19 pandemic cases (covid-19) of roughly 0.8800614 million. Therefore, there is a positive, significant association between the current covid-19 pandemic (covid-19) and the previously unchecked influence of the covid-19 pandemic (covid-19 L1.) in SSA nations.

Table 8.5 also suggests that in SSA countries, given the employment differential (emp) equation, covid-19 pandemic (covid-19) lag one (covid-19 L1) exerts a negative significant influence and/or effect on employment (emp) in SSA countries. The implication of this result is that with rising cases of covid-19 pandemic (covid-19), employment gap (emp) would widen and/or worsen in SSA countries on average by about 50.42391%. Hence, anytime covid-19 pandemic (covid-19) cases rise by a percentage, engagement of the people in productive and meaningful employment (emp) would fall significantly in SSA economies, due to the fact that people would be sick and as such, would be unable to make themselves available for work. This is also true as SSA countries have no reliable internet facilities, steady electricity supply, and other supporting mechanisms to work from home, especially for the services sector. Again, SSA economies are majorly primary and intermediate producers that rely heavily on primary production that requires individual employees to be physical at the workplace and not to work from home. Therefore, given the lockdown policy, social distancing, and other COVID-19 pandemic protocols that require people to work from home, rising cases of COVID-19 pandemic would definitely have a deleterious effect on employment in SSA economies. Therefore, there is an inverse significant correlation between the number of new cases of the covid-19 pandemic (covid-19 L1) in SSA countries and the level of employment at the time (emp).

With respect to health expenditure proxied by out-of-pocket expenditure on health (oophexp) equation, the results suggest that covid-19 pandemic (covid-19) lag one (covid-19 L1) exerts positive significant influence and/or effect on health expenditure measured by out-of-pocket expenditure on health (oophexp) in SSA countries. The implication of this finding is that an increase in the number of cases of the covid-19 pandemic (covid19) would result in about USD0.4202275 billion increase in out-of-pocket health spending in SSA countries. Hence, the more covid-19 pandemic cases are increasing, the more out-of-pocket expenditure on health (oophexp) rises as well. This research reveals a significant positive relationship between the current level of out-of-pocket health spending (oophexp) in SSA countries and the rising incidence of the covid-19 pandemic (covid-19 L1).

Table 8.6 Summary Results of the Panel VAR Stability Test

Eigenvalue		Modulus
Real	Imaginary	
0.8800614	0	0.8800614
0.8549579	0	0.8549579
0.8123850	0	0.8123850
0.2137801	0	0.2137801

All the eigenvalues lie inside the unit circle
pVAR satisfies stability condition
Source Author's computation from available data using STATA 13

Controlling for productivity, the study resorts to the productivity equation to find that covid-19 pandemic (covid-19) lag one (covid-19 L1) maintains an inverse significant effect and/or influence on productivity (produ) in SSA countries. This study has the implication that an increase in the number of covid-19 cases will result in about USD0.2720265 billion decline in productivity (produ) in SSA countries. Therefore, the higher the rising cases of covid-19 pandemic, the less productive (produ) SSA economies would become. This finding again suggests that rising cases of covid-19 pandemic (covid-19 L1.) have a negative significant connection with the current level of productivity (produ) in SSA countries.

8.4.2.1 Panel VAR Stability Test

According to Table 8.6's panel VAR stability test findings, all of the eigenvalues are less than one and as a result, all of them fall inside the unit circle. In line with this finding, the panel VAR satisfies the stability condition. Again, this stability condition is clearly presented in Fig. 8.1.

All of the Eigenvalues' roots are shown to be inside the unit circle in Fig. 8.1. As a result, it may be inferred that the panel VAR process is stationary and that the panel VAR stability test passes the stability criteria. This makes both the tabular and graphic representations to be in consonance with each other, thus showing that the panel VAR model adopted for the study passed the Eigenvalue stability test.

8.4.2.2 Panel VAR Impulse Response Function

The response of the COVID-19 pandemic to employment in SSA nations was examined using the orthogonalized panel VAR impulse response function (oirf). This can be seen as presented in Fig. 8.2.

Figure 8.2 demonstrates how the covid-19 pandemic (covid-19) responds to employment (emp) producing impulse by emitting large slow negative impacts from the first period up to the tenth period, at which point it decays. In other words, a one standard innovation in covid-19 pandemic (covid-19) produces significant negative

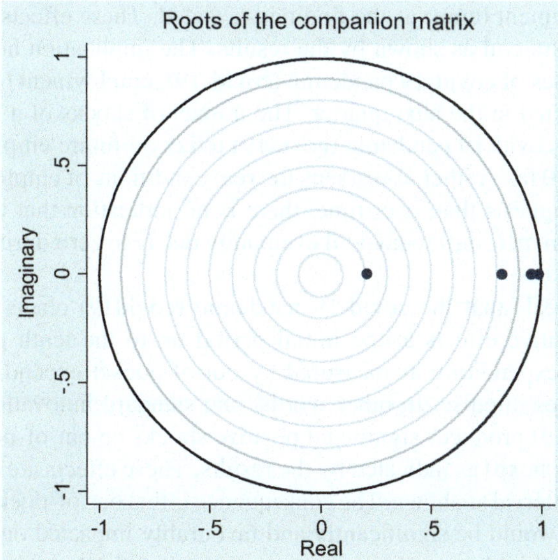

Fig. 8.1 Graph showing the panel VAR stability condition. *Source* Author's computation from available data using STATA 13

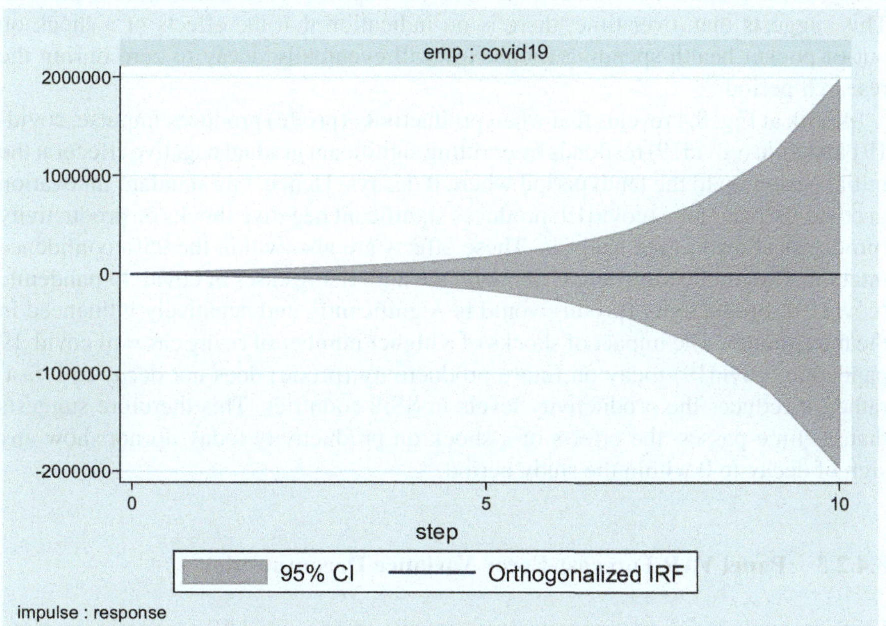

Fig. 8.2 Panel VAR impulse response function of employment and response of Covid-19 pandemic in SSA. *Source* Author's computation from available data using STATA 13

shocks on employment (emp) as the findings revealed. These effects are within the 95% confidence interval as shown by the results. The implication here is that with the high rising cases of covid-19 pandemic (covid-19), employment (emp) would be significantly affected in the next quarter. The impact of shocks of a higher number of rising cases of covid-19 pandemic (covid19) today on future employment (emp) does not decay to 0 fast, rather, it worsens the real conditions of employment in SSA countries. This suggests that, over time, there is no indication that the effects of a shock on employment (emp) today will eventually decay to zero during the research period.

Figure 8.3 reveals that the covid-19 pandemic (covid19) reacts by generating large gradual positive effects at the initial period up to the tenth period when it decays as health expenditure as measured by out-of-pocket expenditure on health (oophexp) provides impulse. In other words, one standard innovation in covid-19 pandemic (covid19) produces significant positive shocks on out-of-pocket expenditure on health (oophexp) as indicated by the results. These effects are also within the 95% confidence interval as shown. The consequence is that out-of-pocket spending on health (oophexp) would be significantly and favourably impacted on the upcoming quarter due to the highly growing instances of the covid-19 pandemic (covid19). The impact of shocks from the rising number of cases of the COVID-19 pandemic (covid19) today on future out-of-pocket health spending (oophexp) does not quickly decay to zero; rather, it worsens the level of oophexp conditions in SSA nations. This suggests that, over time, there is no indication that the effects of a shock on out-of-pocket health spending (oophexp) will eventually decay to zero during the research period.

A look at Fig. 8.4 reveals that when productivity (produ) produces impulse, covid-19 pandemic (covid19) responds by emitting significant gradual negative effects at the initial period up to the tenth period where it decays. Hence, one standard innovation in covid-19 pandemic (covid19) produces significant negative shocks on productivity (produ) as shown in the analysis. These effects are also within the 95% confidence interval. The implication here is that with the high rising cases of covid-19 pandemic (covid19), productivity (produ) would be significantly and negatively influenced in the next quarter. The impact of shocks of a higher number of rising cases of covid-19 pandemic (covid19) today on future productivity (produ) does not decay to 0 fast, rather, it reduces the productivity levels in SSA countries. This therefore suggests that, as time passes, the effects of a shock on productivity today do not show any sign of decay to 0 within the study period.

8.4.2.3 Panel VAR Forecast-Error Variance Decomposition

Since the study is poised to investigate the nexus among covid-19 pandemic, employment differential, and government health expenditure in SSA; it concentrates only on interpreting the response of covid-19 (covid19) variable and its forecast horizon in the panel VAR forecast-error variance decomposition table shown in Table 8.7 presented below.

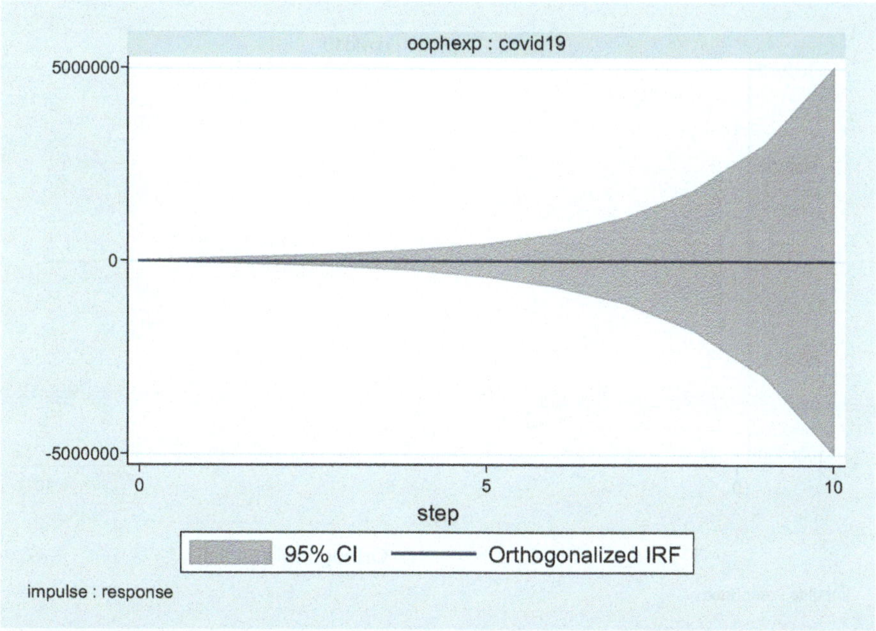

Fig. 8.3 Panel VAR impulse response function of health expenditure and response of Covid-19 pandemic in SSA. *Source* Author's computation from available data using STATA 13

How much of a shock and/or effect is being communicated to one variable, such as employment (emp), health expenditure (oophexp), and productivity (produ), by the covid-19 pandemic (covid19) in SSA economies are shown in Table 8.6, which presents the panel prediction error variance decomposition table results. The results show that 0%, 0.2373412%, 0.7263432%, 0.1413213%, and 0.2233453% of the variance in the forecast error of covid-19 pandemic (covid19) seems to be explained by a unit orthogonal shock in employment (emp) in the first, second, third, fourth and fifth horizons, respectively. However, a unit orthogonal shock in employment (emp) of SSA economies appears to be able to explain 0.3133399%, 0.4093387%, 0.5073283%, 0.6031933% and 0.6963318% of the variance in the forecast error of the covid-19 pandemic (covid19) from the sixth up to the tenth horizon.

In a similar vein, the results also indicated that 0%, 0.7472357%, 0.2293483%, 0.4433641%, and 0.7013249% of the variance in the forecast error of covid-19 pandemic (covid19) seems to be explained by a unit orthogonal shock in health expenditure (oophexp) in the first, second, third, fourth and fifth horizons, respectively. But, from the 6th up to the 10th horizon, 0.9883546%, 0.1293836%, 0.1603534%, 0.1903437% and 0.2193739% of the variance in the forecast error of covid-19 pandemic (covid19) seems to be explained by a unit orthogonal shock in health expenditure (oophexp) of SSA countries.

Again, it was shown by the results that about 0%, 0.4589934%, 0.1403138%, 0.2723936%, and 0.4306332% of the variance in the forecast error of covid-19

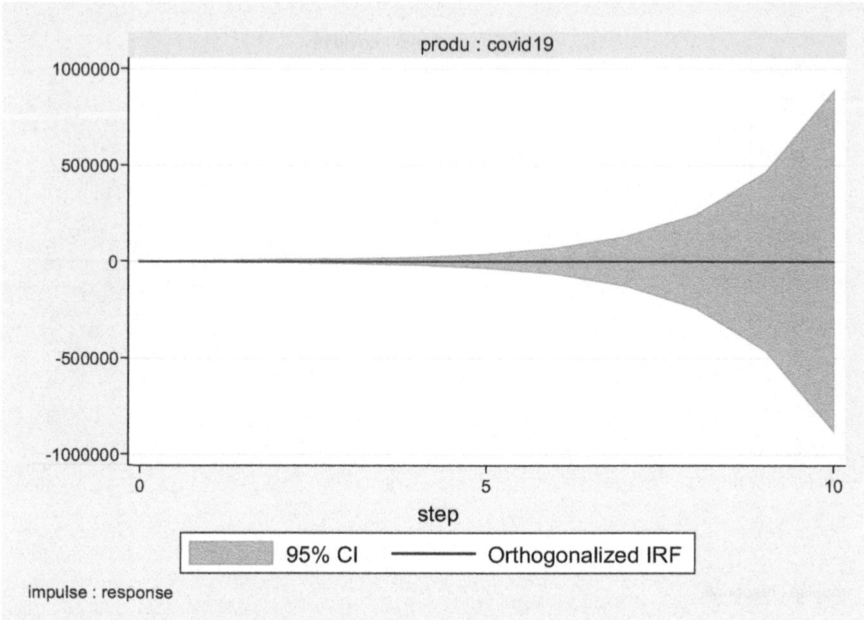

Fig. 8.4 Panel VAR impulse response function of productivity and response of Covid-19 pandemic in SSA. *Source* Author's computation from available data using STATA 13

Table 8.7 Summary results of the panel VAR forecast-error variance decomposition

Response variable and forecast horizon	Impulse variable			
	covid19	emp	oophexp	produ
covid19				
0	0	0	0	0
1	1	0	0	0
2	0.8505152	0.2373412	0.7472357	0.4589934
3	0.8505151	0.7263432	0.2293483	0.1403138
4	0.8406150	0.1413213	0.4433641	0.2723936
5	0.8305123	0.2233453	0.7013249	0.4306332
6	0.8215244	0.3133399	0.9883546	0.6063435
7	0.8201211	0.4093387	0.1293836	0.7923735
8	0.8103290	0.5073283	0.1603534	0.9803239
9	0.8101331	0.6031933	0.1903437	0.1173927
10	0.8004125	0.6963318	0.2193739	0.1359362

Source Author's computation from available data using STATA 13

pandemic (covid19) seems to be explained by a unit orthogonal shock in the productivity (produ) level of SSA countries in the first, second, third, fourth and fifth horizons respectively. However, from the 6th up to the 10th horizon, 0.6063435, 0.7923735, 0.9803239, 0.1173927 and 0.1359362% of the variance in the forecast error of covid-19 pandemic (covid19) seems to be explained by a unit orthogonal shock in the productivity (produ) level of SSA countries.

8.5 Conclusion and Policy Recommendations

The study investigated the nexus among covid-19 pandemic, employment differential and government health expenditure in SSA using the panel vector autoregressive (PVAR) model and panel VAR—impulse response function (PVAR-IRF), and high-frequency time series data obtained from 40 SSA countries from 2020Q1 to 2021Q4. The panel VAR model's empirical results showed that an unchecked increase in COVID-19 pandemic cases in SSA economies would, on average, result in about 0.8800614 million significant increases in the number of current cases of COVID-19 pandemic; additionally, with rising cases of COVID-19 pandemic, the employment gap would, on average, widen and/or worsen in SSA countries by about 50.42391%; and finally, an increase in cases of COVID-19 pandemic.

Again, from the panel VAR—impulse response function, the empirical evidence revealed that when employment produces impulse, covid-19 pandemic responds by emitting significant gradual negative effects at the initial period up to the tenth period where it decays, when health expenditure measured by out-of-pocket expenditure on health produces impulse, covid-19 pandemic responds by emitting significant gradual positive effects at the initial period up to the tenth period where it decays, and that when productivity produces impulse, covid-19 pandemic responds by emitting significant gradual negative effects at the initial period up to the tenth period where it decays. The study recommends however from its empirical findings that:

1. Sub-Sahara African governments need to look out for and explore their peculiarities in the containment of the spread of covid-19, since the study found that covid-19 exerts a negative significant influence and/or effect on employment in SSA countries, given the fact that SSA economies are the primary and intermediate producers, and this does not encourage working from home.
2. Since it was found that rising cases of covid-19 pandemic has a positive significant link with the current level of out-of-pocket expenditure on health, Sub-Saharan Africans need to also look inward towards exploring their abundant natural resources, potentials, and experts in African medicine towards the manufacturing/production of covid-19 vaccine and its total cure. This would allow SSA countries to save some foreign exchanges spent on COVID-19 vaccines, generate more income for the sub-region, and fast-track sustained economic growth and development which Africa craves for.

3. Governments in SSA should as a matter of urgency explore other policy options other than the lockdown policy, since the study revealed that rising cases of covid-19 pandemic have negative significant connection with the current level of productivity in the sub-region. Lockdown policy is not the best option for SSA since the sub-region is majorly dependent on agriculture and as such, are primary and intermediate producers, which may not require locking down the economy due to poverty and hunger.
4. Sub-Saharan governments should as a matter of urgency, encourage the employment of both human (through youth employment specifically) and material resources in the sub-region. Government should encourage a more conducive and favourable business climate in the sub-region through increased infrastructural provision, enhancing the capacities and skills of micro, small, and medium enterprises, and support/encouragement of informal sector businesses. These would definitely increase productivity levels, and fast-track sustainable economic growth and development the sub-region is yearning for.

References

1. Africa CDC (2021) Outbreak brief 52: coronavirus disease 2019 (COVID-19) pandemic. Africa CDC. Last Accessed 18 Jan 2021
2. Africa News (2020) Coronavirus in Africa. https://www.africanews.com/2020/04/04/coronavirus-hub-impact-of-outbreak-across-africa//. https://www.africanews.com/2020/04/04/coronavirus-in-africa-breakdown-of-infected-virus-free-countries/
3. African Economic Outlook (2021) From debt resolution to growth: the road ahead for Africa. African Development Bank
4. African Union (2020) Impact of the coronavirus (COVID-19) on the African economy. African Union Commission. https://www.tralac.org/news/article/14483-impact-of-the-coronavirus-covid-19-on-the-african-economy.html
5. Asogwa HT, Ezenekwe UR, Ukwueze ER, Iwuamadi KC (2021) Impact of Public Health Strengthening Mechanism on Outcome Among Selected African Countries: Implication on Outbreak in Fragile SSA Countries. J Adv Res Soc Sci Humanit (ISSN: 2208–2387), 7(2):01–15
6. Buheji M, Cunha KC, Beka G, Mavrić B, Souza YL, Silva SS, Hanafi M, Yein TC (2020) The extent of COVID-19 Pandemic socio-economic impact on global poverty: A global integrative multidisciplinary review. Am J Econ 10(4):213–224
7. Chakraborty I, Maity P (2020) COVID-19 outbreak: Migration, effects on society, global environment and prevention. Sci Total Environ 728:138882. https://doi.org/10.1016/j.scitotenv.2020.138882
8. Chitungo I, Dzobo M, Hlongwa M, Dzinamarira T (2020) COVID-19: unpacking the low number of cases in Africa. Public Health Pract 1:100038. https://doi.org/10.1016/j.puhip.2020.100038
9. Chowdhury A, Sundaram JK (2020) Reviving the economy, creating the 'New Normal'. http://www.ipsnews.net/2020/06/reviving-economy-creating-new-normal/
10. Dafuleya G (2020) Social and emergency assistance ex-ante and during COVID-19 in the SADC region. Int J Community Soc Dev 2(2):251–268. https://doi.org/10.1177/2516602620936028
11. Dixon J (2016) Social welfare in Africa. Routledge, Abingdon
12. Du Toit A (2020) Outbreak of a novel coronavirus. Nat Rev Microbiol 18(3):123. https://doi.org/10.1038/s41579-020-0332-0

13. Fernandes N (2020) Economic effects of coronavirus outbreak (COVID-19) on the world economy. IESE Business School, Spain. https://papers.ssrn.com/sol3/papers.cfm?abstract_id=3557504
14. Hargreaves JR, Logie CH (2020) Lifting lockdown policies: a critical moment for COVID-19 stigma. Glob Public Health 15(12):1917–1923. https://doi.org/10.1080/17441692.2020.182577
15. International Labor Organization (2020a) Financing gaps in social protection: global estimates and strategies for developing countries in light of the COVID-19 crisis and beyond. ILO brief: social protection spotlight. https://www.ilo.org/secsoc/information-resources/publications-and-tools/Brochures/WCMS_755475/lang--en/index.htm
16. International Labor Organization (2020b) COVID-19 and the world of work. Updated estimates and analysis. ILO monitor. https://www.ilo.org/wcmsp5/groups/public/---dgreports/---dcomm/documents/briefingnote/wcms_743146.pdf
17. International Labour Organization (ILO) (2018) World employment and social outlook: trends for women 2018-global snapshot. International Labour Organization, Geneva. https://www.ilo.org/global/research/globalreports/weso/trends-for-women2018/WCMS_619577/lang--en/index.htm
18. International Labour Organization (ILO) (2020c) Extending social protection to informal workers in the COVID-19 crisis. country responses and policy considerations
19. Johnson AF, Roberto KJ (2020) The COVID-19 pandemic: time for a universal basic income? Public Adm Dev 40(4):232–235
20. Lucero-Prisno DE, Adebisi YA, Lin X (2020) Current efforts and challenges facing responses to 2019-nCoV in Africa. Glob Health Res Policy 5(1):1–3
21. Muhammad LJ, Haruna AA, Sharif US, Mohammed MB (2022) CNN-LSTM deep learning based forecasting model for COVID-19 infection cases in Nigeria, South Africa and Botswana. Health Technol 12:1259–1276. https://doi.org/10.1007/s12553-022-00711-5
22. Njenga MK, Dawa J, Nanyingi M, Gachohi J, Ngere I, Letko M, Otieno CF, Gunn BM, Osoro E (2020) Why is there low morbidity and mortality of COVID-19 in Africa? Am J Trop Med Hyg 103(2):564–569. https://doi.org/10.4269/ajtmh.20-0474
23. Nyakubaya L (2020) Emerging infections: The world is not safe until countries invest in public health infrastructure. A closer look at Sub Saharan Africa (SSA) public health infrastructure during COVID-19 pandemic
24. Oksuz E, Malhan S, Gonen MS, Kutlubay Z, Keskindemirci Y, Tabak F (2021) COVID-19 healthcare cost and length of hospital stay in Turkey: retrospective analysis from the first peak of the pandemic. Heal Econ Rev 11(1):1–12
25. Organization for Economic Co-operation and Development (OECD) (2020) Evaluating the initial impact of COVID-19 containment measures on economic activity. http://www.oecd.org/coronavirus/policy-responses/evaluating-the-initial-impact-of-covid19-containment-measures-on-economic-activity-b1f6b68b/
26. Ossome L (2020) The care economy and the state in Africa's COVID-19 responses. Can J Dev Stud 42(1–2):68–78
27. Shabir AL, Aijaz A (2020) COVID-19 pandemic–an African perspective. Emerg Microbes Infect 9(1):1300–1308. https://doi.org/10.1080/22221751.2020.1775132
28. Shereen MA, Khan S, Kazmi A, Bashir N, Siddique R (2020) COVID-19 infection: origin, transmission, and characteristics of human coronaviruses. J Adv Res 24:91–98. https://doi.org/10.1016/j.jare.2020.03.005
29. UNCTAD (2019) Economic development in Africa report 2019. https://unctad.org/webflyer/economic-development-africa-report-2019
30. United Nations (2020) Impact of COVID-19 in Africa. Policy brief. https://www.uneca.org/publications/policy-brief-impact-covid-19-africa
31. United Nations Development Programme (UNDP) (2020) COVID-19 pandemic. Humanity needs leadership and Solidarity to defeat the Coronavirus. https://www.undp.org/content/undp/en/home/coronavirus.html. Last Accessed 26 Oct 2020

32. World Health Organization (WHO) (2019) World health statistics 2019: monitoring health for the SDGs, sustainable development goals. World Health Organization. https://apps.who.int/iris/bitstream/handle/10665/324835/9789241565707eng.pdf?sequence=9&isAllowed=y
33. World Health Organization (2020) WHO coronavirus disease (COVID-19) dashboard. https://covid19.who.int/
34. World Bank (2020b) COVID-19 to plunge global economy into worst recession since World War II (2020). https://www.worldbank.org/en/news/pressrelease/2020/06/08/covid-19-to-plunge-global-economy-into-worst-recessionsince-world-war-ii. Last Accessed 26 May 2021
35. World Bank (2020c) Global economic prospects, June 2020. Washington, D.C.
36. World Bank (2021) World development indicators. The World Bank Group
37. Worldometer (2022) Worldometer's COVID-19 data. Worldometers Pubs. https://www.worldometers.info/coronavirus/country/Nigeria

Chapter 9
Impact of Foreign Trade and COVID-19 Pandemic on Sri Lankan and Indian Economy: A Comparative Study

Susobhan Maiti and Tanushree Gupta

9.1 Introduction

The Indian economy was impacted particularly hard by COVID-19 and the shutdown was imposed as a precautionary measure. Prior to the pandemic, trade results had not been encouraging and were actually declining relative to the earlier time periods [14]. The onset of COVID-19 was having the same depressing effect on the Sri Lankan economy. Since its independence, Sri Lanka has kept close diplomatic and economic connections to China. During the recent decade, Sri Lanka and China have made great strides in their bilateral economic ties. As a result, China's economic downturn due to COVID-19 may have serious consequences for Sri Lanka [4]. Interruption of international trade is one way in which many countries have been impacted by COVID-19. Since trade is vital to Sri Lanka's small open economy, exports and imports together accounted for 53% of GDP last year. Consequently, supply chain disruptions and a worldwide decline in demand for Sri Lankan exports had an immediate impact. Furthermore, Sri Lanka's imports have exceeded exports over time, worsening the country's trade balance. Exports cover roughly half of the country's imports, while the rest must be funded by foreign remittances and profits from tourism, both of which have been adversely impacted by the spread of COVID-19 [3].

The COVID-19 pandemic has devastated lives, the global economy, and international trade. The epidemic may hurt international trade. The COVID-19 epidemic has disrupted global trade, affecting both supply and demand. The pandemic has slowed international commerce projects worldwide as states focus on the issue [11]. COVID-19 is expected to reduce global logistics gross profit by 6.1%. At worst, 2020

S. Maiti (✉)
Department of Economics, School of Humanities and Social Sciences, JAIN (Deemed-to-be University), Bangalore, India
e-mail: susobhaneco@gmail.com

T. Gupta
School of Commerce and Management Studies, Sandip University, Nashik, Maharashtra, India

R. Bhattacharyya et al. (eds.), *COVID-19 Pandemic and Global Inequality*,
https://doi.org/10.1007/978-981-99-4405-7_9

will see a 7.5% drop in global freight forwarding [36] affecting the economy's reaction to these shocks of uncertainty, which, when slow growth causes a recession, has a negative impact on employment, debt levels, and investment [22]. The worldwide economy has been profoundly affected by the COVID-19 outbreak over the past two years [40]. Cross-border restrictions, port closures, and other logistical issues hurt international trade, which contributed to the worldwide demand drop that caused this severe depression [17]. But earlier predictions of a double-digit contraction in global trade proved to be excessively pessimistic, as global trade had already begun to rebound by the second half of 2020. It is inevitable that the unprecedented public health crisis caused by the current global pandemic of COVID-19 will have far-reaching, negative effects on the global economy, the environment, and international economic and trade cooperation.

This epidemic has had a significant impact on the economy, particularly on major income-generating sectors like agriculture, tourism, the garment and textile industries, and small and medium-sized businesses. Sri Lanka's overall tea export earnings were USD 347.3 million in 2019, down from USD 270.1 million in the first three months of 2020 [34]. Tourism in Sri Lanka and India has been severely impacted by the COVID-19 pandemic, with record low numbers of foreign visitors. Airlines, hotels, travel agencies, tourist stores, etc. have all begun laying off temporary and casual workers, have halted compensation increases, and in some cases have even begun lowering salaries by varying percentages depending on the employee's salary level. Moreover, Sri Lanka's economy became increasingly vulnerable to exogenous shocks like the COVID-19 outbreak because of the twin deficits phenomena, which exacerbated the country's reliance on foreign debt. Government spending in Sri Lanka rose throughout the pandemic period alongside global spending trends, while tax cuts implemented just before the epidemic reduced tax receipts by significant amounts, increasing fiscal deficits and their associated current account deficits [7].

South Asia is one of the world's least economically linked areas despite its closeness to China and India and the existence of bilateral and multilateral free trade agreements (FTAs). Intra-regional trade in South Asia is only 5% of the region's worldwide trade, significantly below its potential due to protectionist policies, high logistics costs, a lack of political will, and a broader trust gap. When compared to East Asia and the Pacific, where intra-regional trade accounts for about 50% of total trade, and Sub-Saharan Africa, where intra-regional trade has improved over the years to 22% thanks to the steps taken by governments to create transparent mechanisms for trade facilitation [12, 16]. The present research is based on two countries that are Sri Lanka and India considering time series analysis. Sri Lanka confronts its biggest economic disaster. The lowest labour force participation rate is in India in 2022, with slowed GDP.

9.2 Background Underpinning

9.2.1 COVID-19 Pandemic and Sri Lanka

International trade disruptions are one way that COVID-19 has had an impact on several nations. Due to its small size and open economy, Sri Lanka depends on commerce; in 2018, exports and imports made up 53% of the country's GDP. As a result, the disruptions to the supply chain and the decline in demand for Sri Lanka's goods and services globally harmed exports in the short term [42]. India is Sri Lanka's top export market, followed by the EU and US, which each receive 33 and 25% of its exports. India and China contributed 21 and 20% of Sri Lanka's total imports in 2017, respectively [32]. The highly potent export markets and goods of Sri Lanka have not improved the issue [31]. The economic performance has had an influence on Sri Lanka's export revenues as well as the country's export capability. Additionally, Sri Lanka's imports have steadily outpaced its exports over time, resulting in a worsening trade deficit; exports only cover roughly half of imports, leaving the other half to be paid by foreign remittances and tourism revenues, both of which have been badly impacted by COVID-19 [42].

The apparel and textile industry, which contributes significantly to national exports, is one of the most negatively impacted industries in Sri Lanka [30] as a result of the drop in demand in its key markets, the US and EU, as well as disruptions in the supply of raw materials and production as a result of the island-wide lockdown, which has since been lifted [42]. Buyers were cancelling contracts, refusing to accept shipments, and unilaterally extending the payment terms, in addition to the supply and production interruptions, which had a negative impact on businesses cash flow and their capacity to pay suppliers and employees, particularly SMEs. While some employees in the garment sector have seen compensation reductions as a result of the loss of incentives, bonuses, attendance payments, and overtime [19], others have lost their positions in the sector. Competitor nations like Vietnam and Cambodia continued to operate while Sri Lankan plants were shut down, which harmed the sector because new orders were made with them [42]. The pandemic also had a significant influence on the export of goods like tea, coconut, rubber, spices, and food and beverages. In comparison to last year, total exports decreased by 26% in the first half of 2020 [42].

9.2.2 COVID-19 Pandemic and India

After the Great Depression of the 1930s, the COVID-19 epidemic has likely dealt the world economy its biggest hit. India was forced to implement the lockdown policy because of its dense population and poor access to medical care. India is not an exception to the global economic downturn [35]. The COVID-19 epidemic and China's manufacturing slowdown have had a $348 million trade impact on India, making it one of the 15 most severely impacted economies. Chemicals, with a trade impact of $129 million for India, followed by textiles and apparel, $64 million, the automotive industry, $34 million, electrical machinery, $13 million, leather items, $27 million in metals and metal products, and wood goods and furniture, $15 million [38]. The impact on India's exports was anticipated to be $348 million, or roughly 0.1% of the country's total goods exports in FY19. The sector of chemicals was expected to have been most negatively impacted, accounting for 36.8% of the overall loss in exports, followed by textile and clothing at 18.4% and automotive at 9.8% [5].

9.2.3 Why Compare India and Sri Lanka?

There are distinct economic difficulties in Sri Lanka and India from one. While Sri Lanka has been on the decline, India is in a much better position to address global concerns. According to the World Bank, Sri Lanka was a model for developing market economies and experienced an average growth of 6.2% between 2010 and 2016 before declining to 3.1% during the following three years. The World Bank now expects the economy to expand by 2.4% this year, down from 3.5% in 2021. But it has stated that the future is rather uncertain. India, on the other hand, has made a strong recovery from its economic recession and is expected to develop the quickest among big economies. India's growth is forecast by the International Monetary Fund to be 8.2% in 2023. The World Bank anticipates 8% growth. The Reserve Bank of India revised its earlier estimate of 7.8% economic growth downward to 7.2% [38].

According to the most recent figures, Sri Lanka's inflation reached a record high in April and has now reached record levels six times in a row. The cost of imported goods is increasing in India. The inflation rate is considerably lower than in Sri Lanka, nevertheless. Additionally, according to the finance ministry, Sri Lanka only has $25 million in usable foreign reserves at the moment, and its overall debt is $51 billion. Although the foreign reserve has decreased in India over the previous several months as well, it is still far bigger than in Sri Lanka. In the six months leading up to March 2022, the foreign exchange reserve decreased by $ 28.05 billion. Despite import limits on non-essential items, the global bank reports that the trade deficit widened in 2020 as a higher import bill offset a rise in export revenues. Currently, Sri Lanka has a fiscal deficit. India's budget deficit is lower than Sri Lanka's [39].

9.3 Literature Review

Foreign trade is very important for the development of any country and when the country is in the group of middle-income countries then foreign trade plays an important role. There are positive effects of export performance on economic growth, including increased specialisation and spill over effects of the export sector's growth, higher capacity utilisation, the externality effect of exports in the diffusion of modern technology across other sectors and industries, and the multiplier effects of economies of scale, industrialisation, and import of capital goods [10]. Development economists have taken a keen interest in the correlation between export growth and GDP expansion in recent years [26, 41].

Being in the same low-income bracket, Sri Lanka and India can both benefit greatly from exports. A 2001 study reveals that low-income nations are making strong efforts to diversify their domestic economy and open doors to global trade and foreign investments, but that they remain less competitive internationally due to persistent political unrest and a history of inward-oriented policies [41]. A high export growth rate has several immediate benefits that boost economic growth [22]. A country can increase imports when exports rise. These imports include capital items, which are crucial to economic progress [26]. The country can buy items from overseas at lower costs by taking advantage of the international division of labour [8, 13, 21]. Competitive pressures also increase export product quality and prevent inefficient export industries from forming [8].

At present, it is widely accepted that India's rising exports are principally responsible for the country's impressive economic development. The rise of India's export sector and the country's increased access to advanced technologies are major contributors to the country's economic prosperity [29]. Exports imply access to a global market and allow for increasing output, trade promotes efficient resource allocation, and trade helps economic growth by creating long-run advantages [27]. The implications of these findings for policy aimed at promoting economic growth in the future are significant.

The import and economic growth around the world from 1962 to 2011 were studied by [37]. To test for the existence of a direct long-run link, an indirect long-run relationship, and an impulse, response function between export and import and economic growth, import variables play a central role in the examination of economic growth output co-integration analysis. The data did support a long-term connection between the factors studied. Long-term economic growth was positively related to imports, as shown. Further, imports significantly and negatively correlated with GDP growth, suggesting that they dampened GDP expansion in the long run. It was also observed by researchers that a shock on imports positively affected GDP growth, but that a shock on imports due to an erroneous term had no discernible impact on GDP growth. As a result of increased competition from imports, domestic manufacturers will be compelled to develop new technologies and improve operational efficiencies which means imports contribute to economic expansion. Those countries still in the process of economic growth greatly benefit from the import of capital goods because of their reliance on foreign capital [24, 43].

9.4 Objectives

The initial goal in this chapter is to measure exports, imports, and GDP growth in two countries. Side by side to determine the relationship between trade-related factors, economic growth, unemployment, and net foreign direct investment. Second, to determine the unidirectional or bidirectional causality of export, import, unemployment rate, net foreign direct investment, and proxy of economic growth in the two nations.

9.5 Methodology and Data Source

9.5.1 Data and Variables

In the present study, five variables are used, i.e., export of goods and services (X), import of goods and services (M), Real Gross Domestic Product (GDP) used as the proxy for economic growth, Unemployment rate (UNE) and Net Foreign Direct Investment (NFDI) have been used. The study is based on time-series data from 1991 to 2022 for two countries, i.e., India and Sri Lanka, collected from World Development Indicators (WDI) published by the World Bank.

9.5.2 Methodology

To understand the linkage between variables, two methods have been used which are as under:

1. Karl Pearson's correlation coefficient and
2. Granger Causality Test

The Pearson product-moment correlation coefficient, generally denoted by r is a measure of the correlation, i.e., linear dependence between two variables X and Y.

The formula for r is

$$r = \frac{\sum_{i=1}^{n} (X_i - \overline{X})(Y_i - \overline{Y})}{\sqrt{\sum_{i=1}^{n} (X_i - \overline{X})^2}\sqrt{\sum_{i=1}^{n} (Y_i - \overline{Y})^2}}$$

where n is the sample size.

A common practice prior to handling time series data and for performing a co-integration test is to determine the stationarity of the series or its degree of integration, I(d). For this Augmented-Dickey–Fuller (ADF) Unit Root Test [6] has been used. It is essential to keep in mind that these tests presuppose the absence of any structural breaks [12].

The present study uses the ADF unit root test to examine the stationarity of the data series. It consists of running a regression of the first difference of the series against the series lagged once, a constant and a time trend. This can be expressed as follows:

$$\Delta Y_t = \alpha_0 + \alpha_1 t + \alpha_2 Y_{t-1} + \sum_{j=1}^{p} \alpha_j \Delta Y_{t-j} + \varepsilon_t$$

The test for a unit root is performed on the coefficient of Yt-1 in the regression in this ADF process. If the coefficient deviates considerably from zero, the hypothesis that Yt has a unit root is rejected. Stationarity is implied by rejecting the null hypothesis [6]

H_0: $\alpha_2 = 0$ i.e., Y_t is a non-stationary series.

H_1: $\alpha_2 < 0$ i.e., Y_t is a stationary series.

The null hypothesis, H0, is accepted and the series is considered nonstationary or not integrated of order zero, I, if the estimated value of the ADF statistic is greater than McKinnon's critical values [9]. If this fails, more differencing must be carried out until stationarity is obtained and the null hypothesis is rejected [1].

To determine whether or not one time period can be helpful in forecasting another, a statistical hypothesis test that can be called the Granger causality test is performed [12]. It is claimed that a time series X is a Granger cause of another time series Y if it can be shown that the values of the time series X convey statistically significant information about the values of Y in the future [2]. The examination is carried out in the following way:

Let y and x be stationary time series.

The null hypothesis is H_0: X does not Granger-cause Y,

The following regression should be used to determine the correct value to use for Y after it has been lagged:

This is the limited model that must be purchased in order to receive SSRR.

The next step is to strengthen the autoregression by including the lag values of x, as shown in the following equation:

$$y_t = a_0 + a_1 y_{t-1} + a_2 y_{t-2} + \cdots + a_m y_{t-m} + b_p x_{t-p} + \cdots + b_q x_{t-q} + residual_t$$

This is the model that does not have any restrictions for obtaining Sum square residual unrestricted (SSRUR).

The following serves as the test statistic in order to put the hypothesis to the test: $F = ((SSR_R\text{-}SSR_{UR})/c)/SSR_{UR}/(n\text{-}l)$.

where c represents the number of lagging terms that were taken, n represents the sample size, and l is the number of parameters that were estimated using the unconstrained equation.

If there are no lagged values of x that are kept in the regression, and then one may accept the null hypothesis that x does not Granger-cause y. This is the only condition under which this hypothesis can be accepted [2, 12].

Johansen Cointegration Test

The Johansen test tests cointegrating relationships between several non-stationary time series data. Compared to the Engle–Granger test, the Johansen test allows for more than one cointegrating relationship. However, it is subject to asymptotic properties (large sample size) since a small sample size would produce unreliable results. Using the test to find the cointegration of several time series avoids the issues created when errors are carried forward to the next step. Johansen's test comes in two main forms, i.e., Trace tests and Maximum Eigenvalue tests.

9.6 Analysis of Results and Discussion

There is a fluctuating pattern in the growth of GDP, exports, imports, NFDI and UNE. Since the COVID-19 epidemic broke out, the world's economy has taken a serious hit. The World Trade Organization (WTO) predicted that global trade would contract by 12.9% in 2020. And it has had a devastating impact on countries across the globe, including those in the South Asian region (Wei et al., 2021). Analyzing the growth tendency between 2020 and 2021 is critical in this context. Nevertheless, the COVID-19 pandemic resulted in a decline in GDP, export, import, NFDI growth and an increase in the unemployment rate for both India and Sri Lanka. In 2020, the growth rate of GDP is −6.7% in India but it is more in Sri Lanka (−3.62%), growth of export is −9.24% in India; whereas, it is −9.71% in Sri Lanka but decrease in the growth rate of import in India (−13.81%) is more than Sri Lanka (−11.42%). The result also indicates that the unemployment rate in India (8%) is more than in Sri Lanka (5.88%) during this period. We found one interesting finding in the case of NFDI, where the growth rate of NFDI in India is positive (42.09%) during this period, but it is negative in Sri Lanka (−37.50%) though the growth rate of NFDI in 2021 is negative in India (−45.18%) (Source: Author's calculation).

The relationship between GDP, export, imports, UNE and NFDI of India and Sri Lanka have been analyzed with the help of the coefficient of correlation. As a result, the Pearson correlation coefficient is used to investigate the relationship between these variables, as presented in Table 9.1. There is a high positive degree of association between GDP and X, and GDP and M, for both countries, which is significant at the 0.01 level of significance. Table 9.1 shows a negative and significant correlation between GDP, UNE, and GDP and NFDI for India and Sri Lanka. In addition, Table 9.1 represents the relationship between X and M, X and UNE, and X and NFDI. There's also a strong and positive correlation that's significant at the 0.001 level of confidence exist between X and M but significant negative relation is found between X and UNE, and X and NFDI for India and Sri Lanka. The correlation table depicts that there is a positive correlation between UNE and M in India, but it is negative in Sri Lanka. Table 9.1 indicates there is a significant negative correlation prevails between NFDI and M. NFDI and UNE is negatively correlated in India but positively related in Sri Lanka.

The regression was run with intercept and trend for GDP, Export, Import unemployment rate and NFDI series of two countries in level and for the first difference with intercept. For the ADF test, the optimum lag is selected based on Schwartz Information Criterion (0–4 lags). It is found that the null hypotheses of unit roots cannot be rejected at conventional significance levels. Therefore, all the series are non-stationary in level but are stationary in first difference. Therefore, all the series are integrated into the first difference. The result of the ADF Unit root is presented in Table 9.2.

Generally, Granger causality test has been undertaken to assess the causal relationship between two variables. It assists in examining the correlation patterns by using the empirical database [23]. Here in the present study, Granger causality is employed to verify whether there is any causal relationship between the variables for both countries, which is presented in Table 9.3. In the case of India and Sri Lanka, the link between X and GDP is characterised by a unidirectional Granger causation relationship. The results support the export-led growth which may be due to the fact that an increase in export i.e. increasing demand in the foreign market which is backed by domestic production leads increase in production as well as income [20]. In the case of India, there is no causal link between M and GDP which may be due to the smaller percentage share of import to GDP,but in the case of Sri Lanka, there is an existing causal relationship from M to GDP may be due to the more share of M to GDP in one hand, on the other hand import helps to enhance efficiency of domestic producer through technological diffusion [25]. In India, the UNE and GDP have a causation link that runs in both directions which is justified by and same line to Okun's law, from UNE to GDP and from GDP to UNE [15]. However, in Sri Lanka, there is no such relationship between these two variables. In India, there is a causation that runs in both directions between NFDI and GDP, on one hand NFDI works as the engine of economic growth on the other hand growing GDP attracts more NFDI inflow which may be due to the greater expected return however, in Sri Lanka, the flow of causality is only in one direction, from NFDI to GDP which may be justified by the engine of economic growth concept acted by NFDI.

The results of the cointegration test for India and Sri Lanka are given in Table 9.4, which shows that at the 0.05 level, there are three cointegrating equations. The variables in the equation are GDP, X, M, UNE, and NFDI. The finding also suggests a long-run link between X and GDP, as well as NFDI and GDP, for both nations. Additionally, the finding suggests a long-run relationship between UNE and GDP in India, and a long-run relationship between M and GDP in Sri Lanka.

Table 9.1 Pearson correlation coefficient of variables for India and Sri Lanka

	India	Sri Lanka	India	Sri Lanka	India	Sri Lanka	India	Sri Lanka	India	Sri Lanka
Variables	GDP		X		M		UNE		NFDI	
GDP	1	1								
X	0.978**	0.974**	1	1						
M	0.971**	0.989**	0.995**	0.981**	1	1				
UNE	−0.908**	−0.865**	−0.727**	−0.911**	0.719**	−0.884**	1	1		
NFDI	−0.927**	−0.846**	−0.901**	−0.827**	−0.886**	−0.869**	−0.676**	0.770**	1	1

Source Author's calculations
*** Correlation is significant at the 0.01 level (2-tailed)*

Table 9.2 ADF unit root test of variables for India

	India	Sri Lanka	India/Sri Lanka	India	Sri Lanka	India/Sri Lanka	India/Sri Lanka
Variables	In levels		Result	In first difference		Result	Conclusion
GDP	1.96	1.19	Do not reject H_0	−4.67***	-3.74***	Reject H_0	I (1)
X	0.49	−0.37	Do not reject H_0	−5.08***	−8.82***	Reject H_0	I (1)
M	0.33	−0.39	Do not reject H_0	−4.86***	−5.26***	Reject H_0	I (1)
UNE	0.29	−2.74	Do not reject H_0	−4.83***	−4.56***	Reject H_0	I (1)
NFDI	−0.36	−0.82	Do not reject H_0	−7.49***	−7.10***	Reject H_0	I (1)

Source Author's calculations
***, **, * Represents statistical significance of 1%, 5% and 10% respectively

Table 9.3 Result of granger causality test of variables for India and Sri Lanka

	India		Sri Lanka	
Null Hypothesis	F-Statistic	Prob.	F-Statistic	Prob.
X does not Granger Cause GDP	6.14	0.00	4.67	0.01
GDP does not Granger Cause X	0.79	0.57	0.13	0.94
M does not Granger Cause GDP	0.66	0.53	3.71	0.03
GDP does not Granger Cause M	1.97	0.16	0.85	0.48
UNE does not Granger Cause GDP	6.80	0.00	0.96	0.43
GDP does not Granger Cause UNE	3.93	0.03	1.25	0.32
NFDI does not Granger Cause GDP	4.76	0.01	5.13	0.01
GDP does not Granger Cause NFDI	4.38	0.01	0.99	0.42

Source Author's calculation

Table 9.4 Result of cointegration test of variables for India and Sri Lanka

	India		Sri Lanka	
Hypothesised No. of CE(s)	Trace statistic	Prob.	Trace statistic	Prob.
None	118.87	0	116.50	0
At most 1	66.30	0	54.48	0.01
At most 2	33.75	0.02	24.32	0.19
At most 3	11.04	0.21	7.97	0.47
At most 4	0.10	0.75	0.26	0.61

Source Author's calculation

9.7 Conclusion and Recommendations

From 1991 through 2022, this study examined export, import, unemployment, net foreign direct investment, and economic growth in India and Sri Lanka. Correlation coefficients showed substantial relationships between India and Sri Lanka's exports, imports, unemployment rate, net foreign direct investment, and GDP. According to the Granger causality conclusion, there are unidirectional and bidirectional causal linkages between these variables. In the case of India and Sri Lanka, the link between X and GDP is characterised by a unidirectional Granger causation relationship. In the case of India, there is no causal link between M and GDP; but in the case of Sri Lanka, there is an existing causal relationship from M to GDP. In India, the UNE and GDP have a causation link that runs in both directions, from M to GDP and from GDP to M. However, in Sri Lanka, there is no such relationship between these two variables. In India, there is a causation that runs in both directions between NFDI and GDP; however, in Sri Lanka, the flow of causality is only in one direction, from NFDI to GDP. The results of the cointegration test indicate that there are three cointegrating equations for both countries. The variables in the equation are GDP, X, M, UNE, and NFDI. The finding also suggests a long-run link between X and GDP, as well as NFDI and GDP, for both nations. Additionally, the finding suggests a long-run relationship between UNE and GDP in India and M and GDP in Sri Lanka.

References

1. Azolibe CB (2020). Banking sector intermediation development and growth of a developing economy: An empirical investigation of Nigeria. Res Sq, 1–18. https://doi.org/10.21203/rs.3.rs-95127/v1
2. Chakraborty C, Jana A (2021) Economic growth and trade-related variables: an empirical study using Indian aata. In Glob Tarif War: Econ, Polit Soc Implic (pp 141–152). Emerald Publishing Limited. https://doi.org/10.1108/978-1-80071-314-720211011
3. Choongjee CH (Ed) (2021) Crisis and fragility: econpmic impact of COVID-19 and policy responses. In KIEP Korean Inst Int Econ Policy (pp 54–67). https://www.researchgate.net/publication/349073744
4. Deyshappriya NRR (2021) COVID-19 and the Sri Lankan economy. Econ Polit Wkly (Engag), 56(29), 1–29. https://www.epw.in/engage/article/covid-19-and-sri-lankan-economy
5. Dhinakaran DP, Kesavan N (2020) Exports and imports stagnation in India during COVID-19-A Review. GIS Bus, 15(4), 1–21. https://www.researchgate.net/publication/341232028_Exports_and_Imports_Stagnation_in_India_During_COVID-19-A_Review
6. Dickey DA, Fuller WA (1979) Distribution of the estimators for autoregressive time series with a unit root. J Am Stat Assoc 74(366a):427–431. https://doi.org/10.1080/01621459.1979.10482531
7. Dolgov SI, Savinov YA (2020) The impact of the new coronavirus outbreak on international trade. Russ Foreign Econ J, 2, 7–18. https://ideas.repec.org/a/alq/rufejo/rfej_2020_02_7-18.html
8. Emery RF (1967) The relation of exports and economic growth*. Kyklos 20(4):470–486. https://doi.org/10.1111/J.1467-6435.1967.TB00859.X

9. Engle R, Granger C (1991) Long-run economic relationships: Readings in cointegration. Oxford university press. https://econpapers.repec.org/bookchap/oxpobooks/9780198283393.htm
10. Feder G (1983) On exports and economic growth. Elsevier 12(1–2):59–73. https://doi.org/10.1016/0304-3878(83)90031-7
11. Gruszczynski L (2020) The COVID-19 pandemic and international trade: temporary turbulence or paradigm shift? Eur J Risk Regul 11(2):337–342. https://doi.org/10.1017/ERR.2020.29
12. Gupta T, Sharma D, Maiti S (2022) Global trade and economic crisis. In https://services.igi-global.com/resolvedoi/resolve.aspx?doi=https://doi.org/10.4018/978-1-6684-5950-8.ch005 (pp 86–111). IGI Global. https://doi.org/10.4018/978-1-6684-5950-8.ch005
13. Habibi Z, Habibi H, Mohammadi MA (2022) The potential impact of COVID-19 on the Chinese GDP, trade, and economy. Economies 10(4):85. https://doi.org/10.3390/ECONOMIES10040073
14. Hazarika D (2021) COVID-19 pandemic and Foreign Trade: A Comparative Analysis in Indian Context. Psychol Educ J, 58(1), 3334–3340. https://doi.org/10.17762/PAE.V58I1.1272
15. Hjazeen H, Seraj M, Ozdeser H (2021) The nexus between the economic growth and unemployment in Jordan. Futur Bus J, 7(1). https://doi.org/10.1186/s43093-021-00088-3
16. Islam MM, Jannat A, Abdullah D, Rafi A, Aruga K (2020) Potential economic impacts of the COVID-19 pandemic on South Asian economies: a review. World 1(3):283–299. https://doi.org/10.3390/WORLD1030020
17. Jaipuria S, Parida R, Ray P (2021) The impact of COVID-19 on tourism sector in India. Tour Recreat Res 46(2):245–260. https://doi.org/10.1080/02508281.2020.1846971
18. Jayasundara JMDP, Fernando PJS (2022) An empirical analysis of the twin deficit hypothesis: the case of Sri Lanka. Sri Lanka J Econ Res 10(1):1–14. https://doi.org/10.4038/SLJER.V10I1.172/GALLEY/233/DOWNLOAD/
19. Kashyap M, Das N, Dubey M (2022) A comparative study of inflation in India and Sri Lanka. Int Res J Mod Eng, 4(5), 1110–1114. www.irjmets.com
20. Kaur G, Sarin V, Dhami JK (2017) Causality between exports and GDP: An empirical evidence from Bimstec region. Curr Issues Econ Financ 77–94. https://doi.org/10.1007/978-981-10-5810-3_6
21. Kontsas S, Stavros K (2022) A conceptual forecasting analysis of international trade aspects based on globalization impact issues article in. Int J Sci Res Manag, 10(1), 2321–3418. https://doi.org/10.18535/ijsrm/v10i1.em6
22. Kotlewski DC (2013) Impact of international trade on economic growth. Gospod Narodowa Pol J Econ, 261(1–2), 5–29. https://doi.org/10.33119/GN/100923
23. Leamer EE (1985) Sensitivity analyses would help. American Econ Rev. 75(3):308–313. https://www.jstor.org/stable/1814801
24. MacDonald JM (1994) Does import competition force efficient production? Rev Econ Stat 76(4):721–727. https://doi.org/10.2307/2109773
25. Maiti S, Chakraborty C (2018) Total factor productivity growth of indian fabrics sector: a firm level analysis, Vidyasagar Univ J Econ, 22, 118–123.http://inet.vidyasagar.ac.in:8080/jspui/bitstream/123456789/5407/1/6%20Susobhan%20Maiti%20%20Total%20Factor%20Productivity%20Growth%20of%20Indian%20Fabrics%20Sector%20A%20Firm%20level%20Analysis.pdf
26. Misfi ML, Jaya TJ, Nur S (2021) The effects pandemic COVID-19 on indonesia foreign trade. J Ekon, 26(2), 277–289. https://doi.org/10.24912/JE.V26I2.750
27. Mishra PK (2011) The dynamics of relationship between exports and economic growth in India. Int J Econ Sci Appl Res, 4(2), 53–70. https://papers.ssrn.com/abstract=1923769
28. Mohammed BZ, Kumar PM, Mahabub ST (2022) An empirical study on customer experience and customer engagement towards electric bikes with reference to Bangalore city, journal of positive school psychology. J Posit Psychol, 6(6), 4591–4597. https://journalppw.com/index.php/jpsp/article/view/8245
29. Petersen MA, Rajan RG (1994) The benefits of lending relationships: Evidence from small business data. J Financ 49(1):3–37. https://doi.org/10.1111/j.1540-6261.1994.tb04418.x

30. PWC (2020) COVID-19 outbreak impact on Sri Lanka and recommendations
31. Rameez A, Fowsar MAM, Lumna N (2020) Impact of COVID-19 on higher education sectors in Sri Lanka: a study based on south eastern university of Sri Lanka. J Educ Soc Res, 10(6), 341–349. http://ir.lib.seu.ac.lk/handle/123456789/5076
32. Robinson J, Kengatharan N (2020) Exploring the effect of COVID-19 on small and medium enterprises: early evidence from Sri Lanka the effects of teacher autonomy, student behavior and student engagement on teacher job satisfaction view project education view project exploring the effect of COVID-19 on small and medium enterprises: early evidence from Sri Lanka. J Appl Econ Bus Res JAEBR, 10(2), 115–125. https://www.researchgate.net/publication/348136545
33. Roshana MR, Kaldeen M, Banu AR (2020) (PDF) Impact Of COVID-19 outbreak on Sri Lankan economy. J CritAl Rev, 7(14), 1–11. https://www.researchgate.net/publication/343587416_IMPACT_OF_COVID-19_OUTBREAK_ON_SRI_LANKAN_ECONOMY
34. Rusniya HF, Nufile AAM (2020) The impact of COVID-19 on Sri Lankan economy. Kalam, Int Res J, 13(4), 11–19. http://ir.lib.seu.ac.lk/handle/123456789/5645
35. Sahoo P, Ashwani. (2020) COVID-19 and Indian economy: impact on growth, manufacturing, trade and MSME sector. Glob Bus Rev 21(5):1159–1183. https://doi.org/10.1177/0972150920945687/ASSET/IMAGES/LARGE/10.1177_0972150920945687-FIG2.JPEG
36. Sivalingam V, Anam. (2021) COVID-19 impact on exports of services: opportunities, challenges and suggestions for India. FIIB Business Review 10(4):315–326. https://doi.org/10.1177/2319714520984676/FORMAT/EPUB
37. Taghavi M, Goudarzi M, Masoudi E, Gashtu HP (2012) Study on the impact of export and import on economic growth in Iran. J Basic Appl Sci Res, 2(12), 12787–12794. https://scholar.google.com/scholar?hl=en&as_sdt=0%2C5&q=Taghavi%2C+M.%2C+Goudarzi%2C+M.%2C+Masoudi%2C+E.%2C+%26+Gashti+%2C+P.+%282012%29.+Study+on+the+Impact+of+Export+and+Import+on+Economic+Growth+in+Iran%2C+Journal+of+Basic+and+Applied+Scientific+Research%2C+2%2812%2912787-12794.+&btnG=#d=gs_cit&t=1670928866675&u=%2Fscholar%3Fq%3Dinfo%3Apqwe7JXun8cJ%3Ascholar.google.com%2F%26output%3Dcite%26scirp%3D0%26hl%3Den
38. The Hindu (2020). COVID-19 Trade impact for India estimated at $348 million: UN report—The Hindu. https://www.thehindu.com/business/Economy/covid-19-trade-impact-for-india-estimated-at-348-million-un-report/article30987932.ece
39. TOI (2022) Explained: "India looks a lot like Sri Lanka"? Read more at: http://timesofindia.indiatimes.com/articleshow/91688911.cms?utm_source=contentofinterest&utm_medium=text&utm_campaign=cppst. https://timesofindia.indiatimes.com/business/india-business/explained-india-looks-a-lot-like-sri-lanka/articleshow/91688911.cms
40. United Nations (2022) Impact of COVID-19 pandemic on trade and development. https://unctad.org/system/files/official-document/osg2022d1_en.pdf
41. Vohra R (2001) Export and economic growth: Further time series evidence from less-developed countries. Int Adv Econ Res, 7(3), 345–350. https://doi.org/10.1007/BF02295403
42. Wijayasiri J (2019) 04 Covid 19 and impact on export sector in sri lanka . https://www.google.com/search?q=Covid+19+and+impact+on+export+sector+in+sri+lanka&oq=Covid+19+and+impact+on+export+sector+in+sri+lanka&aqs=chrome..69i57j0i22i30j0i390.467j0j4&sourceid=chrome&ie=UTF-8
43. Wörz J (2005) Skill intensity in foreign trade and economic growth. Empirica 32(1):117–144. https://doi.org/10.1007/S10663-005-1983-9

Chapter 10
Divergences of Health Expenditures and Role of the Government in Response to COVID-19 Pandemic in Selected Nations—An Investigation

Rajib Bhattacharyya and Arindam Paul

10.1 Introduction

It has often been argued that public investment in social sectors, like health and education generally contributes to the enhancement of human capital, skill formation and knowledge development and thereby increasing productivity and higher returns which stimulates economic growth. Thus, according to this approach, the justification of the role of public policy in the social sector is accepted on the ground that human capital has a positive spill-over effect on economic growth as well as development. So public provisioning of social services is an instrument of human development that has a larger role to play. If we compare the public provisioning of health care services in terms of health expenditure (as a percentage of GDP) in a few selected countries (both developed and emerging market economies) we will find that India's health expenditure (as a percentage of GDP) is the lowest among them all (accounting for 3.54% of its GDP) in 2018 (Fig. 10.1). Even countries like Nigeria have a greater percentage contribution than India.

As per the latest OECD Indicators of Health at a Glance, 2021, before the COVID-19 pandemic, the average health expenditure was approximately 8.8% of their GDP which more or less remained constant since 2013. The United States tops the list by spending 16.8% of GDP. Together a group of the top ten including the US, France, Canada, Japan and the United Kingdom spent more than 10% of their GDP in health (Fig. 10.1). Countries like Brazil and South Africa and a further dozen countries in the next group spent 8–10% of GDP. The next set of countries that spent

R. Bhattacharyya (✉)
Economics, Goenka College of Commerce and Business Administration, Kolkata, India
e-mail: rajib2014hmc@gmail.com

A. Paul
Economics, Jadavpur University, Jadavpur, Kolkata, India

R. Bhattacharyya et al. (eds.), *COVID-19 Pandemic and Global Inequality*,
https://doi.org/10.1007/978-981-99-4405-7_10

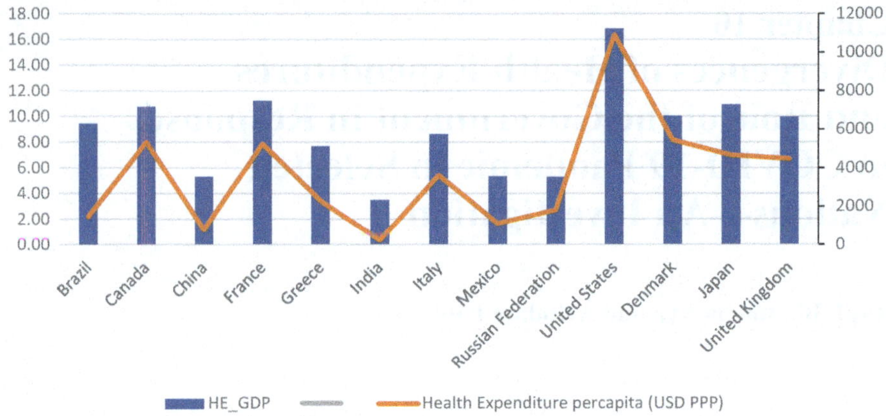

Fig. 10.1 Comparison of health Expenditure (as percentage of GDP) and Health Expenditure per-capita (USD PPP) in selected Countries in 2019. (*Source* Author's Construction based on World Development Indicator (2020) and Global Health Expenditure Database, OECD, 2021)

6–8% of their GDP includes many central and eastern European OECD countries, as well as the newer members from the Latin America region—Colombia and Costa Rica. The expenditure made by Mexico and Turkey along with China and India on health is less than 6% of GDP. So, it is quite clear from the above discussion that there existed a wide range of variation in health expenditure across the globe prior to the pandemic.

But there has been a significant increase in the ratio of health expenditure to GDP for many of the list of countries (already mentioned above). Primary estimates suggest that average health expenditure jumped from 8.8% in 2019 to 9.7% in 2020. Also, countries that were severely affected by the pandemic experienced an appreciable rise owing to combating health disasters and the further spread of the pandemic (for e.g., in the UK it increased from 10.2% in 2019 to 12.8% in the initial part of 2020).

The figure also shows a wide amount of disparity in health Expenditure per capita (USD PPP) across the same set of countries mentioned earlier. India holds the lowest position on both health Expenditure (as a percentage of GDP) and Health Expenditure per capita (USD PPP). The average per capita health spending in OECD countries (USD PPP) was more than USD 4 000, with the US occupying the highest position USD 10,948. But for the next set of countries (Canada, France, Denmark) it is almost half the amount of the US and for Japan and the United Kingdom, it was around the OECD average. China and India are the lowest among the set.

Usually, a variety of financing arrangements are available for individuals or groups of the population to access healthcare facilities. Generally, government financing schemes (at national or subnational levels), compulsory health insurance (managed through public or private entities), out-of-pocket spending (Spending by households both on a fully discretionary basis and as part of some co-payment arrangement), voluntary health insurance—are the most common forms of financing available in many countries.

Denmark and the United Kingdom accounted for 80% or more of national health spending. In Germany, Japan and France more than 75% of spending was covered through a type of compulsory health insurance scheme. While Japan relies on a comprehensive social health insurance, France supplements the public health insurance coverage with a system of private health insurance arrangements, which became compulsory under certain employment conditions in 2016. In the United States, federal and state programmes, such as Medicaid, covered around one-quarter of all US healthcare spending in 2019. Although almost 60% of expenditure was classified under compulsory insurance schemes, these cover very different arrangements. Out-of-pocket payments financed one-fifth of all health spending in 2019 in OECD countries, with the share broadly decreasing as GDP increases. Households accounted for one-third or more of all spending in Mexico (42%), Greece (36%), Russia and China (greater than 35%), India (above 60%), while in France out-of-pocket spending was below 10% (Fig. 10.2). With moves towards universal health coverage, a number of OECD countries have increased spending by government or compulsory insurance schemes in recent decades.

The vast majority of funding for government schemes comes from general government revenues (such as taxation and levies), which are then channelled through budgetary and allocation processes. However, governments might also contribute to social health insurance, for example, by covering the contributions of particular population groups or providing general budget support to insurance funds. Individuals purchase private health insurance through the payment of regular premiums.

Overall public funding can be defined as the sum of government transfers and all social contributions. Private sources consist of the premiums for voluntary and compulsory insurance schemes, as well as any other funds coming from households or corporations. In Denmark, public sources funded more than 80% of health care

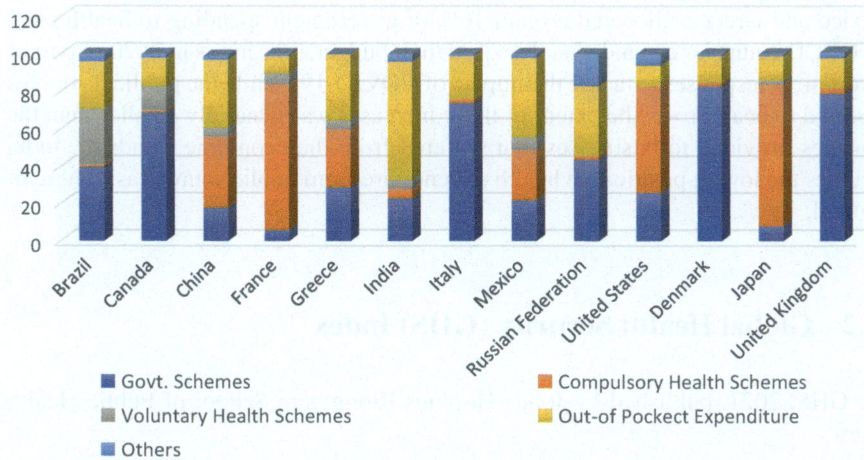

Fig. 10.2 Health Expenditure by Financing Schemes. (*Source* Author's Construction based on World Development Indicator (2020) and Global Health Expenditure Database, OECD, 2021)

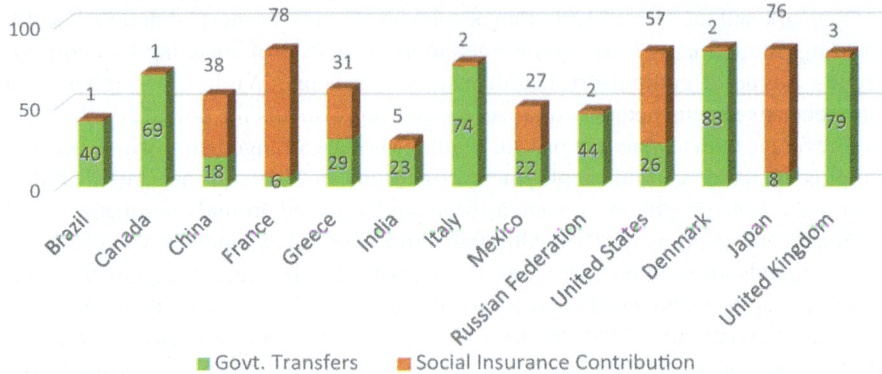

Fig. 10.3 Health expenditure from public sources as a share of total, 2019. (*Source* Author's Construction based on World Development Indicator (2020) and Global Health Expenditure Database, OECD, 2021)

expenditure (Fig. 10.3). In other countries, governments may not pay directly for the majority of health services, but they provide transfers and subsidies [16]. Governments fund a range of public services, and health care competes with other sectors such as education, defense and housing. The level of public funding of health is determined by factors such as the type of health system in place, the demographic composition of the population and government policy. Budget priorities can also shift from year to year due to political decision-making and economic effects. Public funding of health spending (via government transfers and social insurance contributions) accounted for an average of 15% of total government expenditure across OECD countries in 2019. Around 20% or more of public spending was linked to health care spending in Japan, and the United States. At the other end of the scale, Mexico and Greece, allocated around 10% of government spending to health care. All OECD countries expanded and revised their budget allocations in 2020 as part of government responses to tackle the impact of COVID-19. While the public resources allocated to health rose, the extent of these increases was generally smaller than the subsidies provided to businesses that suffered from the economic standstill. India occupies the lowest position on health expenditure from public sources as a share of the total.

10.2 Global Health Security (GHS) Index

The GHS, 2021, published by Johns Hopkins Bloomberg School of Public Health states.

> *Countries continue to suffer harm from the COVID-19 pandemic as a result of insufficient health security capacity. This lack of capacity comes at a time when political and security risks have increased in nearly all countries, and enduring financial investment necessary*

to sustain capacities has yet to be demonstrated. Such weaknesses leave a world acutely vulnerable to future health emergencies, including those potentially more devastating than COVID-19.

It stressed the importance of developing stronger public health coupled with policies and programs that may help people to have universal health coverage, paid sick leave, subsidized childcare, income assistance, food and housing assistance, etc. along with protective public health measures to fight the COVID-19 pandemic.

The GHS Index is based on six pillars with the objective of assessing a country's capability to ***prevent, detect***, and ***respond*** to biological threats along with factors that can be an obstacle to building such capability like ***health systems, norms,*** and ***risks***.

It is clear from the GHS Index that in order to strengthen the preparedness to fight epidemic or pandemic majority of countries, including high-income nations, have not made adequate financial investments. In case of most countries, no improvement has been observed in maintaining a capable and accessible health system. Countries which are exposed to greater political and security risks have also shown greater preparedness deficit. One interesting point to note is that emerging economies like China and India lag behind the other set of countries in all kinds of preparedness required to fight the COVID-19 pandemic (Table 10.1).

Table 10.1 Global Health Security (GHS) Index, 2021

Country	Prevention score	Detection score	Response score	Heath system score	Norms score	Risks score	Overall score
US	79.4	80.1	65.7	75.2	81.9	73.3	75.9
Canada	70.4	70.8	49.2	67.3	79.2	81.8	69.8
UK	63.5	70.8	64.8	68.3	62.5	73.0	67.2
Denmark	64.3	64.6	51.8	64.5	61.1	79.9	64.4
France	59.4	45.7	47.7	70.4	65.3	82.9	61.9
Japan	43.1	71.1	59.5	51.6	66.7	70.9	60.5
Mexico	41.9	54.3	64.8	54.7	68.1	57.9	57.0
Italy	47.2	49.7	43.2	40.2	65.3	65.9	51.9
Greece	44.8	48.9	46.7	46.2	63.9	58.3	51.5
Brazil	49.7	53.6	56.3	50.3	41.7	55.9	51.2
Russia	45.5	43.6	44.7	58.9	51.4	50.5	49.1
China	43.9	48.5	38.5	51.8	38.9	63.4	47.5
India	29.7	43.5	30.3	46.1	47.2	60.2	42.8

Source Hopkins Bloomberg School of Public Health States.

10.3 Divergences in Fiscal Support in Response to COVID-19

There has been a significant difference in fiscal support measures in response to the COVID-19 pandemic which has failed to arrest the quick spread of the pandemic. The strong recovery from the last two years is not only due to the vaccination programmes but also due to the massive and quick monetary and fiscal of the government. Figure 10.4 shows to what extent the fiscal support in the US widely diverged from other strong economies of the world.

In order to fight the deep recession caused by disruptions in supply chain and lockdown measures, developed advanced countries have been able to mobilize a considerable amount to support and stimulate their domestic economies. But in contrast, developing countries with limited resource bases could not provide financial support and stimulus packages adequately given the size of most developing economies and their limited fiscal space, the per capita amount of such packages is limited in comparison with both their needs and the magnitudes mobilized by developed countries (Fig. 10.4a). If we analyze the fiscal stimulus package (as a % of GDP) of these sets of countries we will observe that Japan, Italy, the US, the UK and Canada are heading the list. But compared to them the other developing countries a way lagging behind. So, from the point of view of government support, there exists a huge divergence between them (Fig. 10.4b).

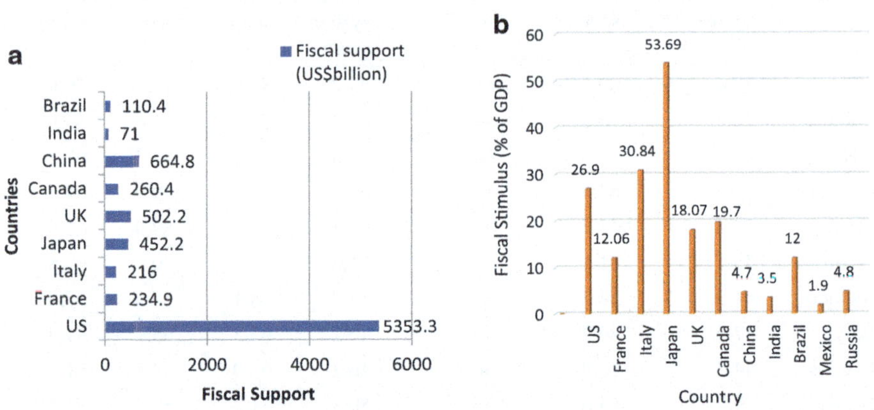

Fig. 10.4 **a** Fiscal Support in Nations (US $ billion). **b** Fiscal Stimulus (as % of GDP). (*Source* Moody's Analytics—Global Fiscal Policy in the Pandemic, February, 2022 and https://www.statista.com/statistics/1107572/covid-19-value-g20-stimulus-packages-share-gdp)

10.4 Literature Survey

An enormous body of literature has developed with the objective of explaining the issue of convergence/divergence of health expenditure, the development of public health infrastructure and the role of government in pursuing policies to mitigate the negative impact of the COVID-19 pandemic. However the problem of testing a hypothesis lies in the fact that only two years of scattered and non-uniform data sets are available. Here we cite a few good works of literature that are available along with their major findings. OECD [17], Health at a Glance 2021, compares key indicators for population health and health system performance across OECD member countries and key emerging economies. They have tried to focus on health status, risk factors for health, access to health care, quality of health care, health system capacity and resources. García et al. [9] explore some of the key drivers of efficiency and find that lower income inequality, less corruption, and health interventions oriented at expanding population access to basic health services are associated with greater efficiency. Balakrishnan and Namboodhiry [1] in their study tried to emphasize the need for developing a strong public health system, with evidence on health expenditures across the states of India. They found that the average level of expenditure on health is found to be low both in itself and in relation to spending by governments in South and Southeast Asia. They arrived at two important conclusions: (a) some of the mortality from COVID-19 is policy-induced and (b) assume that assuring health security to the Indian population would require a radical restructuring of the spending priorities of the states Fallahi [8] tried to examine the issue of convergence in the ratio of total health expenditures to GDP for a sample of OECD countries over the period 1960–2006. Stochastic convergence is tested using unit root tests, without and with a structural break. Moreover, β convergence is examined by applying a method that allows for a structural break and is robust to the presence of unit roots and serial correlation in the errors. The results support the existence of stochastic convergence for all countries. β Convergence, however, is supported for some countries only before the break points (regime 1). In regime 2 (the period after the break points) all countries are experiencing divergence. Barro and Martin [2, 3] talk about an important economic question is whether poor countries or regions tend to converge toward rich ones. They based their main analysis on a growth equation that derives, as a log-linear approximation, from the transition path of the neoclassical growth model for closed economies. Assuming x_i^* to be the steady-state per capita growth rate, $\widehat{y_{it}}$ is output per effective worker, $\hat{y}_{it}^*$ is the steady-state level of output per effective worker, T is the length of the observation interval, the coefficient β is the rate of convergence, and u_i, is an error term. They found that the process of convergence within the European countries is in many respects similar to that of the United States. In particular, the rate of convergence is again about 2% a year. In a 1992 paper, they considered the neoclassical growth model as a framework to study the convergence of per capita income and product across 48 contiguous US States. They found clear evidence of convergence across the US States. Moreover, the book on Economic Growth [4, 2nd edition] has a separate chapter relating the empirical analysis of convergence, discussing in detail about *both the* β *and* σ convergence criteria. Hembram & Halder [14] attempted to re-examine the standard debate of β, σ, and club convergence empirically in India with respect to per capita net state domestic product (PCNSDP) across 22 states over time (viz. 1980–1981 to 2015–2016). They went beyond the σ convergence, and the distribution-sensitive inequality measure such as generalized entropy is used to explore the pattern of distribution of PCNSDP among states over time. They found σ divergence, a rising trend of inequality of PCNSDP with a higher sensitivity to the right tail of the distribution. The results show that there exists absolute β divergence but conditional β convergence. Hembram & Halder [13] made a comprehensive study on the global convergence of income based on β, σ inequality across 187 countries over a period from 1990 to 2018 at a disaggregated level. Most of the recent studies have found the absence of absolute convergence but the presence of conditional convergence [6, 18]. Cherodian and Thirlwall [6] have found the presence of absolute divergence but weak conditional convergence across 32 Indian states for the period, 1999–2000 to 2010–2011. Chakraborty and Chakraborty [5] have considered a dynamic panel of 28 states and 14 years (viz. 2001–2014); the conditioning variables are public capital spending, gross fixed capital formation, credit deposit ratio, commercial credit by the banking sector, literacy rate, infant mortality rate (IMR), and total fertility rate (TFR). They have argued that public investment in health plays a crucial role in conditional and club convergence.

10.5 Objective of the Study, Data and Methodology

We consider panel data which includes a total of fourteen major Covid-affected countries and twenty-two time points (2000–2021). The countries can be subdivided into two major categories viz. low-income group and high-income group. The former group consists of six countries and the latter group consists of eight countries. Moreover, the time span can be sub-divided into two sub-spans. Since Covid hit in the last quarter of 2019 we consider the time span 2000–2019 to be the pre-Covid period and the time period 2020 is the Covid shock period. Our main indicator is the health expenditure of the countries. Therefore, we consider the Current Health Expenditure per Capita in PPP (Che_pc_ppp) and two main determinants, viz., Domestic general government health expenditure per capita, PPP (dgghe_pc_ppp) and Domestic private health expenditure per capita, PPP (dpghe_pc_ppp). We do the convergence exercise for the pre-covid time span. Using the convergence outcome and analyzing the Covid shock period individually try to predict what happened to the convergence of health expenditure after the covid era.

In the case of the convergence exercise, we have used *both the* β *and* σ convergence criteria. The σ convergence of any indicator depends on the dispersion of the value of that indicator between different countries over time. If the dispersion over time decreases, we say that sigma convergence occurs among the group of countries

Table 10.2 Explaining Different GE Measures (where $A_L = \{i|x_i \leq \overline{x}\}$ and $A_H = \{i|x_i \geq \overline{x}\}$)

Value of α	Formula of $GE(\alpha)$	Name of $GE(\alpha)$	Tail of the distribution received a larger weight
0	$\frac{1}{n}\sum_{i \in A_L} ln\left(\frac{\overline{x}}{x_i}\right)$	Mean log deviation	Lower-tail
1	$\frac{1}{n}\sum_{i \in A_H} \left(\frac{x_i}{\overline{x}}\right) ln\left(\frac{x_i}{\overline{x}}\right)$	Theil measure of Inequality	Both the tails received equal weights
2	$\frac{sd(x)}{2\overline{x}}$	Half of the Coefficient of Variation	Upper-tail

Source Authors own construction based on the knowledge from relevant papers

in case of long-run occurrence of that particular indicator. Since standard deviation is very much dependent on the unit of measurement and the Gini-measure of inequality is very much distribution insensitive along with not perfectly sub-group decomposable, therefore we consider the Generalized Entropy (GE) measures. The GE measure of inequality is

$$GE(\alpha) = \frac{1}{n\alpha(\alpha - 1)} \sum_{i=1}^{n} \left[\left(\frac{x_i}{\overline{x}}\right)^{\alpha} - 1\right]$$

where α is the distribution sensitivity parameter, x_i be the value of the indicator (x), n be the number of countries and $\overline{x}$ be the mean of the indicator x. If α is low enough then $GE(\alpha)$ put more weight to the lower tail of the distribution and vice-versa. We consider three main distributional weights in terms of values of α viz. ($\alpha \in \{0, 1, 2\}$). Table 10.2 describes these particular GE measures corresponding to the value of α.

Following Barro and Sala-i-Martin [2], we have also used the fixed effect model to check the β convergence of the per capita health expenditure and its two major components namely per capita domestic general government health expenditure and domestic private health expenditure at PPP.

10.6 Empirical Analysis

10.6.1 Analysis of σ Convergence

We will do the σ convergence analysis for the current per capita health expenditure, domestic general government per capita health expenditure and domestic private per capita health expenditure respectively one after another. Table 10.3 in the Annexure shows the values of different measures of σ convergence for the current health expenditure per capita and correspondingly Fig. 10.5a, b and c, respectively, depict the plot

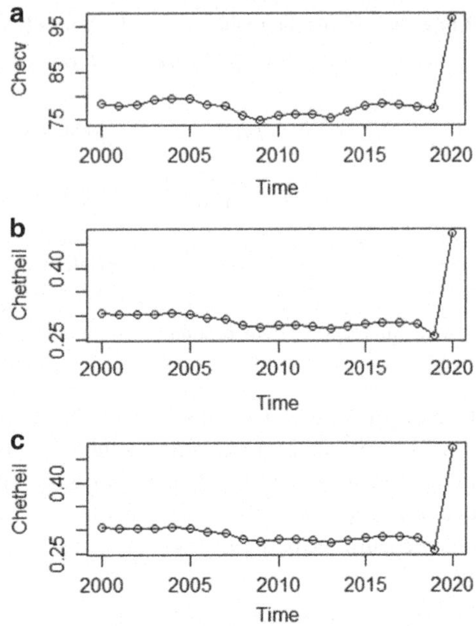

Fig. 10.5 **a** Coefficient of variation of Che_pc_ppp across countries for the period 2000–2020. **b** Theil's measure of Che_pc_ppp across countries for the period 2000–2020. **c** Mean log deviation of Che_pc_ppp across countries for the period 2000–2020. *Source* Generated by the authors

of coefficient of variation, Theil measure and mean log deviation for the current per capita health expenditure over the year 2000 to 2020.

In the case of all the three measures, we can observe a downward move up to the year 2013 but then there is an increasing trend after 2013 in particular for the cv measure and Theil measure. Hence, our conclusion is there may be a tendency of convergence before 2013 but after that, the situation became worse in terms of current health expenditure per capita. Therefore, we are unable to conclude any about the σ convergence of current per capita health expenditure.

Table 10.4 in the Annexure show the values of different measure of σ convergence for the domestic general government per capita health expenditure and correspondingly Fig. 10.6a, b and c are, respectively, the plot of coefficient of variation, Theil measure and mean log deviation for the domestic general government per capita health expenditure over the year 2000–2019.

In case of all the three measures, one can observe a downward move up to the year 2013 but then there is an increasing trend after 2013 in particular for cv measure and Theil measure. Hence, our conclusion is there may be a tendency of convergence before 2013 but after that, the situation became worse in terms of current health expenditure per capita. Therefore, we are unable to conclude any about the σ convergence of domestic general government per capita health expenditure. It should be noted that in case of both indicators, the mean log deviation tells us a different story. Therefore, when we put larger weight to the lower part of the distribution,

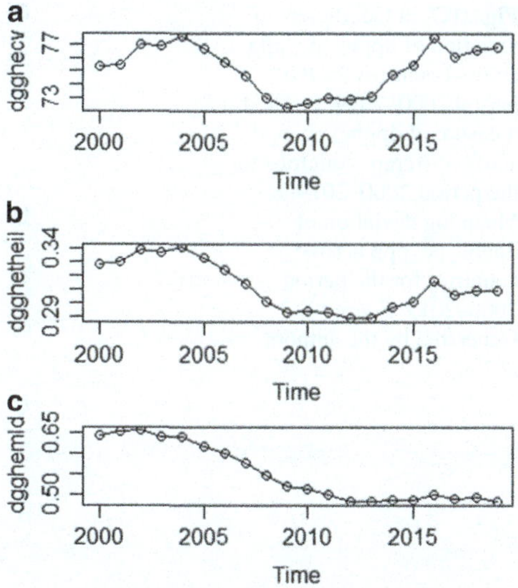

Fig. 10.6 **a** Coefficient of variation of dgghe_pc_ppp across countries for the period 2000–2019. **b** Theil measure of dgghe_pc_ppp across countries for the period 2000–2019. **c** Mean log deviation of dgghe_pc_ppp across countries for the period 2000–2019. *Source* Generated by the authors

we may get sigma convergence across these countries. Hence, there may be an incidence of σ convergence among the low-income group but in generally the outcome is inconclusive.

Table 10.5 in the Annexure show the values of different measures of σ convergence for the domestic private per capita health expenditure and correspondingly Fig. 10.7a, b and c, respectively, represent the plot of coefficient of variation, Theil measure and mean log deviation of the domestic private per capita health expenditure over the period 2000–2019. It is clearly visible that all three measures of σ convergence for the domestic private per capita health expenditure are falling over the period 2000–2019. Hence, we can conclude that for the domestic private per capita health expenditure we have the incidence of σ convergence.

10.7 Shock Period Analysis

The shock period analysis is shown in the Table in Annexure. Before the Covid shock period the range value of the coefficient of variation, Theil measure and mean log deviation of current per capita health expenditure were, respectively, (75–81)%, 0.26–0.3 and 0.36–0.45. However, During the Covid shock period the value of coefficient of variation, Theil measure and mean log deviation of current per capita health expenditure are, respectively, increased to 96%, 0.46 and 0.73. Hence, during the Covid shock period all the indicator of the σ convergence indicates that the gap between the counties increases in term of current per capita health expenditure. If this gap increase will have a significant effect on the process of the stock of Health capital formation, then the observed divergence tendency after 2013 for current per

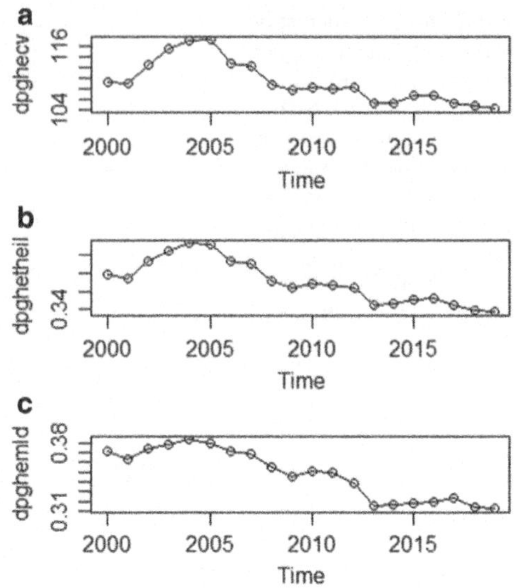

Fig. 10.7 **a** Coefficient of variation of dpghe_pc_ppp across countries for the period 2000–2019. **b**: Theil measure of dpghe_pc_ppp across different countries for the period 2000–2019. **c**: Mean log deviation of dpghe_pc_ppp across countries for the period 2000–2019. *Source* Generated by the authors

capita health expenditure will lead to the divergence of current per capita health expenditure.

10.8 Analysis of β Convergence

Following Barro and Sala-i-Martin [2], we now use the fixed effect model to check the β convergence of the per capita health expenditure and its two major components namely per capita domestic general government health expenditure and domestic private health expenditure. Then, we estimate the following model using our panel data

$$\gamma_{it} = \alpha + \beta ln\left(x_{i(t-1)}\right) + \mu_i + \epsilon_t + u_{it} \tag{10.1}$$

where $\gamma_{it} = ln\left(x_{it}/x_{i(t-1)}\right)$ is the log value of the growth ratio of any indicator x of country i at time point t, μ_i is the country-specific error component and ϵ_t is time specific error component.

In Annexure, we present the estimation result of the Fixed effect model separately for the current per capita health expenditure, the domestic general government per capita health expenditure and the domestic private per capita health expenditure. Since our analysis requires only the value of the estimated β coefficient and whether it is significant or not. Therefore, let us concentrate on the Table 10.6 only.

It is observed that the estimated β coefficient for the estimated fixed effect model for all three variables are negative, significant and absolute value lies between zero and unity. A negative value of the estimated β coefficient confirms that there is a

Table 10.6 Panel Fixed Effect Model outcome *(for detail see appendix table 10.7)*

Variable under fixed effect model		Estimated β coefficient	Significant status
Without shock effect	Che_pc_ppp	−0.060956	Significant at 1% level
	dgghe_pc_ppp	−0.047236	Significant at 1% level
	dpghe_pc_ppp	−0.157344	Significant at 1% level
With shock effect	Che_pc_ppp	−0.048940	Not significant

Source Authors

negative relation between the growth ratio of any time point to the previous year's value of the indicator. Hence, we have the β convergence for all the three indicators. Further, the absolute value of the estimated β coefficient for domestic general government per capita health expenditure is less than the estimated β coefficient for domestic private per capita health expenditure. Therefore, domestic private per capita health expenditure converges at a faster rate than the domestic general government per capita health expenditure. However, when we include the shock period the beta coefficient gets insignificant. Hence, the trend of convergence is not confirmed due to Covid shock.

10.9 Conclusion

Though there were clear trends of divergence in social sector expenditure in the pre-COVID-19 era between low-income and high-income countries, it became more prominent with the outbreak of the COVID-19 pandemic. In case of the development of public health infrastructure, there exist significant variations across countries which was a major constraint to fight against this kind of pandemic globally. The evidences from COVID-19 clearly demonstrates the need for investing in the public health care system in order to mitigate the devastations from these kinds of pandemics. China and India, being two fastest growing emerging nations of the world, are lagging way behind in public health care provisioning. In terms of health expenditure (as a percentage of GDP), health Expenditure per capita (USD PPP), variety of financing arrangements are available for individuals or groups of the population to access healthcare facilities, health expenditure from public sources as a share of the total—it demonstrates the significant gap between rich and poor nations and there is no tendency for these gaps to narrow down in the long term. Empirical analysis to examine the trends in expenditure on health care facilities (current health expenditure per capita in PPP and its two main determinants viz., domestic general government health expenditure per capita, PPP and domestic private health expenditure per capita, PPP) in selected 14 low and high-income countries, confirms that there is no case for convergence in health divergences between these sets of countries. Moreover, if we include the shock period (2020) the spikes of divergences are even more significant. Using the coefficient of variation, Theil's measure and mean log deviation for σ

convergence and panel fixed effect model for β convergence, the study does not find any trends of convergence in health expenditure. Hence, the authorities like WHO should take care of the issues to minimize the differences in the per capita health expenses in the low and high income earning countries by means of global policy packages.

Annexture

See Tables 10.3, 10.4 and 10.5

Table 10.7 Panel data analysis (fixed effect model)

Table 10.3 Different measures of σ convergence for Che_pc_ppp

	Year	cv	mld	Theil
1	2000	77.61258	0.444887	0.294547
2	2001	77.63307	0.444332	0.294725
3	2002	79.6869	0.451684	0.305661
4	2003	80.69132	0.447904	0.307543
5	2004	81.06987	0.447634	0.309322
6	2005	80.56804	0.437425	0.303882
7	2006	79.15489	0.42917	0.295837
8	2007	78.55282	0.419609	0.290232
9	2008	76.24088	0.404494	0.277549
10	2009	75.13194	0.391942	0.270825
11	2010	75.81109	0.395302	0.274728
12	2011	75.70547	0.38984	0.273482
13	2012	75.64985	0.375537	0.269758
14	2013	74.92272	0.360328	0.264183
15	2014	76.52376	0.364993	0.270939
16	2015	77.53538	0.366833	0.274935
17	2016	78.76225	0.375077	0.282991
18	2017	77.16671	0.375042	0.274278
19	2018	77.45255	0.371224	0.274908
20	2019	77.55016	0.365124	0.273826

R Outcome of Fixed Effect Model for Che_pc_ppp for Pre Shock Period

Two ways effects Within Model

Call:

plm(formula = gche ~ log(lag(che, 1L)), data = PanelFinal, effect = "twoways", model = "within").

Balanced Panel: $n = 14$, $T = 19$, $N = 266$.

Residuals:

Min	1st Qu	Median	3rd Qu	Max
−0.26849541	−0.01815846	−0.00048993	0.01771452	0.26103531

Table 10.4 Different measures of σ convergence for dgghe_pc_ppp

	Year	cv	mld	Theil
1	2000	75.38344	0.642937	0.327252
2	2001	75.45889	0.652194	0.329513
3	2002	76.95094	0.655783	0.338902
4	2003	76.84399	0.640234	0.336479
5	2004	77.54218	0.640261	0.340295
6	2005	76.63863	0.617558	0.332692
7	2006	75.67681	0.599301	0.323292
8	2007	74.64878	0.577026	0.313718
9	2008	73.02976	0.547201	0.300579
10	2009	72.25629	0.519509	0.292381
11	2010	72.65838	0.514525	0.293447
12	2011	72.96607	0.498849	0.292583
13	2012	72.90769	0.483769	0.288964
14	2013	73.09539	0.481307	0.288167
15	2014	74.69603	0.486819	0.296479
16	2015	75.42856	0.484902	0.300296
17	2016	77.49199	0.500281	0.315394
18	2017	76.00564	0.488632	0.30554
19	2018	76.55121	0.493075	0.308675
20	2019	76.75024	0.482275	0.308409

Table 10.5 Different measures of σ convergence for dpghe_pc_ppp

	Year	cv	mld	Theil
1	2000	109.3779	0.370815	0.377456
2	2001	109.0118	0.36313	0.373808
3	2002	112.7306	0.374714	0.393087
4	2003	115.5491	0.378806	0.404291
5	2004	117.015	0.383345	0.412057
6	2005	117.2981	0.379526	0.410891
7	2006	112.9123	0.371456	0.392681
8	2007	112.4642	0.36806	0.38893
9	2008	108.9633	0.354581	0.370858
10	2009	107.8315	0.34545	0.363909
11	2010	108.4257	0.350864	0.368475
12	2011	108.1966	0.349444	0.366967
13	2012	108.2509	0.338288	0.363218
14	2013	105.2566	0.315054	0.345252
15	2014	105.4434	0.317492	0.346697
16	2015	106.8115	0.318222	0.350544
17	2016	106.9596	0.319832	0.352128
18	2017	105.2451	0.324068	0.344387
19	2018	104.7455	0.314447	0.33942
20	2019	104.2379	0.312039	0.337018

Coefficients:

	Estimate	Std. Error	*t*-Value	Pr(>|*t*|)
log(lag(dpghe, 1))	−0.060956	0.022536	−2.7049	0.007338**

Signif. codes:

'***' 0.001 '**' 0.01 '*' 0.05 '.' 0.1 '' 1

Total Sum of Squares: 0.54594.

Residual Sum of Squares: 0.52932.

R-Squared: 0.030444.

Adj. *R*-Squared: −0.10271.

F-statistic: 7.31623 on 1 and 233 DF, *p*-value: 0.007338.

R Outcome of Fixed Effect Model for Dgghe_pc_ppp for Pre Shock

Two ways effects Within Model

Call:

plm(formula = gdgghe ~ log(lag(dgghe, 1L)), data = PanelFinal, effect = “twoways”, model = “within”).

Balanced Panel: $n = 14$, $T = 19$, $N = 266$.

Residuals:

Min	1st Qu	Median	3rd Qu	Max
−0.2781945	−0.0238835	−0.0012419	0.0250152	0.2693519

Coefficients:

	Estimate	Std. Error	*t*-Value	Pr(>|*t*|)
log(lag(dgghe, 1))	−0.047236	0.016775	−2.8159	0.005281**

Signif. codes:

‘***’ 0.001 ‘**’ 0.01 ‘*’ 0.05 ‘.’ 0.1 ‘’ 1

Total Sum of Squares: 0.77151.

Residual Sum of Squares: 0.74612.

R-Squared: 0.032911.

Adj. *R*-Squared: −0.099908.

F-statistic: 7.92921 on 1 and 233 DF, *p*-value: 0.005281.

R Outcome of Fixed Effect Model for Dpghe_pc_ppp for Pre Shock Period

Two ways effects Within Model.

Call:

plm(formula = gdpghe ~ log(lag(dpghe, 1L)), data = PanelFinal, effect = "twoways", model = "within").

Balanced Panel: $n = 14$, $T = 19$, $N = 266$.

Residuals:

Min	1st Qu	Median	3rd Qu	Max
−0.27541533	−0.02728384	−0.00048104	0.02276403	0.22126890

Coefficients:

	Estimate	Std. Error	*t*-Value	Pr(>|*t*|)
log(lag(dpghe, 1))	−0.157344	0.033029	−4.7639	3.341e−06 ***

Signif. codes:

'***' 0.001 '**' 0.01 '*' 0.05 '.' 0.1 '' 1

Total Sum of Squares: 0.75069.

Residual Sum of Squares: 0.68406.

R-Squared: 0.088756.

Adj. R-Squared: −0.036394.

F-statistic: 22.6944 on 1 and 233 DF, p-value: 3.3411e-06.

R Outcome of Fixed Effect Model for Che_pc_ppp with Shock Period

Two ways effects Within Model

Call:

plm(formula = gche ~ log(lag(che, 1L)), data = PanelFinal, effect = "twoways", model = "within").

Balanced Panel: $n = 13$, $T = 20$, $N = 260$.

Residuals:

Min	1st Qu	Median	3rd Qu	Max
−1.6000521	−0.0285992	−0.0081296	0.0261584	0.4985668

Coefficients:

	Estimate	Std. Error	*t*-Value	Pr(>|*t*|)
log(lag(che, 1))	−0.048940	0.068573	−0.7137	0.4761

Total Sum of Squares: 4.9891.

Residual Sum of Squares: 4.9779.

R-Squared: 0.0022389.

Adj. *R*-Squared: –0.13841.

F-statistic: 0.509359 on 1 and 227 DF, *p*-Value: 0.47615.

References

1. Balakrishnan P, Namboodhiry SK (2021) The importance of investing in a public health system: evidence from COVID-19 mortality. Indian Econ Rev Springer. [https://doi.org/10.1007/s41775-021-00116-7]
2. Barro RJ, Martin XS (1991) Convergence across states and regions. Brook Pap Econ Act 1(107):182
3. Barro RJ, Martin XS (1992) Convergence. J Polit Econ 100(2):223–51. [JSTOR, http://www.jstor.org/stable/2138606. Accessed 31 Dec. 2022]
4. Barro RJ, Martin XS (2004) Economic growth (2nd Edition). The MIT Press Cambridge, Massachusetts, London, England
5. Chakraborty P, Chakraborty L (2018) Federalism, fiscal asymmetries and economic convergence: evidence from Indian states, NIPFP working paper series, working paper no. 232. [Available at: http://www.nipfp.org.in/publications/working-papers/1827/]
6. Cherodian R, Thirlwall AP (2015) Regional disparities in per capita income in India: convergence or divergence? J Post Keynes Econ 37(3):384–407
7. Escribano GM, Juarros P, Mogues T (2022) Patterns and drivers of health Spending efficiency, IMF Working Papers 22/48 (Washington: International Monetary Fund)
8. Fallahi F (2011) Convergence of total health expenditure as a share of GDP: Evidence from selected OECD countries [Available at: Online at https://mpra.ub.uni-muenchen.de/51324/MPRAPaperNo.51324]
9. García AB, López PA, Balado BY, Lema RE, País GM, Marchán-L (2022) J Healthc Qual Res 2023 Jan–Feb 38(1):61–62. Spanish. https://doi.org/10.1016/j.jhqr.2022.08.002. Epub 2022 Aug 26. PMID: 36114120; PMCID: PMC9411145. [Translated as—A pending agenda on post-COVID-19 quality of life: Comments on the study by Moya-Salazar J.]

10. Global Health Security (GHS) Index (2021) John Hopkins Bloomberg School of Public Health, Centre for Health Security. Available: www.GHSIndex.org
11. Global Health Expenditure Database (GHED) (WHO) [Available at: https://apps.who.int/nha/database/country_profile/Index/en]
12. Global Fiscal Policy in the Pandemic, Moody's Analytics.Available at www.moodysanalytics.com
13. Hembram S, Haldar SK (2021) Revisiting global income convergence: 1990–2018. A disaggregated analysis. Econ Bull 41(3):952–974
14. Hembram S, Haldar SK (2019) Beta, sigma and club convergence: Indian experience from 1980 to 2015, Indian Economic Review. J Delhi Sch Econ. Springer [Indian Economic Review https://doi.org/10.1007/s41775-019-00056-3]
15. IMF Fiscal Monitor. [Available at https://www.imf.org/COVID19policytracker]
16. Mueller M, Morgan D (2017) New insights into health financing: First results of the international data collection under the System of Health Accounts 2011 framework. Health Policy 121(7):764–769. https://doi.org/10.1016/j.healthpol.2017.04.008
17. OECD (2021) Health expenditure on primary health care, in Health at a Glance 2021: OECD Indicators. OECD Publishing, Paris. https://doi.org/10.1787/0bb3b147
18. Sofi AA, Durai SRS (2017) Income convergence in India: evidence from nonparametric panel data. J Econ Stud 44(3):400–411
19. Solow RM (1956) A contribution to the theory of economic growth. Q J Econ 70(1):65–94
20. Wold Bank group (2021) World Development Indicator. [Retrieved from https://databank.worldbank.org/source/world-development-indicator]

Chapter 11
Examining the Relationship Between COVID-19 and Different Macroeconomic Variables of the Indian Economy: A Cointegration Analysis

Ruby Sarma

11.1 Introduction

The global pandemic COVID-19 has touched the life of everyone. No country in the world could get rid of SARS SARS-CoV-2 virus. All the countries across the globe somehow managed the same. Macro-economic indicators of the economies of the world have undergone drastic changes. As part of this, sectors of the economies also have been very much affected. Maybe it is of stock market indicators, of inflation, of unemployment, of tourism and hospitality, of trade disruptions, of government debt, of inequality between rich and poor, and many more destabilizations within and outside the economy.

Countries had to undertake policies on public expenditure in health [1], policies on sanitation [2], policies on healthcare support, i.e., number of acute care beds, hospital beds and number of physicians [3], and social support [4], etc. There has been so much of theoretical evidence that countries with higher GDP rates are able to provide their people with better living standards, public health programs, education and environmental sanitation. All of these lead to enhanced prevention, treatment of disease, better health and life expectancy in these affluent countries [5–8].

GDP per capita is an important variable in assessing economies' level of development. In developing countries, the majority are poor and the households have to experience economic struggles due to their limited budget [9]. Countries with lower national income, lower health care expenditure, lower quality of government, and lower social transfers have higher inequalities in mortality.

Having considered theoretical and empirical dimensions, it can be hypothesized that poorer countries, characterized by lower economic performance, and limited

R. Sarma (✉)
Rangia College, Assam, India
e-mail: ruby55.sarma@gmail.com

R. Bhattacharyya et al. (eds.), *COVID-19 Pandemic and Global Inequality*,
https://doi.org/10.1007/978-981-99-4405-7_11

health and fiscal capacities of governments might underperform in tackling the COVID-19 pandemic.

This has repercussions in the post-pandemic period too. Because of mismanagement of macro-economic variables, the problems aggravate further. Traditionally, because of the weak nature of governance, the poor countries are supposed to face acute inequalities in the distribution of income and wealth. Contrary to this, Deaton shows that richer countries after the pandemic, experienced larger economic contractions than poorer countries in 2020 [10]. Francisco [11] showed that despite their advantages, richer countries have shown a larger loss in life years due to the pandemic than many poorer countries. Thus, the pandemic proves to be responsible for a massive global recession. As part of this, inequality within many countries is on the increase. It is because of the evidence of rising poverty and rising billionaire incomes. Moreover, when differences in GDP per capita are weighted by population, inequality between countries has increased [10] after the pandemic.

The economy of India marked vulnerable to unemployment and poverty even prior to the pandemic. Naturally, the pandemic was a big blow to it. The economic crisis after March 2020 affected all the sectors of the Indian economy. Broken supply chains, lack of market outlets, poor demand and falling output prices—all acted as hindrances for the farmers. In industry, micro and small enterprises were the most affected. The crisis led to a loss of employment to the tune of at least 15 million. At the first wave, nearly 10 million labourers returned to their homes. As projected by the International Labour Organisation, 400 million people in India would fall into poverty, both in the extensive margin (headcount) and intensive margin (deprivation depth). Unemployment levels had spiked to 23.5% but with a mid-June recovery to 8%. Similarly, the service sector was also affected. Services contribute over half of GDP. However, it remained low at 33.7% in 2020. Thus, the economy is withstanding both supply and demand shocks, all resulting in a decline in wholesale and retail price indices, along with unemployment and poverty. To mitigate the damage, the Government of India had announced fiscal stimulus of 20 trillion rupees (10% of GDP). RBI also announced expansionary monetary policy. In spite of the efforts, banks accessed only 520 billion rupees out of the emergency guaranteed credit window of 3 trillion rupees. Just like investment, recovery through consumption has stalled. Even if consumption of electricity, petrol and diesel has started to recover, they are still below the pre-pandemic period.

The structural adjustment process initiated by the Government of India is supposed to have far-reaching effects on the entire economy, and across the sectors. The present paper tries to examine the relationship between COVID-19 and different macroeconomic variables: inflation, exchange rate and nifty fifty.

11.2 Review of Literature

Rao et al. [12] analysed the negative effects of inflation in India, especially, its effect on common people. With statistical data, the study analysed food inflation and suggested appropriate government policies to correct the same. Victor et al. [13] investigated the inflation–unemployment dynamics during the recession and COVID-19 times in India and the UK. Their study revealed that the recession and COVID-19 pandemic had given way to stagflation in India. Armantier et al. [14] used the New York Fed's Survey of Consumer Expectations (SCE hereafter) to study how U.S. households' inflation beliefs, including inflation expectations, uncertainty and disagreement, were affected during the first six 3333 months of the COVID-19 pandemic. Their study found immediate and unprecedented increases in individual inflation uncertainty and in inflation disagreement across respondents. Barry et al. [15] articulated that the Reserve Bank of India is the best target of inflation of the economy as a whole. It considers the output gap in setting policy rates. However, this capacity to target has become challenging during the Covid crisis. Bobeica and Hartwig [16], Orkideh and Lee [17] examined structural shocks in the Western world after COVID-19 and proposed a model to forecast future price levels in pandemic. Santacreu and LaBelle [18] investigated the role of Global Supply Chain disruptions in the Producer Price Index (PPI) in the U.S. economy and found that the prices of the output of those industries increased which relies on foreign countries for inputs.

Ebrahimy et al. [19] examines the potential drivers and dynamics of inflation during the COVID-19 pandemic. They distinguished between the lockdown phase and the reopening phase. They found no evidence of expected inflation to rise. However, they found a rise in the variance of expected inflation indicating significant uncertainty and a potential risk of de-anchoring. The global pandemic not only influenced the inflation rate across the world, but also severely affected the exchange rate. Narayan [20] examined the Yen-US dollar exchange rate's resistance to shocks and concluded that COVID-19 has changed the resistance of the Yen to shocks. Feng et al. [21] explore the impact of COVID-19 and the relevant government response policies on exchange rate volatility in 20 countries during the period of January 13, 2020 to July 21, 2020. The empirical results of their study indicated that an increase in confirmed cases significantly raised the exchange rate volatility. Here, they found two types of results: the various policies adopted by governments in response to the pandemic, such as the closing of schools, restrictions on internal movements, and public information campaigns that inhibit exchange rate. On the contrary, the economic response policies implemented by governments during the pandemic, such as income support, fiscal measures, and international aid, have a restraining effect on exchange rate volatility.

Li et al. [22] attempted to highlight the impact of COVID-19 confirmed cases and deaths occurring in the most affected countries of the world such as China and the USA, especially in the context of their respective currencies. The study has found that response policies implemented by governments during the pandemic, including income support, fiscal measures, and international aid, have a restraining effect on exchange rate volatility.

Banerjee et al. [23] examined the effect of COVID-19 on the Foreign Exchange Rate and Stock Market of the Indian economy. They used secondary data over a span of 112 days spanning between March 11 and June 30, 2020. The study tries to explore any causality among the growth rate of confirmed cases, exchange rate and SENSEX value. Using vector autoregressive (VAR) models, they found a positive correlation between the growth rate of confirmed cases and the growth of the exchange rate and a negative correlation between the growth of confirmed cases and the growth rate of SENSEX value. However, the study observed that an increase in confirmed COVID-19 cases causes no significant change in the values of exchange rate and SENSEX index. Also, they found variation of results if the analysis is split across different time periods: before lockdown, the first phase of unlock, and the four phases of lockdown.

Dinh and Pham [24] compared the economies of India and Vietnam on the basis of two aspects: gold price volatility and several COVID-19 indicators such as daily confirmed cases, cumulative totals, daily death cases, cumulative death cases, etc. The study has found that COVID-19 indicators have the opposite effect on gold prices in India and Vietnam. The study used GARCH(1,1) model and the date of COVID-19 cases and the death of COVID-19 deaths as two dummies. The study found no evidence of the COVID-19 dummy's effect on gold price volatility in India. However, in the case of Vietnam, it has been found a negative impact of the same indicators.

Salim [25] explores interactions between COVID-19 cases, political responses, and exchange rates among countries. The study considers foreign exchange rates as a proxy for global economic response to the growing number of COVID cases and political reactions and responses to the pandemic. The study finally finds and increase in demand for as well as the value of the dollar. Sing et al. [26] try to find out the relationship between COVID-19 infections, Exchange Rates, Stock Market Return, and Temperature in G7 Countries. They applied the Partial and Multiple Wavelet Coherence technique during the period January 4 to July 31, 2021. The study has found that increases in temperature in G7 countries have a significant bearing on spreading the novel coronavirus. Moreover, the study has found that confirmed COVID-19 cases have a significant bearing on exchange rates and stock market returns. In addition to these, when the effects of temperature and equity market returns are taken into consideration, a stronger correlation between the exchange rate returns of the various countries and the rise in COVID-19 cases is seen. Co-movements are more noticeable when taking into consideration the impact of temperature and exchange rate returns, as well as the rise in the confirmed number of coronavirus-infected cases and equity returns.

Yarovaya et al. [27], using both stock indexes and stock index futures, give empirical evidence on the patterns of intra- and inter-regional information transmission across 10 developed and 11 emerging markets in Asia, the Americas, Europe, and Africa. The study, through the analysis of return and volatility spillovers around the most recent crises based on the generalized vector autoregressive framework, the main transmission channels were explored for the period from 2005 to 2014. The research shows that local and regional volatility shocks are more likely to affect markets than inter-regional contagion. Yarovaya et al. [28] examine how volatility spreads across stock index futures in six important Asian developed and emerging markets. The study investigates the potential sensitivity of the widely used volatility spillover tests to the use of range volatility estimators. The findings show that markets in the Asian region are strongly interconnected, demonstrating that the markets that receive signals are vulnerable to both positive and negative volatility shocks, demonstrating the asymmetric nature of volatility transmission channels. Moreover, the study highlights the close connections across markets in the Asian area, highlighting how both positive and negative volatility shocks can affect markets that receive signals. This highlights the asymmetric character of volatility transmission channels.

11.3 Materials and Methods

11.3.1 Data Source

World Development Indicator data were gathered for all explanatory variables. We looked at the relationship between COVID-19 and a few selected variables using monthly data from 2000 to 2022 for all variables. As a result of the log transformation, which reduced the scale range over which the variables are assessed, the data were subsequently transformed into logarithmic form. For denoting the log form of the variables Covid 19, Exchange rate Inflation, and Nifty 50, respectively, we have used LNCOIVD19, LNER, LNINFLATION, and LNNIFTY.

11.3.2 Stationarity Test

Unit root or non-stationarity in the time series analysis must be tested in order to prevent erroneous regressions. For all of the logarithmic series and their initial differences, we ran the Augmented Dickey–Fuller (ADF) unit root test to check whether the data were stationary. The following has been included for the intercept and trend components in the ADF test of the estimated relation:

$$\Delta X_t = \varphi_0 + \beta t + \rho X_{t-1} + \sum_{i=1}^{P} \gamma_i \Delta X_{t-1} + \varepsilon_t \tag{11.1}$$

The ADF test is the t-statistics calculated with the estimated coefficient of ρ, and the probability distribution of that is a functional of the Weiner process that is used to explain the Brownian motion of a particle with a large number of molecular shocks. According to ADF statistic, if the calculated values are less than their critical values then the variable series (LNCOIVD19, LNER, LNINFLATION and LNNIFTY) are said to be stationary or integrated of zero order that is $I(0)$. If the tests are insignificant, then again both the tests are performed on the first difference of variable X (i.e. ΔX). Now, we said that the X is integrated of order 1 that is $I(1)$.

11.3.3 Cointegration

The study used a cointegration test to identify the stable and non-spurious relationship among the chosen variables after assessing the stationarity of the data. Here, we used the cointegration technique proposed by Johansen & Juselius (1990). The Maximum Eigenvalue Test and the Trace Test are the two tests used in this method to ascertain the quantity of cointegrating vectors that are present. The test statistics are computed using the formula below.

$$\text{Trace} = -T \sum_{i=r+1}^{p} Ln(1 - \lambda_i) \tag{11.2}$$

where $\lambda_{r+1}, \ldots\ldots \lambda_p$ are $p - r$ smallest estimated Eigenvalues. The likelihood ratio test statistic for the null hypothesis of r cointegrating vectors against the alternative of $r + 1$ cointegrating vectors is the Maximal Eigenvalue test and is given by

$$\lambda_{\max} = -T[\ln(1 - \lambda_i)] \tag{11.3}$$

We can reject the null hypothesis of no cointegration if the calculated Trace statistic or Max Eigen Value surpasses the critical value.

11.4 Results and Analysis

11.4.1 Outcomes of Stationary Test

As mentioned in the materials and methodology part, the study has applied the ADF test to identify the stationary properties of the selected variables. Stationarity is primarily tested via unit root tests. The test findings also aid in determining the needed order of integration, or the number of times the data point needs to be varied. In order to eliminate a unit root or specific trend, the study applies the Augmented Dickey–Fuller (ADF) test to all the variables. The outcomes of ADF unit root test is displayed in Table 11.1.

Following the test statistics, the study observed that all the selected variables are non-stationary at levels but stationary in first differences. Thus, we conclude that all the data series are $I(1)$.

Table 11.1 Outcome of stationary test

Series	Augmented Dickey–Fuller test statistics	
	Level	First difference
LNCOVID 19	−2.387	−5.047*
LNER	−1.003	−5.790*
LNINFLATION	−3.212	−3.993**
LNNIFTY	−2.091	−7.783*

Source Author

11.4.2 Outcomes of Cointegration Tests

In Table 11.2, the estimated results of Johansen's cointegration tests have been shown. The table displays the total number of cointegrating vector results for the provided specification. Trace statistics have been used to demonstrate these. Similar evidence is presented in the second section of the table, which uses the maximum eigenvalue test to identify the cointegrating vectors. The null hypothesis is rejected in each case of trace statistics based on *p*-values at 5% significance. At the 5% level of significance, the trace statistic is always higher than the crucial value. Four cointegrating correlations between the variables are shown by the trace test. Similarly, under the maximum eigenvalue test also the study observed four cointegrating equations. Thus, both the trace test and the max-Eigen value test have indicated four cointegrating equations at the 1% level.

In short, the statistics are consistent with the evidence that the COVID-19 cases, NIFTY, and economic indices like inflation and exchange rate have a long-term association. Outcomes of the study suggest that every sphere of the economy, including the stock markets, was impacted by the COVID-19 virus' quick spread. The stock markets of industrialized and emerging nations have both experienced significant volatilities. However, the impact of COVID-19 on stock market performance may only be temporary because of the robust foundations of developed country stock markets, and those markets may rebound during the economic recovery.

Table 11.2 Result of the cointegration test

Trace Test				
Hypothesized				
No. of CE(s)	Eigenvalue	Trace Statistic	0.05 Critical Value	Prob.**
None*	0.507118	53.82299	40.17493	0.0013
At most 1	0.433908	33.30593	24.27596	0.0028
At most 2	0.300596	16.80497	12.3209	0.0083
At most 3	0.199049	6.436706	4.129906	0.0133
Maximal Eigenvalue Test				
Hypothesized				
No. of CE(s)	Eigenvalue	Max-Eigen Statistic	0.05 Critical Value	Prob.**
None *	0.507118	20.51706	24.15921	0.1444
At most 1	0.433908	16.50096	17.7973	0.0774
At most 2	0.300596	10.36826	11.2248	0.0705
At most 3	0.199049	6.436706	4.129906	0.0133

*Denote rejection of the hypothesis at the 0.05 level.
**Mackinnon–Haug–Michelis (1991) *p*-values.
Trace test indicates 4 cointegrating equations at the 0.05 level.
Maximal Eigenvalue test statistics indicate 4 cointegrating equations at 0.05 level.
Source Author

11.5 Conclusion

The present chapter tries to examine the relationship between COVID-19 and different macro variables of the Indian economy. To fulfil the objectives, the study has used monthly data of selected variables during the year 2020 to 2022. Initially, the study has employed a unit root test to examine the stationary property of the variables. In addition to this, the study has also applied a co-integration test to examine the long-run relationship among the variables. The study has found that all the variables used are integrated of order one, that is, they are non-stationary at a level and become stationary at first difference. After identifying the order of integration, we have applied the co-integration technique as mentioned above. The outcome of the co-integration test implies that there is a long-run relationship among the selected variables.

The global pandemic compels the policymakers across the globe to re-design, and re-thought the public policies of national interest. In order to mitigate the difficulties of the pandemic, some country-specific prescriptions are to be followed. Policies concerning the macro variables should be such that they create confidence, and resilience on the part of the government as well as of the public, not only to gear up from the present uncertain and dangerous situation but also to face further difficulties.

References

1. Ng WL (2020) To lockdown? When to peak? Will there be an end? A macroeconomic analysis on COVID-19 epidemic in the United States. J Macroecon 65:103230. https://doi.org/10.1016/j.jmacro.2020.103230
2. Caruso BA, Freeman MC (2020) Shared sanitation and the spread of COVID-19: risks and next steps. Lancet Planet Health 4:e173. https://doi.org/10.1016/S2542-5196(20)30086-3
3. White DB, Lo B (2020) A framework for rationing ventilators and critical care beds during the COVID-19 pandemic. JAMA 323:1773–1774. https://doi.org/10.1001/jama.2020-5046
4. Bavel JJVK, Baicker PS, Boggio V, Capraro A, Cichocka M, Cikara MJ et al (2020) Using social and behavioural science to support COVID-19 pandemic response. Nat Hum Behav 4:460–471. https://doi.org/10.1038/s41562-020-0884-z
5. Mackenbach JP, Looman CWN (2013) Life expectancy and national income in Europe, 1900–2008: an update of Preston's analysis. Int J Epidemiol 42:1100–1110. https://doi.org/10.1093/ije/dyt122
6. Krieger N (2011) Epidemiology and the people's health. Theory and context. Oxford University Press, Oxford
7. Kunitz SJ (2007) The health of populations. General theories and particular realities. Oxford University Press, Oxford
8. Smith JP (1999) Healthy bodies and thick wallets: the dual relation between health and economic status. J Econ Perspect 13:145–166. https://doi.org/10.1257/jep.13.2.145
9. McKee M (2009) The public health effect of economic crises and alternative policy responses in Europe: an empirical analysis. Lancet 374:315–323. https://doi.org/10.1016/S0140-6736(09)61124-7
10. Deaton A (2021) "COVID-19 and Global Income Inequality." NBER Working Paper 28392, National Bureau of Economic Research, Cambridge, MA
11. Ferreira FHG (2021) Inequality in the Time of Covid-19. Financ Dev
12. Rao et al. (2013) A Study on Inflation in India. Int Res J Soc Sci 2(12):51–55
13. Victor et al. (2021) From a recession to the COVID-19 pandemic: inflation–unemployment comparison between the UK and India. Economics 9:73. https://doi.org/10.3390/economies9020073
14. Armantier et al. (2021) How economic crises affect inflation beliefs: Evidence from the Covid-19 pandemic. J Econ Behav Organ 189:443–469
15. Eichengreen B, Gupta P, Choudhary R (2020) Inflation targeting in India: an interim assessment; policy research working paper. No. 9422. © World Bank, Washington, DC. https://openknowledge.worldbank.org/entities/publication/825942ec-e861-5e0d-9212-19391f49a91c License: CC BY 3.0 IGO
16. Bobeica, Hartwig (2023) The COVID-19 shock and challenges for inflation modelling. Int J Forcasting 39:519–539
17. Gharehgozli O, Sunhyung L (2022) Money supply and inflation after COVID-19. Economies 10:101. https://doi.org/10.3390/economies10050101
18. Santacreu, LaBelle (2022) Global supply chain disruptions and inflation during the COVID-19 pandemic. Federal Reserve Bank of St. Louis Review
19. Ebrahimy et al. (2020) The impact of COVID-19 on inflation: potential drivers and dynamics. IMF 2020 Special Notes series on covid19
20. Narayan PK (2020) Has COVID-19 changed exchange rate resistance to shocks? Asian Econ Lett 1(1) https://doi.org/10.46557/001c.17389
21. Feng et al (2021) What is the exchange rate volatility response to COVID-19 and government interventions? Econ Anal Policy 69(2021):705–719
22. Li et al. (2022) COVID-19 and currency market: a comparative analysis of exchange rate movement in China and USA during pandemic. Econ Res-Ekon Istraživanjas 35(1):2477–2492. https://doi.org/10.1080/1331677X.2021.1959368

23. Banerjee I, Kumar A, Bhattacharyya R (2020) Examining the Effect of COVID-19 on foreign exchange rate and stock market – an applied insight into the variable effects of lockdown on Indian Economy. ArXiv: Statistical Finance
24. Dinh Van S, and Pham Tuan A (2022) The influence of COVID-19 on gold price volatility – a comparative study of India and Vietnam. J Trade Sci
25. Salim I (2022) COVID-19 and the foreign exchange market: an analysis of the pandemic's effect on exchange rates. Honors College Theses 770. https://digitalcommons.georgiasouthern.edu/honors-theses/770
26. Sing et al. (2021) Nexus Between COVID-19 Infections, Exchange Rates, Stock Market Return, and Temperature in G7 countries: novel insights from partial and multiple wavelet coherence. Front Environ Sci Sec. Environ Econ Manag 9. https://doi.org/10.3389/fenvs.2021.772783
27. Yarovaya L, Brzeszczyński J, Lau CKM (2016) Intra-and inter-regional return and volatility spillovers across emerging and developed markets: evidence from stock indices and stock index futures. Int Rev Financ Anal 43:96–114
28. Yarovaya L, Brzeszczyński J, Marco Lau CK (2016) Volatility spillovers across stock index futures in Asian markets: Evidence from range volatility estimators. Financ Res Lett 17:158–166. https://doi.org/10.1016/j.frl.2016.03.005 https://www.sciencedirect.com/science/article/pii/S1544612316300174
29. Berkman FL, Kawachi I, Glymour MM (2014) Social epidemiology. Oxford University Press, Oxford, p 23

Chapter 12
Women Matter: An Analysis of Italian women's Employment Between Two Crises

Leonardo Salvatore Alaimo, Antonio Corasaniti, and Luisa De Vita

12.1 Introduction

The strongest impacts of economic downturns are often on female employment. However, this is not a generalized decrease, but has mainly affected specific economic sectors. The COVID-19 crisis has affected some of the fields in which women are most present, such as trade, tourism, and care services. The impacts also differ according to the employment contract and age. In Italy, for example, the protection measures activated by the government, such as the freeze of individual and collective *layoffs* for *redundancy*, have protected above all adult permanent employees. This contribution, focusing on the Italian situation, provides a comparison of the impacts on women's employment of two very different crises: the financial crisis of 2008 and the one generated by COVID-19. The aim is to show that, despite the different trends with an increase in female employment in the first case and a fall in the second, we have always the same problem: the quality of female employment.

While the great proportion of employed women in Italy is those with high educational attainments, women continue to have more atypical, lower-paid contracts and to be concentrated in *low*-tech and high labor-intensity *industries*. This prevents the improvement in conditions for working women those crises contribute to exacerbate. If the financial crisis has raised the level of women's employment, especially in low-skilled and low-wage occupations, the pandemic has hit just these occupations, pushing women even further out of the market.

L. S. Alaimo (✉) · A. Corasaniti · L. De Vita
Department of Social Sciences and Economics, Sapienza University of Rome, Rome, Italy
e-mail: leonardo.alaimo@uniroma1.it

A. Corasaniti
e-mail: antonio.corasaniti@uniroma1.it

L. De Vita
e-mail: luisa.devita@uniroma1.it

R. Bhattacharyya et al. (eds.), *COVID-19 Pandemic and Global Inequality*,
https://doi.org/10.1007/978-981-99-4405-7_12

The chapter will attempt, through an analysis of the microdata collected in the European Labour Force Survey (hereafter ELFS) for the 2009, 2011 and 2020, to analyse these mechanisms in detail.

The chapter is organized as follows. In the first paragraph, we discuss the long-term trends in female employment in Italy showing how crises, regardless of origin, contribute to the polarization of female employment. The second part presents the methodology and data analysis of the ELFS. The last part, together with the discussion of results, provides several insights for policymakers especially for rescheduling the investments planned in the post-pandemic recovery strategies.

12.2 Crisis and Quality of Female Employment in Italy

The deep employment crisis generated by the COVID-19 pandemic is mainly a crisis of female employment. Looking at the ISTAT data of December 2020, it is immediately obvious how there were more than 370 thousand fewer employed women compared to the same period in 2019. Of the total 445 thousand jobs lost in one year, 70% are women. However, the impacts are highly diversified across economic sectors like all economic downturns. As is well known, for example, during the 2008 financial crisis, which lasted with varying fluctuations until 2013, it was mainly women's employment that was holding out. Indeed, while heavily masculinized sectors such as finance or construction have suffered major losses, the demand for goods and services such as education, health, personal services, etc., has remained the same, thus favouring women massively employed in these sectors.

The crisis from COVID-19 19 on the contrary, has affected two of the industries where women are most present, trade and tourism, including the food service sector, which alone explains the largest share of the losses. In addition to differential impacts by sector, contractual differences are also significant. The layoff freeze and the wage guarantee fund have mainly protected permanent employees by exacerbating the inequalities in the labor market. Looking at the data, it was mainly fixed-term employment that declined with 22.7% fewer employed; self-employment dropped by 5.1% as did part-time work and collaboration. The collapse is also concentrated on young women, i.e., those mostly employed with more unstable contracts and therefore penalized by these employment dynamics. The only encouraging data is the retention of employment for educated women. Gender gaps decrease as educational attainment increases. In 2020, women with an upper-secondary degree have an employment rate 25.5 points higher than that of their peers with low levels of education, an advantage almost double that of men, and the difference between the rates of female college graduates and high school graduates is 16.6 points, an advantage three times higher compared with what occurs for male employment.

Employment outcomes are affected both by the greater employability in the labor market of higher educational qualifications and by the interest in participating in the labor market, which increases as the level of education attained rises" As evident from the data, in fact, the inactivity rate falls by more than 40 points in the transition from lower secondary school to college graduation." These advantages, however, diminish when looking at disciplinary pathways. Even during the crisis, male employment in STEM fields has grown while women, despite holding a degree in these disciplines, face greater entry difficulties. The occupational rate of women with degrees in STEM fields is 10% lower than that of men.

The recent pandemic crisis and the economic crisis of 2008, rather than marking a setback, serve as a magnifying glass of the historical problems affecting women's employment in Italy, which relate to 3 macro factors.

The first concerns the division of domestic and care work and services for children and the elderly, especially for the frail and dependent older adults. The second concerns the quality of employment with reference to working conditions, wages, protections, and career advancement. Finally, the third is related to the need to implement policies to also invest and allocate resources to those sectors where women are most present, namely the service sectors where essential and strategic products and services are offered for social inclusion and collective well-being.

On the first point, Covid and forced confinement provided further proof of the overwhelming gender asymmetry in domestic and care work division. The strong variability in employment rates between women with children and without children highlights the strong penalizing role that children play in women's access to and retention in the labor market as well as in their career paths [17]. As variously shown, women are forced to leave work at the birth of their first child in almost 20% of cases, and when they re-enter the labor market they usually do so with part-time contracts and low labor intensity. Even during the lockdown imposed in Italy, although it was plausible to expect some rebalancing in homebound families, no significant changes seem to have happened. In fact, research has shown that beyond minor adjustments, especially in younger and more highly educated families, it was mostly women who bore the burden of caregiving [8, 11], exacerbated also by the need to follow and organize distance education [5].

Policy initiatives often have prioritized the increase of the flexibilization of work, for example with the increased use even in the post-pandemic period of remote work. While less has been invested in the expansion of services. With respect to childcare services, the number of available places, especially in public services, is dramatically insufficient [10]. The coverage rate does not exceed 30%, and in 50% of cases, these are private facilities with fees that are often too high for many families. Also, very strong are the territorial gaps, in several southern Italian regions the coverage rate does not exceed 3% of the potential supply. In addition to the scant number of available services, these are services that are inadequate for the needs of female workers and need more flexible arrangements both in access criteria and on opening and closing times.

With respect to services for long-term care, the absolute prevalence of monetary transfers and the low investment in services not only does not create new employment but also prevents the development of the social infrastructure that is so much needed to boost the country's productive capacity. The investment in these services, in addition to providing new employment, also makes it possible to invest in human capital and professionalize a sector with a strong female presence that still suffers from disadvantageous working conditions in terms of both social recognition, wages and social protection.

The disadvantage is greatest for the most vulnerable women. As clear not only with the pandemic crisis but also since the economic crisis of 2008, those who have suffered the greatest disadvantages have been women with lower education and precarious working conditions. If indeed the crisis of 2008, had favoured women's employment but contributed to a sharp decline in the quality of work, the pandemic crisis wiped out especially low-educated women employed in low-skilled occupations.

As mentioned, highly educated women enjoy a better position although this is still a relative advantage and only compared to uneducated women since the gap with men with equal education remains constant.

Although women are better educated and have better peer performance, they have the finest results both on time to degree and get higher evaluations, but the performance in terms of employment still needs to improve. In addition to having uneven labor market participation, women have fewer chances for career advancement and earn significantly less than their male peers [22]. On the gender pay gap, the problem is mainly related to the greater concentration of women in those sectors where wages are lower. With respect to top positions, on the other hand, women experience a real "pay effect" whereby they are paid less for their work for the same qualifications, and this is especially true for managerial positions. Even the debated Gulfo–Mosca law on gender quotas, while achieving very important results in terms of presence on the boards of listed companies, has not produced significant effects for other managerial positions. For example, the presence of women in middle management positions has not improved either in numerical terms or with respect to pay [7, 19].

Finally, the third point regarding the need to devote more attention and resources to the service sector, especially personal services. As we know, these are highly feminized sectors that are considered essential to the functioning of socioeconomic systems that are often considered non-strategic or low value-added.

On the contrary, as pointed out earlier, investment in social infrastructure is strategic in a win–win logic in which both workers, especially women, and the broader social community benefit. Strengthening investment in essential sectors where women are the majority would ensure on the one hand the possibility of qualifying the sector, especially from the point of view of the skills employed, by improving working conditions which means higher wages and better social protections.

On the other hand, it would enable the provision of more qualified services, which would also have a positive impact on the quality of life of citizens.

From this point of view, investments directed to sectors in the hi-tech, digital, and those related to the green transition impact mainly in male-dominated sectors. It, therefore, seems crucial that investment in these sectors should also go in the direction of increasing the presence of women with expendable skills in these supply chains with important impacts in terms of the quality of female employment. On the other hand, supply chains related to care, personal services, trade, tourism and catering without investment are bound to remain underdeveloped. These jobs where women are massively employed are characterized by high informality, low productivity and thus low wages with very negative spillover effects on GDP as well.

12.3 Data and Methods

12.3.1 Data Description

We want to analyze the effects of a set of explanatory variables on the level of income of women in Italy in three years, 2009, 2011 and 2020. In order to do this, we use data from the Eurostat's Labor Force Survey. Table 12.1 reports the variables used in this work.

The dependent variable is the level of income by decile (INCLEVEL), obtained by recoding the decile of income (INDECIL). Figure 12.1 reports the percentage distribution of INCLEVEL in the three years considered. We can observe how the distributions are quite similar, with a prevalence of women reporting low-income levels (around 40% in all years); as expected, the lowest percentages are for high incomes.

Figures 12.2, 12.3, and 12.4 in Appendix report the percentage distributions of the considered explanatory variables.

As shown in Table 12.2, among the high-skilled occupations, during the three years observed only the "Professional" group showed a marked increase. In contrast, female managers went from accounting for 1.3% of the total employed in 2009 to 0.8% in 2020. The same trend for the group of "Technicians and associate professionals", who went from weighing in at 26.2% of the total in 2009 to nearly 17% in 2020. At the same time, for medium- and low-skilled occupations, female workers employed in "services and sales" occupations increase as a percentage of the total, while the percentage of those employed in elementary occupations does not show a consistent change between 2009 and 2020.

Taking into consideration the type of employment (Table 12.3), the occupational groups that show clear changes between 2009 and 2020 are the "Professionals" and the "Services and sales workers" on the one hand, which see their weight increase in percentage terms as far as full-time jobs are concerned, while on the other hand, a decreasing trend can be identified among "Technicians and associate professionals" and "Elementary occupations", which go from representing 29.8 and 10.6% of full-time female workers in 2009 respectively, to 18.7 and 8% for 2020.

With regard to part-time work, it is the medium- and low-skilled occupational groups that see their weight increase in the total computation of part-time workers: in fact, the group of "Services and sales workers" over the three years registers a steady increase in this regard, rising from 24.3% in 2009 to 32.3% in 2020, and the "Elementary occupations" which, while in the transition from 2009 to 2011 see their weight increase from 22 to 24.6%, despite a slight decrease registered for 2020 (23.1%) fail to return to the 2009 levels.

Table 12.1 Variables used: names; descriptions and modalities

Variable name	Description	Modalities
INCDECIL	Monthly (take home) pay from main job (deciles)	From 1 (Below the 1st decile) to 10 (More or equal to the 9th decile
INCLEVEL	Level of income by decile	Low: from 1 (below the 1st Dec.) to 3 (between 2nd and 3rd Dec.) Medium: from 4 (between 3rd and 4th Dec.) to 7 (between 6 and 7th Dec.) High: form 8 (between 7 and 8th Dec.) to 10 (more or equal to the 9th Dec.)
HATLEV1D	Level of education	Low: Lower secondary; Medium: Upper secondary; High: Third level
AGE	Age class of population	15–19; 20–39; 40–54; 55–69
REGIONW	Macro-area of place of work	North; Centre; South
ISCO1D/ IS881D	Occupation classification (coded 1 digit)	1: Managers. 2: Professionals. 3: Technicians and associate professionals. 4: Clerical support workers. 5: Service and sales workers. 6: Skilled agricultural, forestry and fishery workers 7: Craft and related trades workers. 8: Plant and machine operators and assemblers. 9: Elementary occupations
FTPT	Full-time/ Part-time distinction	Full-time job; Part-time job
TEMP	Permanency of the job	Person has a permanent job or work contract of unlimited duration; Person has temporary job/work contract of limited duration
CHILD 0–8	Presence of children aged less than 9 years in the household	Yes; No

Source Compiled by the authors using Eurostat's Labor Force Survey

Most occupational groups show within them a decrease in female full-time workers over the 12-year period considered (Table 12.4). This is most evident for groups connoted by medium and low qualifications, such as Service and Sales workers (-6.8 percentage points) and Elementary Occupations (-14.4 percentage points). Obviously, these are the groups where, on the other hand, the share of part-time female workers increases in percentage terms, while for the group of Managers, as well as the group of Craft and related trades workers, the decrease in the incidence of part-time work in the total number of employed women is quite clear in the group as a whole.

In every group except the armed forces, the presence of women with a child aged 0–8 years decreases (Table 12.5). This generalized trend, however, is not the same for all groups; in fact, it is mainly female workers in the Managers, Services and sales workers, Skilled and agricultural workers, and Craft related trades workers groups that show a significant increase in percentage terms between 2009 and 2020. Consequently, it is precisely these groups that have marked a sharp decrease in percentage terms within them of women with children 0–8. For the remaining groups, however, the variations are small in both cases.

12.3.2 Model Specification

We want to analyze the effects of a set of explanatory variables on the level of income (in a scale from 1—Low to 3—High), an ordinal variable. Ordinal variables are often analyzed with the linear regression model. However, such variables violate the assumptions of the linear models, which can lead to incorrect conclusions [14, 16, 25]. For this type of variable, we know the categories are ordered (running from high to low or low to high), but the distance between the categories is unknown [12, 13]. That is, unlike continuous variables, the distance between values 1 and 2 need not be the same as the distance between values 2 and 3. With ordinal outcomes, it is much better to use ordinal response models that avoid the assumption that the distances between categories are equal and, consequently, the problems of treating ordinal variables as though they are continuous. There is more than one ordinal regression model. One of the most popular models is the so-called proportional odds model [14], also known as the proportional odds version of the cumulative

Fig. 12.1 Percentage distributions of income's deciles for women: year 2009, 2011, 2020

Table 12.2 Distribution of employed women per Isco per year (100% per column)

ISCO	2009 (%)	2011 (%)	2020 (%)
Armed forces	0,1	0,1	0,1
Managers	1,3	0.9	0,8
Professionals	10,5	17,1	19,0
Technicians and associate professional	26,2	17,7	16,9
Clerical support workers	21,0	21,6	21,2
Services and sales workers	16,9	20,5	22,6
Skilled agricultural, forestry and fishery workers	0,3	0,3	0,3
Craft and related trades workers	5,3	4,2	2,8
Plant and machine operators—assemblers	4,1	3,7	3,2
Elementary occupations	14,2	14,1	13,2
TOT	100	100	100

Source Computed by the authors

Table 12.3 Composition of Full-time and Part-time job per Isco (Employed women; 100% per column)

ISCO	2009		2011		2020	
	FT (%)	PT (%)	FT (%)	PT (%)	PT (%)	FT (%)
Armed forces	0,1	0,0	0,1	0,0	0,2	0,0
Managers	1,7	0,5	1,2	0,2	1,2	0,1
Professionals	13,0	4,8	22,1	7,3	25,4	7,6
Technicians and associate professional	29,8	18,2	18,1	13,2	18,7	11,8
Clerical support workers	20,0	20,7	20,7	19,7	21,3	20,8
Services and sales workers	14,2	24,3	18,1	28,5	18,2	32,3
Skilled agricultural, forestry and fishery workers	0,4	0,3	0,3	0,3	0,4	0,3
Craft and related trades workers	5,0	6,8	4,3	4,3	3,0	2,2
Plant and machine operators and assemblers	5,1	2,4	4,7	2,0	3,7	1,8
Elementary occupations	10,6	22,0	10,3	24,6	8,0	23,1
TOT	100	100	100	100	100	100

Source Computed by the authors

Table 12.4 Full-time and Part-time distribution per Isco (Employed women; 100% per row)

ISCO	2009		2011		2020		TOT (%)
	FT (%)	PT (%)	FT (%)	PT (%)	FT (%)	PT(%)	
Armed forces	98,4	1,6	92,9	7,1	98,6	1,4	100
Managers	90,2	9,8	92,8	7,2	95,3	4,7	100
Professionals	87,2	12,8	87,6	12,4	86,8	13,2	100
Technicians and associate professional	80,5	19,5	76,2	23,8	75,8	24,2	100
Clerical support workers	70,8	29,2	71,0	29,0	66,9	33,1	100
Services and sales workers	59,5	40,5	59,7	40,3	52,7	47,3	100
Skilled agricultural, forestry and fishery workers	76,5	23,5	71,6	28,4	69,4	30,6	100
Craft and related trades workers	64,9	35,1	69,7	30,3	73,0	27,0	100
Plant and machine operators and assemblers	84,1	15,9	84,6	15,4	79,9	20,1	100
Elementary occupations	54,9	45,1	49,5	50,5	40,5	59,5	100

Source Computed by the authors

Table 12.5 Percentage of female workers with at least one child aged less than 9 within the household (100% per raw)

ISCO	2009		2011		2020		TOT (%)
	No (%)	Yes (%)	No (%)	Yes (%)	No (%)	Yes (%)	
Armed forces	83,3	16,7	80,0	20,0	77,8	22,2	100
Managers	80,0	20,0	80,6	19,4	83,9	16,1	100
Professionals	77,2	22,8	77,2	22,8	79,0	21,0	100
Technicians and associate professional	73,9	26,1	71,1	28,9	78,8	21,2	100
Clerical support workers	76,3	23,7	76,5	23,5	79,6	20,4	100
Services and sales workers	77,6	22,4	79,3	20,7	82,4	17,6	100
Skilled agricultural, forestry and fishery workers	75,0	24,7	80,0	20,0	84,0	16,0	100
Craft and related trades workers	74,7	25,3	77,4	22,6	81,2	18,8	100
Plant and machine operators and assemblers	81,3	18,7	74,3	25,7	81,5	18,5	100
Elementary occupations	81,3	18,7	81,6	18,4	83,7	16,3	100

Source Computed by the authors

logit model [1], an extension of the binary logistic model for the cases in which the dependent variable assumes ordered categorical values. Such a model, probably the most frequently utilized in practice for ordinal response variables, uses cumulative probabilities which do not overcome a threshold. In this way, it makes the whole range of ordinal categories binary at that threshold. It is based on the cumulative distribution function:

$$\Pr(y \le m) = \pi\_1 + \pi\_2 + \cdots + \pi\_m = \frac{\exp\alpha_m + \boldsymbol{\beta X}}{1 + \exp\alpha_m + \boldsymbol{\beta X}}$$

where $m = 1, \ldots, J$ is the outcome category; $\boldsymbol{X}$ is the matrix of the explanatory variables; α_m the intercept and $\boldsymbol{\beta}$ (the vector of coefficients) are the parameters, we must estimate. $Pr(y \le m)$ measures the probability of y below a given m. From the previous equation, we can define the odds that an outcome is less than or equal to m given $\boldsymbol{x}$:

$$\Omega_{\le m|>m}(\boldsymbol{x}) = \frac{\Pr(y \le m|\boldsymbol{x})}{1 -. \Pr(y \le m|\boldsymbol{x})} \text{ for } m = 1, \ldots, J-1$$

If the cumulative odds are less than 1 (more than 1), the response is associated with a shift towards the right (left) of the response scale, namely a rise in the probabilities in the higher categories. The model can be estimated by calculating the natural logarithms of the odds, assumed to equal:

$$\ln\Omega_{\le m|>m}(\boldsymbol{x}) = \tau_m - \boldsymbol{x\beta}$$

where τ_m is the cut-point to estimate. In the case of three categories (like that of this work) and considering only one independent variable, where we are fixing the intercept to equal 0 and estimating the cut-points, the model is

$$\ln\frac{\Pr(y \le 1|\boldsymbol{x})}{1 - \Pr(y \le 1|\boldsymbol{x})} = \tau_1 - x\beta$$

$$\ln\frac{\Pr(y \le 2|\boldsymbol{x})}{1 - \Pr(y \le 2|\boldsymbol{x})} = \tau_2 - x\beta$$

$\boldsymbol{\beta}$ is the vector of p coefficients, each of which describes the influence of the p explanatory variables on the logit and the α_m parameter is related to the outcome category and not used in the interpretation of the results. This effect does not change for all the $J-1$ cumulative logits. One of the main assumptions of this logit formulation is the common effect of $\boldsymbol{\beta}$ in the $J-1$ equations. Therefore, each logit has its own intercept (α_m), but the regression coefficients ($\boldsymbol{\beta}$) do not depend on m, implying that the model assumes that the relationship between x_m and y is independent of m [14]. Consequently, because the regression parameters are independent of and invariant to the outcome category, the odds ratios (OR) are the same over each logit, and the common log odds ratio provides a single estimate of the log odds ratio over the cut-off points. This estimate is the optimum one obtained using the maximum likelihood methods. This assumption, the so-called parallel regression assumption or the proportional odds assumption, establishes that the relationship between each pair of outcome groups must be the same. Because the relationship between all pairs of groups is the same, there is only one set of coefficients (only one model). If this assumption is violated, there is no parallelism between the categories and, consequently, interpretations of the results will be wrong and we would need different models to describe the relationship between each pair of outcome groups. Models violating the parallel regression assumption should be used with care since they raise identification and interpretation issues [1].

We fitted proportional odds models to the data for the different years considered and tested the proportional odds assumption using the test proposed by [4]. For the three models, the tests reject the parallel regression assumption. When the hypothesis is rejected, we can use alternative models that do not impose the constraint of parallel regressions (see, for instance: [3, 14, 18, 23]), but this violation is never a reason to use linear regressions [13]. In this work, we opted for the generalized ordered logit model [6, 13, 15]. The parallel regression assumption, as previously written, results from assuming the same coefficient vector in all the $J-1$ equations. The generalized ordered logit model allows $\boldsymbol{\beta}$ to differ for each of the $J-1$ equations:

$$\ln\Omega_{\leq m|>m}(\boldsymbol{x}) = \tau_m - \boldsymbol{x}\boldsymbol{\beta}_m \text{ for } m = 1, \ldots, J-1$$

where predicted probabilities are computed as follows:

$$\Pr(y = 1|\boldsymbol{x}) = \frac{\exp\tau_1 - \boldsymbol{x}\boldsymbol{\beta}_1}{1 + \exp\tau_1 - \boldsymbol{x}\boldsymbol{\beta}_1}$$

$$\Pr(y = j|\boldsymbol{x}) = \frac{\exp(\tau_j - \boldsymbol{x}\boldsymbol{\beta}_j)}{1 + \exp(\tau_j - \boldsymbol{x}\boldsymbol{\beta}_j)} - \frac{\exp\left(\tau_j - \boldsymbol{x}\boldsymbol{\beta}_{j-1}\right)}{1 + \exp\left(\tau_j - \boldsymbol{x}\boldsymbol{\beta}_{j-1}\right)} \text{ for } j = 2, \ldots, J-1$$

$$\Pr(y = J|\boldsymbol{x}) = \frac{\exp\tau_{J-1} - \boldsymbol{x}\boldsymbol{\beta}_{J-1}}{1 + \exp\tau_{J-1} - \boldsymbol{x}\boldsymbol{\beta}_{J-1}}$$

12.4 Results

We start with the analysis of the association between the dependent variable (INCLEVEL) and the set of selected explanatory variables. To do this, we construct the contingency tables between the dependent variable and each independent variable (reported in Appendix). In Table 12.6 we report the χ^2 statistics and the Cramer's V index of each contingency table in different years. Because the χ^2 values are always significant, we could claim that there are relationships between INCLEVEL and the considered variables. Obviously, we can only claim that the distributions are different, because the χ^2 test is not directional. The Cramer's V index allows us to have a measure of association in a range from 0 (no association) to 1 (maximum association). We can observe that the values are practically the same in all years. The highest level of association (more than 0.5 in all years) is observed between INCLEVEL and the variable regarding full-time/part-time job distinction. Medium values of the association are observed for the occupation classification. All the other variables show weak levels of association with INCLEVEL, with the Macro-area of job and the presence of children aged less than 9 years in the household having 0 values.

At this point, we estimate three generalized ordered logit models, one for each considered year, by using STATA statistical software. Table 12.7 reports the results.

For each model, we have two sets of odds ratios labelled LOW and MEDIUM; the odds ratios indicate the factor change in odds of observing a value above the listed category versus observing values at or below the listed category. For each considered variable, we indicate the base level in parentheses.

In general, we can observe that the independent variables almost always show the same signs in different years. Specifically, regardless of the year considered, we can observe that:

- Women with higher educational qualifications are more likely to belong to a higher income decile. For instance, looking at 2009, women with a high education level have 2.497 times higher odds of having a medium or high-income decile than do women with a low level of education; women with high education have 4.205 times higher odds of having high-income decile than do women with a low level of education. Similar considerations apply to 2011 and 2020.
- Managers in almost every case are more likely to belong to a higher income decile. For 2009 alone, professionals have the higher probability, among the various groups, of belonging to higher income deciles, and only for those whose base income is low. As one moves into lower-skilled occupations, the probability tends to decrease more and more.
- Geographic area data also show the same result throughout the years, regardless of income bracket. The geographic variable shows that those who work in northern Italy are more likely to belong to a higher income decile, with the probability decreasing as one moves toward the South of the country.
- The presence of children between the ages of 0 and 8 within the household, while found to be statistically significant in determining higher probabilities of belonging to medium or high incomes for all three years examined, in the case where the starting point is lower-middle incomes are not significant for 2011 and 2020, but only for 2009. For the latter case, women with children belonging to this age group have 1.149 times higher odds of having high-income decile than do women without children aged between 0 and 8.
- Finally, focusing on the type of employment and the type of contract, the data show that women who are employed on a permanent basis and those with full-time contracts are more likely to belong to the upper income deciles than those who are employed on a permanent basis and those with part-time contracts. Similar considerations apply for all years taken in consideration.

Table 12.6 Association between level of income and different explanatory variables: χ^2 statistics; Cramer's V index. Years 2009, 2011, 2020

Variables	df	2009			2011			2020		
		χ2	Pr	Cramer's V	χ2	Pr	Cramer's V	χ2	Pr	Cramer's V
Level of education	4	1.10E + 04	0.000	0.281	1.10E + 04	0.000	0.278	1.00E + 04	0.000	0.284
Age class	6	4.00E + 03	0.000	0.171	4.00E + 03	0.000	0.169	2.00E + 03	0.000	0.126
Macro-area of job	4	326.414	0.000	0.049	436.4547	0.000	0.056	308.506	0.000	0.049
Occupation classification	10	2.20E + 04	0.000	0.403	2.30E + 04	0.000	0.411	2.10E + 04	0.000	0.410
Full/Part-time distinction	2	2.20E + 04	0.000	0.563	2.00E + 04	0.000	0.532	2.20E + 04	0.000	0.585
Permanency of the job	2	3.30E + 03	0.000	0.220	3.40E + 03	0.000	0.220	2.60E + 03	0.000	0.201
Presence of children aged less than 9 years	2	142.691	0.000	0.046	115.71	0.000	0.041	52.4568	0.000	0.029

Source Computed by the authors

Table 12.7 Generalized ordered logit regression models of income level of Italian women in 2009, 2011 and 2020, on a set of explanatory variables: odds ratios and z values by robust error estimation

		2009				2011				2020			
		LOW											
		Odds ratio	Std. Err.	z	P > |z|	Odds ratio	Std. Err	z	P > |z|	Odds ratio	Std. Err	z	P > |z|
Education (Low)	High	2.497	0.105	21.7	0	2.454	0.095	23.12	0	2.348	0.097	20.74	0
	Medium	1.504	0.044	14.03	0	1.394	0.039	11.82	0	1.571	0.05	14.33	0
Age Class (15–19)	20–39	2.088	0.074	20.9	0	1.878	0.068	17.52	0	1.766	0.08	12.58	0
	40–54	3.939	0.131	41.25	0	3.25	0.109	35.15	0	2.745	0.111	24.89	0
	55–69	4.967	0.233	34.22	0	3.891	0.169	31.34	0	3.286	0.146	26.73	0
Isco (Managers)	Professionals	1.29	0.164	2	0.046	0.599	0.1	−3.07	0.002	0.509	0.117	−2.93	0.003
	Technicians	0.75	0.09	−2.39	0.017	0.426	0.071	−5.14	0	0.345	0.079	−4.62	0
	Clerical workers	0.477	0.058	−6.13	0	0.266	0.044	−8	0	0.21	0.048	−6.79	0
	Service/sales workers	0.2	0.024	−13.25	0	0.081	0.013	−15.15	0	0.061	0.014	−12.19	0
	Elementary workers	0.061	0.007	−22.83	0	0.037	0.006	−19.71	0	0.037	0.009	−14.25	0
Macro-area (North)	South	0.429	0.011	−32.29	0	0.448	0.011	−31.73	0	0.456	0.013	−27.66	0
	Center	0.704	0.021	−11.53	0	0.638	0.018	−15.64	0	0.656	0.019	−14.38	0
Presence of Children (No)	Yes	1.294	0.037	8.96	0	1.2	0.033	6.57	0	1.168	0.038	4.82	0
Permanency of the job (Temporary)	Permanent	2.329	0.07	27.98	0	2.401	0.074	28.58	0	2.368	0.08	25.49	0

(continued)

Table 12.7 (continued)

		2009				2011				2020			
		LOW											
		Odds ratio	Std. Err.	z	P > |z|	Odds ratio	Std. Err	z	P > |z|	Odds ratio	Std. Err	z	P > |z|
Full-Time/ Part-Time (Full-time)	Part-time job	0.044	0.001	116.4	0	0.063	0.002	108.76	0	0.061	0.002	110.46	0
Constant		1.815	0.23	4.7	0	2.979	0.506	6.42	0	4.593	1.078	6.5	0
		MEDIUM											
		Odds ratio	Std. Err	z	P > |z|	Odds ratio	Std. Err	z	P > |z|	Odds ratio	Std. Err	z	P > |z|
Education (Low)	High	4.025	0.195	28.81	0	4.448	0.213	31.22	0	3.883	0.22	23.92	0
	Medium	2.14	0.092	17.79	0	2.04	0.088	16.45	0	2.03	0.109	13.25	0
Age Class (15–19)	20–39	1.831	0.086	12.86	0	1.781	0.09	11.42	0	1.519	0.089	7.15	0
	40–54	4.034	0.179	31.47	0	3.564	0.17	26.7	0	2.594	0.139	17.74	0
	55–69	6.19	0.319	35.42	0	5.636	0.299	32.54	0	3.754	0.211	23.48	0
Isco (Managers)	Professionals	0.526	0.043	−7.89	0	0.238	0.026	−13.33	0	0.174	0.023	−13.47	0
	Technicians	0.278	0.022	−16.36	0	0.187	0.02	−15.51	0	0.143	0.019	−14.89	0
	Clerical support workers	0.133	0.011	−25.15	0	0.087	0.009	−22.45	0	0.067	0.009	−20.61	0

(continued)

Table 12.7 (continued)

		2009				2011				2020			
		LOW											
		Odds ratio	Std. Err.	z	P > |z|	Odds ratio	Std. Err	z	P > |z|	Odds ratio	Std. Err	z	P > |z|
	Service/sales workers	0.058	0.005	−32.45	0	0.035	0.004	−29.52	0	0.023	0.003	−27.8	0
	Elementary workers	0.013	0.002	−36.87	0	0.013	0.002	−32.94	0	0.01	0.002	−29.2	0
Macro-area (North)	South	0.532	0.014	−23.93	0	0.529	0.014	−23.69	0	0.496	0.014	−24.23	0
	Center	0.735	0.022	−10.2	0	0.726	0.022	−10.5	0	0.67	0.02	−13.39	0
Presence of children (No)	Yes	1.149	0.034	4.75	0	1.023	0.03	0.77	0.443	1.04	0.034	1.19	0.236
Permanency of the job (Temporary)	Permanent	2.519	0.111	20.92	0	2.871	0.134	22.63	0	2.785	0.13	21.92	0
Full-Time/ Part-Time (Full-time)	Part-time job	0.102	0.004	−54.5	0	0.134	0.005	−50.83	0	0.145	0.006	−50.29	0
Constant		0.186	0.019	−16.57	0	0.263	0.033	−10.49	0	0.417	0.063	−5.76	0

(continued)

Table 12.7 (continued)

2009				2011				2020			
LOW											
Odds ratio	Std. Err.	z	P > |z|	Odds ratio	Std. Err	z	P > |z|	Odds ratio	Std. Err	z	P > |z|
N = 68,743				N = 69,566				N = 63,325			
AIC = 98,700.3 (df = 32)				AIC = 100,660.9 (df = 32)				AIC = 91,360.5 (df = 32)			
BIC = 98,992.7 (df = 32)				BIC = 100,953.7 (df = 32)				BIC = 91,650.3 (df = 32)			

Source Computed by the authors

12.5 Discussion and Conclusion

The presented data confirm the strong segmentation of the Italian labor market, which penalizes, especially the weakest categories. Although it is not yet possible to assess the effects on female employment due to the pandemic, the 2020 data currently available still allow us to highlight a downward trend.

Unsurprisingly, as educational qualifications increase, the probability of being in a middle- or upper-income level increases in all three years considered. The two crises have different outcomes, in fact, if the long-term effects of the financial crisis in 2008 pushed women's employment with an increase also of less qualified women, the first effects of the crisis from COVID-19 resulted in the market exit only for women in elementary occupations. The growth trend in female employment is unchanged for managers while it has increased for professionals. Looking at the data, elementary occupations were 14.6% of total female employment in 2011 became 13.15% in 2020 with professionals increasing from 17.6 to 19, 4%. Particularly significant is the data on income distribution that confirms inequalities in comparison with males even for highly educated women. The data clearly show how highly educated women placed in the highest income deciles in 2020 are only 13%, a downward trend since 2009, while men are almost 42%. On the contrary, if we look at low-educated women in 2020 almost 50% are placed in the last 2 deciles compared to 16% of men.

As widely expected, inequalities related to care loads are very strong. The Italian labor market continues to be hostile to women with children, and the 2020 data show a further worsening. Out of the total number of employed women between 2009 and 2020, the percentage of employed women with children decreased by 2.5% with a reduction mainly related to women placed in elementary occupations. This group after a slight growth between 2009 and 2011, where women with children in elementary occupations increased, collapsed again with the first effects of the pandemic crisis. In 2020, only 43.3% of women in elementary occupations had at least one child compared to 51.75 for professionals. Thus, the number of employed women with children up to the age of 8 declines further highlighting once again how the most disadvantaged is the low-skilled women. These results are also evident in the ordered logit regression model. Indeed, the probability of having a middle and high income is higher if one has children in the 0–8 range, and this is precisely related to the higher presence of professionals, who therefore have higher income, among women with children.

The data then confirm how sectors related to personal services, where most women's employment is concentrated, are the most likely to have occupations placed in the lowest income deciles. Moreover, these sectors from 2009 to 2020 have seen an increase in the number of employed women but the growth is mainly in part-time employment contracts from 45% in 2009 to 53.15 in 2020. The increase in part-time employment, which is predominantly involuntary in Italy, impacts also on wages, which, as evidenced by the regression model, decreases the probability of being in the highest income deciles.

Overall, the data presented on the quantity and quality of women's employment highlight how the crises only exacerbate Italy's difficulties as it struggles to make the most of women's human capital, even compared to educated women.

There are two main trends.

On one hand, the proportion of women among skilled professionals continues to increase, as does progress towards wage equality, albeit at a slower pace. Indeed, while the gender quota law introduced in Italy in 2011 has produced an increase in the number of women on the boards of listed companies, there have been no trickle-down effects either in management positions, where there are still few women, or in companies that are not required to comply with quotas.

To provide an example if we look at the data the law on gender quotas that forced publicly listed companies to increase the percentage of women on boards has generated important progress. Women on the boards of Italian listed companies (productive sectors excluding finance) in 2022 is almost 43% which ranks Italy above the European average. However, if we look at executive roles the presence of women remains at 14%, and the percentage of CEOs remains very low.

On the other hand, the employment conditions of the most vulnerable women (with children, low education, etc.) are found to be much worse, emerging of strong segregation among women. These impacts appear to be the result of the neo-liberal turn of gender equality policies aimed at valuing especially women who have high credentials and thus can meet the demands of competitive markets that, however, force the most fragile women to accept extremely disadvantageous conditions to stay employed [9, 20, 21].

Meaningful on this issue is the data on the working poor, which are mainly concentrated in the personal services sector where women are overrepresented. According to INPS's (Italian National Institute of Social Security) data, in 2018 women accounted for 38% of workers at risk of low wages. Furthermore, when comparing women and men in the same household, after the birth of a child, women are almost three times more likely to experience a wage downturn.

Against this backdrop, the pandemic crisis by affecting the sectors with the highest concentration of women has exacerbated inequalities, making it urgent to intervene on a broader scale, including from the investments planned under the National Recovery and Resilience Plan (NRRP).

With respect to the NRRP's planned investments, the most encouraging indications concern the planned investments to increase the supply of services, especially for children. As confirmed by OECD 2020 data, women receive pay for only 45% of working time, compared to 67% for men precisely because of women's greater commitment to domestic and care activities. In this sense, the plan has tried to provide a response by, on the one hand, funding the construction of new services especially in the most deprived areas and, on the other hand, increasing the share of services open both morning and afternoon.

The intention to act with skill-enhancing interventions to increase labour market opportunities is also positive. Actions are planned to work on digital skills and technical-scientific knowledge, the so-called STEM disciplines that offer important opportunities for fostering skilled employment and on which women are still under-trained. Likewise, support for female entrepreneurs, who still face many difficulties in accessing credit is also positive. Despite they represent a qualified and often very innovative pool with a clear vocation to offer products and services that are more sustainable and attentive to the needs of a broader community [24], resources for women's enterprises have been at a standstill for many years.

Fewer resources, on the other hand, are allocated to the highly feminized and essential services sector, which, as was tragically evident in the pandemic, are often considered non-strategic or low value-added. On the contrary, investment in social infrastructure is strategic in logic in which both workers, especially women, and society as a whole win. Strengthening investment in essential sectors where women are the majority would ensure on the one hand the possibility of qualifying the sector, especially from the point of view of the skills employed, by improving working conditions which means higher wages and better social protections. On the other hand, it would enable the provision of more services at higher quality with consequent positive effects on the quality of life of citizens as well. The use of NRRP funds, on the other hand, seems to favour mainly hi-tech, digital, and green transition-related sectors. While these are highly strategic sectors, it is important to remember that they are highly masculinized sectors thus is mandatory to increase the presence of women with expendable skills in these sectors.

So if renewal is expected from the NRRP, it seems to be necessary to enhance all women's human capital, making women key players and supporting more inclusive economic and social systems based on good quality employment for all.

Appendix

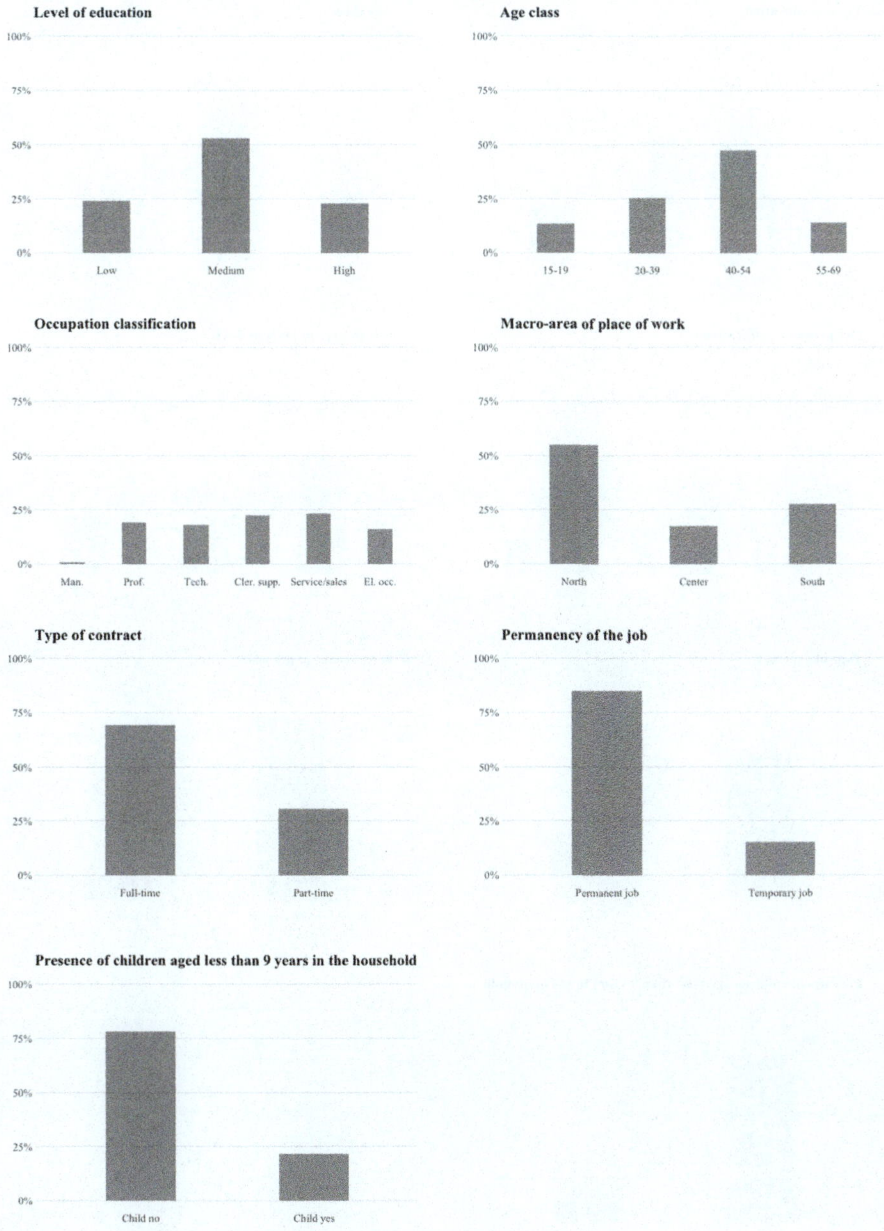

Fig. 12.2 Distributions of selected explanatory variables: year 2008

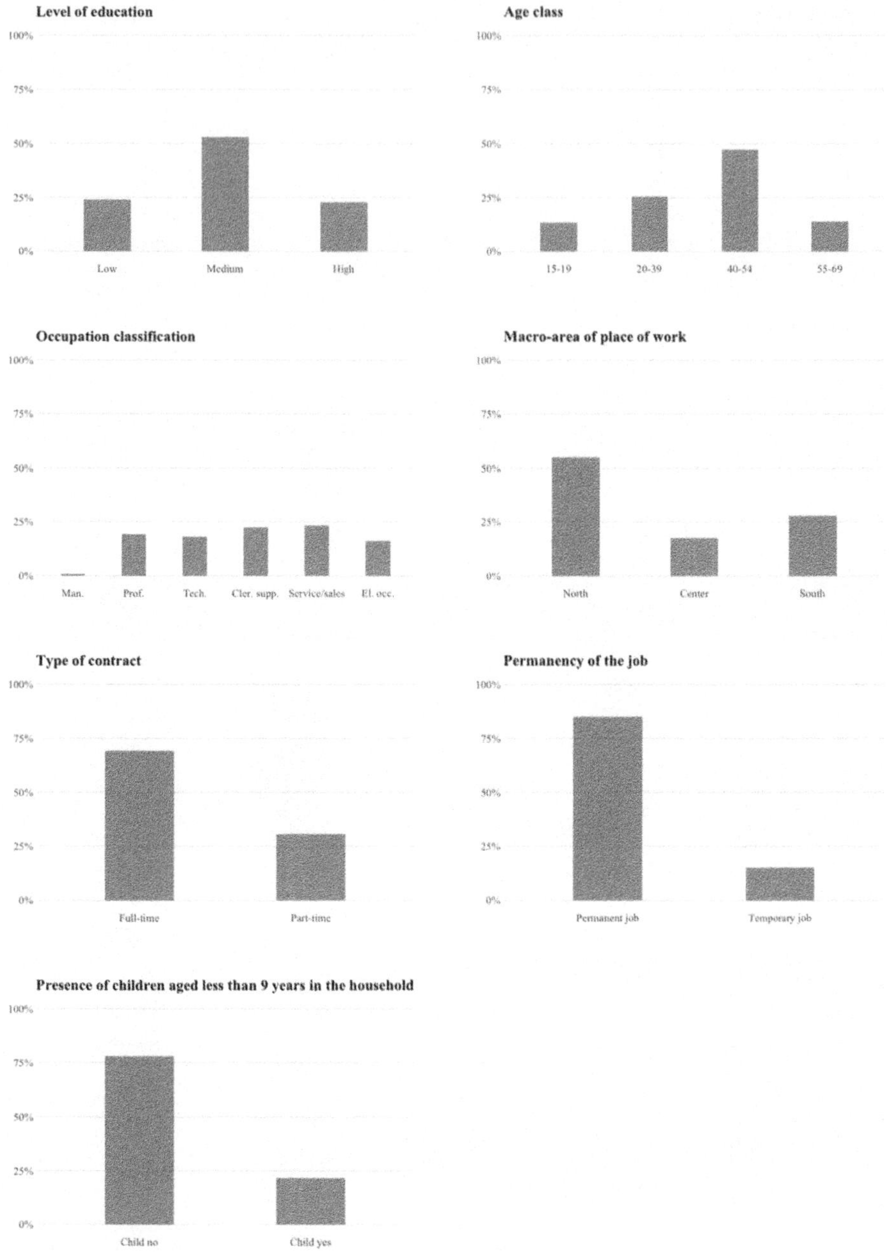

Fig. 12.3 Distributions of selected explanatory variables: year 2011

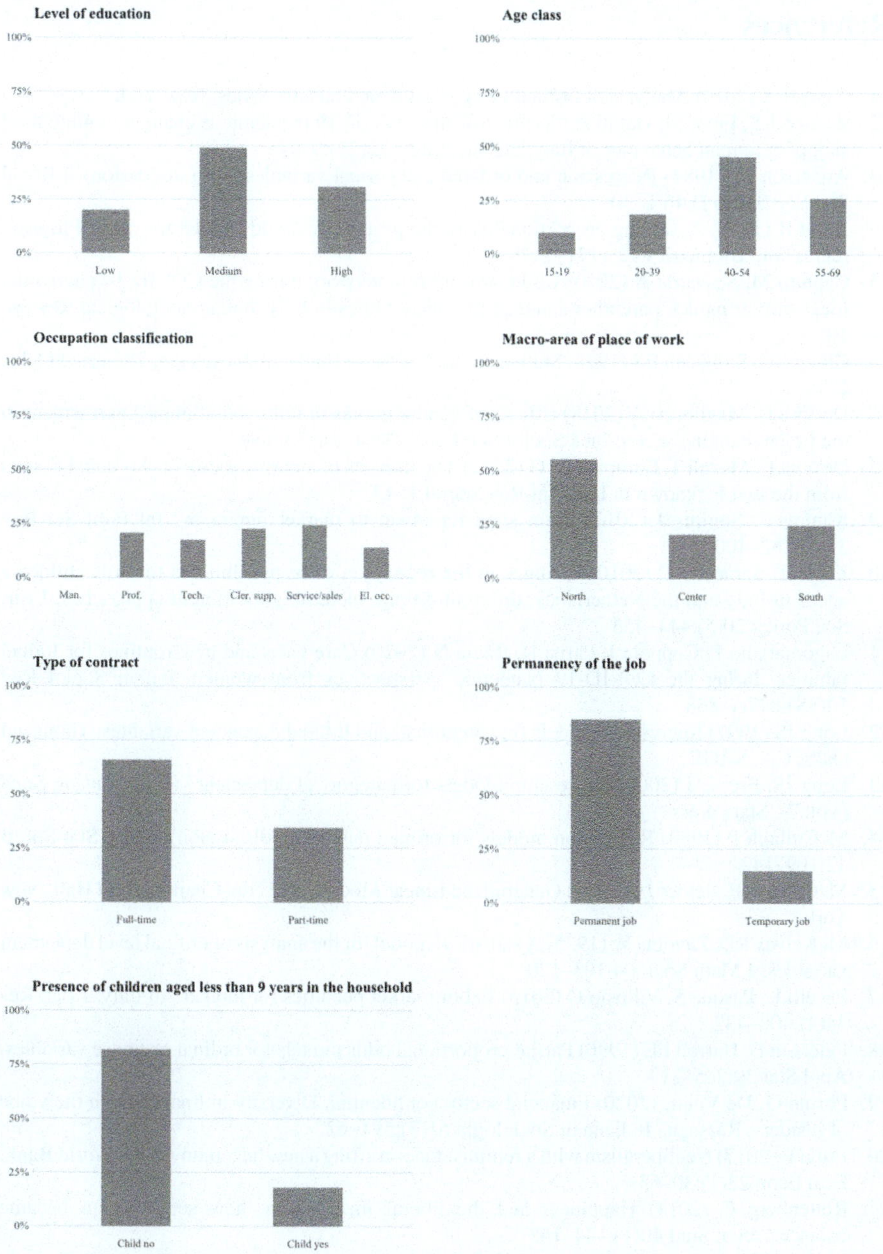

Fig. 12.4 Distributions of selected explanatory variables: year 2020

References

1. Agresti A (2010) Analysis of ordinal categorical data, 2nd edn. Wiley, New York
2. Alaimo LS, Fiore M, Galati A (2020) How the COVID-19 pandemic is changing online food shopping human behaviour in Italy. Sustainability 12(22):9594
3. Anderson JA (1984) Regression and ordered categorical variables (with discussion). J Royal Stat Soc Series D 46:1–30
4. Brant R (1990) Assessing proportionality in the proportional odds model for ordinal logistic regression. Biometrics 42:1171–1178
5. Cannito M, Scavarda A (2020) Childcare and remote work during the COVID-19 pandemic. Ideal worker model, parenthood and gender inequalities in Italy. Italian Sociological Review, 10
6. Clogg CC, Shihadeh ES (1994) Statistical models for ordinal variables. Sage, Thousand Oaks, CA
7. De Vita L, Magliocco A (2018) Effects of gender quotas in Italy: a first impact assessment in the Italian banking sector. Int J Sociol Soc Policy 38(7–8):673–694
8. De Vita L, Mazali T, Campanella G (2022) The impacts of smart working on women. Lessons from the first lockdown in Italy. Int Rev Sociol 1–17
9. Kantola J, Squires J (2012) From state feminism to market feminism? Int Polit Sci Rev 33(4):382–400
10. Knijn T, Saraceno C (2010) Changes in the regulation of responsibilities towards childcare needs in Italy and the Netherlands: different timing, increasingly different approaches. J Eur Soc Policy 20(5):444–455
11. Lagomarsino F, Coppola I, Parisi R, Rania N (2020) Care tasks and new routines for Italian families during the COVID-19 pandemic: perspectives from women. Italian Sociol Rev 10(3S):847A–868
12. Long JS (1997) Regression models for categorical and limited dependent variables. Thousand Oaks, CA: SAGE
13. Long JS, Freese J (2006) Regression models for categorical dependent variables using Stata (Vol. 7). Stata press
14. McCullagh P (1980) Regression models for ordinal data (with discussion). J Roy Stat Soc B 42:109–142
15. McCullagh P, Nelder JA (1989) Generalized Linear Models, 2nd edn. Chapman and Hall, New York
16. McKelvey RD, Zavoina W (1975) A statistical model for the analysis of ordinal level dependent variables. J Math Sociol 4:103–120
17. Pacelli L, Pasqua S, Villosio C (2013) Labor market penalties for mothers in Italy. J Lab Res 34(4):408–432
18. Peterson B, Harrell FE (1990) Partial proportional odds models for ordinal response variables. Appl Stat 39:205–217
19. Porino G, De Vita L (2020) Financial sector confidential. Diversity in finance from the voice of insiders. Rassegna Italiana di Sociologia 61(3):591–622
20. Prügl E (2017) Neoliberalism with a feminist face: crafting a new hegemony at the World Bank. Fem Econ 23(1):30–53
21. Rottenberg C (2014) Happiness and the liberal imagination: how superwoman became balanced. Fem Stud 40(1):144–168
22. Rubery J, Grimshaw D, Figueiredo H (2005) How to close the gender pay gap in Europe: towards the gender mainstreaming of pay policy. Ind Relat J 36(3):184–213
23. Skrondal A, Rabe-Hesketh S (2004) Generalized latent variable modeling: multilevel, longitudinal, and structural equation models. Chapman & Hall/CRC Press, Boca Raton, FL
24. Unioncamere (2020) IV Rapporto nazionale sull'imprenditoria femminile
25. Winship C, Mare RD (1984) Regression models with ordinal variables. Am Sociol Rev 49(4):512–525

Chapter 13
COVID-19, Online Education and Role of Mentoring in Developing Economies—A Theoretical Build-Up with an Empirical Overhaul

Nilendu Chatterjee and Tonmoy Chatterjee

13.1 Introduction

We all know how badly the Pandemic named Covid-19 hit every part of the world. Although first heard of in November 2019 in Wuhan province of China, but the rapid pace at which this disease has spread across the universe, its severity and its fast-changing nature—all are certainly not unknown to any of us. A disease that could transmit through almost anything could decide the life and death of individuals within a few days. Such severity with its awful nature along with a lack of knowledge about its treatment had shaken the world.[1] Since this disease does not care about any division of money, power, religion, region, caste, etc. it was transmitted and affected every part of the world with individuals of every social category. The consequent was quite expected, that is, lockdown or shutdown of economic and social activities to break the chain of transmission. The modern human civilization of twenty-first century, being powered by every sort of advancement, could hardly believe such an enforced shutdown of activities but for the sake of life, we all had to accept it in every part of the world.

By the end of March 2020, almost the whole of the world was compelled to go into lockdown, and as a result, economic and social activities came to a halt for an indefinite period. No one knew how long that shutdown would continue and its deadly

[1] Although the World has witnessed a pandemic in every 100 years for the last three centuries, but on every occasion the nature of the disease has been different and so has been its treatment. Covid -19, being absolutely a new disease was very hard to be diagnosed.

N. Chatterjee
Department of Economics, Bankim Sardar College, South 24 Parganas, Halapara, India

T. Chatterjee (✉)
Department of Economics, Bhairab Ganguly College, Kolkata, India
e-mail: tonmoychatterjee.economics@gmail.com

R. Bhattacharyya et al. (eds.), *COVID-19 Pandemic and Global Inequality*,
https://doi.org/10.1007/978-981-99-4405-7_13

impact on our future. But one thing was certain—life would never be like before in the post covid era. At the beginning of the lockdown period, entire civilization went into shock mode and hence at least for two to three weeks all sorts of activities were halted. So were the activities of the education sector. But the show should go on. For the sake of civilization and the future of millions of students, educational activities could not be stopped indefinitely. After a few months of lockdown, all the sectors gradually but surely started to open up again in order to restore normalcy but the sector that suffered the most is the Education Sector. Together with other sectors, education sector went into lockdown but unlike them, it could not open up maintaining various covid protocols. It has suffered from a prolonged and certainly the longest period of lockdown than any other sector, of more than eighteen months. In between this period, whenever any attempt of opening up was taken, it failed miserably because of the nature of activities involved with this sector.[2] Now the education sector has gradually opened up and we can only hope for the best to happen for both teachers and students. But one cannot forget the prolonged eighteen to twenty months which could be regarded as the "period of darkness, uncertainty but with a bright ray of light and hope". Even if educational sector has opened up, we know it won't be easy for both teachers as well as students, since it won't be like pre-pandemic era because a lot of things and practices have changed in between and the education system in India is on the verge of facing a paradigm shift in which online education is going to be the inevitable wing. Again, in this era of normalcy, we have to abide by the covid protocols and stop the spreading of the disease, as we do not know when this pandemic would surely come to an end.[3]

The questions that started to take central stage as soon as the lockdown started are—what will happen to the stakeholders of education, now? What will be the future of teaching–learning evaluation? As the number of cases of Covid kept on increasing, the lockdown got extended.[4] Questions that started to haunt were—will the students suffer by losing the academic year? Or, will the exams be postponed indefinitely? As the academic year went on, there needed to be more certainty about completing the remaining syllabus.[5] But, with the innovations and inventions of scientific tools and their appropriate use in teach-learning pedagogy through hand-held devices made the continuation of teaching–learning possible. In this circumstance of indefinite uncertainty, the approach that was taken all over the world was to continue the study through electronic medium, that is, online study was started and became predominant. It seemed appropriate to keep the students active without wasting the academic year, that is, without pushing them one step further into uncertain future. So, initiatives of

[2] By "nature of activities" we mean huge gathering of students which is almost impossible to avoid and norms of social distancing are hard to implement.

[3] The sudden and rapid upsurge of "Omicron" variant of Covid once again developed "cloud of fear" worldwide. Secondly, there are news of upsurge of covid cases in several parts of the world, just like China is going through another wave.

[4] Especially, for the education sector.

[5] Even UGC, Government Bodies and Education Departments of various states had changed their recommendations, policies and dates several times regarding exam of the students, such were the effects of the disease and uncertainty of using offline mode.

online were started to be taken by almost all academic institutions.[6] Hence, continuation of education at all levels was considered as "emergency" both by educators and students and both the communities started to continue teaching–learning activities process by adopting systems in which they were not used to.[7]

At the same time, other important questions that came up were: Is it possible to start studying, in online mode, in a developing economy like India? Even if it is possible in the metro Cities, can it be feasible or possible for the poor people of the backward regions of rural India? Are all types of students aware of that electronic medium? Are the students suffering from mental depression due to this long-reigning lockdown of education sector? What should be the way of providing them with study materials? Will these be handful for them? What are the factors that could have an influence over online education? What could be the possible positive and negative externalities of using such mode? All such questions began to come up which would be investigated in this paper with the help of primary data taken from the students who have been participating in online mode of education ever since the lockdown began.

Eventually, we all know, the online classes started in India also once it was realized that the lockdown is going to be a prolonged one, from the month of April 2020. Since then, the online classes in almost all parts of India continued until institutions opened and even after opening up in November 2021. Now, Government has announced New Education Policy 2020 and it is already implemented in different states of India. New Education Policy 2020 has given immense importance to the online learning in order to increase the gross enrolment ratio in higher education system. Hence, the mode of learning that came into practice significantly during Covid is being recognized as indispensable for future development of the education system. But the criticism and doubts have continued to prevail. Is the quality of these classes good enough like that of offline classes? Are the online study materials good enough? Are these study materials lacking in quality compared to hard copy books? Are the Students getting help from the teachers and libraries every day like they used to get before the lockdown was announced? Are the classes being held regularly? Is it possible for the students of backward regions, poor families to attend and continue such classes on a regular basis? All such questions became immensely important [9]. Starting from the month of July 2020, till now several College level and University level examinations have been held by online mode in which open-book mode of examinations has been followed. So, are the students prefer online examination mode? Or, have they been facing any problem with online mode of examination? We have looked to get an idea of such burning, controversial issues based on the views provided by students of both rural areas as well as urban and semi-urban areas.

---

[6] In this regard, one must not forget to mention the contribution made by electronic platforms, especially that provided by the live meeting software.

[7] Certainly, in developing nations like India where magnitude of online learning was almost insignificant.

A common perception among people is that online classes are that it can be somewhat smoothly conducted[8] in Urban areas where all sorts of infrastructural facilities along with good economic conditions prevail. But it is almost impossible to conduct in backward parts or rural areas or even in semi-urban areas due to a lot of problems. This paper would make a special focus on this viewpoint and its truthiness.

If we look at the field of literature, we would see that there are quite a few works regarding online education or even distance education both before Covid-19 as well as within the pandemic period. We all know that every new approach has its advantages, disadvantages and challenges as well. All these along with the rise and popularity of online educational software as a business during this pandemic have been discussed by [1] by applying SWOT analysis. Several qualitative factors do lead to the success and failures of online learning such as design of course outline, instructional technique, students' perception, etc. [2]. Few outcomes or ways to success have been suggested by the authors as well. Online learning has the great advantage of being flexible. It has also been observed even before the pandemic period that online and offline modes of education do not have significant differences as far as the ranking of students and preferences between genders are concerned [3]. The work by Chakraborty et al. [7] has focused on the opinion of Undergraduate students regarding online education. They have surveyed 358 students and found that more than 65% of students preferred offline education mode but around 40% supported courses from government portals such as MOOCs. Again, they have dealt with various aspects of online education, where they have observed that almost 69% students opined that the quality of online teaching has been improving since its beginning in March'2020 and around 78% found online mode to be useful in the pandemic scenario. It is also correct that there is no common prescribed strategy of online education that can be followed. The teaching–learning pedagogy does vary across nations and within different regions or even across institutions. Everywhere, the suitable; feasible pedagogy, for both teachers and learners, was followed for the sake of continuation of teaching–learning process [4]. Studies found that students have gone through mental depression, suffered from emotional distress during this pandemic and they did not feel encouraged to join online classes with enough productivity and hence it asks for different methods of online teaching to bring this section back to teaching–learning process [5].

So, one can see that the existing works on online education during pandemic and even before pandemic are mostly descriptive in nature Almost no work has considered the whole range of issues of online education, beginning from economic condition of the household to the regional division of technology, quality of education and even the issue of mental depression. Very little work has covered students from both rural and urban areas and compared between them. In this work, we shall look to fill up these gaps which have been our prime motivation behind the work.

Rest of the chapter is organized as follows. Section 13.2 will analyze the build-up and analysis of the theoretical background of the paper. Section 13.3 will be used

[8] Not entirely, due to internet connectivity problems and negative economic impacts of this ongoing pandemic on every sphere of people.

for discussing data and methodology used in our study. Section 13.4 will discuss about econometric findings of our study along with a rural–urban comparison which is the prime focus of this study and finally concluding remarks along with policy recommendations will be made in Sect. 13.5.

13.2 Theoretical Background

Though education is a public good by virtue and hence it is treated as almost free good in developing economies, however, it has been attached with few associated costs. For instance, transportation cost to reach institutes, cost associated with food consumption during the stay in the institute and miscellaneous. We refer this cost as cost of offline education (COE) and denote it as C_o. Again, cost of education through online (CNE) is also positive and we denote it as C_N. For example, expenditure associated with internet charges, etc. Now for brevity of our understanding of rational situation we assume $C_o > C_N$. Following the said inequality, we can derive the demand for education under both offline and online modes in the following manner-

$$D_o = D_o(P_o, P_N, I, T_o);\ D_0^1 < o,\ D_0^2 > o,\ D_0^3 > o,\ D_0^4 > o \tag{13.1}$$

where, price of offline education (P_o) is approximated by COE and it is assumed that an increase in C_o also increases expenditure or willingness to pay for offline education directly and indirectly. Again, by virtue of partial substitutability between offline and online education modes, the price of online education, that is, P_N has its adverse effect on the preference pattern of offline education. If online education becomes cheaper compared to the offline one, students may opt for online education mode for given quality of education level. Apart from price issue, the income of the consumers (I) and taste (T_o) over or biasedness over offline education positively impact the preference of offline education.

Similar to the case of offline education demand, here we express the demand or preference of online education in terms of expression (13.2).

$$D_N = D_N(P_N, P_o, I, T_N);\ D_N^1 < o,\ D_N^2 > o,\ D_N^3 > o,\ D_N^4 > o \tag{13.2}$$

where, price of online education (P_N) is approximated by CNE and it is assumed that an increase in C_N also increases expenditure or willingness to pay for online education directly and indirectly. Again, from behavioural instinct of partial substitutability between offline and online education modes, the price of offline education, that is, P_O has its adverse effect on the preference pattern of online education. For instance, if offline education becomes cheaper compared the online system, students may choose offline education mode for give quality of education level. Effects of income and taste (T_N) on demand of online education remain same as it is in case of offline education. Now here, T_o remains fixed at $\overline{T}_o$ level by choice of students. However, T_N depends on mentoring factor (M_N), that is, how and in which way proper mentoring can positively influence the preference over online education through taste channel. Mathematically we can express it as-

$$T_o = \overline{T}_o \quad (13.3)$$

and

$$T_N = T_N(M_N, / T_o = \overline{T}_o); \quad T_N^{/} > 0 \quad (13.4)$$

Therefore, following Eqs. (13.1)–(13.4) we can derive the preference between offline and online education depending upon the following factors, one, $C_o > C_N$ and $T_N^{/} > 0$.

Utility maximization of the representative student gives us the following condition;

$$\mathrm{MU_o/P_o} = \mathrm{MU_N/P_N} \quad (13.5)$$

Following the above-stated inequality, i.e., $C_o > C_N$, from Eq. (13.5) we get

$$\mathrm{MU_o/P_o} < \mathrm{MU_N/P_N} \quad (13.6)$$

Inequality (6) tells us that students prefer online education over offline education following the above cost discrimination. This inequality may be more biased towards online education if we augment mentoring aspect in terms of Eq. (13.4) and hence inequality (6) can be rewritten as

$$\mathrm{MU_o/P_o} < \mathrm{MU_N}(T_N)/\mathrm{P_N} \quad (13.7)$$

Following, $P_N < P_o$ and $MU_o\,(T_O) < MU_N\,(T_N)$ inequality (7) reveals that under better mentoring under online education can influence students more towards online education mode relative to offline education.

Here we have started with demand functions to compare online and offline education systems. Further to categorise the significance of online education, we have inserted the mentoring factor. To perform all these, we have implicitly assumed that the demand functions are determined following the utility maximization of representative participants. It is to be noted that even if we have started with utility maximization and introduced envelope theorem our main outcomes remain unchanged.

13.3 Data and Methodology

In this study, we have collected primary data directly from students of UG level covering both General Courses as well as Honours Courses through google forms from both rural areas as well as urban areas. We have collected data of 1500 students from ten Degree Colleges of Rural area and 1465 students from eleven different degree colleges in Kolkata. One can say that that we have followed randomness in our survey since both the respondents as well as his intention to reply or not—both were unknown to us. Although our questionnaire contained several questions on socio-economic and academic aspects, our main question was whether a student likes to join online classes or not and what would be the way to deal with the issue of mental depression so that during the prolonged lockdown period students always motivated to attend online classes and do not feel any boredom or suffer from any emotional depression. Students had to answer either "YES" or "NO". So, our dependent variable (Y) is binary in nature. "YES" was assigned the value of 1 and "NO" was coded as 0. Here we have performed logistic regression. It implies that our dependent variable Y is categorical where the logit of Y has been used, instead of Y, in our regression equation. So, it is expected that if online classes have a positive effect on the utility level of a student, then he or she would say "YES" to the question, else "NO" should be the reply.

The choice of either a YES or a NO for willingness to attend online classes implies the fact that the students are facing a situation like an individual does in a free market scenario. Here, the respondent student is allowed to judge whether he or she prefers online classes or not. Let's look at the Random Utility version of this Dichotomous Choice elicitation method. We will see that a student will reply by saying a YES if he or she gets more utility in online classes than offline classes. If the opposite happens, then we will get a NO as reply.

Hence, one can say that if $(U_{online} - U_{offline}) \geq 0$, the respondent student will express his or her eagerness to attend online classes by replying with a YES. $(U_{online} - U_{offline}) < 0$, then there is a NO by the respondent is the expected outcome.

But the thing is that neither the level of utility of an individual respondent from the two forms of classes are observable or measurable, nor the difference between the two forms of classes can be measured. But the factors which guide the willingness or unwillingness towards either of the two forms are certainly very much observable which helps us to specify the following forms of the utility function.[9]

$$U_{online}(1, E; S) = \theta(1, E; S) + e_1 \tag{13.8}$$

$$U_{offline}(0, E; S) = \theta(0, E; S) + e_0 \tag{13.9}$$

[9] This part is briefly modified from the theoretical methodology of Harou, Markandya, Bellu and Cistulli (1998).

From the above two equations, it is notable that willingness to attend online classes or a YES is represented by 1 and the unwillingness is represented by 0 (zero), E is the education-related variables and S stands for variables related to the socio-economic aspects of the students or their families which includes income as well. Here, e is the random error part that arises because of the limited knowledge regarding the utility function.

From the Eqs. (13.8) and (13.9), we get to see that a difference between the two utility functions can be derived in the following manner.

From Eqs. (13.8) and (13.9) we can write

$$\Delta U = \Delta\theta - e \tag{13.10}$$

where $(U_{online} - U_{offline}) = \Delta$U, $(e_1 - e_0) =$ e, and [θ(1, E S) – θ(0, E, S)] = Δθ, given Eq. (13.10), one can write that if

$$\Delta\theta = e \rightarrow \text{the respondent will be willing towards online classes and he or she would reply by saying a YES} \tag{13.11}$$

$$\Delta\theta < e \rightarrow \text{the respondent will not prefer online classes and he or she would reply by saying a NO} \tag{13.12}$$

Two forms of models, that is, either logit or probit model can be used to estimate such types of Dichotomous Choice models. Here the logit model (logistic distribution of the error term) for our analysis has been considered.[10]

The probability that an individual student is willing to attend online classes can therefore be expressed as

$$P(\text{Willingness to attend Online Classes}) = P(Y = 1) = P(e = \Delta\theta) = F(\Delta\theta) \tag{13.13}$$

where Y is the observed dichotomous variable, willingness = 1, unwillingness = 0.

If we assume that the random part e is following a probability distribution of logistic pattern, we can write that –

$$P(\text{Willingness to attend Online Classes}) = F(\Delta\theta) = 1/[1 + exp(-\Delta\theta)] \tag{13.14}$$

[10] One can follow either the logit or the probit model for analysing DC models. This choice or specification is again dependent upon the probability distribution of the random error part. If the error part follows a normal distribution is the suitable one but if it follows logistic distribution then logit is the appropriate one, but for being simple to deal with logit regression is the one that is predominantly used.

Table 13.1 Independent variables used in the study

Income	Total monthly income from all sources
Sex	Dummy variable. 0 for Males, 1 for Females, 2 for others
Caste	Dummy variable. 0 for General Caste, 1 for OBC, 2 for SC, 3 for ST
Duration of online classes	Dummy variable. 0 for less than 3 h daily, 1 for 3–5 h daily, 2 for More than 5 h daily
Quality of teaching	Dummy variable. 0 for high, 1 for Medium, 2 for Bad
Internet connectivity	Dummy variable. 0 for not a problem, 1 for if it is a problem
Cost effectiveness	Dummy variable. 0 for Yes, 1 for No
Effectiveness of online study materials	Dummy variable. 0 for very good, 1 for good, 2 for medium, 3 for Bad
Centralized routine	Dummy variable. 0 for Yes, 1 for No
Nature of course	Dummy variable. 0 for Honours, 1 for General
Mentoring by teacher throughout the year	Dummy variable. 0 for Yes, 1 for No

Source Computed by the authors

So, in order to estimate the willingness of a student to attend online classes, we have used the logit model[11] which contains the following variables.

Dependent Variable:

$$l_n \frac{P_i}{1 - P_i}$$

where P_i is the probability of willingness to say "YES" to attend or like online classes. So, it represents the probability of $Y = 1$.

$l_n \frac{P_i}{1-P_i}$ is the log-odds ratio.[12]

The independent variables used in the model are described in Table 13.1.

We have used several socio-economic aspects by using dummy. These dummy variables have been deliberately used because these attributes are expected to play important roles in the responses of the students regarding online classes.

[11] We have selected our variables in the model after carefully going through the existing literature related to this line of study.

[12] Along with an increase in P_i, there is an increase in the log-odds ratio as well, since it represents the ratio of probability of Willingness to attend online Classes (P_i) and that of unwillingness to attend ($1-P_i$).

13.4 Results and Discussion

Out of 1500 responses from the college of rural area, we have found 944 students prefer online classes and 556 do not. In the urban area, out of 1465 students, these figures are 955 in favour of attending classes and rest of the 510 students are unwilling. One can refer to these number of unwilling students as "protest respondents". There may be several influencing factors behind one's willingness or unwillingness over online system, although all of them enjoy the facilities of online classes. So, we cannot omit those respondents. The respondents have responded to the offered question by either saying "YES" or "NO". In order to estimate the factors that have a significant impact on willingness to attend online classes or even which factors are responsible for unwillingness, we have used a logit model, and the results of our model are stated in the following table.

Table 13.2 gives us meaningful outcomes. Here we can see that all variables are not significant, yet they have meaningful interpretations in the context of our study. Income, caste, sex—these three variables are insignificant which means this practice of online classes was forcefully imposed upon all of us to save ourselves from this pandemic. So, irrespective of level of income, caste or gender, we have to accept this reality and adjust ourselves with this practice. Although, initially there were objections coming regarding affordability of the poorer section to attend online classes, since it needs a bit of investment in the form of having an android mobile phone along with internet connectivity but as the days have passed, as the pandemic got prolonged, the results show that even the poor families have accepted to incur this investment for the sake of education of their child. So, people across all income levels, caste, sex, region have adjusted themselves with this mode of education. The quality of teaching is an issue, as it always is. As the qualities of teaching and study notes fall, the willingness to attend online classes also decrease in both rural as well as in urban areas. Same can be said about the duration of classes. As the duration of classes per day rises, the willingness to attend classes fall in both regions. There could be several factors, including internet data pack; lack of classroom atmosphere, behind that. Our findings suggest that people in both areas believe that this system of online classes is cost-effective in nature and bears significant impact on willingness, although the level of significance varies across regions.

It is a fact, in the era of online classes, one has to bear lesser cost than pre-pandemic era. A student does not have to bear the daily cost of going to college and tuition. He or she, in the modern era of e-books and study materials, can easily have access to them, and such facilities help in lowering down the costs. We can see that as the connectivity becomes poor it affects the willingness to join classes in both study areas and it has a higher significance in rural areas than in urban areas. Having a centralized online routine structure, as expected, always helps the students positively in attending classes. We can see that there are differences of opinions between students of rural areas and urban areas over the two variables—nature of course and mentoring. These two factors are very much related to each other and both play significant parts in policy suggestions. In the rural areas, there is no issue

Table 13.2 Results of the logit model for online classes of rural & urban areas

Variable	Rural area		Urban area	
	Coefficient	Marginal effects (dY/dX)	Coefficient	Marginal effects (dY/dX)
Income	0.00021 (0.54)	0.000287 (0.73)	0.00031 (0.73)	0.000168 (0.88)
Sex	0.00058 (0.31)	0.000402 (0.26)	0.00097 (1.01)	0.000311 (0.57)
Caste	0.00065 (0.88)	0.00324 (0.70)	0.00021 (0.19)	0.000240 (0.62)
Duration	−0.00223** (−2.01)	−0.00201** (−2.09)	−0.00045* (1.91)	−0.000198* (1.88)
Quality of teaching	−0.00369*** (−5.54)	−0.00410*** (−4.21)	−0.00068*** (−7.24)	−0.000852*** (−5.88)
Internet connectivity	−0.05001*** (−9.21)	−0.04665*** (−6.24)	−0.00288* (−1.79)	−0.000626* (−1.80)
Cost effectiveness	0.00540* (1.81)	0.00102* (1.82)	0.00241*** (5.24)	0.000819*** (7.21)
Study notes	−0.00432** (−1.99)	−0.00366** (−1.92)	−0.00042*** (−3.21)	−0.000228*** (−4.88)
Centralized routine	0.00204*** (5.66)	0.00247*** (6.11)	0.000267*** (6.22)	0.000069*** (7.21)
Nature of course	−0.00229 (0.29)	−0.00314 (0.33)	−0.00654*** (−4.22)	−0.000984*** (−5.45)

(continued)

Table 13.2 (continued)

Variable	Rural area		Urban area	
	Coefficient	Marginal effects (dY/dX)	Coefficient	Marginal effects (dY/dX)
Mentoring	0.00468*** (9.25)	0.00422*** (8.24)	−0.00871 (0.11)	−0.000688 (0.71)
Constant	6.4266*** (6.97)		4.1258*** (5.21)	
Log-likelihood	290.402		254.218	
LR chi-square	279.66		291.75	
Prob > chi-quare	0.000		0.000	
Pseudo R^2	0.7754		0.5478	
Total no. of observations	1500		1465	

The values in the parentheses for both coefficient and marginal effects are the t-values
*** denotes significant at 1% levels
** denotes significance at 5% levels
* denotes significance at 10% levels

Source Computed by the authors

regarding nature of course, that is, students of both honours or major course and general or pass course are willing enough to attend classes but in urban areas as we move from honours course to general course, the willingness fall. So, students of honours course are more willing to attend classes in urban areas. The main reason behind that is the factor of mentoring. In our studied institution of rural area, there is continuous process of mentoring throughout the year that not only helps students in attending online classes regularly but helps them overcoming several other problems including mental; emotional depression through which almost everyone went through during this period. Mentoring not only helped them to stay aware of every college related, study-related programmes but they could share their family problems, mental issues with the mentors that helped them overcoming several problems. The role of mentor played by teachers of the institution, in this regard, plays the important role of keeping all students in touch with studies throughout the year. In the institutions of urban area, there were no such presence of mentoring which could have played the decisive role in the willingness to attend online classes by "general degree course or pass course students". All these factors have been reflected in the fitness of our models as well. In the rural area, our fitted model has the R—square value of more than 77% and for the urban area it is over 54%, for a cross-section data, we can say our models are well fitted but the model of rural area gives us a better picture. This could be because of the fact that students of honours courses are judged as better ones, as far as academic merit is concerned. But, in state like West Bengal, number of general or pass course students is many times higher than that in honours courses. Hence, encouraging those pass-course students to attend classes regularly is a challenge and here mentoring plays the game changing role. Most of our variables are significant at either 1% level or 5% level. The mean variance inflationary factors (VIF) of our models are 3.08 and 3.91, respectively for rural and urban areas which shows the problem of multicollinearity is not a serious issue for our study.[13] We have also calculated the marginal effects for all the variables that show for one unit of change in the dependent variable, holding other variables constant, how the probability to attend the online classes change.

We have also estimated the Lower Bound (LB) and Upper Bound (UB) values of the variables of our concern at 95% confidence interval.[14] The results are reported in Table 13.3.

The table gives us actually the predictability power of our model. It tells us that on 95% of the cases the values of the co-efficient are going to lie within the given range of Lower Bound and Upper Bound.

[13] Since it is below 5. If VIF is above 5, then it is considered as causing serious problems in estimation process.

[14] It should be noted that the reported confidence intervals are asymmetric because the log-odds ratios represent the transformed forms of the logit-coefficients which are non-linear.

Table 13.3 Results of confidence intervals at 95% level of significance

Variable	Rural area		Urban area	
	95% confidence interval		95% confidence interval	
	LB	UB	LB	UB
Income	0.00015	0.00032	0.00017	0.00048
Sex	0.00024	0.00061	0.00070	0.000101
Caste	0.00038	0.0088	0.00009	0.00030
Duration	−0.00198	−0.00245	−0.00035	−0.00059
Quality of teaching	−0.00330	−0.00387	−0.00055	−0.00089
Internet connectivity	−0.04827	−0.05201	−0.00255	−0.000289
Cost effectiveness	0.00510	0.00575	0.00201	0.000289
Study notes	−0.00390	−0.00481	−0.00029	−0.00066
Centralized routine	0.00108	0.00178	0.000155	0.000248
Nature of course	−0.00208	−0.00289	−0.00330	−0.000878
Mentoring	0.00288	0.00408	−0.00605	−0.000988
Constant	3.0898	11.0285	2.0088	9.5878

Source Computed by Authors

13.5 Concluding Remarks and Policy Suggestions

By July 2020 Covid-19 had a negative impact on over 1.7 billion students of all forms[15] worldwide, covering 200 nations (UN, 2020) and hence overnight shift to e-learning and online learning became the only possible mode of teaching learning process. In developing nations like India, cursed with various forms of inequalities and dualities, there were several questions regarding success of such pedagogy. In the wake of sudden upsurge of Omicron variant and many more uncertainties regarding Covid to come in future, online learning or even mixed mode of learning would certainly continue for a considerable period. Although the number of Covid cases have gone down and educational institutions have opened up, but the importance given to this mode of learning in New Education Policy 2020 makes the outcomes of our chapter even more relevant. Under such circumstances, online classes would continue alongside offline classes, as students will be given the options to choose any one of the two modes and during pandemic period it was the safest mode for all the stakeholders. Our study over higher educational institutions of rural and urban areas based on primary data suggests that we need to look after few factors which may become crucial in increasing the attendance of students and hence deciding the success of this pedagogy. Firstly, the nature or quality of teaching and study notes has to be good, otherwise the students may not feel interested in attending classes, secondly, duration of the classes has to be fixed in such a way so that the students do not feel any pressure. Similar things can be said about having a centralized routine

[15] Primary education to higher education.

that bears a positive impact. The issue of cost-effectiveness has to be kept in mind, including the issue of internet connectivity along with the amount of Giga Bytes (GB) a student has to spend per day. Most importantly, mentoring should be started and continued across all institutions not only for the sake of encouraging the larger section of students to attend online classes regularly but from the social point of view as well. We know people have been going through various forms of problems during this pandemic period and being teachers, we should play the role of "guide" in order to guide a student on several aspects and help him or her overcome several other problems and continue education. Given that people from all socio-economic classes have accepted this form of education and teaching communities, both students and teachers have adjusted to it, and we may require to continue it for the sake of living, few factors can decide the success of such classes should be taken care of.

References

1. Dhawan S (2020) Online learning: a panacea in the time of COVID-19 crisis. J Educ Technol Syst 49(1):5–22
2. Yang Y, Cornelius LF (2004) Students' perceptions towards the quality of online education: a qualitative approach. *Mimeo*
3. Paul J, Jefferson F (2019) A comparative analysis of student performance in an online vs. face-to-face environmental science course from 2009 to 2016. Frontiers in Computer Science. https://doi.org/10.3389/fcomp.2019.00007
4. Doucet A, Netolicky D, Timmers K, Tuscano FJ (2020) Thinking about pedagogy in an unfolding pandemic (An Independent Report on Approaches to Distance Learning during COVID-19 School Closure). Work of Education International and UNESCO. https://issuu.com/educationinternational/docs/2020_research_covid-19_eng
5. Petrie C (2020) Spotlight: quality education for all during COVID-19 crisis (hundrED Research Report #01). United Nations. https://hundred.org/en/collections/qualityeducation-for-all-during-coronavirus
6. Chatterjee N (2014) Willingness to pay for drinking water in some selected dryland areas of West Bengal: a contingent valuation approach. Vidyasagar Uni J Econ XIX(2014–15):14–37
7. Chakraborti P, Mittal P, Gupta MS, Yadav S, Arora A (2020) Opinion of students on online education during the COVID-19 pandemic. Wiley. https://doi.org/10.1002/hbe2.240
8. Haraou P, Markandya A, Bellu L, Cistulli V (1998) Environmental economics and environmental policy: a workbook. Economic Development Institute (EDI) of World Bank
9. Muthuprasad T, Aiswarya S, Aditya KS, Jha Girish K (2021) Students' perception and preference for online education in India during COVID -19 pandemic. Soc Sci Human Open 3(1):100101. ISSN 2590–2911. https://doi.org/10.1016/j.ssaho.2020.100101
10. United Nations (2020) Policy brief: education during COVID-19 and beyond. United Nations. https://www.un.org/development/desa/dspd/wp-content/uploads/sites/22/2020/08/sg_policy_brief_covid-19_and_education_august_2020.pdf

Chapter 14
The Role of Government Education Spending in Low and Lower-Middle Income Countries in a Post-Covid World

Haimanti Banerjee and Sucharita Ghosh

14.1 Introduction

The last few decades have seen a rapid expansion of the education sector worldwide with the mass education of the population being an important policy directive in most developing economies. One of the Millennium Development Goals set in September 2000 was to ensure universal primary education by 2015; this resulted in primary school net enrolment in the developing world increasing from 83 to 91% between 2000 and 2015 [40]. Currently, one of the key Sustainable Development Goals (SDG) for 2030 is to ensure free, equitable, and quality primary and secondary education for all. On an ambitious mission to achieve this SDG target, global spending on education has increased over the last 10 years. In fact, prior to the Covid-19 pandemic, low- and middle-income countries registered the fastest growth in real spending on education worldwide, increasing by 5.9% a year from 2009 to 2019 [17].[1] Governments contributed the highest to global education over this period at 82%, followed by households and development assistance at 17 and <1%, respectively. There has

[1] The economic literature has long established a strong relationship between education and economic growth which is based theoretically on the endogenous growth models of Lucas [27], Romer [35] where an educated labor force by increasing the level of human capital formation leads to an increase in productivity and adoption of new technology. Several studies [8, 15, 6] have found a positive relationship between the accumulation of human capital, as measured by rising educational attainment, and economic growth. An extensive review of the education and growth literature is provided in Krueger and Lindahl [24], Pritchett [32], Hanushek and Woessmann [22].

H. Banerjee (✉)
Marketing and Business Economics, Joseph M. Katz Graduate School of Business, University of Pittsburgh, Pittsburgh, PA, USA
e-mail: hab102@pitt.edu

S. Ghosh
Department of Economics, College of Business, The University of Akron, Akron, OH, USA
e-mail: sghosh@uakron.edu

R. Bhattacharyya et al. (eds.), *COVID-19 Pandemic and Global Inequality*,
https://doi.org/10.1007/978-981-99-4405-7_14

been an increase in educational opportunities for children in low and middle-income countries despite the wide gap between the average $1,300 invested in the average child's education by a low-income country's government versus the $110,000 spent by the average high-income country [2].

This increase in spending on education is also due to the recognition that a more educated population can positively impact economic growth by raising the health and quality of the workforce [10], attracting trade and foreign investment [11]; increasing life expectancy [13], improving institutional quality [20], improving the cognitive ability of the population [22], and increasing the knowledge and the innovative capacity of an economy [8].

Empirical studies in the literature have shown the positive impact that government spending on education can have on several education metrics such as students' cognitive performance outcomes, primary school enrollment rates, school completion rates, and the Human Capital Index, all of which also highlight that governments should focus on educational investments in early years [14]. This fact is borne out in the average Human Capital Index (HCI) score of 0.56 across low- and middle-income countries which implies that by the age of 18, a child born today will be only 56% as productive as a child would be under the benchmark of complete education and full health.[2] Efficiency of government expenditure has also achieved macro development outcomes such as reduction in income inequality, poverty rates, and increasing urbanization levels [31]. Studies also show that government effectiveness and robust structural guidelines play a crucial role in the disbursement of funds and lead to improved learning outcomes [17].

Despite the vast literature showing the positive linkages between government investment in human capital and outcomes, the post-pandemic world remains uncertain and poses a severe threat to the education budget as developing economies have to pursue fiscal austerity measures. After the start of the Covid-19 pandemic in 2020, 41% of low and lower-middle income countries decreased their spending on education with an average spending decrease of 13.5% [18]. Since the start of the Covid-19 pandemic, two-thirds of low and lower-middle income economies have cut their allocation to education spending. In contrast, only one-third of high and upper-middle-income countries have reduced their education spending which leads to an inherent divergence between these two groups of countries going forward [17]. Moreover, existing data reveals considerable heterogeneity in gains attained within the low-income and lower middle-income countries over the past decade which are now bound to be exacerbated in the post-pandemic world. Given that public budgets have been impacted significantly because of the Covid-10 pandemic, the sustained increase in government spending on education over the last decade is not likely to be maintained. Consequently, the impact of the Covid-19 pandemic impact on education financing could possibly increase the gap in learning outcomes between lower and higher income countries. It is therefore very important to understand how effective government spending has been over the past decade, and, more importantly, to understand how to improve the effectiveness of public education spending.

[2] https://www.worldbank.org/en/topic/education/brief/ending-learning-poverty.

This chapter uses panel data analysis to investigate the impact of education spending of approximately 78 low and lower-middle income economies and 111 upper-middle and high-income countries on education outcomes over the sample period, 1999–2020. The chapter will identify and discuss the efficacy of financial channels through which the education sector receives funding. The results from this study will allow governments in low- and middle-income countries gain greater insight into how to better channel their scarce resources in order to make more impactful policy decisions for the future.

This chapter will proceed as follows. Section 14.2 provides a brief literature review of the impact of government education spending on education outcomes. In Sect. 14.3 we empirically evaluate how government spending on education has impacted education outcomes in low- and middle-income countries over the past decade, which is followed in Sect. 14.4 on understanding the impact of the Covid-19 pandemic on government spending and learning losses in low- and middle-income countries. Section 14.5 concludes.

14.2 Government Education Expenditures and Education Outcomes: A Brief Literature Review

Government expenditure on education as a percentage of the GDP for low and lower-middle income countries showed significant increase from 3.7% to an average of 4.5% from 2015 onwards. While the increase is a positive step in the right direction, relative to high-income and upper-middle-income countries for the sample period studied (1999–2020), the share of education spending in low- and middle-income countries was persistently lower.[3] Unless we see higher than average economic growth in low- and middle-income countries, the disparity in government spending on education between low- and middle-income countries and high-income countries will not decrease.

In low- and middle-income countries, governments have implemented new initiatives and increased spending to encourage greater enrollment and attendance at the school level [23]. However, when determining at which level of education (primary, tertiary, or secondary) to focus their spending, governments face a policy trade-off. This trade-off impacts the composition of human capital in the economy and arises from the choice between public policies that open up education possibilities for the masses by increasing literacy rates or policies that further improve high-skill education. While the private benefits of education for individuals such as better employment opportunities and higher salaries are well recognized, public benefits

[3] While we do not focus on the impact of government education expenditures on economic growth, there is a vast literature that studies this dimension of government education expenditures. A meta-analysis by Churchill et al. [5] considered 29 papers that specifically looked at the impact of government education expenditures on economic growth and found that a 1% increase in government expenditures as a percentage of GDP increases growth by 0.2–0.3%.

such as increased tax revenues and improved quality of public services are often less recognized. This often explains why governments ignore public investment in tertiary education which, in a knowledge economy, can help developing countries keep up or catch up with more technologically advanced economies [9]. An analysis of economic rates of return, especially in the 1970 and 1980s, took into account the full costs of the different levels of education, including foregone earnings, and compared them to the benefits of lifetime earnings [33]. For example, Psacharopoulos and Patrinos (2002) reviewed 98 country studies from 1960 to 1997 and found that the average public rate of return for primary education was 18.9% while for tertiary education it was 10.8%. Results like this often cause the conventional government education policy in developing countries to be to invest more in primary education and to cut back on public subsidies to tertiary education.[4]

The Dakar framework for Action [42] decided on a target allocation of 20% share of education expenditures in the overall spending of the government.[5] As evident from the data, the pre-Covid19 average share of education spending has been approximately 16% and lower than the target.[6] With a constrained education budget, there is little room to invest in resources to enhance educational outcomes beyond staff compensation. For example, an analysis of education spending in the West and Central Africa region [38] reports that only 27% of low- and lower-middle income countries have an operating digital learning policy.

Al-Samarrai et al. [3] reports that countries with the lowest government spending on education will see the biggest impact on educational outcomes such as enrollment rates if they were to even slightly increase their spending. However, the efficacy of government spending declines for countries with already moderately higher government spending. A policy brief (2021) analyzing education spending in the West and Central Africa region (WCAR) reports that countries could improve their primary education and secondary education completion rates by approximately 40% keeping current levels of spending constant and by creating an improved financial management system. Miningou [28] finds the average efficiency for low-income countries are about 75% and Governance-related factors and labor market conditions can contribute to the efficient usage of government education expenditure. Grigoli [21] suggests reducing student-to-teacher ratios and easing access to education facilities will improve efficiency in education spending. Alternatively, a study conducted by Trabelsi [37] find that countries with very low educational quality measured in PISA scores will not achieve economic growth despite investment in

[4] INDIA provides a classic example of this public policy trade off. The government of India gives high priority to education which is reflected in the enormous increase in public education spending as a percentage of total government spending from about 2.3% in the early 1990s to 6.1% in 2000–2001 [23]. The Indian government's priority towards early education is further reflected in the passage of the Right of Children to Free and Compulsory Education (RTE) Act which came into force in 2010 mandating universal elementary education, defined as education in grades one to eight.

[5] World Education Forum [42] adopted the Dakar Framework for Action: Education for All.

[6] Analysis of education spending in the West and Central Africa region [38] reports governments in the region allocated an average of 17% of their total budgets to education.

education, implying that efficiency of government spending is again tied to endogenous factors. Finally, a comprehensive study conducted by OECD, Education at a glance [30], reports that governments faced with fiscal challenges and rising requirements of investments in higher education, will need to mobilize, allocate and manage financial resources with insight gained from successful practical experiments, policy evaluations in other countries.

14.3 Impact of Government Spending on Education Outcomes in Low and Lower-Middle Income Countries Over the Past Decade

It is important to understand how government spending has impacted education outcomes in the last decade before we can analyze how best a government could allocate its scarce resources in a post-pandemic world. We begin by explaining the empirical model, the data used in the empirical model, and then discuss the empirical results.

14.3.1 Empirical Model

We empirically assess the impact of government expenditure in education on educational outcomes proxied by enrollment rates at primary, secondary, and tertiary levels of schooling using a fixed effects model.

$$GER_{ijt} = \alpha_0 + \alpha_1 GOVEXP_{ijt} + \alpha_2 ODA_{jt} + \alpha_3 A_{jt} + \varepsilon_t$$

where GER_{ijt} is the gross enrollment rate for i th educational level (primary, secondary, and tertiary) of country j at time t. $GOVEXP_{ijt}$ denotes the three measures of government expenditure used in the analysis for the ith educational level of country j at time t: (i) $GOVEXP\_EDU$ is total government expenditure on education; (ii) $GOVEXP\_Level$ is government expenditures on primary, secondary, and tertiary levels of education, respectively; and (iii) $GOVEXP\_Levelperstudent$ is government expenditure per student on primary, secondary, and tertiary levels of education. Official development assistance loans by the Development Assistance Committee are denoted by ODA_{jt}.[7] Finally, A_{jt} is a set of control variables that impact educational outcomes. These variables are explained in further detail in the next subsection.

[7] The OECD Development Assistance Committee is an international forum of many of the largest providers of aid, including 31 members. Further details are available here: https://www.oecd.org/dac/development-assistance-committee/.

14.3.2 Data Description

We use World Bank panel data for 78 low-income countries and lower-middle income countries over the period 1999–2020.[8] The summary statistics for all variables are reported in Table 14.1 (given at the end of the chapter).

We use educational outcome as our dependent variable by utilizing a direct measure of participation by students in primary, secondary, and tertiary levels of education which helps us analyze the impact on specific levels of education. We choose gross enrollments, defined as GER, instead of net enrollment measures to accommodate students who are officially lagging behind in terms of age for the specified educational level, especially for low- and lower-middle income countries. As summarized in Table 14.1, the average gross enrollment rate for primary education is at 101% whereas gross secondary and gross tertiary enrollment rates lag behind at 53 and 15% respectively. Typically, low-income countries have made great strides in increasing literacy rates at the primary level, but have not been able to achieve higher estimated returns at secondary and tertiary levels.[9]

The main explanatory variable in this study is Government Expenditures on Education. We use three different measures to capture public education expenditures. The first measure, $GOVEXP\_EDU$, refers to the overall government expenditure on education as a percentage of gross domestic product (GDP). In the past two decades, governments on average have spent about 4% of their GDP on education as reported in Table 14.1. To measure the change in government education expenditures particularly in the last ten years, we segment the data across two sub-periods, 2010–2014 and 2016–2020, and then average the data over five years to smooth out any fluctuations.

Figure 14.1 shows the range in changes in government spending on education as a percentage of GDP from an increase of more than 50% to a decrease of 48%, which could be due to increases in GDP not keeping pace with increased allocations of government education expenditure in the budget, or because there has been no significant economic growth for some low-income countries.[10] To get a better picture of the government's prioritization of education, Fig. 14.1 also includes the change in government education expenditures as a percentage of overall government expenditure. We find that the general trend is that countries with increased overall government spending show an increased allocation toward education expenditures with a few exceptions. For example, Angola (AGO) shows a 32% decline in government education expenditures as percentage of GDP, but a 47% rise in the share of education expenditure in overall government expenditure.

[8] We do not include 2021 in the analysis due to the scant data available for all the countries in the sample for this year.

[9] Barro and Lee [7] report that developing countries have successfully reduced illiteracy rates, especially amongst the younger cohorts.

[10] Education Finance Watch [17] reports that the rates of growth in education spending were much faster in low- and middle-income countries, where spending on education rose by 5.9% over 2009–2019.

Table 14.1 Summary statistics for 78 low and lower middle income countries from 1999 to 2020

Variable description	Mean	Std. dev	Minimum	Maximum
School enrollment, primary (% gross)	101.5433	19.72921	20.88291	149.9568
School enrollment, secondary (% gross)	53.01242	24.91327	5.29104	104.3128
School enrollment, tertiary (% gross)	15.38331	15.2128	0.25662	82.67118
Government expenditure on education (% of GDP)	4.170898	2.174927	0.62247	13.51266
Government expenditure on education (% of government expenditure)	16.12698	5.539649	4.67327	44.8018
Expenditure on primary education (% of government expenditure on education)	43.85543	12.05908	15.6148	74.36318
Expenditure on secondary education (% of government expenditure on education)	31.09652	10.39685	0.82897	71.58674
Expenditure on tertiary education (% of government expenditure on education)	18.91647	8.601918	0.0058	59.02014
Government expenditure per student, primary (% of GDP per capita)	12.22009	5.811499	3.03459	37.32327
Government expenditure per student, secondary (% of GDP per capita)	21.61847	13.84108	0.72783	88.90806
Government expenditure per student, tertiary (% of GDP per capita)	137.2895	253.0967	0.03371	2489.753
Net ODA received (% of GNI)	8.51684	9.419813	−0.2891	92.14146
GDP per capita growth (annual %)	1.926124	4.627324	−36.5569	28.676
Current health expenditure (% of GDP)	5.378792	2.324396	1.505006	20.41341
Individuals using the Internet (% of population)	12.54687	16.09962	0	84.12036
Voice and Accountability: Estimate	−0.60988	0.726439	−2.23327	1.175147

Source Authors

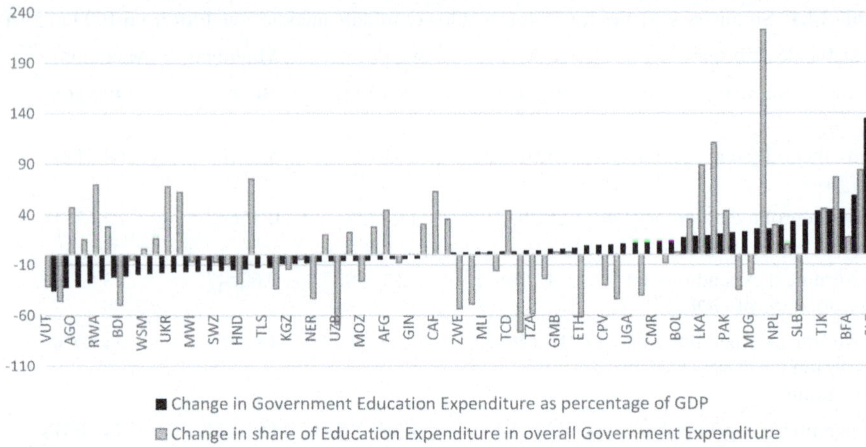

Fig. 14.1 Change in government expenditure on education as a percentage of GDP between 2010–2014 and 2016–2020. *Source* Drawn by the authors

We illustrate the changes in gross enrollment rates for primary, secondary, and tertiary levels of education between the time periods 2010–2014 and 2016–2020 in Figs. 14.2, 14.3, and 14.4, respectively.

Figure 14.2 shows the impact of changes in government spending over these two time periods. Since primary enrollment rates were already high prior to 2010, we see that the maximum cluster of countries exhibits changes within ± 10% of the existing levels in the 2010–2014 period. Figure 14.3 shows the impact of changes in government spending as a share of total government spending on changes in

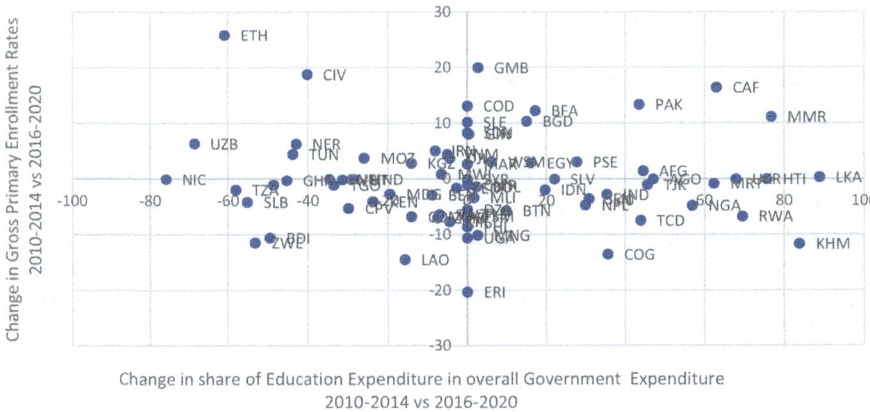

Fig. 14.2 Change in gross primary enrollment rates (2010–2014 vs. 2016–2020) due to change in share of education spending in total government spending (2010–2014 vs. 2016–2020). *Source* Drawn by the authors

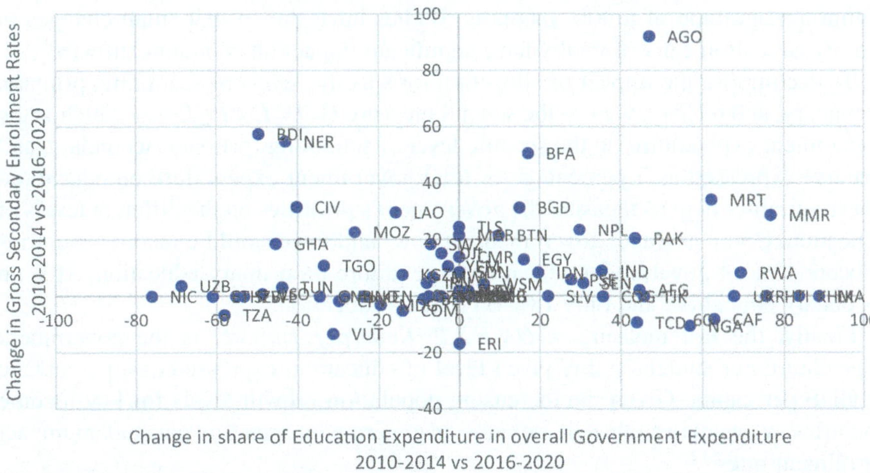

Fig. 14.3 Change in gross secondary enrollment rates (2010–2014 vs. 2016–2020) due to change in government education expenditures in overall spending (2010–2014 vs. 2016–2020). *Source* Drawn by the authors

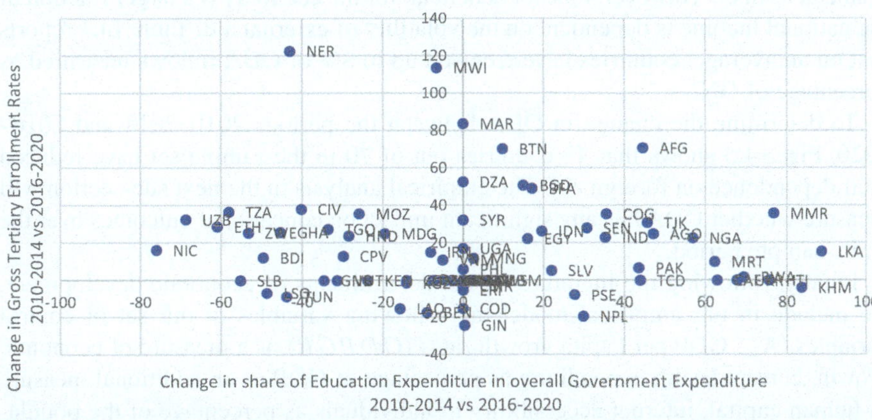

Fig. 14.4 Change in gross tertiary enrollment rates (2010–2014 vs. 2016–2020) due to change in government education expenditures in overall spending (2010–2014 vs. 2016–2020). *Source* Drawn by the authors

secondary enrollment rates. We find a larger positive change with a higher magnitude of 20% for a broad group of countries in the 2016–2020 period relative to the earlier 2010–2014 period. It is worth noting that the increase in secondary enrollment rates has occurred despite a fall in government spending for some countries. Figure 14.4 shows the impact of changes in government spending as a share of total government spending on changes in tertiary enrollment rates. We find the highest increase across all education levels during the 2016–2020 time period with a big cluster of countries within a magnitude of a 40% increase. Studies have shown that small changes in tertiary education can eventually have significant impact on economic growth.[11]

To decompose the impact of allocation for specific levels of schooling, primary, secondary, and tertiary, we use the second measure $GOVEXP\_Level$ which is the government expenditure on the specific level of schooling (primary, secondary, and tertiary) expressed as a percentage of total government expenditure on education. These variables help us measure the government's priorities on the different levels of education. On an average, governments in low- and lower-middle income countries allocate 43% of government education expenditure on primary education, 31% on secondary education, and only 18% on tertiary education.

Finally, the last measure, $GOVEXP\_Levelperstudent$, is the government expenditure per student at any given level of education, expressed as a percentage of GDP per capita. Given the increasing population growth levels for low-income countries, we want to analyze if increases in government spending per student impact enrollment rates.[12]

The independent variable, Official Development Assistance (ODA), measures net development assistance provided to least-developed countries, expressed as a percentage of Gross National Income (GNI). This is an alternative channel for low-income countries to promote economic development and welfare at concessional financial terms.[13] However, it is not beneficial for the economy if a larger fraction of the national income is dependent on the volatility of external aid. Table 14.1 reports that on an average, countries have received up to 8% of ODA inflows measured as percentage of GNI.

To determine the change in ODA between the periods 2010–2014 and 2016–2020, Fig. 14.5 shows that 43 countries out of 70 in the sample set have reduced their dependence on foreign aid. The empirical analysis in the next sub-section will measure whether ODA has any significant impact on educational outcomes over the entire sample period.

Finally, following the literature on the determinants of economic development, we include in our empirical model the following variables in our set of control variables, A_{jt}: GDP per capita growth rates ($GDPGR$) as a measure of economic growth, current health expenditure as percentage of GDP as an additional measure of human capital, internet accessibility to individuals as percentage of the population to proxy for basic infrastructure, and voice and accountability estimates from World Governance Indicators as a parameter for democratic power of the citizens in

[11] Castelló-Climent and Mukhopadhyay [12] show that in less developed countries, tertiary education may be crucial in shaping the economic performance.

[12] A World Bank study [17] on how the Covid-19 pandemic has affected on education financing reports that due to larger populations in low- and middle-income countries, the share of GDP spent on education is insufficient to achieve the improved quality of education.

[13] Dreher et al. [16] find that higher per capita aid for education significantly increases primary school enrollments.

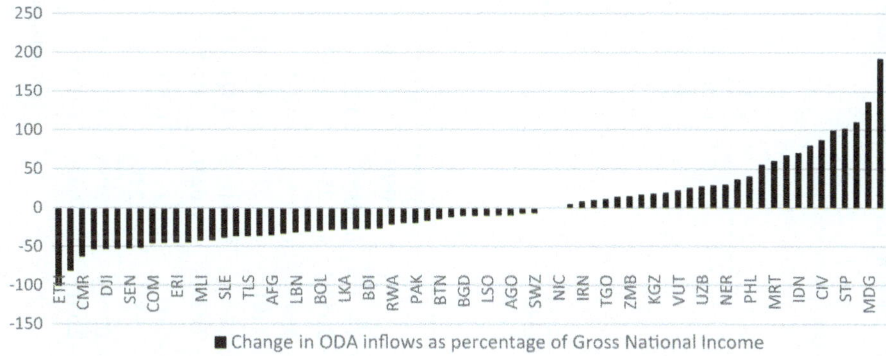

Fig. 14.5 Changes in net inflow of official development assistance as a percentage of gross national income between 2010–2014 and 2016–2020. *Source* Drawn by the authors

the economy.[14] All else equal, the control variables should positively contribute to economic growth which, in turn, could positively impact education enrollment rates.

14.3.3 Empirical Results

We estimate five models for each educational level for low and lower-middle income countries, the results are shown in Table 14.2. We begin by analyzing whether government expenditures at the primary, secondary, and tertiary levels have a direct impact on educational outcomes at each educational level for low- and lower-middle income countries. For enrollment rates at the primary level, we find that government expenditures on education as a percentage of GDP is statistically significant role as shown in Models 1.1 at the 5% level of significance and 1.5 at 1% level of significance. We also find primary-level specific government expenditure per student to be statistically significantly as shown in Model 1.3 at the 5% level of significance. The negative coefficient reveals that despite larger enrollments, per student funding levels are on the decline over time. For secondary level enrolment rates, we find similar results with the measure, government expenditure on education as a percentage of GDP; it is statistically significant as shown in Model 2.5 at the 5% level of significance. Moreover, secondary-level specific government expenditure is statistically significant in Model 2.2 at the 5% level. At the tertiary enrollment level, government expenditure as a percentage of GDP in Model 3.5 is significant at the 1% level. As illustrated in Fig. 14.4, despite declining government spending on education, tertiary enrollment

[14] The control variables, *Health Expenditure* and *Individuals with access to Internet*, were included following Prasetyo and Zuhdi [31] which investigates the impact of integrated government spending on health and education on the Human Development Index, and the Asian Development Outlook (2021) which reports 86% internet access in high-income economies and about 41% internet access in lower-middle income economies.

Table 14.2 Effect of government spending and ODA on gross enrollment rates for primary, secondary, tertiary levels of schooling for low income and lower middle-income countries

Independent variable	Dependent variable: gross enrollment primary					Dependent variable: gross enrollment secondary				
	Level: Primary					Level: Secondary				
	1.1	1.2	1.3	1.4	1.5	2.1	2.2	2.3	2.4	2.5
Government expenditure in education (% GDP)	2.298** (−1.003)				2.359*** (−0.354)	0.701 (−0.79)				0.703** (−0.33)
Government expenditure on **'Level'** education (as % of Government expenditure on education)		−0.111 (−0.076)					0.147** (−0.072)			
Government expenditure per student on **'Level'** education (% of GDP per capita)			−0.336** (−0.148)					−0.388*** (−0.051)		
Net ODA received (% of GNI)				−0.232*** (−0.067)	−0.139* (−0.081)				−0.536*** (−0.066)	−0.661*** (−0.090)
Health expenditure (as % of GDP)	1.256* (−0.669)	1.830*** (−0.473)	1.724*** (−0.46)	1.344*** (−0.274)	1.379*** (−0.321)	−0.129 (−0.728)	0.338 (−0.392)	0.374 (−0.357)	0.508** (−0.25)	0.26 (−0.297)
GDP per capita growth rate (annual %)	0.415*** (−0.125)	0.262* (−0.145)	0.168 (−0.132)	0.340*** (−0.081)	0.402*** (−0.0963)	0.13 (−0.127)	0.152 (−0.122)	0.0359 (−0.101)	0.162** (−0.071)	0.0856 (−0.088)
Individuals using Internet (% of the population)	0.127** (−0.053)	0.163** (−0.063)	0.189*** (−0.053)	0.108*** (−0.026)	0.120*** (−0.0321)	0.586*** (−0.0846)	0.556*** (−0.048)	0.517*** (−0.038)	0.504*** (−0.024)	0.524*** (−0.030)
Voice and accountability	3.954 (−3.859)	11.72*** (−2.597)	10.50*** (−2.467)	5.405*** (−1.31)	4.601*** (−1.531)	−1.278 (−3.778)	2.731 (−2.181)	3.457* (−1.985)	0.954 (−1.23)	0.301 (−1.491)
Constant	87.15*** (−7.501)	104.4*** (−4.575)	103.5*** (−3.403)	99.07*** (−1.829)	87.82*** (−2.733)	43.65*** (−6.716)	40.07*** (−3.301)	54.02*** (−2.551)	49.07*** (−1.694)	47.85*** (−2.539)

(continued)

Table 14.2 (continued)

Independent variable	Dependent variable: gross enrollment primary					Dependent variable: gross enrollment secondary				
	Level: Primary					Level: Secondary				
	1.1	1.2	1.3	1.4	1.5	2.1	2.2	2.3	2.4	2.5
Observations	858	428	456	1,163	847	670	331	352	906	659
R-squared	0.129	0.161	0.159	0.094	0.143	0.395	0.416	0.527	0.459	0.465

Independent variable	Dependent variable: gross enrollment tertiary				
	Level: Tertiary				
	3.1	3.2	3.3	3.4	3.5
Government Expenditure in Education (% GDP)	−0.154 (−0.45)				−0.342* (−0.19)
Government expenditure on **'Level'** education (as % of Government expenditure on education)		0.256*** (−0.049)			
Government expenditure per student on **'Level'** education (% of GDP per capita)			−0.000406 (−0.002)		
Net ODA received (% of GNI)				−0.103** (−0.0409)	−0.0924* (−0.0552)
Health expenditure (as % of GDP)	0.794 (−0.519)	0.567** (−0.259)	0.503 (−0.314)	0.729*** (−0.164)	0.810*** (−0.19)

(continued)

Table 14.2 (continued)

Independent variable	Dependent variable: gross enrollment tertiary				
	Level: Tertiary				
	3.1	3.2	3.3	3.4	3.5
GDP per capita growth rate (annual %)	−0.0555 (−0.066)	−0.120* (−0.066)	−0.0869 (−0.069)	−0.0414 (−0.0408)	0.00206 (−0.0472)
Individuals using Internet (% of the population)	0.352*** (−0.052)	0.453*** (−0.025)	0.449*** (−0.0261)	0.306*** (−0.0121)	0.339*** (−0.0151)
Voice and accountability	−3.373 (−2.399)	−3.557*** (−1.078)	−3.996*** (−1.056)	−3.378*** (−0.662)	−4.049*** (−0.755)
Constant	6.408** (−3.129)	3.145* (−1.737)	8.267*** (−1.901)	6.102*** (−1.022)	6.964*** (−1.38)
Observations	698	422	412	896	692
R-squared	0.512	0.576	0.521	0.511	0.527

Robust standard errors in parentheses
***$p < 0.01$, **$p < 0.05$, *$p < 0.1$
Source Authors

rates have increased significantly during the past decade. In terms of magnitude, a 1% change government spending on education leads to a 2.3% change in primary enrollment levels for low-income countries, a 0.7% change in secondary enrollment rates, and 0.3% change in tertiary enrollment rates. While enrollment rates have increased, it is still necessary for policy initiatives and actions to be directed toward secondary and tertiary levels of education.

Focusing on ODA's impact on education outcomes, we find ODA to be statistically significant at the 1% level for primary enrollment rates in Model 1.4. The negative sign of the coefficient does not necessarily imply that higher ODA is detrimental to educational outcomes. Rising enrollment rates despite falling ODA levels depict lower dependence on aid and a higher contribution by the Government.[15] We find similar results for secondary enrollment rates in Model 2.4 and tertiary enrollment rates in Model 3.4, respectively. Overall, we find that low and lower-middle income economies rely on ODA significantly but the decline in dependence is an important step toward achieving development goals. However, when compared to ODA, we find that across all levels of educational enrollments, government spending allocations have had a greater impact on education outcomes.[16]

In order to compare the impact of government spending on high-income countries, we conduct a similar fixed effects analysis for 111 upper middle-income countries and high-income countries over the same time period of 1999–2020. We do not include ODA as an explanatory variable in the analysis since inflow of foreign aid at concessional terms is not relevant for majority of the high-income countries. The results are presented in Table 14.3 (given at the end of the chapter). We find that government spending on education is statistically significant at tertiary enrollment levels unlike low income countries. Primary and secondary enrollment rates are close to saturation or at maximum levels in high-income countries and we find relatively low impact from additional government spending. However, in direct contrast to low-income countries, an increase of 1% in government spending will lead to a 2.4% change in tertiary enrollment rates in high-income countries vis-à-vis a 0.15% change in low-income countries. Returns to tertiary education have been found to have the biggest impact on higher earnings and higher income growth for countries.[17] The differences in the effectiveness of government spending to increase tertiary enrollment rates between high- and low-income countries will continue to persist unless greater government initiatives are directed both at the secondary and tertiary education levels in low-income countries.

---

[15] Kyne [25] finds that ODA provided for educational purposes are relatively small compared to other allocations of aid.

[16] The Centre for Global Development finds that the vast majority of education expenditure continues to be domestically financed. https://www.cgdev.org/blog/state-global-education-finance-seven-charts-update.

[17] Montenegro and Patrinos [29] find returns to tertiary education have increased from 13% in the 1980s to more than 17% in the early part of the twenty-first century.

Table 14.3 Effect of government spending on gross enrollment rates for primary, secondary, tertiary levels of schooling for upper middle income and high income countries

Independent variable	Dependent variable: gross enrollment primary			Dependent variable: gross enrollment secondary		
	Level: Primary			Level: Secondary		
	1.1	1.2	1.3	2.1	2.2	2.3
Government expenditure in education (% GDP)	−0.156 (−0.537)			1.699** (−0.695)		
Government expenditure on **'Level'** education (as % of Government expenditure on education)		0.106*** (−0.0385)			−0.0394 (−0.0656)	
Government expenditure per student on **'Level'** education (% of GDP per capita)			−0.0389 (−0.0506)			−0.319*** (−0.0796)
Health expenditure (as % of GDP)	0.272 (−0.549)	1.195*** (−0.221)	1.281*** (−0.228)	0.0561 (−0.713)	1.669*** (−0.46)	2.085*** (−0.427)
GDP per capita growth rate (annual %)	−0.0578 (−0.0523)	0.0764** (−0.0386)	0.0605 (−0.0386)	0.164** (−0.0761)	0.189** (−0.0838)	0.159** (−0.0778)
Individuals using Internet (% of the population)	−0.0607*** (−0.018)	−0.0806*** (−0.00892)	−0.0794*** (−0.00886)	0.188*** (−0.0316)	0.152*** (−0.018)	0.150*** (−0.0163)
Voice and accountability	−3.558** (−1.58)	−4.080*** (−1.103)	−4.660*** (−1.131)	−6.839 (−5.524)	−0.22 (−2.421)	0.927 (−2.269)
Constant	107.6*** (−3.777)	99.65*** (−2.119)	103.1*** (−1.594)	84.50*** (−5.654)	80.35*** (−4.363)	81.24*** (−3.212)
Observations	1,247	779	863	1,160	748	835
R-squared	0.086	0.145	0.12	0.269	0.203	0.2

(continued)

Table 14.3 (continued)

Independent variable	Dependent variable: gross enrollment tertiary		
	Level: Tertiary		
	3.1	3.2	3.3
Government expenditure in education (% GDP)	2.424** (−1.063)		
Government expenditure on **'Level'** education (as % of government expenditure on education)		0.409*** (−0.0764)	
Government expenditure per student on **'Level'** education (% of GDP per capita)			−0.279*** (−0.0308)
Health expenditure (as % of GDP)	1.001 (−1.46)	1.302*** (−0.421)	0.930** (−0.401)
GDP per capita growth rate (annual %)	0.185 (−0.136)	0.196*** (−0.0688)	0.0607 (−0.0664)
Individuals using Internet (% of the population)	0.335*** (−0.0382)	0.320*** (−0.0158)	0.308*** (−0.015)
Voice and accountability	1.644 (−4.086)	2.135 (−2.102)	3.081 (−1.997)
Constant	15.13 (−12.33)	18.61*** (−3.459)	38.57*** (−3.133)
Observations	1,092	756	783
R-squared	0.532	0.531	0.559

Robust standard errors in parentheses
***$p < 0.01$, **$p < 0.05$, *$p < 0.1$
Source Authors

14.4 Learning Losses Due to Covid-19 and the Role of Government Spending

Prior to Covid-19, government spending on education as a percentage of GDP increased for 35 out of the 78 low and lower-middle income countries studied in the sample between the time periods of 2010–2014 and 2016–2020. These countries also showed an increased allocation toward education expenditures as a fraction of total government expenditure. After Covid-19, looking at the World Bank data for a reduced sample of 62 low and lower-middle income countries from 2019 to 2020, we find that 46 countries showed an increase in government education expenditure as a fraction of GDP with an average increase of 6%. Only 35 countries showed a marginally increased allocation in education as a share of government expenditures. While the proportion of education spending from the government budget has not seen a decline, we do find that the overall Government Education Expenditure has declined. The Covid-19 pandemic created institutional problems for education, especially for low-income countries. Decline in household income levels, prolonged school closures, lack of access to digital devices or instructional content, and eventual school dropouts will severely undermine the positive aspects that have been demonstrated in the empirical analysis of the past decade.[18]

The significant learning deficits cannot be adequately captured by any single quantitative determinant of educational outcomes such as Gross Enrollment Rates. A composite measure that consists of both quantitative (expected years of schooling) and qualitative (standardized test scores harmonized across countries) aspects of learning such as Learning Adjusted Years of Schooling (LAYS) is more pertinent.[19] We use World Bank-calculated LAYS estimates based on the methodology in Filmer et al. [19] to summarize our findings in Fig. 14.6.

The data on LAYS is still in its early stages and very incomplete. The picture that emerges between 2017 and 2020 shows a gradual change for low-income and lower-middle income countries from 5.7 LAYS to 5.8 LAYS for 9.4 average years of schooling. In comparison, the high-income and higher middle-income countries exhibit 9.1 LAYS for 12.5 average years of schooling in 2020. The divergence in learning is significant and requires greater government allocation of resources, which is likely to be exacerbated given the impact of Covid-19 on government budgets in low- and middle-income countries. Asian Development Outlook (2021) estimates learning losses for developing economies in Asia from 23 to 38%. The learning deficit and the worsening divergence in LAYS should be a priority for government policy directives going forward.

Many low-income countries have reduced government education expenditure as a share of total spending with the onset of the pandemic. Despite the limited availability

[18] For example, a survey conducted in Bangladesh in 2021 shows that 53% of households reported incomes less than expenditures while school closures have varied from 50 days to as long as 300 days across most countries in developing Asia (Asian Development Outlook, 2021).

[19] LAYS is calculated as a product of expected years of schooling and standardized test scores harmonized across countries. The metric is calculated for primary and secondary levels of schooling.

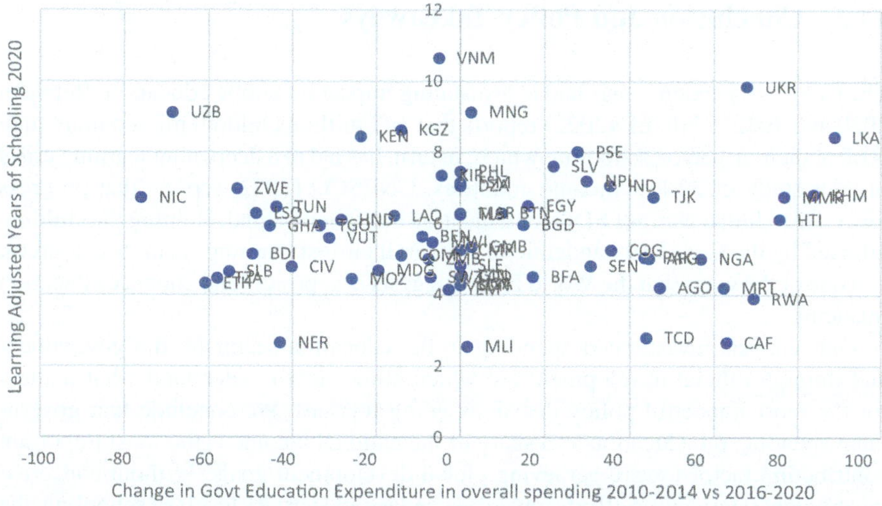

Fig. 14.6 Learning Adjusted Years of Schooling (LAYS) in 2020 versus Change in government education expenditure in overall spending (2010–2014 vs. 2016–2020). *Source* Drawn by the authors

of 2021 data, we find that GDP (expressed in current international dollars, converted by purchasing power parity) has increased in 2021 relative to 2020 data. Using 2020 data on share of education spending as a percentage of GDP, Fig. 14.7 shows the projections of increase in government spending for 2021.

We find that the Government Education Expenditures as a fraction of GDP can increase by a very modest 8% as it does from 2019–2020, ranging from a 0.5% increase to an increase of 17% in low- and lower-middle income countries.

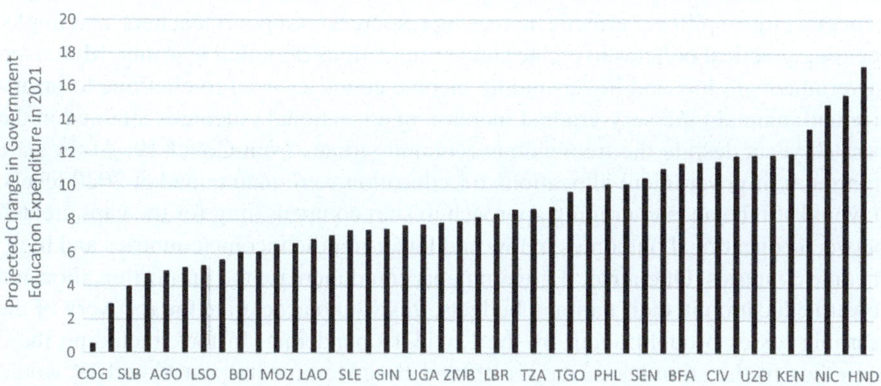

Fig. 14.7 Projections of increase in government spending in low income and lower middle-income countries in 2021 using education expenditure shares from 2020 as percentage of GDP. *Source* Drawn by the authors

14.5 Conclusion and Policy Takeaways

The Covid-19 pandemic has had a devastating impact on public education. Between 2020 and 2022, UNICEF (2022) reports that 147 million children missed more than 50% of their in-person schooling which, in turn, has led to a deepening learning crisis in their study of 32 low-income countries. UNESCO (2022) reports that progress toward the United Nations SDG for education has fallen behind. Helping the children affected by the Covid-19 pandemic to recover their lost learning requires resources, and one of the ways that the World Bank suggests is to protect and enhance education financing.

Our analysis investigated spending in the education sector by the government and through official development aid which allows us to understand what matters for the most impactful policy decisions going forward. We conclude that government spending on education as a share of the national income is the most important contributing factor toward achieving global development goals. Without concerted government intervention efforts toward secondary and tertiary levels of schooling, the divergence in educational outcomes between low and lower-middle income countries versus high-income countries and subsequent earnings will continue to persist.

Low and lower-middle income countries need to maximize the effectiveness of government funding on education by addressing some of the inherent inefficiencies within the education sector so that each dollar spent achieves the highest possible level of student outcome. We know that the strategies and practices used to maximize student outcome levels depend on the specific student population that each school must serve [1]. Thus, there is no blanket policy that can be prescribed for all countries since schools in different countries have different ways of being efficient; this holds within a country too. However, some of the ways to maximize the effectiveness of government funding on education include linking funding to graduation rates, orienting funds toward relevant tertiary education components that have the ability to generate larger spillover effects, increasing resources to support teachers, and implementing practical policies to create stable foundations of digital learning. Moreover, governments in low and lower-middle income countries need to continue to prioritize and maintain the very gradual increase in educational outcomes attained in the past 10 years despite the tremendous economic losses from Covid-19. At the bare minimum, if government allocations for education were maintained at 2020 levels, it would still be an encouraging approach to start compensating for the gaps created between educational outcomes in low and lower-middle income countries and high-income countries. Of course, if governments could increase the proportion allocated toward education in their national budgets, this would accelerate the recovery of the learning losses brought about by the Covid-19 pandemic. In fact, including these increases in the stimulus packages offered by governments post Covid-19 would further facilitate the recovery of learning losses [41].

References

1. Agasisti T, Zoido P (2019) The efficiency of schools in developing countries, analysed through PISA 2012 data. Socioecon Plann Sci 68:100711
2. Al-Samarrai S, Gangwar M, Gala P (2020) The impact of the COVID-19 pandemic on education financing. World Bank, Washington, DC
3. Al-Samarrai S. Cerdan-Infantes P, Lehe JD (2019) Mobilizing resources for education and improving spending effectiveness: establishing realistic benchmarks based on past trends. Policy Research Working Paper No. 87. World Bank, Washington, DC
4. Asian Development Bank (ADB) (2021) Learning and earning losses from COVID-19 school closures in developing Asia. Mandaluyong, Philippines.
5. Awaworyi Churchill S, Ugur M, Yew SL (2017) Does government size affect per-capita income growth? A hierarchical meta-regression analysis. Econ Rec 93(300):142–171
6. Barro RJ (1991) Economic growth in a cross section of countries. Q J Econ 106(2):407–443
7. Barro R, Lee JW (2010) A new dataset of educational attainment in the world, 1950–2010. NBER Working paper No. 15902
8. Benhabib J, Spiegel MM (1994) The role of human capital in economic development evidence from aggregate cross-country data. J Monet Econ 34(2):143–173
9. Bloom D, Canning D, Chan K (2006) Higher education and economic development in Africa, vol 102. World Bank, Washington, DC
10. Bloom D, Canning D, Sevilla J (2004) The effect of health on economic growth: a production function approach. World Dev 32(1):1–13
11. Borensztein E, De Gregorio J, Lee JW (1998) How does foreign direct investment affect economic growth? J Int Econ 45(1):115-135
12. Castelló-Climent A, Mukhopadhyay A (2013) Mass education or a minority well educated elite in the process of growth: the case of India. J Dev Econ 105:303–320
13. Castelló-Climent A, Doménech R (2008) Human capital inequality, life expectancy and economic growth. Econ J 118(528):653–677
14. Del Boca D, Monfardini C, See SG (2018) Government education expenditures, pre-primary education and school performance: a cross-country analysis. CESifo Working Paper Series 6934, CESifo
15. Dinopoulos E, Thompson P (2000) Endogenous growth in a cross-section of countries. J Int Econ 51(2):335–362
16. Dreher A, Nunnenkamp P, Thiele R (2008) Does aid for education educate children? Evidence from panel data. World Bank Econ Rev 22(2):291–314
17. Education Finance Watch (EFW) (2021). World Bank Group, Washington, DC. http://documents.worldbank.org/curated/en/226481614027788096/Education-Finance-Watch-2021. Accessed 3 Jan 2023
18. Education Finance Watch (EFW) (2022). EFW-2022-Jul1.pdf (https://www.worldbank.org). Accessed 3 Jan 2023
19. Filmer DP, Rogers FH, Angrist N, Sabarwal S (2018) Learning-Adjusted Years of Schooling (LAYS): defining a New Macro Measure of Education. Policy Research working paper WPS 8591. World Bank Group, Washington, DC
20. Glaeser EL, La Porta R, Lopez-de-Silanes F, Shleifer A (2004) Do institutions cause growth? J Econ Growth 9(3):271–303
21. Grigoli F (2014) A hybrid approach to estimating the efficiency of public spending on education in emerging and developing economies. IMF Working Paper series. No. 2014/019
22. Hanushek EA, Woessmann L (2008) The role of cognitive skills in economic development. J Econ Literat 46(3):607–668
23. Hill S, Chalaux T (2011) Improving access and quality in the Indian education system. OECD Economics Department Working Papers, No. 885. OECD Publishing. https://doi.org/10.1787/5kg83k687ng7-en
24. Krueger AB, Lindahl M (2001) Education for growth: Why and For Whom? J Econ Literat 39(4):1101–1136

25. Kyne D (2008) An empirical investigation of relationships between official development assistance (ODA) and human and educational development. Int J Soc Econ 35:202–221
26. Li Z, Sharma U, Maheen M (2021) Impact of COVID-19 on primary school students in disadvantaged areas of Bangladesh. Asian Development Bank Briefs, Manila, Philippines
27. Lucas RE (1988) On the mechanics of economic development. J Monetary Econ 22(1):3–42
28. Miningou EW (2019) Quality education and the efficiency of public expenditure: a cross-country comparative analysis. Policy Research Working Paper 9077, World Bank, DC
29. Montenegro CE, Patrinos HA (2014) Comparable estimates of returns to schooling around the world. The Policy Research Working Paper Series, Working Paper 7020, World Bank Group
30. OECD: Education at a Glance 2022: OECD Indicators. https://gpseducation.oecd.org/review educationpolicies/#!node=41709&filter=all. Accessed January 2023
31. Prasetyo AD, Zuhdi U (2013) The government expenditure efficiency towards the human development. Procedia Econ Financ 5:615–622
32. Pritchett L (2006) Does learning to add up add up? The returns to schooling in aggregate data. In: Hanushek EA, Welch F (eds) Handbook of the economics of education. North Holland, Amsterdam, pp 635–695
33. Psacharopoulos G (1982) The economics of higher education in developing countries. Comp Educ Rev 26(2):139–159
34. Psacharopoulos G, Patrinos HA (2004) Returns to investment in education: a further update. Educ Econ 12(2):111-134
35. Romer PM (1990) Human capital and growth: theory and evidence. In: Carnegie-Rochester conference series on public policy, vol 32, pp 251–286. North-Holland
36. Shafuda CP, De UK (2020) Government expenditure on human capital and growth in Namibia: a time series analysis. J Econ Struct 9:1–14
37. Trabelsi S (2017) Public education expenditure and economic growth: the educational quality threshold effect. Region et Developpement 45:99–112
38. UNICEF (2022) Analysis of education spending in the West and Central Africa region. https://www.unicef.org/wca/media/7131/file/Reimagining-Financing-for-Education-Policy-Brief.pdf. Accessed January 2023
39. UNICEF (2022) Primary education. Current Status + Progress. https://data.unicef.org/topic/education/primary-education/. Accessed January 2023
40. United Nations (2015) Millennium development goals report. https://www.un.org/millenniu mgoals/2015_MDG_Report/pdf/MDG%202015%20rev%20(July%201).pdf. Accessed April 2023
41. World Economic Forum (2022) Severe learning losses and worsening inequalities in education. https://www.weforum.org/agenda/2022/01/global-education-crisis-children-stu dents-covid19/. Accessed January 2023
42. World Education Forum (2000) Dakar Framework for Action. Available at https://www.right-toeducation.org/sites/right-to-education.org/files/resource-attachments/Dakar_Framework_for_Action_2000_en.pdfLast accessed January 2023.

Chapter 15
The Impact of COVID-19 on Institutional Single Family Institutional Investors in Growing U.S. Markets

Kenneth Chilton

15.1 Introduction

The U.S. housing market is radically different today than 15 years ago. Before the 2008 market crash, private equity investors and real estate investment trusts (REITs) were no significant single-family rental market players. However, that changed in 2010 as banks and mortgage finance companies sold large portfolios of foreclosed homes to institutional investors. In turn, these companies converted thousands of single-family homes to single-family rentals. Before 2010, the single-family rental market was primarily mom-and-pop investors, regional investment groups, and house flippers. This change has had significant impacts on the U.S. housing situation.

The prominent companies that dominate the single-family rental (SFR) market are as follows:

- Progress Residential (private equity, owns 80,000 + homes)
- American Homes 4 Rent (REIT, owns 56,000 homes)
- Invitation Homes (REIT, owns 82,000 homes)
- Tricon Residential (REIT, owns 27,000 homes)
- Amherst Capital (REIT, owns 23,000 homes)

These institutional investors operate differently than investors who advertise "we buy houses." Such enterprises are typically local and involve brokers who actively seek homes to buy. Likewise, the major SFR players do not operate like Offerpad or other buyers who earn fees quickly buying and selling homes. Offerpad works with individual sellers motivated to use their digital platform to accommodate quick transactions—typically without real estate agents.

While the universe of homes owned by corporate institutional investors is relatively small compared to the overall single-family supply in the U.S. (about 2% of

K. Chilton (✉)
Tennessee State University, Nashville, USA
e-mail: kchilton@tnstate.edu

R. Bhattacharyya et al. (eds.), *COVID-19 Pandemic and Global Inequality*,
https://doi.org/10.1007/978-981-99-4405-7_15

all homes), the companies operate only in select markets. They focus on growing suburban communities near large U.S. metropolitan areas. They are particularly active in southern and southwestern states that experiencing strong population growth. Coincidentally, many of the states have weak tenants' rights laws. Texas, Arizona, Florida, Georgia, North Carolina, and Tennessee have experienced large influxes of SFR REIT investors. SFR investors own more than 11,000 single-family homes in Mecklenburg County, NC (Charlotte, NC) alone. In suburban Nashville, TN, SFR investors own about 10% of all homes in Rutherford County—with a market share of 30–40% in some neighborhoods.

A recent Urban Institute report found that major institutional investors own newer, larger homes (median year built is 1999), in higher-income census tracts than smaller investors and mom-and-pop landlords [10]. In addition, communities with higher concentrations of institutional investor ownership tend to be more racially integrated.

15.2 COVID and Demographic Trends

According to popular media, COVID catalyzed a change in consumer living preferences. The pandemic created conditions more conducive to suburban tastes. The desire for less dense urban and multifamily coupled with newfound freedom to work remotely led to an influx of suburban residents. That is the popular narrative, but critical analyses of such claims are limited. A Cleveland Fed study analyzed migration flows and found evidence of growth in suburban communities in 2020 [18]. However, they concluded that the term "exodus" is misleading because it implies a high magnitude of out-migration. The movement toward suburban locales was consistent across most metropolitan areas in the study, but it was not an overwhelming flight to suburbia. In addition, the suburban flight was not solely attributed to COVID. High housing costs in central cities pushed some residents to lower-cost communities outside the urban area.

Ozimek and O'Brien [14] found that families with young children drove the out-migration to suburban areas in major cities. They found substantial population declines between 2020 and 2021 for "under 18" and "under 5" age cohorts. [7] analyzed data from 88 U.S. cities with populations greater than 250,000 and found "unprecedented" population losses in 2020–21. Population loss was most pronounced in large cities such as New York and San Francisco, but 51 cities experienced population loss. In those cities experiencing population gain, it tended to be more modest than previous years. Growth cities tend to align well with the target markets of institutional SFR investors.

Demographers need to be more certain about the cause of migration trends. COVID is most certainly a part of the story, but many trends prior to the pandemic are likely contributors to suburban population growth. Concerns about urban crime (whether valid or not), school quality, and high housing costs likely contributed to changing consumer demands and preferences over the last several years. Low interest rates led to substantial increases in home prices which likely contributed to urban displacement and a suburban cost advantage. The main point is that COVID was one of multiple contributing factors to changes in real estate markets over the last 5-years. Institutional investors were and remain active purchasers of homes in markets that fit their business model.

15.3 COVID and Impacts on Institutional Investors

The growth of SFR investors coincided initially with the foreclosure crisis. COVID is a different type of crisis, though. It is not based on a housing market failure that produced millions of foreclosures. Public health emergencies are qualitatively different than market failures. One consequence of the COVID epidemic is changing consumer preferences related to residential choice and home office work. According to SFR investors, more and more consumers want to rent single-family homes in suburban locations. Some renters would prefer to own homes, but a combination of factors related to household debt burdens, lack of credit, supply, rising interest rates, and high housing prices have all boosted the appeal of renting homes in suburban locales. Changes in homework environments have only served to increase demand for an already limited supply of suburban rental homes.

MetLife Investment Management predicts "institutional SFR ownership is likely to grow significantly over the next decade" [5]. They also point out that a rising interest rate environment will likely increase opportunities for institutional SFR investors to buy and build more rental homes. SFR investors rely on technology to position themselves in local markets. Using algorithms, they can identify and make cash-only offers on houses within 10 min of a house hitting the market. This is an incredible competitive advantage over first-time and traditional single-unit buyers who often must apply for credit, plan inspections, and negotiate with buyers over repairs and prices. Institutional investors often buy sight unseen and make all-cash offers.

15.4 SFR Industry Genesis

The growth of institutional investors is directly attributable to the foreclosure crisis after 2008. The housing crash created tremendous opportunities for investors to buy bargain-priced single-family residential homes. The investors did not necessarily have a strong business model in place, but the industry professionalized and evolved over time.

Some of the investment companies are organized as Real Estate Investment Trusts (REITs). REITs have been around since the 1960s. They were designed to encourage average Americans to invest in real estate. REITs cover an array of real estate options: multi-family apartments, self-storage facilities, shopping centers, office parks, and senior housing project to name just a few. REITs allow profits to flow through a corporate entity with taxes levied on individual investors. As mentioned earlier, SFR REITs were not established until 2012. Institutional investors targeting single-family rentals also include private equity investors.

Given the industry's infancy, the literature on institutional investors and single-family housing is limited. Plenty of articles have been written about the industry in trade magazines and in the popular media. The academic literature is limited. There needs to be scholarly literature on the impact of COVID on institutional investors buying or building single-family rental homes.

The corporatization of the single-family rental industry started after the foreclosure crisis of 2009–2010. The scale of foreclosures permitted large companies to accumulate sizable portfolios of single-family houses in a short period. Outside of mom-and-pop landlords and some regional investment groups, the corporate single-family rental model has unheard of prior to 2010. The business model that converted foreclosed single-family housing units to rental properties was, in a way, developed on the fly.

Chilton et al. [3] analyzed the growth on SFR investors in the Nashville region and found limited research on SFR REITs. At the time, it was a small niche issue. Immergluck [11] has documented the growth of SFR investors in the Atlanta region and labeled the city as a private equity "strike zone." The UNC-Charlotte Urban Institute conducted a similar analysis of Charlotte, NC, and Mecklenburg County [15] and found major market growth over the last decade. While acquisition strategies tend to be similar among institutional SFR investors, Charles [2] found many variations in community demographics where investors are most active.

The industry's growth is documented, but empirical evidence on the impact on local property markets, homeownership rates, and quality of life remains to be discovered. The growth of institutional ownership coincides with price and rent escalation in most U.S. and global markets. Isolating the impact of institutional investors on overall housing affordability, for example, remains a methodological problem.

Another area for improvement in analyzing institutional investor impacts on regional housing markets is perspective. If a critic views home ownership as a socially desirable outcome for households, then the growth of corporate landlords might be interpreted as a bad omen. Homeownership has historically been the major pathway to individual household wealth creation and the primary means of intergenerational wealth transfer. From this perspective, the growth on institutional investors might be considered negatively. In contrast, institutional investors are efficient if industry growth is viewed as an outcome of competitive market forces that creates wealth for shareholders.

15.5 Corporate Business Model

The business model that has evolved uses technology as its lynchpin. Fields [8] argues the emergency and growth of corporate SFR firms to their use of technologies. She refers to them as "automated landlords." Technology is the key to property acquisition, customer service, and portfolio management. Most institutional investors use a three-prong growth strategy. First, they continue to compete with one another and individuals for houses listed for sale. This process is referred to as "sharp shooting." Sometimes, corporate investors work with local real estate brokers to identify and purchase properties. The second strategy is to partner with national builders to construct build-to-rent neighborhoods. This can be a win–win for both developers and investors. Developers can contract with institutional investors to deliver an entire community with certainty. Plus, developers only have to deal with one buyer. The developer can deliver a homogenous product that meets the needs of one customer who is unlikely to break a contract due to financing concerns or changing tastes for amenities. Finally, some of the corporate investors, such as American Homes 4 Rent, engage in land banking. They acquire parcels in select markets to build future rental housing communities.

As the business model has evolved, institutional SFR investors are technology companies. They have developed proprietary algorithms that make swift investment decisions. As Progress Residential's CEO explained during a real estate Podcast:

> The vast majority of those were acquired one at a time off the MLS. And we've done that by investing heavily in the technology and the analytic systems to support those acquisitions... Essentially the way it works is we get an automatic feed every 15 min for every home in our buy box across our markets. So when a home goes on the market within 15 min we get a feed. If it meets our criteria, we have an algorithm that quickly scores it and helps, does the underwriting. And we're constantly tweaking the inputs to that based on the performance and the data of our overall portfolio... and that allows us to really tweak the model. We have an acquisition team that has a couple of inputs. They put in the rents and the renovation budget, and they try to generally get an offer out within a couple of hours of the home going on the market. We're able to analyze it very quickly, make an offer—our offers are all cash—very flexible closing, basically whenever the seller wants to move out" (Chaz Mueller, CEO Progress Residential).

The variables in the "buy box" are proprietary. But, most institutional investors focus on buying newer suburban homes in areas with perceived higher-quality public schools. Since COVID encouraged urban residents to seek less dense suburban communities, they often found a strong competitor for single-family homes: Institutional investors. As Progress's CEO makes clear, their all-cash offers are a better deal for sellers who do not have to worry about last-minute glitches in buyer financing. Corporate investors remain well-positioned for changes in consumer tastes that value suburban living over urban lifestyles.

According to Dowdall et al. [6], "the proportion of the rental market owned by sole proprietors has approximately halved, going from 77% to 41% of all rental units" over the last 30 years. Today's housing market is radically different than in the past. Institutional investors and out-of-town landlords own a larger market share that continued to grow during COVID. The long-term implications of this change are unknown, but the growth in corporate absentee landlords has attracted federal attention. Senator Elizabeth Warren has raised concerns about corporate landlords driving up housing prices and increasing rents [17].

It is difficult to discern if institutional investors ramped up purchasing homes because of COVID. Estimates do not disaggregate totals and allocate shares based on the type of investor. Data shows that investor purchases of single-family homes skyrocketed after the second quarter of 2020. According to [1], investors accounted for 18.4% of U.S. homes purchased in the fourth quarter of 2021. The investor share was 32.7% in Atlanta, 32.1% in Charlotte, 29.8% in Jacksonville, 29.2% in Las Vegas, and 28.4% in Phoenix.

Investor home purchases peaked in February 2022, accounting for 28% of all single-family house purchases [12]. However, the major institutional investors are only active in some U.S. markets. The major institutional investors—American Homes 4 Rent, Invitation Homes, Progress Residential, Tricon, and Amherst CPI—have focused primarily on fast-growing markets in the southwest and south. Investor presentations of American Homes 4 Rent (AMH) explain the geographic strategy of these companies. A "Migration Trends Favor AMH Footprint" map shows the primary markets that capitalize on "outbound migration from coastal urban centers to higher quality of life markets." Las Vegas, Phoenix, Dallas, Austin, Houston, Tampa, Orlando, Jacksonville, Nashville, Atlanta, Charlotte, and Raleigh are highlighted as growth regions.

15.6 Methods

To analyze the impact of COVID on the single-family residential and rental markets, the author interviewed elected officials and urban planners in Tennessee and, to a lesser extent, Georgia. Both states have experienced an influx of institutional investors who buy single-family residential homes and convert them to rental properties. Institutional investor market shares in both the Atlanta and Nashville regions have grown since 2012.

The interviews followed an informal discussion process with property appraisers and planners over the Summer and Fall of 2022. The discussions took place at two conferences of the Tennessee Appraisers Association and the Georgia Planning Conference. Appraisers are publicly elected in Tennessee, and the author has attended and presented at 4 Tennessee Appraiser conferences in the last 2 years.

This paper also includes secondary data derived from the U.S. Census Bureau and real estate trade publications that track investor activity, property values, and rent changes in major U.S. metro areas. In addition, corporate annual reports and investor relations publications from publicly traded institutional investors are used to glean information on industry perspectives and trends.

15.7 Housing Market Trends

Prior to delving more deeply into COVID-related impacts, it is important to frame the discussion based on different perspectives. This section starts with the perspective of the primary investors. We will analyze their projections and business practices in a rapidly changing pandemic and post-pandemic environment. We will then highlight the perceptions of elected property assessors to changes in local property markets. Finally, we will discuss how local land use planners view the issue and highlight their concerns.

According to the Federal Reserve Bank of St. Louis (FRED), the number of privately-owned housing units authorized in permit-issuing places building permits plummeted from 1.8 million units in October 2005 to 364,000 in December 2008. Since that time, the number of permits in the US has recovered has experienced an uneven recovery. Housing permits dropped substantially during COVID before recovering slightly in 2021. One of the key marketing points institutional investors use is that the housing supply needs to keep up with demand. The shortage of housing units has increased home prices and elevated demand for rental houses. They are simply filling a market niche. Before, during, and after COVID, institutional investors have continued their buying activities. Institutional investors sometimes purchased unfinished homes and vacant lots in unfinished subdivisions after the foreclosure crisis. Investors argue that they are community assets who provide much-needed housing supply in communities where demand is strong. They also claim that many millennials are less interested in homeownership than previous generations—adding to the appeal of rental homes. Finally, the companies argue that the cost of renters in many of their markets is cheaper than ownership costs. These claims focus on the present. They do not take consider the potential cost benefits of locking into a 30-year mortgage that maintains a constant payment for 30 years.

The COVID pandemic created some unique barriers to institutional investors. The federal government initially implemented an eviction moratorium to protect renters who lost jobs or income during the economic slowdown. The Supreme Court struck down that policy, but many states enacted similar eviction limitations [13]. A Senate Subcommittee on the Coronavirus crisis found that corporate landlords Progress Residential and Invitation Homes evicted more tenants than publicly acknowledged. Some evicts had applied for federal rental assistance and were awaiting aid [16].

Corporate landlords report occupancy rates in excess of 97% and use those numbers as evidence of strong demand and satisfaction with their product. The pandemic and economic disruption it caused in the lives of thousands of tenants potentially threatened occupancy rates and profits. However, COVID should have undercut the value proposition made by corporate landlords. Namely, the COVID crisis dovetailed with growing demand for SFR houses in select suburban communities. According to Chun et al. [4], "The decoupling of workplace location and residential preferences suggests that home buyers may prefer homes in smaller and less dense counties that offer lower living costs and larger living spaces during and even after the pandemic." Corporate landlords also market suburban amenities such as better public schools, private yards for pets, and exclusivity.

15.8 Interviews with Local Officials

Based on conversations and interviews with planners and property assessors, there needs to be a consensus on the merit of institutional investors buying local properties. Officials in counties with higher market shares of SFRs tend to be more aware of the trend and wary of it. Others live in jurisdictions with limited or no institutional investor presence. They tend to be aware of property brokers who advertise "we buy houses" and a growing presence of limited liability companies buying houses in their jurisdictions. In general, investors are considered a legitimate player in the real estate market and they should not be more heavily regulated than any other entity.

Institutional investors operate outside the view of most local taxpayers. They buy properties in segmented markets within a large region. Residents living outside the algorithm buy box are likely unaware of institutional investors. Within communities with a higher share of institutional investor concentration, homeowners are more aware of them. The companies acquire properties in newer communities that do not require hefty renovation costs. Thus, even within a market such as Nashville, the concentration of investor activity is limited to mostly to communities built after 1995. Mayors, council members, and state legislators often need to be made aware of changes in property markets because they are happening outside their electoral districts. When discussing the emergence of the industry with professionals in the appraisal industry, an underlying assumption is this is the proper outcome of a market-driven process. Government interference in the property market is not an option in Tennessee and Georgia. Building a strong political coalition to fight back against the institutional investor model is difficult because the impacts are geographically limited.

Short-term rentals have generated more publicity in some markets, such as Nashville, because they are often associated with loud parties and neighborhood disruption. The home owned by an institutional investor looks the same as a home owned by local resident. The impact of short-term rentals can be viscerally experienced by residents who have to deal with nuisances unique to tourists (noise, parking). These quality-of-life concerns are less prevalent in single-family suburban neighborhoods.

Opposition to institutional investors business practices is an area of consumer concern. Multiple social media groups that are highly critical of Progress Homes, Invitation Homes, and American Homes 4 Rent have formed. In general, current and former tenants complain about shoddy maintenance, excessive fees, annual rent increases, and difficulty reaching customer assistance. These online groups have been contacted by news media and researchers seeking input on corporate landlords' business practices. Users share stories, photos and advise potential renters to seek alternative landlords. This type of awareness, though, only sometimes attracts the attention of homeowners and elected officials.

The newness of institutional investors buying single-family homes coupled with concentrated impacts makes it particularly difficult to build a political or regulatory consensus. In some neighborhoods—many of which have homeowner associations—up to 50% of homes are investor-owned. More affluent communities might have little to no investor ownership several miles away. Similarly, large institutional investors have largely ignored low-income communities to focus on upper-middle-class households. Given this reality, awareness and concern about corporate investment in local property markets is low.

In discussions with local property assessors, awareness is dependent on investment patterns. Appraisers in rural communities are not typically concerned. Appraisers in more urban communities experiencing robust investment activity are more aware of the growth in LLCs buying and owning single-family houses. Levels of concern vary from county to county. In the Nashville region, the property appraiser most concerned about institutional investors serves the community with the highest market share. He also views institutional investors as threats to community quality of life and homeownership rates. Appraisers and staff members are less concerned about the industry in counties with smaller investment footprints. Some were surprised that institutional investors have proliferated, but it is outside of their sphere of influence.

The bulk of institutional investor ownership in Tennessee is in suburban Nashville and Memphis. In interviews, many appraisers share belief that homeownership is part of the larger American Dream. As elected officials, though, their role is to appraise properties and send out tax bills. Those interviewed believe state legislators should handle any regulation.

A few appraisers believe institutional investors should be treated like short-term rental properties. According to one county appraiser, "We send thousands of tax bills to a handful of out-of-town investors. Those companies essentially operate as commercial enterprises and should be taxed as such." This change would require legislation and some are concerned that any additional commercial taxes generated would be passed on to existing and future renters. Another appraiser pointed out that institutional investors are now lobbying rural state legislators (who are not impacted by the industry) to pass legislation friendly to corporate landlords. For instance, the Tennessee Legislature recently passed a bill that further dilutes the ability of Home Owner Associations (HOAs) to limit corporate ownership of homes in HOA-governed communities—a strategy adopted by HOAs to fight back against investors.

The appraisers interviewed did not see any direct impacts of COVID on the activities of corporate landlords. Some voiced concern about rising interest rates on housing affordability. Most agreed that COVID-induced demand for suburban lifestyles and housing reinforces strong demand for institutional investor rental properties. All acknowledged that corporate landlords' purchasing, building, and leasing activities are all legal. Willing buyers and renters engaging in commerce is exceedingly difficult to regulate and manage. Their preference for individual home ownership aside, they are pessimistic about the ability of the government to regulate the corporate landlord industry.

Appraisers did not directly attribute population growth and demand for housing directly to the COVID pandemic. According to many of those interviewed, population growth was occurring both before and during COVID. Some did acknowledge that the corporate landlord business model appeals to households seeking more space and private dwelling instead of multifamily living. The growing cost of housing and rent in Davidson County (Nashville proper) has likely contributed to an exodus of middle-income households seeking single-family rentals and/or lower rents in outlying counties.

Land use planners need to be made aware of the corporate landlord phenomena. In general, new communities are planned in accordance with local zoning ordinances. Planners are not interested in who owns or resides in the dwelling unit. For planners, the issue is about something other than commercial or residential appraisal rates. Land use planners became more interested in the corporate landlord sector when the business model expanded to include build-to-rent (BTR) communities. These are neighborhoods that corporate investors plan as strictly rental housing. Investors have partnered with national builders to create new single-family neighborhoods that are not sold to individual homeowners.

In discussions with land use planners, awareness of the corporate landlord issue is low. Planners generally review and approve development projects across an entire jurisdiction. Some residential developments might include institutional investors, but the bulk does not. In two cases we discovered, planners approved development plans for single-family neighborhoods and those development rights were later transferred to institutional investors. In both cases, land use planners expressed concern about transparency. The projects were marketed to the community as traditional single-family neighborhoods, not single-family rental communities that are 100% renter-occupied. As one planner put it, "this was a case of bait and switch."

This awareness has yet to translate into aggressive regulatory actions against institutional investors. However, it has spurred one jurisdiction near Atlanta to disallow transferrable development rights for BTR communities. If a development is approved for a local or national developer, that approval cannot then be transferred to institutional investors or others. The corporate landlord would be required to go through the review and community input process anew.

Municipalities in the Atlanta region have been most aggressive in attempts to limit the growth of SFR REITs, private equity landlords, and BTRs. According to Furth [9]:

- The city of Alpharetta has restricted most of its residential zones to "For-Sale" development since earlier than 2014.
- Clayton County has banned BTR homes entirely.
- The city of Woodstock has restricted communities in which 20% or more of homes are rentals to its R3 zone and added costly exterior material requirements.
- The city of Holly Springs requires planned BTR districts to apply for discretionary approval.
- Cherokee County limits single-family developments in which 10% or more of homes are rentals to its RD3 zone.

- Forsyth County has instructed staff to prepare an ordinance limiting BTR homes.

The legality of these actions will likely be challenged in court. According to two interviewees, institutional investor lobbyists are very active in Georgia trying to limit restrictions and regulations on corporate landlords. They are also more prevalent in Tennessee than they were pre-COVID.

Regardless of the regulatory environment, planners did not attribute the growth of the industry to COVID. Many of the plans to expand in and around the Atlanta region predated COVID. In addition, the companies have been engaged in land banking to fuel future BTR communities across the country for several years. COVID likely sparked renewed interest among some households to escape dense urban and multifamily environments. When they sought housing in suburban environments, consumers often discovered the large market share of institutional investors in suburban locales.

15.9 COVID, Crisis and Future Growth

According to those interviewed and literature, COVID has yet to have a major impact on institutional single-family rental investors. The companies have long-term plans, are highly capitalized, and can survive market fluctuations. Their product has strong consumer demand that continued during and after the initial COVID crisis. The companies remain engaged in strategic planning, including land banking and partnering with national developers. For example, American Homes 4 Rent's investor report shows it has over 15,000 lots in the development pipeline. All major SFR investors are planning for time horizons well beyond COVID. The data show that institutional investor purchases of single-family homes in Nashville did not slow down in 2020.

However, American Homes 4 Rent sees an opportunity in uncertain economic conditions. According to its December 2022 investor presentation, "economic disruption ahead is likely to create growth opportunities that AMH is positioned to take advantage of." It further points out that the company has "dry powder" capacity that can be strategically used to grow the company. The equation used by the company is as follows: "Elevated Borrowing Costs + Market Uncertainty + Liquidity Needs = Potential Growth Opportunities." They see an opportunity to grow market share and profits as a direct consequence of economic instability.

Institutional investors all use similar business strategies. Their strategic partners and acquisition channels are slightly different but each of them uses traditional MLS acquisition pipelines, they partner with developers to buy new houses/developments, and their core competency is technology. They are positioned to take advantage of market disruptions. COVID is one example of a market disruption and investors have gained valuable experience managing that crisis. All of the major players grew their portfolios during COVID. They are better prepared today to react to future market disruptions as a result of this experience.

At present, the literature on COVID and its impact on SFR institutional investors needs to be more extensive. That could be because the pandemic did not negatively impact institutional investors active in the SFR space. In fact, future studies should examine how supply chain problems and price inflation in raw materials contributed to lower housing supply and higher housing costs. The combination of factors may create a home-purchasing market more favorable to highly capitalized investors over middle-income house hunters. This research did not find any direct negative impacts of the COVID pandemic on single-family rental institutional investors' market share, occupancy rates, and growth.

15.10 Conclusion

After the 2009–2010 mortgage foreclosure crisis, a new type of landlord bought up tens of thousands of single-family homes and converted them to single-family rental (SFR) homes. The companies were organized as Real Estate Investment Trusts (REITs) and are now traded on Wall Street. Private Equity investors mimicked the REIT model and have entered the market forcefully since 2015. This chapter explored how COVID-19 had impacted single-family rental institutional investors and the growth of their portfolios. The analysis has come to the conclusion that institutional investors are well-capitalized and positively positioned to take advantage of further economic turmoil related to COVID-19. It is further stated that COVID-19 has yet to have a major impact on institutional single-family rental investors. The companies are observed to have long-term plans, are highly capitalized, and can survive market fluctuations. Their products still have robust consumer demand which continued during and after the initial COVID-19 crisis. The companies remain involved in strategic planning including land banking and associating with national developers.

References

1. Anderson D, Bokhari S (2022) Real estate investors are buying a record share of U.S. Homes. RedFin News. https://www.redfin.com/news/investor-home-purchases-q4-2021/
2. Charles SL (2019) The financialization of single-family rental housing: an examination of real estate investment trusts' ownership of single-family houses in the atlanta metropolitan area. J Urban Aff 42(8):1321–1341. https://doi.org/10.1080/07352166.2019.1662728
3. Chilton K, Silverman RM, Chaudhry R, Wang C (2018) The impact of single-family rental REITS on regional housing markets. Societies 8:4
4. Chun Y, Haupert T, Roll S, Fox-Dichter SR, Grenstein-Weiss M (2022) Did the pandemic advance new suburbanization? Brookings. https://www.brookings.edu/blog/up-front/2022/05/23/did-the-pandemic-advance-new-suburbanization/
5. Conroy B (2022) As Rates Skyrocket, 'Wall Street' Single Family Rental Investors See Opportunity. Housing Wire. https://www.housingwire.com/articles/as-rates-skyrocket-wall-street-single-family-rental-investors-see-opportunity/

6. Dowdall E, Goldstein I, Katz B, Preis B (2022) Investor home purchases and the rising threat to owners and renters: tales from 3 cities. Drexel University, Nowak Metro Finance Lab. https://drexel.edu/~/media/Files/nowak-lab/220923_InvestorHomePurchases_Final.ashx?la=en
7. Frey WH (2022) Report: big cities saw historic population losses while suburban growth declined during the pandemic. Brookings: https://www.brookings.edu/research/big-cities-saw-historic-population-losses-while-suburban-growth-declined-during-the-pandemic/
8. Fields D (2022) Automated landlord: digital technologies and post-crisis financial accumulation. Environ Plan A Econ Space 54(1):160–181. https://doi.org/10.1177/0308518X19846514
9. Furth S (2022) https://www.mercatus.org/research/policy-briefs/build-rent-housing-bans-case-zoning-overreach
10. Goodman L, Zinn A, Reynolds K, Noble E (2023) A profile of institutional investor-owned single-family rental properties. Urban Institute
11. Immergluck D (2022) Atlanta as a private-equity "Strike Zone" in Wall Street's single-family rental boom. Nonprofit Quarterly, Sept. 28. https://nonprofitquarterly.org/atlanta-as-a-private-equity-strike-zone-in-wall-streets-single-family-rental-boom/
12. Malone T (2022) The beginning of the end? Single-family investor activity takes a step back in Q2. CoreLogic Intelligence, Aug. 24. https://www.corelogic.com/intelligence/the-beginning-of-the-end-single-family-investor-activity-takes-a-step-back-in-q2/
13. National Low Income Housing Coalition (2021). Court rulings on the federal eviction moratorium. https://nlihc.org/sites/default/files/Court-Rulings-on-the-Federal-Eviction-Moratorium.pdf
14. Ozimek A, O'Bryan C (2022) Families with young children led exodus from major cities during COVID. Economic Innovation Group. https://eig.org/family-exodus/
15. Portillo, E. & Lane, J. (2021). Wall-Street Backed Landlords Now Own More than 11,000 Single-Family Homes in Charlotte. UNC-Charlotte Urban Institute: https://ui.charlotte.edu/story/wall-street-backed-landlords-now-own-more-11000-single-family-homes-charlotte
16. Select Subcommittee on the Coronavirus Crisis (2022). Examining pandemic evictions: a report on abuses by four corporate landlords during the coronavirus crisis. Staff Report, July. https://coronavirus.house.gov/sites/democrats.coronavirus.house.gov/files/2022.07.28%20SSCC%20Staff%20Report%20Examining%20Pandemic%20Evictions.pdf
17. Warren E (2022) Warren calls out private-equity backed firms for increasing rents, driving up housing costs, and raking in profits amid housing shortage. Elizabeth Warren Website, https://www.warren.senate.gov/newsroom/press-releases/warren-calls-out-private-equity-backed-firms-for-increasing-rents-driving-up-housing-costs-and-raking-in-profits-amid-housing-shortage
18. Whitaker S (2021) Did the COVID-19 Pandemic Cause an Urban Exodus? Federal Reserve Bank of Cleveland, District Data Brief. https://www.clevelandfed.org/publications/cleveland-fed-district-data-brief/2021/cfddb-20210205-did-the-covid-19-pandemic-cause-an-urban-exodus

Chapter 16
Digital Movement, Implications on Sustainable Development in Post Pandemic Time: An Introspection with Special Reference to India

Debashis Mazumdar and Mainak Bhattacharjee

16.1 Introduction

During the last few years, particularly during the Covid-afflicted years, our country has experienced a massive expansion in digital movement starting from online transactions to online education. Now, the onset of this pandemic has pressed mankind into the virtual world of work from the actual work and thereof has gone a long way in aiding the digital revolution find deeper penetration and this transition is seemingly self-reinforcing and perpetuating in nature, for a myriad of socio-economic and political reasons. However, such transition process will wade through entailing cost, implicit but poignant in nature, as against the obvious benefit, so far, the less-developed and underdeveloped countries are concerned. To put this in a more specific way, the less-developed and the underdeveloped nations are conspicuously marked by gross inequality in income and wealth, so much so that the access to technologies supporting this very virtual world of work becomes largely unequal among people across different socio-economic strata. In this paper, an attempt has been made to give an overview of this digitization process in different fields of economic and social activities as well as an estimation of digital absorption based on some basic indicators. Besides, in this current wave of technological transition, the radical revamping of production methods is vividly emergent, which has potentially risk of rampant job loss, to be suffered by semi-skilled and unskilled at large without any alternative; notwithstanding that such revamping can indeed foster a condition for the

D. Mazumdar
Department of Economics, The Heritage College, Kolkata, India
e-mail: debashis.mazumdar@thc.edu.in

M. Bhattacharjee (✉)
Economics, Loreto College, Kolkata, India
e-mail: mainakbh4@gmail.com

R. Bhattacharyya et al. (eds.), *COVID-19 Pandemic and Global Inequality*,
https://doi.org/10.1007/978-981-99-4405-7_16

laying emphasis on skill-imparting education largely at deficit along with triggering sustained growth in innovation and growth. This poses a dichotomous state of being where the present-day technological revolution will inevitably enhance the growth capacity of the less developed countries, but at the cost of growing socio-economic inequality, at least in the short run or during the immediately following period, so to say and thus in turn will be antithetical to the goal sustainable development. Thus it is this very backdrop reiterating the popular growth-development trade-off, the study shows that though the growth rate of digital absorption has been commendable onwards 2014–17, there are clear signs of a digital divide which can ultimately intensify the inequalities in the access to such digital services and, hence, can put some obstacle to the creation of 'capabilities' among the common people.

16.2 Objective of the Study

The principal objectives of this study are: (i) to indicate the growth trajectory of digital payments in India during 2017–21, (ii) to indicate the growth trend in internet-using people in India during 2000–2019, (iii) to evaluate the position of India in terms of digital absorption based on the indicators like digital foundation, digital reach and digital value, (iv) to show the extent of digital divide in India and (v) to suggest some policies so as to overcome these obstacles in the process of 'digital India' movement. As against the backdrop of these, the study goes on to developing a theoretical model based on Jones [1, 2], Baladi and Marjit [3] to illuminate on political economic implication of digital movement in the direction of distributive justice.

16.3 Date Source and Methodology

This study is primarily based on secondary data sources like the reports and data bank of World Bank, Statista (USA), R.B.I, Ministry of Electronics & IT, Government of India, NSSO data on Social Consumption of Education [4], etc. Simple statistical methods (like charts and tables) have been used to analyse the secondary data. In addition, a simple microeconomic analysis has been made to show the impact of digital divide.

16.4 Literature Survey

The Ministry of Electronics & Information Technology (MeitY), Government of India, in its report entitled 'India's Trillion-Dollar Digital Opportunity' [5], which is a research collaboration with McKinsey & Company, shows that India is among the top three global economies in terms of the number of digital consumers. In 2013,

India had 238.71 million internet subscriptions and this figure went upto 560 million in 2018 making India as the second-largest internet subscriptions market in the world.

Further, the study (viz. ICUBE [6]) made by the Kantar Group, a data analytics and brand consulting company, based in London, UK, has shown that the number of active internet users in India has been growing at a steady pace in spite of challenging years during 2019–20 [6]. The ICUBE is an annual syndicated study of Kantar, which was launched in 1998, to measure the reach and frequency of Internet users in India. As per ICUBE [6] estimates, out of a population of 1433 million individuals in India, 622 million individuals are active internet users. This translates to about 43% of the total population across urban and rural India who have used internet at least once in the last one month from the date of the survey. The ICUBE [6] covered about 75,000 respondents across 390+ cities and urban locations and about 1300+ villages.

There is no doubt that digital technology will reduce office costs, cut down travel expenses (and time), besides avoiding the geographical restrictions for hiring employees with lower salary expectations, but our societies will likely shift towards more individualistic entities with less human interactions in the labour market [7].

Based on a primary survey on the teachers of urban and rural areas, another study has shown that access to critical preconditions for conducting online classes, such as power, good internet connection, internet data pack and computing devices like laptops, was limited to a small proportion of the teachers surveyed [8].

Massive online education without addressing the huge access gap and disparities in digital infrastructure would not only exclude a vast majority of students from learning opportunities but also exacerbate the existing socio-economic disparities in educational opportunities [9].

Suitability of online teaching as a surrogate has also been questioned in many studies. Researchers are of the opinion that the classroom in physical form by itself is a radical and transformatory space for many. It creates an alternative sociality; it is often a space for lasting friendship; it has the potential to break the bonds of the social givens, particularly if nurtured consciously in that direction by the teachers. Thus online classes cannot suitably substitute the offline classes [10].

Some studies have indicated the impact of digital divide upon the healthcare system. Disparities in health outcomes are a well-documented and worrisome part of the health care system in India. These disparities persist and are occasionally exacerbated by new technologies that are intended to improve health care system. This results in a digital divide in which populations that have poorer health outcomes continue to have poorer health outcomes despite technological improvements [11].

Use of tele-health/ tele-medicine platforms has been on the rise over the past several years. Tele-health has been lauded as a means to close the healthcare gap to rural populations. Taken within the context of several social determinants of health, we can see how the digital divide occurs and can perpetuate inequity based on various social factors [12].

This problem of digital divide was present even in some of the developed countries of the world. This becomes evident from some research studies [13] which indicate negative correlation between rurality and internet speed at the county level of USA during the COID pandemic, highlighting the struggle for rural areas. The schools in those areas tackled the challenges of providing equitable educational access by attempting to provide internet access for students, while even households with internet service struggled to maintain sufficient internet speed and its affordability. Essential activities moved online, yet sufficient Internet was an essential public service that remained unattainable for many US households.

16.5 Indications of Silver Lining

Digital India, a flagship program of Ministry of Electronics & Information Technology (MeitY), Government of India launched in July 2015, has been implemented with a vision to transform India into a knowledge economy and digitally empowered society by realizing the full potential of fast-paced technological advancement. Digital services like e-Hospital, BHIM-UPI, online scholarships, DigiLocker, Umangapp, e-Courts, Tele Law, e-Way Bills, etc. have improved ease of living for citizens. The Government e-Marketplace (GeM) has not only made government procurement transparent but has also enabled small businesses and even Start-Ups to sell their products and services to government organizations (Annual Report, MeitY, 2020–21).

Resurgence of electronic manufacturing has made India the manufacturing location for the second largest number of mobile phones in the world. The production of mobile phones has gone up from about 6 crore in 2014–15 to about 33 crore in 2019–20. The domestic production of electronic items has increased substantially, from INR 1,90,366 Crores (USD 29 billion) in 2014–15 to INR 5,33,550 Crores (USD 75.7 billion) in 2019–20 at a compound annual growth rate (CAGR) of 23%. India's share in global electronics manufacturing has grown from 1.3% in 2012 to 3.6% in 2019 (Annual Report, MeitY, 2020–21).

On one hand, the world's largest digital literacy program Pradhan Mantri Grameen Digital Saksharta Abhiyan (PMG DISHA) is working to boost digital inclusion by making 6 Crore rural adults digitally literate, and on the other hand, 233 BPO units have been set up under BPO Promotion Schemes to create new job opportunities for young men and women. A total of 7300 crore online transactions on e-Gov applications in 2020 reveal the volume of the impact of Digital India in transforming India. In fact, emerging technologies like 5G, internet of things, advanced data analytics, artificial intelligence, cloud computing, augmented and virtual reality, 3D printing, robotics and blockchain, etc., will redefine the future of technology-led transformation in India.

If we review the growth of digital payments in India in the recent past (2017–21), we find that the volume of this payment increased from USD 83,730 million in 2017 to USD 1,39,262 million in 2021 (Table 16.1 and Fig. 16.1) showing a slight downward trend during pandemic period, viz. in 2020. Table-1 shows that while the share of digital commerce in these payment was maximum among all the reasons or modes of digital payments (like digital commerce, digital remittance and mobile POS payment) it also increased by about 45% during that period. The growth of mobile POS payments indicates a spectacular growth of 1216% during that period (from USD 1,477 million in 2017 to USD 19,441 million in 2021). The World Bank data regarding the percentage of population using internet in India also shows a tremendous hike during 2017–19 (Fig. 16.2). The figure reveals that only about 1% of India's total population used internet service during 2000–01 and this figure went up to 20% in 2017, and in 2019 it increased to about 40%.

India has also experienced the second-fastest rate of growth of digital adoption in comparison with seventeen mature and emerging digital economies such as Brazil, China, Indonesia, Russia, South Korea, Sweden, and the United States (Table 16.2). India's digital index score has moved from 17 in 2014 to 32 in 2017 (on a scale of 0 to 100), which shows a second-fastest rise after Indonesia [5]. India has also performed well on e-governance and digital identity and in terms of the uptake of digital media by online consumers. For instance, India's monthly mobile data consumption per user, at 8.3 gigabytes (GB) per month in 2017, is found to be over 54 times the figure in mid-2016 and higher than countries like China at 5.5 GB per user, and it was comparable to digital leaders like South Korea at 8–8.5 GB per user.

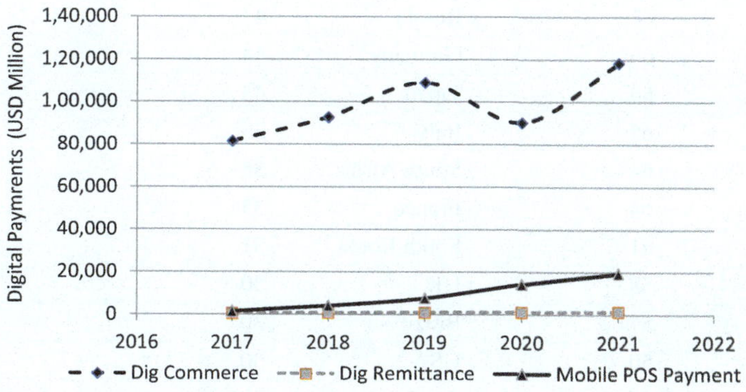

Fig. 16.1 Digital payments in India during 2017–21 (in USD Mill). *Source* Based on Table 16.1

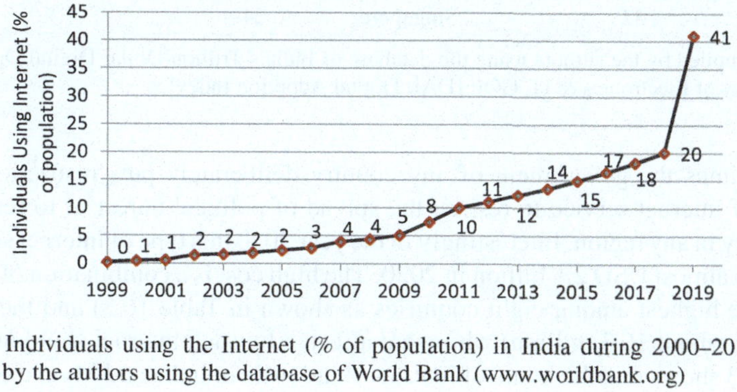

Fig. 16.2 Individuals using the Internet (% of population) in India during 2000–2019. *Source* Compiled by the authors using the database of World Bank (www.worldbank.org)

Table 16.1 Trend of digital payments in India during 2017–21

Year	Digital payment in India (in USD million)			
	Dig commerce	Dig remittance	Mobile POS payment	Total payments
2017	81,638	615	1,477	83,730
2018	92,769	783	4,132	97,684
2019	1,09,119	1,031	7,629	117,779
2020	90,281	1,128	14,291	105,700
2021	1,18,405	1,416	19,441	139,262

Source Statista (www.statista.com), USA

Table 16.2 Digital adoption index: a comparison across nations

Country	DAI in 2017	Country	Growth in DAI during 2014–17
South Korea	75	Indonesia	91
Sweden	73	**India**	90
UK	67	China	45
Singapore	67	Russia	44
USA	66	Germany	44
Australia	66	Japan	43
Canada	65	Italy	36
Russia	64	South Africa	35
Japan	64	France	35
Germany	61	South Korea	31
France	58	UK	30
Italy	57	Brazil	30
Brazil	50	USA	30
China	46	Sweden	27
Indonesia	40	Canada	25
South Africa	40	Australia	25
India	32	Singapore	24

Source Compiled by the authors using the database of India's Trillion-Dollar Digital Opportunity [5], Ministry of Electronics & IT, GOI; [DAI: Digital Adoption Index]

Sometimes the government of any country deliberately puts restrictions upon the use of internet service to restrict the spread of political unrest or to restrict the insurgency in any region. Interestingly in the year 2020 this type of internet shutdown cost India almost USD 2.8 billion in 2020. The high cost is a combination of the long hours (the highest among eight countries as shown in Table 16.3) and the number of people (about 10.3 million) who were affected by such internet shutdowns [14]. Table 16.3 shows that the hours of internet shutdowns in India and Myanmar remain almost the same in 2020 but the higher economic costs for India signify how it

Table 16.3 Economic Cost of major Internet shutdowns across nations in 2020

Country	Internet shut-downs in 2020 (hours)	Economic cost of major internet shut-downs (in USD million)
India	8,927	2,779
Belarus	218	336
Yemen	912	237
Myanmar	8,808	189
Azerbaijan	1,128	123
Ethiopia	1,536	111
Sudan	36	69
Turkey	18	51

Source Compiled by the authors using the database of the cost of Internet shutdowns, Statista

has affected greater number of people involved in economic activities using internet service.

16.5.1 Flipside of this Process

So far, our discussion has revealed the growth aspect of 'digital movement' in India. According to Warschauser [15], 'What is most important about ICT is not so much the availability of a computing device or the Internet line, but rather the people's ability to make use of that device and line to engage in meaningful social practices'.

Let us first look into the factors which determine the Digital Adoption Index (DAI). The DAI is prepared on the basis of three broad pillars, viz. digital foundation of a country, digital reach of the people and the digital value generated through the usage of digital technology. This DAI is measured on the basis of 30 metrics divided between those three pillars. Principal component analysis is conducted to estimate the relative importance of the three pillars: 0.37 for digital foundation, 0.33 for digital reach and 0.30 for digital value [5]. Within each pillar, each element is assigned equal value, with indicators normalized into a standard scale of 0–100 (0 indicating lowest possible value). A simple average of the normalized values was then used to calculate the index [5].

The digital foundation, in turn, takes into consideration four important factors, viz. fixed-line or land-line infrastructure of telecommunication, mobile telephone infrastructure, e-governance platforms and the affordability of the people in using these services. A close introspection of the relative position of India to 16 other countries (as already indicated in Table 16.2) in terms of the matrices used for showing the position of India regarding digital foundation during 2014–17 clearly shows that (i) average price of using internet was much higher in India, (ii) international internet bandwidth per user was much lower and (iii) the download speed on internet data was also lower in India (Table 16.4). Thus, digital foundation was not very strong in India during 2014–17.

Similarly, the digital reach in a country is determined by (i) the number of devices (say, smart phones per 100 people), (ii) data usage by the people and (iii) Number of Apps and content. In this case also, we find that the number of smartphones per 100 people, mobile broadband subscription per 100 people, fixed broadband subscriptions per 100 people, etc., remained at a low level in India during 2014–17 (Table 16.5).

The third pillar of DAI, viz. the digital value consists of the factors such as (i) digital payments, (ii) e-commerce transactions as percentage of total retail transactions, (iii) Average data usage for entertainment, etc. Table 16.6 clearly shows that the position of India in many of these dimensions (say, number of cashless consumer transaction per person, e-commerce transactions as percentage of total retail transactions) remained at a low level compared to 16 other nations under study [5].

Table 16.4 India's position in relation to 16 other countries in digital foundation during 2014–17

Parameters	Best performing country	India's position
Allocated Spectrum <1 GB per Km^2, 2014 and 2017	58.3	0.3
Allocated Spectrum >1 GB per Km^2, 2014 and 2017	221.3	0.9
4G availability, 2015–2017	100%	86.%
Average mobile download speed, 2014 and 2017	26.0 Mbps	4.9 Mbps
International Internet Bandwidth per internet user, 2013 and 2016	960 Kbps	16
Average fixed line download speed, 2014 and 2017	28.6 Mbps	6.5 Mbps
No. of public Wifi hotspots per 1 lac people, 2014 and 2017	614.4	21.5
Average price per GB of mobile data, 2013 and 2017	0.07% GNI per capita	0.37% GNI per capita
Average fixed broadband subscription charge, 2014–2017	0.1% GNI per capita	0.45% GNI per capita
Government Online Service Index, 2013–2017	100%	100%
Digital identity program assesment	100%	100%

Source India's Trillion-Dollar Digital Opportunity [5], Ministry of Electronics & IT, Government of India

Table 16.5 India's position in relation to 16 other countries in digital reach during 2014–17

Parameters	Best performing country	India's position
No. of smart phone user per 100 people, 2013 and 2017	95.8	**22.2**
No. of basic phone user per 100 people, 2013 and 2017	49.9	34.8
Mobile phone subscription per 100 people, 2016 and 2016	1617	87
Mobile internet subscription (2G, 3G, 4G or 5G) per 100 people, 2016 and 2016	178.6	80.9
Mobile broadband subscription (2G, 3G, 4G or 5G) per 100 people, 2016 and 2016	144.4	38.7
Average mobile data consumption per user per month, 2013 and 2017	86 GB	1 GB
Fixed broadband subscription per 100 people, 2014 and 2016	42.4	1.4
Average fixed-line consumption per user per month 2014 and 2017	153.6 GB	18.3 GB
No. of app dowloading, 2014 and 2017	81.7	45.7

Source Same as Table 16.4

Table 16.6 India's position in relation to 16 other countries in digital value during 2014–17

Parameters	Best performing country	India's position
E-participation Index, 2014 and 2017	100%	76%
% of people using WhatsApp, Wechat & other popular instant messaging app, 2014 and 2017	73%	28%
Average time spent on social media sites per user per week, 2014 and 2017	25.6 h	17 h
% of people engaged in one purchase/e-commerce, 2014 and 2017	78%	26%
% of people engaged in social media, 2014 and 2017	85%	19%
E-commerce as a % total retail, 2015 and 2017	20%	5%
% of users searching for product information online before online purchase, 2014 and 2017	85%	19%
Average data usage for music per user per month	1.3 GB	27.5 MB
Average data usage for video per user per month, 2013 and 2016	59.2 GB	335.4 MB
No. of cashless consumer transactions per person, 2013 and 2016	802.7	767.6

Source Same as Table 16.5

16.6 Extent of Digital Divide

When different segments of the society fail to avail the benefits of digital movements, it shows a sign of digital divide, say, the access to digital infrastructure may be higher for urban people compared to rural people. In this regard, we shall particularly focus our attention to the problem of digital divide with respect to online education during the pandemic period. It is true that online education can benefit students to access digital libraries, to complete short-term internship programmes and enhance their knowledge domain at lower opportunity cost (since they can save their time which would have been required to pay regular visits to libraries or training centres). However, the success of online education is critically contingent upon the availability of digital infrastructure. A student may have a smartphone but may not have adequate access to internet (with the required speed. Thus, access to internet service along with the possession of a proper digital device (say, in the form of a desktop computer, laptop computer, notebook, palmtop, tablet or similar handheld devices) can be considered as the ideal combination for availing online education.

However, NSSO data on social consumption of education (2017–18) in India clearly reveals that only about 9% of the students who were enrolled in any course had access to essential digital infrastructure, viz. a computer with internet access (Fig. 16.3). In urban areas, this percentage was much higher (21%) compared to the rural areas (4%). This divide between rural and urban areas was also prominent in respect of access to internet service and availability of computers.

Therefore, the online education system which was being followed during the pandemic period cannot be considered as inclusive when 75% of the enrolled students did not have access to internet and 91% of the enrolled students did not have computer with internet. Hence, the extent of exclusion seemed to have surpassed the benefit of inclusion in this regard. This divide was also clear in respect students across social groups (viz. SC, ST, OBC and General category students).

Figure 16.4 clearly reveals that students belonging to SC, ST and OBC groups remained far behind the students belonging to general category in terms of the possession of a computer along with internet access. The NSSO Report on the social consumption of education (2017–18) indicated that such measly access to digital infrastructure is enmeshed with huge socio-economic and spatial disparities. Thus,

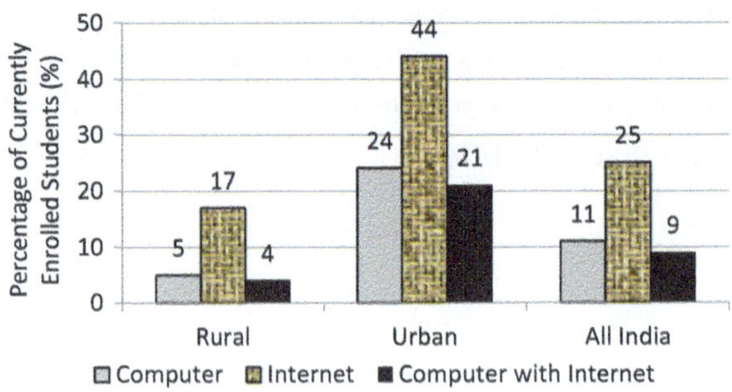

Fig. 16.3 Percentage of enrolled students in india with access to digital infrastructure in 2017–18. *Source* Compiled by the authors using the database of NSSO on social consumption on education (2017–18)

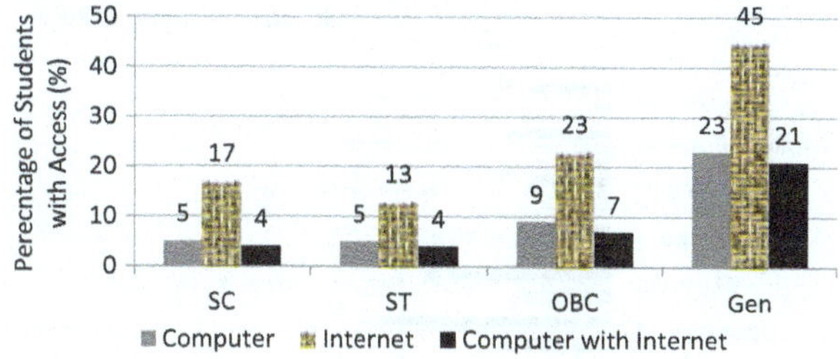

Fig. 16.4 Digital divide among the students across social groups in India in 2017–18. *Source* Same as Fig. 16.3

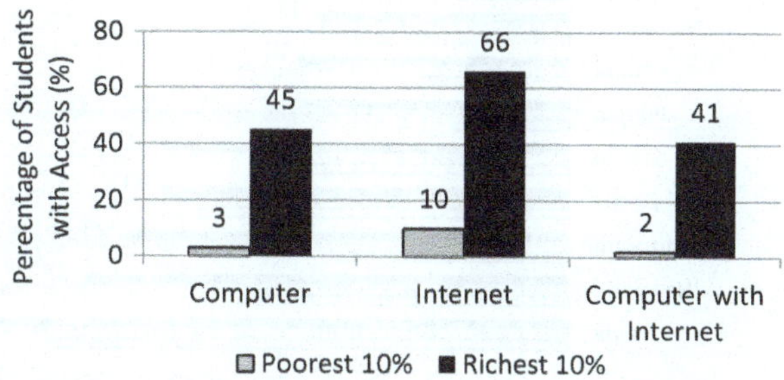

Fig. 16.5 Digital divide among the students across income groups in India in 2017–18. *Source* Same as Fig. 16.4

this digital divide was also acute among students across the income groups. It has been observed that about 41% of the students belonging to the richest 10% households had possessed computer with access to internet service but only 2% of the students belonging to the poorest 10% households enjoyed this opportunity (Fig. 16.5).

There were also inter-state variations with regard to that digital divide. Across the states, Goa emerges as the best performer with 30% of the enrolled students having access to computer with internet. The states such as Uttarakhand, Maharashtra, Haryana, Himachal Pradesh, Tamil Nadu, Punjab, Sikkim, Kerala, Mizoram and Nagaland remained above the All-India average in this regard whereas the states like Odisha, Bihar, Madhya Pradesh and Tripura remained below the All-India average (Fig. 16.6).

In this connection, we can refer to a real-life story published in the Times of India on 5 July, 202. It is all about the financial difficulty faced by a poor family in Chhattishgarh. The report states that Lakshmi Sahu and her husband Purushottam Sahu together used earn Rs 5,400 a month and during June 2021 they had to spent Rs 14,000 on a smartphone for their 12-year-old son to facilitate his online learning. This poor family, already burdened with debt, found it difficult to afford the monthly data recharge and on some days they did not have money to buy groceries. Thus, this might have happened to many other poor families in India.

This apart, a student does not only need a gadget and internet connectivity for attending online classes, a congenial physical space around them is also very crucial. It should be ideally a quiet and isolated space where the student is not disturbed by the presence of others. But in many cases, particularly in urban areas, getting such a physical space is also very difficult. Even in rural areas, economically and socially

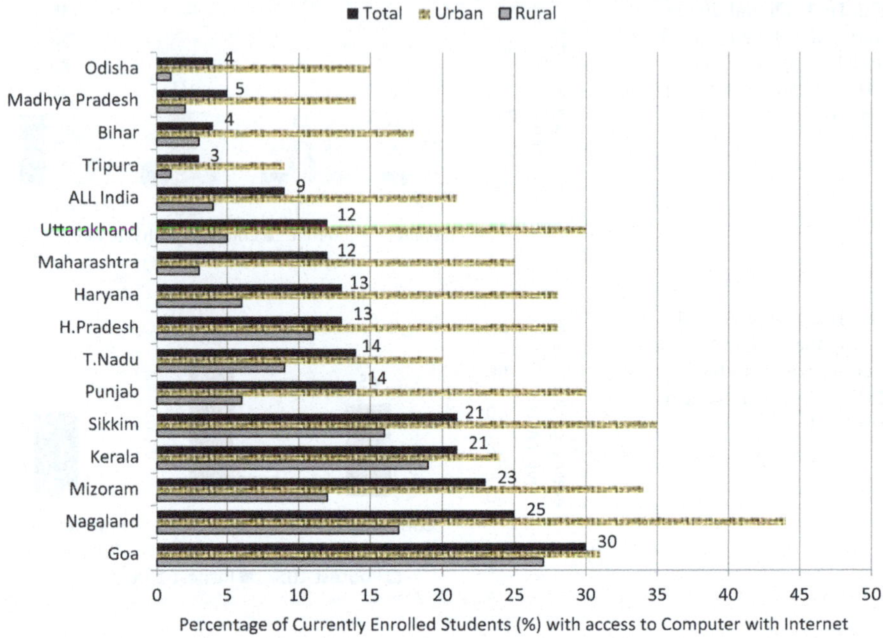

Fig. 16.6 Digital divide among the students across the states in India in 2017–18. *Source* Same as Fig. 16.5

disadvantaged students who do not have access to the privacy of well-endowed domestic spaces face similar problems.

The physical space of the schools and colleges in general and the classrooms in particular are not merely a space for the transaction of knowledge, it is often a space for lasting friendship and a means for creating a permanent social bondage. A physical classroom has the potential to break the gaps created out of our narrow social taboos particularly in cases where some dedicated teachers are engaged in inculcating value judgments among the students.

Despite all these negative aspects of online teaching, education planners in India advocated for this mode of teaching as the future of higher education. During the pandemic period, several documents and statements of the high functionaries of the Ministry of Human Resource Development (MHRD), University Grants Commission (UGC) and NITI Aayog have emphasized upon online learning [10]. The National Education Policy (NEP) [16] of the government of India calls for carefully designed and appropriately scaled pilot studies to determine how the benefits of online/digital education can be reaped while addressing or mitigating the downsides. However, this policy stresses the need for optimization and expansion of the existing digital platforms and ongoing ICT-based educational initiatives to meet the current and future challenges in providing quality education for all [16].

16.7 A Theoretical Model on Digital Movement in Context of Developing Nations

The context of digital movement has enough potential to trigger socio-economic and political commotion in developing and less-developed nation where the distributive is largely impaired due to persistent and yawning income inequality among different functional groups. Now of late, this technological wave of transition dawned a substantial amount of uncertainty and thereof attracted enough political remonstration from the potential sufferer, particularly the groups of people who anticipate a fair amount of threat on their livelihood. To be precise, there is strong consensus on the apprehension that such technological would result in large displaced of semi-skilled and low-skilled who are in majority in less-developed countries for want of modern technical education who are the real sough after to let this new technological epoch to surface and persist. However, the interesting flipside of this dispensation is based on the contention that this technological revolution is what necessary only to suit the production needs of the current time but to aid the developing nation enhance their competitive edge in global trade and economy. Moreover, with the developing nations transiting into a phase of advancement of technical education and progressing with it, this digital movement has become indispensable for creating suitable job openings required to employ the large generation of youths equipped in modern skill sets which otherwise will find the way to expatriation in search of coveted livelihood and that in turn will amount a potential brain drain and exodus of skilled labour, slogging the process of economic growth and to that end the economic developed. Hence, the bottom line that comes from quite obviously the developing countries are required to introduce dynamism in their economic growth by having effective policy instruments that are capable of offsets the potential fallout of digital movement on distributive justice as what is the seemingly rational roadmap to sustainable development amidst this new wave of technological progress. Now the model described below is attempt to set an appropriate to this line of rumination on the disruptive aspect(s) of the digital revolution/ movement extant and the potential implication for sustainable development in developing and less-developed nations.

The structure of the model, drawing on as noted earlier in the objective, is based on a three-sector small open economy namely, X (a modern technology-intensive sector) operating with high skilled labour (S) and specific capital (K′), Y (urban sector) operating with semi-skilled and less-skilled labour (L) and traditional capital (K) and a rural sector (Z) operating with L and K. Now, it is hereby assumed that X runs with a fixed coefficient production technology, so is Y, while Z runs with flexible coefficient. In this backdrop, we allow for high-skilled labour force being partly employed for want of suitable job opportunity for want of the specific capital, whereas, L and K are fully employed. Moreover, wage rate of L-workers in Y institutionally given as, $\overline{W}$ and there is migration of L between Y and Z. Besides, all three sectors are open to foreign trade and thereof the price of the output produced by each is exogenously given. Thus, we have the following equations.

$$P_X = a_{SX} W_S + a_{K'X} r' \tag{16.1}$$

$$P_Y = a_{LY} \overline{W} + a_{KY} r \tag{16.2}$$

$$P_Z = a_{LZ} W + a_{KZ} r \tag{16.3}$$

$$\overline{W} \left(\frac{a_{LY} Y}{L - a_{LZ} Z} \right) = W \tag{16.4}$$

$$a_{SX} X < S \tag{16.5}$$

$$a_{SX} X = K' \tag{16.6}$$

$$a_{LY} Y + a_{LZ} Z = L \tag{16.7}$$

$$a_{KY} Y + a_{KZ} Z = K \tag{16.8}$$

Now, as what is quite evident, that there are seven equation seven unknown, namely, W_S, W, r', r, X, Y, Z [Note: (5) is inequation].

16.7.1 Advent of Digital Movement and Its Implications on Wage-Inequality

Here we shall analyse the potential consequences of the introduction digital revolution on the economy. To begin with, the eve of digital movement will create negative among the semi-skilled and low-skilled workers out of fear about displacement owing to the adoption of digital technology involving both digitization and digitalization. This will pull down the bargaining power of L-workers and thereof will cause significant fall in $\overline{W}$. Thus, we have the following result.

$$\widehat{W} = \underset{+}{\left[\frac{1 + \left(\frac{L_Z^0}{L_{fY}^0} \right) \sigma_Z \theta_{KZ} \left(\frac{\theta_{LY}}{\theta_{KY}} \right)}{L_{fY}^0 - \left(\frac{L_Z^0}{L_{fY}^0} \right) \sigma_Z \theta_{KZ}} \right]} \left(\frac{d\overline{W}}{\overline{W}} \right) \tag{16.9}$$

[Hints to the derivation has been cited in the appendix]

Hence, for $\left(\frac{d\overline{W}}{\overline{W}} \right) < 0$ we get, $\widehat{W} < 0$. Let us explain the rationale behind this result. Following the worsening of urban wage of L-workers, the expected wage-earning in Y will contraction and in effect fewer workers employed in rural sector will be willing to migrate or there may happen a reverse migration owing to the extent of fall in W_Y may be too intense to afford the cost of living over there. This will increase the supply of L in Z and hence W will witness a decline. Therefore, we have the following proposition.

Proposition 16.1 *Assuming there is wage inequality between high-skilled workers on the one hand and semi-skilled and low-skilled workers on the other, being already extant, the advent digital movement would work to exacerbate such inequality and hence as its immediate impact such technological transition in production will militate against the distributive justice. Besides in the circumstance of pandemic, such negative development would add to the misery of the economically marginalized section of the nation. Moreover, if assumed further that sector Z produces the wage goods at large, fall in W and consequently, a contraction in purchasing of workers at large, demand for goods produced Z will get squeezed in resulting contraction of its output and thus a further fall in W and thereof a surge in rural -urban wage disparity.*

16.7.2 Introduction of Digital Technology in Urban Sector and Its Consequences

In this section, we shall address the potential consequences of the introduction of digital technology in urban sector as a drive towards modernization. To this end, the production function corresponding sector can re-thought as what follows.

$$Y = \text{Min}[f(L, S), K/a_{KY}] \tag{16.10}$$

Let us now try and elicit the underlying intuition of this modified production function. This is so that post the introduction digital technology in Y sector, for obvious reason, there will arise the condition for substitution of low-skilled workers by high-skilled counterpart (at least partly to begin with) as complimentary to K. Thus, makes sense to keep the overall production function in standard Leontief form, where (L, S) will operate with K as complimentary input, while retaining the substitutability of between L and S [Note: f is linearly homogenous in (l, S)]. Hence, reducing (16.10) to unit isoquant form we get,

$$1 = f(a_{LY}, a_{SY}) \tag{16.10'}$$

Besides, these the zero-profit condition of Y-sector will change into:

$$P_Y = a_{LY}W_Y + a_{KY}r + a_{SY}W_S \tag{16.2'}$$

Now with no change in exogenously given P_Y, and factor prices, Eq. (16.11) suggests a reduction in a_{LY} and rise in a_{SY} as sufficient for its own fulfillment. Hence, we introduce a parameter ρ signifying the degree of the usage of digital technological in Y sector, such a_{LY} is falling ρ while a_{SY} is rising in ρ, where, a_{LY} and a_{SY} are cost-minimizing in nature. Besides, it is reasonable with the onset of digital drive the unutilized skilled labour finds vent to utilization leading the situation to full employment. However, this full employment will quite reasonably come against departure from of L, particularly for the reason of wage rigidity in urban sector and not all the displaced workers will be able to find alternative employment in the rural sector. Thus, in this backdrop, the previously mentioned full employment conditions will change into what follows.

$$a_{SX}X + a_{XZ}(\rho)Z = S \tag{16.5'}$$

$$a_{LY}Y + a_{LZ}Z < L \tag{16.7'}$$

Now let us come to the precise dispensation of aftermath of this development on W_S, W, r and r' as what follows.

$$\widehat{W} = \varepsilon^Y_{L\rho}\hat{\rho} < 0 \tag{16.11}$$

$$\widehat{W_S} = -\left[\frac{\{(\theta_{KY}/\theta_{KZ})\theta_{LZ} - \theta_{LY}\}\varepsilon^Y_{L\rho} + \varepsilon^Y_{S\rho}\theta_{SY}}{\theta_{SY}}\right]\hat{\rho} \tag{16.12}$$

$$\hat{r} = -(\theta_{LZ}/\theta_{KZ})\varepsilon^Y_{L\rho}\hat{\rho} > 0 \tag{16.13}$$

$$\hat{r}' = -(\theta_{LZ}/\theta_{KZ})\widehat{W}_S \tag{16.14}$$

[Note: $\varepsilon^Y_{i\rho}$ is the technological elasticity of the employment of factor $i = L, S$ and $\hat{\rho} > 0$].

Let us explain these results. It is well that the introduction of digital technology in Y-sector will drive out L from being replaced by S as what is a necessity quite obviously. This will cause downward adjustment in W in rural as what is required for the rural sector to absorb the displaced workers, but such an adjustment would not be enough to keep with full employment since, in anticipation of such an abject fall in wage many displaced to may refuse to migrate to the rural sector and instead, will find alternative livelihood through self-employment or settle with relatively less low paying informal jobs. Now to absorb a part of these displaced workers the demand for capital would rise, notwithstanding the internal substitution of labour by scale or the rising demand for capital may come on the back of the need for increasing scale of production in Z-sector. Now let us assume that the rate displacement of L in Y-sector brought about introduction of digital technological is substantially higher than that of the absorption of S then, the term in the numerator in negative, provided that (a) Y-sector is more K-intensive relative to Z and (b) Z-sector is more L-intensive relative to Y-sector. Consequently, we have $\widehat{W_S} > 0$ and thereof, $r' < 0$. While the flip side, although a trivial one, so to say, is that $\widehat{W_S} < 0$ and henceforth, $r' > 0$. Now in this case one interesting point that arises quietly logically, that the rate of fall in W_S is higher relative to that in W, what is evident from the following.

$$\widehat{W_S} - \hat{W} = -\left[\left[\left[\frac{(\theta_{KY}/\theta_{KZ})\theta_{LZ} - \theta_{LY}}{\theta_{SY}}\right] + 1\right]\varepsilon^Y_{L\rho} + \varepsilon^Y_{S\rho}\right]\hat{\rho} > 0 \quad (16.15)$$

Thus, we have the following proposition.

Proposition 16.2 *Introduction of digital technology in the urban sector comes with two distinct dichotomous ramifications as on the overall income inequality. One end is that, if the high skilled rises in the aftermath of such technological transition, given that wage earning low skilled and poorly skilled workers will witness an in evitable decline, the wage disparity will shoot. Moreover, this extends to the similar income disparity between the tradition capital and specific capital. Thus, the income inequality problem will get furthered within the functional groups. The other end is that, if high skilled wage falls (although a trivial possibility) then the within the group income inequality can potentially down, however the between group inequality will rise. Hence, overall status income inequality remains a little ambiguous in this case.*

16.8 Conclusion

The present study brings out the potential aftermath of digital movement for developing nations in general and India in particular, as on the distributive justice notwithstanding its role in enhancing the overall factor productivity of the economy and at the same time mitigating unemployment and underemployment of skilled labour as what can be considered as the product modern technical education. Now in this study, it well vivid that the inception of digital revolution or movement as big shot technological transition is a significant threat to distributive justice, a what seems to be true, particularly true, for a developing country or less developed one with preponderance of semi-skilled or low skilled workers in labour force, so far labour is displacing character is concerned. There, the advent of digital technology and a additionally drive towards enabling its faster penetration across different sectors in a less developed country will bring about a severe loss of employment and an sharp in unemployment in the immediate term or even during the considerable period-of-time offing, which in turn will amount to a marked increase socio-economic inequality and thus jeopardization of distributive justice. This will create a ripe condition for the dichotomous of society led by the decimation of the middle class (or low middle class or) and consequently, the marginalization of common people, as what resembles 'missing middle phenomenon' [17]. To this end the current chapter can be seen as caveat for developing and less developed nations which have not only embarked on this digital movement but have gone into the task of enabling its furtherance in order they can cope with the new global economic order.

Appendix

The result indicated by Eq. (16.9) [vide: Proposition 16.1] has been derived using the standard hat-algebra [1] as illustrated below.

$$\theta_{SX}\hat{W}_S + \theta_{K'X}\widehat{r'} = 0 \tag{16.16}$$

$$\theta_{LY}\left(\frac{d\overline{W}}{\overline{W}}\right) + \theta_{KY}\hat{r} = 0 \tag{16.17}$$

$$\theta_{LY}\widehat{W} + \theta_{KY}\hat{r} = 0 \tag{16.18}$$

$$\widehat{W} = \left(\frac{d\overline{W}}{\overline{W}}\right) - \left(\frac{\sigma_Z\theta_{LZ}\theta_{KZ}}{L^0_{fY}/\overline{L}}\right)\left(\widehat{W} - \hat{r}\right) \tag{16.19}$$

Similarly, can be derived, Eq. (16.15) [vide: Proposition 16.2].

References

1. Jones R (1965) The structure of simple general equilibrium models. J Polit Econ 73(6):557–572
2. Jones R (1971) A three-factor model in theory, trade and history. In: Bhagwati J, Jones R, Mundell R, Vanek J (eds) Trade, balance of payment and growth, Amsterdam, North-Holland
3. Beladi H, Marjit S (1996) An analysis of rural-urban migration and protection. Can J Econ 29(4):930–40
4. NSSO (75th Round) (2017–18) Key indicators of household consumption on education in India. Ministry of Statistics & Programme Implementation, National Statistical Office, Government of India
5. Ministry of Electronics & Information Technology (MeitY), Government of India (2019) India's trillion-dollar digital opportunity, website
6. Kantar (2021) Internet adoption in India. ICUBE-2020, June, website
7. Rossi E, Balsa-Barreiro J (2020) The future of work in the post-COVID-19 world. Econ Polit Week 55(44):23–25
8. Singh AK, Satyavada RS, Goel T, Sarangapani P, Jayendran N (2020) Use of EdTech in Indian School Education during COVID-19: a reality check. Econ Polit Week 55(44):16–19
9. Reddy AB, Jose S, Vaidehi R (2020) Of access and inclusivity digital divide in online education. Econ Polit Week 55(36):23–26
10. Bhattacharya S (2020) What is so wrong with online teaching? Econ Polit Week 55(23):19–21
11. Saeed SA, Masters RM (2021) Disparities in health care and the digital divide. Curr Psychiatry Rep 23:61. https://doi.org/10.1007/s11920-021-01274-4

12. Ramsetty A, Adams C (2020) Impact of the digital divide in the age of COVID-19. J Am Med Inform Assoc 27(7):1147–1148
13. Lai EJ, Widmar NO (2021) Revisiting the digital divide in the Covid-19. Appl Econ Perspect Policy 43(1):458–464
14. Buchholz K (2021) The cost of Internet shutdowns. Statista, 6 January, website
15. Warschauser M (2004) Technology and social inclusion. Rethinking the digital divide. MIT Press, Cambridge, MA, website
16. MHRD (2020) National Education Policy, Ministry of Human Resource Development, Government of India
17. Krueger A (2013) The missing middle in eds economic reform in India: challenges, prospects and lessons by T.N. Srinivasan, Nicholas C. Hope, chap 9, Anjini Kochar, Roger Noll and T.N. Srinivasan. Cambridge University Press

Chapter 17
Effect of Externalities like Choice Overload, Nudges and Unconscious Bias on Consumer Choice and Their Convergence in Student Groups

Chyanika Mitra, Arindam Paul, and Annesha Neogy

17.1 Introduction

Consumer choice and decision making are frequently inclined by various concealed and unintentional factors in the day to day lives, also known as externalities. With the consumers being subject to such externalities, they might be prone to take suboptimal decisions that lead to inefficient choices. One such *inefficiency* is 'choice paradox' which evidently means that all things constant, a consumer finds it difficult to make an optimal choice when presented with several options but also faces equal, if not stronger level of dilemma when choosing between two equally preferred items. Moreover, choice paradox and other inefficiencies driven by the externalities lead to a difference between private and the social value of consumption. Therefore, it leads to a distortion in social welfare. Hence, it is very crucial to measure the externality on the demand side to evaluate the policies prescribed by the planners. On the other hand, the advent of the COVID-19 Pandemic was followed by worldwide lockdowns and stunted economic growth, which inevitably led to large-scale employment losses. As far as the demand side is concerned, the effect of COVID-19 is conspicuous as it led to a momentous shift of consumption behaviour from offline, physical mode to the virtual, online mode.

This study aims to explore and analyse the change in the purchasing patterns, the prevalence of choice paradox, the decision-making process behind them (if any) such as choice overload, nudges and unconscious bias. Choice overload is an inability to

C. Mitra · A. Neogy
Economics, Goenka College of Commerce and Business Administration, Kolkata, India
e-mail: chayanika.mitra@sxuk.edu.in

A. Paul (✉)
Economics, Jadavpur University, Jadavpur, Kolkata, India
e-mail: arindamp.economics@jadavpuruniversity.in

R. Bhattacharyya et al. (eds.), *COVID-19 Pandemic and Global Inequality*,
https://doi.org/10.1007/978-981-99-4405-7_17

make a decision due to overthinking a problem. Example: Indecision while having to choose from several brands of a commodity at a grocery store, spending excessive amount of time browsing through online shopping sites trying to make the optimum purchase, deciding which stock to invest in etc. A Nudge is any aspect of the choice architecture that alters people's behaviour in a predictable way without forbidding any options or significantly changing their economic incentives. To count as a mere nudge, the intervention must be easy and cheap to avoid. For instance, putting fruit at eye level counts as a nudge. Banning junk food does not. Unconscious biases are attitudes that are held subconsciously and affect the way individuals feel and think about others around them. Unconscious bias refers to how our mind can take shortcuts when processing information. A classic example of unconscious bias may be opting for a shortcut to make a positive/negative decision about a book without even having had read it.

The methodology of the study is empirical which is based on a primary survey[1] conducted for 500 sample students residing in India. A comprehensive online survey over two months (August–October) in 2021. The questions are inclusive of focal aspects of consumers' lives such as employment status, household income, local and online shopping, eating at a restaurant, real estate, automobiles, vocational and educational interests, investments and future planning. Even though this survey is subject to 'Response Bias' (the tendency for participants to respond inaccurately or falsely to questions), the extensive questions have aided to minimise the bias. In addition, they have provided with a reliable response base for further analysis.

Using this data, we have measured each of the aforementioned externalities using Principal Component Analysis. We also checked the correlation between each externality and how they are affected by the individual's demographic factors. Our results show that there is a positive correlation between the externalities which implies that if an individual is highly susceptible to being influenced by nudges, then unconscious bias also plays a strong role behind their decision-making process and the inability to make an optimal, rational choice is also prevalent. Moreover, we found that the nudges significantly affect one gender, meaning, female individuals have more tendency of getting influenced by nudges. However, choice overload among individuals is significantly affected by annual household income and the highest level of education in the family. Choice overload is positively affected by annual household income which implies that an individual has a larger choice set when he/she has larger income level. Choice overload is negatively affected by the highest level of education in the family, which implies that higher education allows an individual to contract their choice set rationally. Finally, unconscious bias is significantly affected by all the demographic factors that we considered, such as number of members in the family, annual household income, highest level of education in the family and gender.

---

[1] Owing to restrictions imposed by the government to contain the spread of the coronavirus, it was not feasible to conduct social experiments, which would have led to unbiased insights into the actual mechanisms that are at work behind an individual's decision-making process.

Further, we check the effect of COVID-19 over these externalities via the comparison between the role of online consumption behaviour and the role of offline consumption behaviour in determining these externalities. We also established that there is a convergence of these externalities in the student groups. Intuitively this means students' choice decisions are more affected by all three externalities. This study is important because in literature, the externalities have been mentioned individually whereas, our study considers all these externalities together and also checks how they are related to each other.

17.2 Literature Review

The existing literature have discussed choice overload, nudges and unconscious bias individually. Therefore, we can classify the entire literature into three groups.

Kurien et al. [6] discuss 'analysis paralysis' (over-analysing or over-thinking a situation) principle in the consumer decision-making process when choosing a product through a series of experiments for sales of FMCG and Electronics goods for ten years in different types of stores and outlets. The authors observed that when customers have more choices, they buy less, consumers postpone buying decisions when they are spoilt for choices, while they have closed deals quicker when fewer options are available. Additionally, more choices lead to greater dissatisfaction because expectations are raised. However, concluding the 'magic' optimum number of choices is tricky. The phenomenon can be defined as a situation where the opportunity cost of decision analysis exceeds the benefits gained by taking some decision or an informal situation where the utter volume of options swamps the decision-making process itself, thus preventing a decision.

Scheibehenne et al. [10] through a meta-analysis of 63 conditions from 50 published and unpublished experiments shows that an increase in the number of options may lead to adverse consequences such as a decrease in the motivation to choose or satisfaction with the final preferred option. The research found a mean effect size of virtually zero but a considerable variance between studies. The meta-analysis further confirmed that 'more choice is better' if decision-makers had well-defined preferences before choice. The paper positively identifies some potentially essential preconditions for choice overload to occur.

Further, Park and Jang [9] consider that tourism suppliers offer a wide variety of products, the paper tries to determine whether the aspect of choice overload persists in tourism and its vendible. By incorporating the scenario method, respondents were randomly assigned to one of ten different scenarios ($2_{\text{Destinations}} \times 5_{\text{Choice}}$ sets). The authors highlighted that having more than 22 choices propelled the tendency of not choosing anything regardless of the destination type. This suggested that choice overload indeed persists in the tourism industry. The research also pointed out that when fewer than 22 choices were provided, participants who made a choice perceived less regret than those who made 'no choice'.

Another study by Chernev et al. [2] highlights the significance of assortment decisions for retailers and manufacturers that various research articles have overlooked. It further throws light on whether large assortments can lead to 'choice overload'. The authors have attempted to identify factors that reliably moderate the impact of assortment size on choice overload and generalise them into an overarching conceptual framework.

Study by Mann [7] interprets 'root cause analysis' as a crucial step in the problem-solving system. The paper proposes an alternative and better way—*root contradiction analysis*—which requires way less time and effort and, more often than not, is capable of delivering more robust solutions. Two case studies have supported the same. Problems may be addressed to control and prevent interruptions, obstacles, errors, and counter-quality occurrences: root causes of issues that prevent the problem when removed. However, root cause analysis requires lots of data. In addition, the cost and time involved in capturing that data can often be prohibitive.

Besedeš et al. [1] investigate some sequential choice architectures that facilitate the choice basket to remain large while potentially reducing the effect of choice overload. The paper examines experimentally the ability of varying choice architectures to improve decision making. Choice architectures are considered to reduce a significant decision problem into fragments of more manageable ones. Such practices approach a problem sequentially, eliminating a few options at a time. Despite the greater likelihood of a better option being available, a larger number of choices may lead in choice overload, greater regret, and more indecision.

Recent study by Talbert [12] emphasises that the primary way one comes to know what others are thinking is by interacting with them. The interactive context requires real-time engagement such that conscious intellectual deliberation is disruptive in that it disturbs the flow of the interaction. Understanding that part of what one knows when one knows others comes from non-propositional, noncognitive know-how in a joint context can help elucidate the common wisdom behind the claims about how we should not overthink our interactions with other people.

Sunstein [11] highlights how cognitive psychologists and behavioural economists have been incorporating empirical findings of human behaviour into various economic models. Those findings have transformed the understanding of regulation and its likely consequences. *For example, choice architecture*, understood as the background against which decisions are made, has significant effects on decisions and outcomes alike. Moreover, minor, inexpensive policy initiatives, making modest design changes, can significantly affect energy, environment, health, savings and much more. This paper explores relevant evidence, catalogues behaviourally informed practices and reforms and discusses some implications for regulatory policy. Galizzi [3] stresses that it is often unclear which aspect of a policy formulation the term 'behavioural' refers to, and practitioners, policy-makers and researchers often use or assume quite different definitions of 'behavioural'. The paper further scrutinised theelationnship between the conceptual core of behavioural policies and behavioural science. Thaler [13] insists that the current generation of behavioural economists is using all the contemporary tools of economics, from theory to big data to structural models to neuroscience. They apply those tools to most of the domains in which economists practice their craft. The author also skillfully highlighted that people have been nudging as long as they have been trying to influence other people, but not all nudging is nudging for good. For example, some firms actively use behaviourally informed strategies to profit from the lack of scrutiny most shoppers apply. The author calls this kind of exploitive behaviour 'sludge', which is the opposite of a good nudge.

17.3 Data Descriptions

The data was collected via online primary survey, with questions pertaining to focal aspects of the lives of consumers such as consumption of food, purchasing of appliances, real estate, investment in stock market, etc. The population consists of 507 respondents. The sampling technique is a purposive sampling technique.

The study compiles them in the forms as presented in Table 17.1. It can be seen from the table that for the most part, the respondents belong to the age group of 20–35 years, who are mainly students. It can be noted half of the respondents are either students or involved in part-time jobs along with their studies. The next sizeable portion of the population is engaged in full-time jobs. The respondent's family structures look more or less equitable. While 32% claim that no one else is dependent on them financially, 22% respondents live in 3-person nuclear families.

While trying to understand consumer behaviour from various economic strata of the country, it was found that over 31% of the respondents had an annual household income of more than 15,00,000 INR. More than half of the respondents' highest education attained by self or close family member is a master's degree, closely followed by a bachelor's degree (33%). A majority of 95.66% engage in shopping online. This is inclusive of essentials (like grocery and vegetables) and leisure shopping both. It was notably observed that while around 60% of the respondents engaged in leisure shopping a few times a month, over 15% admitted to doing it once a week. It was also observed that over 68% of the respondents admitted to relying more on online shopping since the outbreak of the pandemic. However, 7.5% claim that they have significantly reduced shopping online during the same time frame, for reasons that haven't been tapped in this study.

17.4 Methodology

In this section, we have provided a brief overview of the data collected from the respondents in the sub section Description of the data. In the next sub section, we have provided a brief overview on Principal Component Analysis.

Table 17.1 Description of the variables

Variables	Percentages
Age group	
15–20	18
20–35	57
35–45	6
Above 45	19
Gender	
Male	47.93
Female	51.68
Employment Status	
Working Full Time	35.31
Working Part Time/ Student	49.9
Homemaker	7.3
Other	7.5
Average family size	3.5
Annual household income of more than 15,00,000 INR	31.32%
Qualification of respondents as postgraduate	52%
Engagement in online shopping	99%
Engagement in leisure shopping	60%
Relying on online shopping	68%

Source Authors' Calculation

17.5 An Overview on PCA

In order to understand the extent of effect of choice overload, nudges and unconscious bias among the respondents, the questions were first categorised, then each individual response was assigned a numerical value. Following this, STATA was used to run Principal Component Analysis for each externality individually and then calculate the correlation between the three externalities. In addition, Varimax Rotation and Scree Plots were also run for each of the externality individually and later compared.

The methodology of Principal Component Analysis (PCA) is elaborated below. Principal Component Analysis is a method of dimension reduction of the original dataset. Given a dataset of n variables PCA tries to find out a certain number (which is less than n) of orthogonal factors that explains the maximum variations of the dataset. The fact that the factors are not observable disqualifies regression and other methods previously examined. However, that under certain conditions the hypothesized factor model has certain implications, and these implications in turn can be tested against the observations.

Let us consider three variables Y_1, $Y_2 and Y_3$ which are explained by two factors $F_1 and F_2$ such that factors are linearly related to Y variables.

$$
\begin{aligned}
Y_1 &= \beta_{10} + \beta_{11}.F_1 + \beta_{12}.F_2 + \varepsilon_1 \\
Y_2 &= \beta_{20} + \beta_{21}.F_1 + \beta_{22}.F_2 + \varepsilon_2 \\
Y_3 &= \beta_{30} + \beta_{31}.F_1 + \beta_{32}.F_2 + \varepsilon_3
\end{aligned}
\tag{17.1}
$$

In the matrix form, the Eq. (17.1) is the following,

$$Y = \beta.F + \varepsilon \tag{17.2}$$

Y is 3 ×1 matrix of Y variables, F is a matrix of factors with a dimension 2 ×1, β is a matrix of factor loadings with a dimension 3 ×2 and ε is the error with a dimension of 3 ×1.

The errors $\varepsilon_1, \varepsilon_2 and \varepsilon_3$ explains the measurement errors of variables $Y_1, Y_2 and Y_3$, respectively. The errors are independent of each other and have constant variance. Now, β_{ij} are called the factor loadings which explains the correlation between Y_i and F_j. The unobserved factors are orthogonal to each other. It may appear that the loadings can be estimated and the expectations tested by regressing each Y against the two factors. Such an approach, however, is not feasible because the factors cannot be observed. An entirely new strategy is required.

It is possible to show that the variance of Y variables and the covariances are functions of factor loadings. Hence, the extraction of the factor loadings can explain the overall variations of the dataset.

From Eq. (17.2), we can derive the variance of $Y = \beta Var(F)\beta' +$ Var(ε).

The choice of β is such that it maximizes the Var(Y) subject to a normalizing condition

$$\beta.\beta' = I$$

The maximizing problem becomes

$$Max_{\beta} \beta Var(F)\beta' subject to \beta.\beta' = I$$

The Lagrange of the problem is $L = \beta Var(F)\beta' + \lambda(I - \beta.\beta')$

$$\frac{\partial L}{\partial \beta} = Var(F).\beta - \lambda.\beta = 0$$

$$(Var(F) - \lambda)\beta = 0$$

Here, λ is the eigenvalues of $Var(F)$ matrix and β is the corresponding eigen vector.

Note that, the first eigenvector β_1 maximises $Var(F)$ most and the factor loadings corresponding to β_1 comes first in terms of variation explanation of Y. So, $F_1 = \beta_1.Y$ will explain the highest variation followed by F_2.

Finally, an OLS regression was run, keeping the demographic factors as the independent variables and each of the externality as the dependent variable respectively. Further, OLS regression was run again without the demographic component of 'Employment Status' in order to distinguish and identify the effect of 'student population' in determining the results.

17.6 Results and Discussion

Table 17.2 provides the results of the PCA for Nudges, Choice Overload and Unconscious bias. It can be seen that for Nudges, there are three components explaining 52.68% of the data variations. It is also supported by Fig. 17.1 where three factors have eigenvalues more than 1. Hence, three out of ten factors are explaining the data.

For Choice Overload, there are four components explaining 51.88% of the data variations. It is also supported by Fig. 17.2 where four factors have eigenvalues more than 1. Hence, four out of ten factors are explaining the data.

For Unconscious Bias, there are four components explaining 55.77% of the data variations. It is also supported by Fig. 17.3 where four factors have eigenvalues more than 1. Hence, four out of ten factors are explaining the data.

We have obtained the predicted values of the principal components.

Table 17.3 reveals the correlation between different principal components. It can be seen that the correlation coefficient between Nudges and Choice Overload is 0.4052. The correlation coefficient between Nudges and Unconscious Bias is 0.5344. However, the correlation coefficient between Choice Overload and Unconscious Bias is 0.2996. Hence, it can be said that the Nudges are more positively correlated with other Choice Overload and Unconscious Bias, but the Choice Overload and Unconscious Bias are not correlated to that extent.

Table 17.4 presents the effects of different demographic variables on the different dimensions of choice paradox for the respondents who are not students. It can be seen that the effects of these variables are not uniform across all the choice paradoxes. The number of family members have positive effect on unconscious bias but insignificant for other paradoxes. This is because when the number of family members increases then the probability of making unconscious miss takes is generally increases. Considering the factor of household income, we can see that the households with larger income will likely have higher choice overload and households with smaller income will likely have larger unconscious bias. We can also see that the female members will have more externalities in Nudges and Unconscious bias.

More educated members will have more choice overload externality, but they will have less unconscious bias. Since, education is positively correlated with income of the households therefore we have the same type of outcome in case of education and households' income.

These three pie charts (Figs. 17.4, 17.5 and 17.6) reflect the online shopping behaviour of the respondents in the post-pandemic period. A sweeping majority of 95.66% engage in shopping online. This is inclusive of essentials (like grocery and vegetables) and leisure shopping both. It was notably observed that while around 60% of the respondents engaged in leisure shopping a few times a month, over 15% admitted to doing it once a week.

Table 17.2 The principal component analysis for nudges, choice overload and unconscious bias

Nudges

Component	Eigenvalue	Difference	Proportion	Cumulative
Comp1	2.97979	1.70409	0.2980	0.2980
Comp2	1.27571	.262719	0.1276	0.4255
Comp3	1.01299	.0461717	0.1013	0.5268
Comp4	.966815	.140132	0.0967	0.6235
Comp5	.826683	.0313695	0.0827	0.7062
Comp6	.795313	.11364	0.0795	0.7857
Comp7	.681673	.105591	0.0682	0.8539
Comp8	.576083	.0693998	0.0576	0.9115
Comp9	.506683	.12842	0.0507	0.9622
Comp10	.378263	.	0.0378	1.0000

Principal components (eigenvectors)

Variable	Comp1	Comp2	Comp3	Comp4	Comp5	Comp6	Comp7	Comp8	Comp9	Comp10
nvar1	0.2561	0.2429	0.5961	0.0150	-0.2078	-0.5129	0.1650	0.4121	0.1100	-0.0666
nvar2	0.2387	0.1489	0.6207	0.1668	0.1217	0.6395	0.0388	-0.2734	-0.0484	0.0735
nvar3	0.3482	0.4788	-0.2788	-0.1711	0.1681	0.1518	0.0343	0.1335	-0.2479	-0.6409
nvar4	0.3293	-0.0782	0.0596	0.0174	0.6551	-0.2748	-0.5898	-0.0373	0.1267	0.1083
nvar5	0.3262	0.5251	-0.2903	-0.1964	-0.0767	-0.0495	0.1712	-0.1845	0.1261	0.6384
nvar6	0.3516	-0.3774	-0.0439	-0.3837	-0.0524	0.1415	0.2175	-0.0724	0.6802	-0.2162
nvar7	0.3256	-0.4556	0.0304	-0.3628	0.1090	0.0518	0.2350	0.2603	-0.5919	0.2568
nvar8	0.3765	-0.1785	-0.0126	0.1775	-0.3724	-0.3377	-0.0676	-0.6586	-0.2612	-0.1882
nvar9	0.3363	-0.0880	-0.1807	0.2600	-0.4991	0.2987	-0.5007	0.4194	0.0505	0.1070
nvar10	0.2386	-0.1346	-0.2412	0.7251	0.2764	-0.0312	0.4849	0.1396	0.0910	0.0253

CHOICE OVERLOAD

Component	Eigenvalue	Difference	Proportion	Cumulative
Comp1	2.13831	.301452	0.1782	0.1782
Comp2	1.83686	.606176	0.1531	0.3313
Comp3	1.23068	.211502	0.1026	0.4338
Comp4	1.01918	.0556975	0.0849	0.5188
Comp5	.963483	.0211135	0.0803	0.5990
Comp6	.942369	.128338	0.0785	0.6776
Comp7	.814031	.0661186	0.0678	0.7454
Comp8	.747913	.0345275	0.0623	0.8077
Comp9	.713385	.10244	0.0594	0.8672
Comp10	.610945	.0890546	0.0509	0.9181
Comp11	.521891	.060936	0.0435	0.9616
Comp12	.460955	.	0.0384	1.0000

Principal components (eigenvectors)

Variable	Comp1	Comp2	Comp3	Comp4	Comp5	Comp6	Comp7	Comp8	Comp9	Comp10
covar1	0.1968	0.4678	-0.2958	-0.2809	0.1518	0.0084	0.1126	0.1624	-0.0026	-0.3365
covar2	0.1902	0.4550	-0.2921	-0.2268	0.3059	0.0297	0.2276	0.0738	0.0431	0.2416
covar3	0.5029	-0.1039	0.1361	-0.1344	-0.1927	-0.0172	0.1977	-0.3599	0.0737	0.1389
covar4	0.2700	0.2885	-0.2350	0.2004	-0.1427	0.0409	-0.6497	-0.5150	-0.0270	-0.0766
covar5	0.4549	-0.1912	0.2404	-0.2324	-0.0619	0.0218	0.3424	-0.2343	-0.0053	-0.2000
covar6	0.1874	0.1669	0.1790	0.2996	-0.1780	0.8121	0.0640	0.2681	-0.2115	-0.0313
covar7	0.3562	-0.2353	0.0398	-0.2184	-0.0092	0.0387	-0.4496	0.5113	0.5427	-0.0404
covar8	0.1228	-0.2404	-0.5618	0.4263	-0.0004	0.1033	0.2808	-0.0429	0.3580	0.3607
covar9	0.1518	-0.2327	0.0998	0.2991	0.8288	0.0842	-0.0544	-0.1313	-0.0276	-0.2976
covar10	0.4180	-0.0716	-0.0062	0.1693	0.0488	-0.3758	-0.1280	0.3546	-0.6057	0.3494
covar11	0.1290	0.3148	0.1822	0.5621	-0.2124	-0.4202	0.2212	0.1743	0.2559	-0.3727
covar12	-0.0279	0.3796	0.5506	0.0639	0.2364	-0.0094	-0.0610	-0.0999	0.3024	0.5301

UNCONSCIOUS BIAS

Component	Eigenvalue	Difference	Proportion	Cumulative
Comp1	2.0943	.792119	0.2094	0.2094
Comp2	1.30218	.125535	0.1302	0.3396
Comp3	1.17665	.176466	0.1177	0.4573
Comp4	1.00018	.0353517	0.1000	0.5573
Comp5	.96483	.117413	0.0965	0.6538
Comp6	.847417	.0391382	0.0847	0.7386
Comp7	.808279	.0757364	0.0808	0.8194
Comp8	.732543	.0506847	0.0733	0.8926
Comp9	.681858	.290099	0.0682	0.9608
Comp10	.391759	.	0.0392	1.0000

Principal components (eigenvectors)

Variable	Comp1	Comp2	Comp3	Comp4	Comp5	Comp6	Comp7	Comp8	Comp9	Comp10
ubvar1	0.1035	-0.3834	0.4779	0.1073	0.3485	-0.5575	-0.2140	-0.2996	0.1768	0.0581
ubvar2	0.4168	-0.0641	0.1207	-0.2917	0.3064	0.2135	0.2926	-0.2621	-0.6211	0.2072
ubvar3	0.5161	-0.1543	-0.0868	0.1495	-0.3046	-0.1569	-0.2276	0.0937	-0.2913	-0.6458
ubvar4	0.5109	0.0324	-0.2437	-0.1054	-0.1708	-0.1742	-0.3390	0.2764	0.1319	0.6318
ubvar5	0.3293	-0.0377	-0.0661	0.6271	-0.1761	0.2563	0.3230	-0.4292	0.2976	0.1367
ubvar6	0.1352	-0.5596	0.3205	-0.0648	0.0283	0.3862	0.2152	0.5510	0.2466	-0.0307
ubvar7	0.3652	0.3325	-0.0414	-0.4476	0.2968	0.1284	0.0041	-0.1566	0.5601	-0.3336
ubvar8	0.1545	0.4722	0.1303	0.4238	0.4213	-0.2376	0.2675	0.4926	-0.0859	-0.0338
ubvar9	0.0237	0.3384	0.5785	0.1496	-0.0830	0.4531	-0.5511	-0.0366	-0.0885	0.0529
ubvar10	0.0611	0.2480	0.4792	-0.2647	-0.5987	-0.3092	0.4195	-0.0087	0.0492	0.0501

Source Authors' Calculation

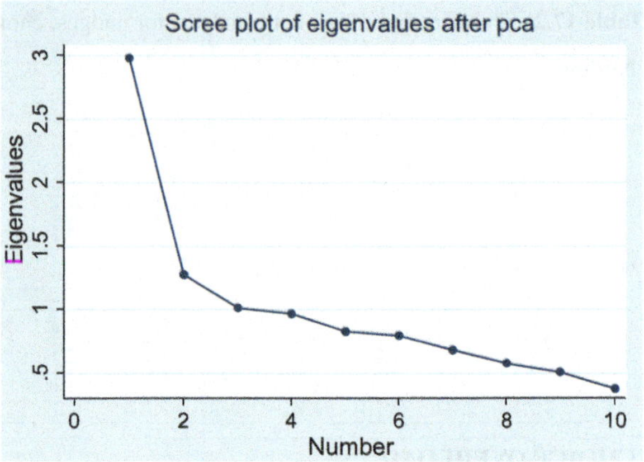

Fig. 17.1 Scree plots for nudges. *Source* Authors' Calculations

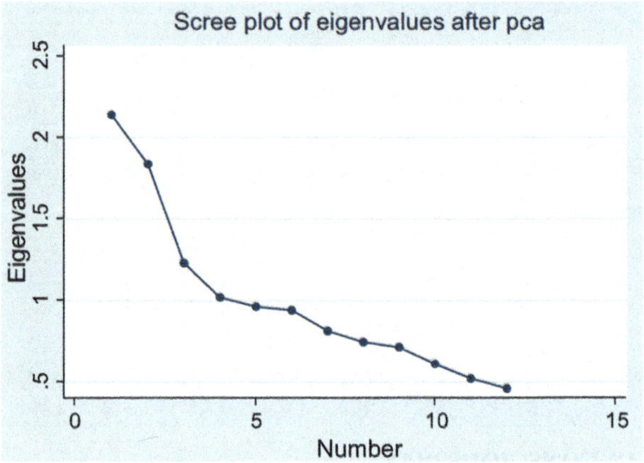

Fig. 17.2 Scree plots for choice overload. *Source* Authors' Calculations

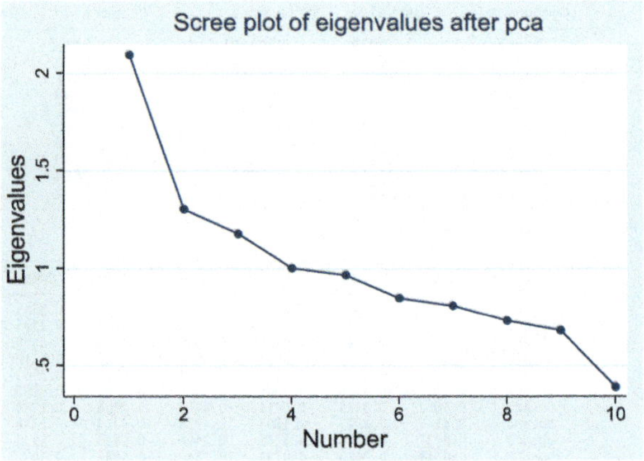

Fig. 17.3 Scree plots for unconscious bias. *Source* Authors' Calculations

Table 17.3 Correlation matrix of principal components

	Nudges	Choice overload	Unconscious bias
Nudges	1		
Choice Overload	0.4052	1	
Unconscious Bias	0.5344	0.2996	1

Source Authors' Calculation

Table 17.4 Regression analysis for three choice paradoxes excluding students

Explanatory variables	Principal components		
	Nudges	Choice overload	Unconscious bias
Number of family members	−0.007 (0.045)	−0.045 (0.036)	0.064* (0.035)
Annual household income	0.00018 (0.00035)	0.000014* (0.00023)	−0.00024** (0.0046)
Gender	0.271*** (0.153)	−0.155 (0.094)	0.230** (0.125)
Education level	−0.121 (0.118)	0.191** (0.032)	−0.248** (0.087)
Constant	1.211** (0.305)	2.201** (0.809)	3.201** (0.677)

Note Figures in the parentheses are the standard errors for the corresponding coefficients
Source Authors' Calculation

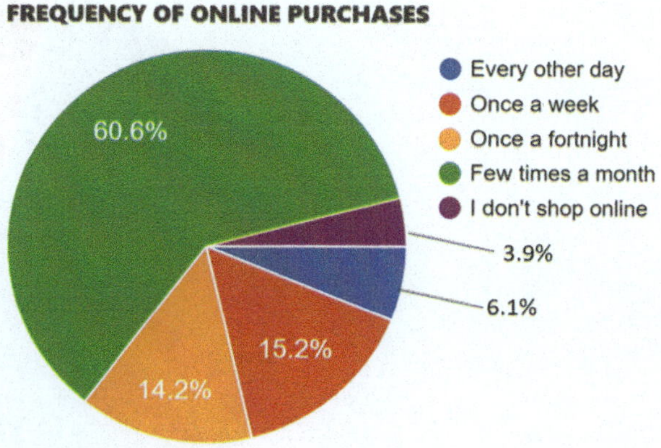

Fig. 17.4 Frequency of online purchases. *Source* Drawn by the Authors

It was also observed that over 68% of the respondents admitted to relying more on online shopping since the outbreak of the pandemic. However, 7.5% claim that they have significantly reduced shopping online during the same time frame, for reasons that haven't been tapped in this study.

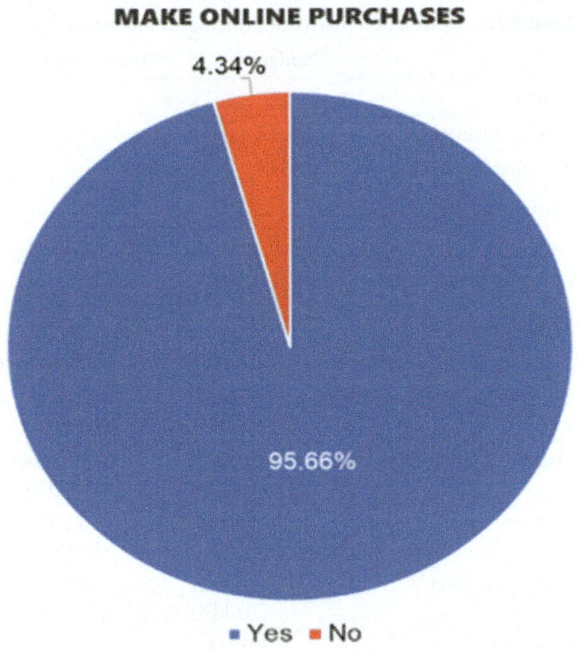

Fig. 17.5 Post-pandemic shopping behavior. *Source* Drawn by the Authors

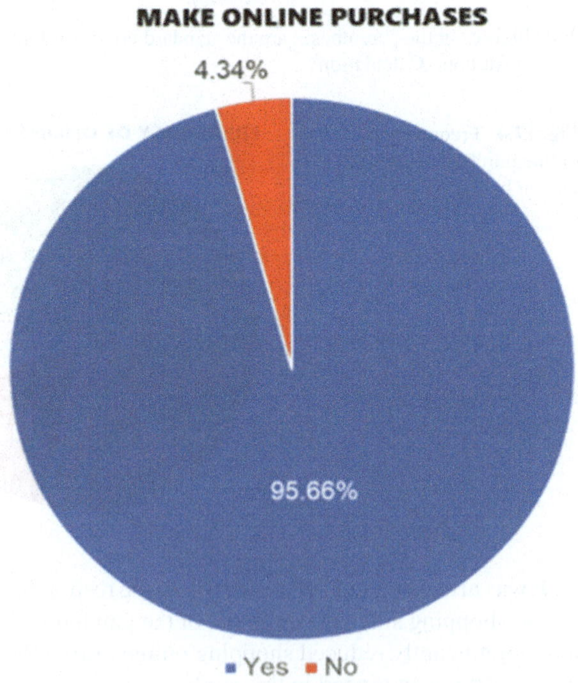

Fig. 17.6 Make online purchases. *Source* Drawn by the Authors

The Indian e-commerce market has been one of the biggest beneficiaries of the pandemic, as containment measures introduced millions to the convenience of online shopping and prompted seasoned online shoppers to buy more.

Social distancing compulsions throughout the year, massive smartphone base and reliable broadband galvanised e-commerce uptake beyond metros, deep into smaller cities and towns bring an element of 'trust in online commerce. The outbreak necessitated the use of new technology tools and non-contact formats to cater to unprecedented demand. Analysts said these shifts in consumer shopping traits are here to stay, post-pandemic.

The pandemic brought about a 'structural shift' in shopping behaviour with more and more customers and businesses relying on e-commerce. Players like **Amazon** and **Flipkart** as well as industry watchers noted that the need for social distancing and prioritizing safety during the pandemic led to millions of people turning to e-commerce platforms this past year, not only in metros but also in tier III regions and beyond. From changes in category preferences to the emergence of 'new essentials', and from the adoption of native languages to a surge in new-age forms of payments—the past year bore witness to an array of unique consumer trends.

For example, Amazon also saw similar trends as thousands of neighbourhood **Kirana** stores and offline retailers also came onboard to leverage digital technology to reach customers' doorstep. A Grofers spokesperson said that amongst all new users on its platform in the last one year, 64% were first-time online grocery shoppers, while 20% were totally new to e-commerce. Flipkart witnessed new user growth of close to 50% soon after the lockdown, with tier III regions and beyond registering the highest growth of 65% during the 'Unlock' (July–September) phase last year (Fig. 17.7).

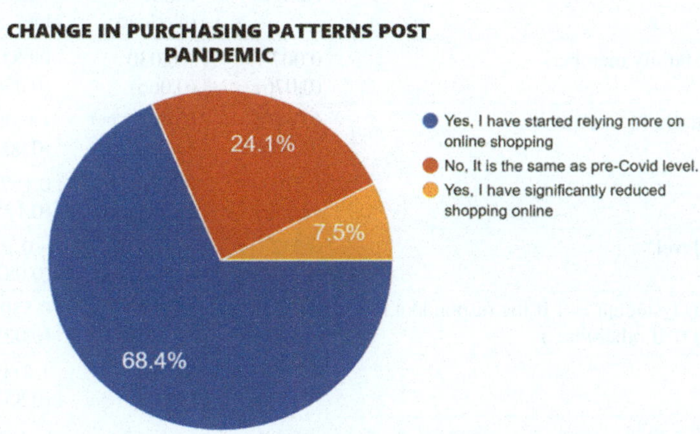

Fig. 17.7 Change in purchasing patterns post pandemic. *Source* Drawn by the Authors

17.7 Convergence Within Student Group

Table 17.5 represents the effect of demographic factors on these consumption externalities after including the students as well.

It can be seen that coefficients of D student which is the dummy for students are statistically significant for these choice externalities. Hence, it can be said that there is a convergence of these externalities in the student groups. Townsend [15] first highlights the prevalence of consumption externalities among young adults including students in USA. He showed that the demand function for tobacco and alcohol becomes less price elastic for students and young adults as compared to other age groups. Greenfield et al. [4] has also highlighted that the young tend to ignore personal risks of intoxication and their consumption pattern is less responsive to an increase in tax regime for tobacco and alcohol. Now, in our study, we have not strictly restricted our respondents as consumers of alcohol and tobacco. However, these three types of externalities are mostly observed among typical commodities used for regular consumption. It can be seen that the existence of these externalities still prevails among the students who are a subset of young adults even if the consumption goods are considered. Intuitively this means students' choice decisions are more affected by all three externalities. The convergence in our study reflects the existence of tall three externalities in one single demographic group (students). As a result, we can claim that these externalities are converging among the student group.

Table 17.5 Regression analysis for three choice paradoxes including students

Explanatory variables	Principal components		
	Nudges	Choice overload	Unconscious bias
Number of family members	0.007 (0.076)	−0.030 (0.066)	0.081** (0.036)
Annual household income	0.00022 (0.00089)	0.000027** (0.00013)	−0.00013 (0.00096)
Gender	0.217 (0.353)	0.138 (0.195)	0.167 (0.125)
Education level	0.332 (0.208)	−0.117 (0.221)	−0.203** (0.082)
D_student (D_student = 1 if the respondent is a student and 0, if otherwise.)	0.449*** (0.145)	0.466*** (0.133)	0.550*** (0.023)
Constant	1.590** (0.305)	2.236** (0.211)	1.211** (0.857)

Note Figures in the parentheses are the standard errors for the corresponding coefficient
Source Authors' Calculation

17.8 Conclusion

We conclude our contribution in the following ways. First, the choice paradox in terms of Choice overload, Nudges and Unconscious bias is very much dependent upon the demographic factors of the individuals such as education, gender and number of family members and economic factors such as the household's income. Further, these dependency is not uniform. Therefore, government policy to tackle these choices paradox will be in targeted in nature. Secondly, we found that if the individual is a student then all the three types of choice paradox are present. Therefore, controlling the choice paradox the policy must target the student group of society.

References

1. Besedeš T, Deck C, Sarangi S, Shor M (2015) Reducing choice overload without reducing choices. Rev Econ Stat 97(4):793–802
2. Chernev A, Böckenholt U, Goodman J (2015) Choice overload: a conceptual review and meta-analysis. J Consum Psychol 25(2):333–358
3. Galizzi (2018). Behavioural aspect of policy formulation: experiments. Mater Insights Nudges
4. Greenfield TK, Ye Y, Kerr W, Bond J, Rehm J, Giesbrecht N (2009) Externalities from alcohol consumption in the 2005 US National Alcohol Survey: implications for policy. Int J Environ Res Public Health 6(12):3205–3224
5. John P (2016) Behavioral approaches: How nudges lead to more intelligent policy design. In: *Contemporary approaches to public policy* (pp. 113–131). Palgrave Macmillan, London
6. Kurien R, Paila AR, Nagendra A (2014) Application of paralysis analysis syndrome in customer decision making. Procedia Econ Financ 11:323–334
7. Mann D (2002) Analysis paralysis: When root cause analysis isn't the way. TRIZ J (May)
8. Newell BR, Shanks DR (2014) Unconscious influences on decision making: a critical review. Behav Brain Sci 37(1):1–19
9. Park JY, Jang SS (2013) Confused by too many choices? Choice overload in tourism. Tour Manage 35:1–12
10. Scheibehenne B, Greifeneder R, Todd PM (2010) Can there ever be too many options? A meta-analytic review of choice overload. J Consum Res 37(3):409–425
11. Sunstein CR (2013) Nudges. gov: Behavioral economics and regulation. Forthcoming, Oxford
12. Talbert B (2017) Overthinking and other minds: The analysis paralysis. Soc Epistemol 31(6):545–556
13. Thaler RH (2018) From cashews to nudges: The evolution of behavioral economics. Am Econ Rev 108(6):1265–1287
14. Thaler RH, Ganser LJ (2015) Misbehaving: The making of behavioural economics
15. Townsend J (1996) Price and consumption of tobacco. Br Med Bull 52(1):132–142
16. Zamir E, Teichman D (2018) Behavioral law and economics. Oxford University Press

Chapter 18
COVID-19 and Impact on Income Inequality: The Indian Experience

Sovik Mukherjee

18.1 Background

The COVID-19 pandemic has had a significant impact on India's economic growth and income distribution. Research suggests that India's economic slowdown is the only factor responsible for the recent reversal of the long-term fall in global income inequality (weighted for the share of population) which was happening since the 1990s [12]. Nonetheless, despite a decline in worldwide inequality, India's economic disparity rose from 1990 to 2019. According to the World Inequality Database (WID), the percentage of the top 1% of the population's national income has increased from 11% in 1990 to 21% in 2019 [41]. There is a rich literature that demonstrates that pandemics cause inequality and poverty to worsen (see for e.g. [10, 14, 28, 30, 35]).

It needs to be mentioned that conceptually consumption inequality is treated similarly like income equality but in terms of estimated measurements are quite different [17]. In the Indian context during the COVID-19 period, it was estimated that consumption inequality shrunk less than income inequality, likely due to consumption smoothing [20]. Malani and Ramachandran [26], find that excess deaths during COVID disproportionately affected high incomes. Prior to COVID-19, death rates were greater for lower income groups. However, the top terciles' death rates increased more during the pandemic. As a result, death rates were constant across terciles by July 2021. Because of this reason and to have a clearer picture about the position of inequality in India, this chapter contributes to the literature on the impact of COVID-19 pandemic on income inequality and not consumption inequality per se.

S. Mukherjee (✉)
Department of Commerce (Morning Section), Faculty of Commerce and Management, St. Xavier's University, Kolkata, India
e-mail: sovik1992@gmail.com

R. Bhattacharyya et al. (eds.), *COVID-19 Pandemic and Global Inequality*,
https://doi.org/10.1007/978-981-99-4405-7_18

In the Indian context, papers like Banerjee and Piketty [2] and Chancel and Piketty [4] give us an idea about the trends in income inequality in general. COVID-19 pandemic has increased global inequality, reversing the decline of the previous two decades [8]. Weak recoveries in emerging markets and developing economies (EMDEs) have raised between-country inequality [24]. Within-country income inequality is also estimated to have increased somewhat in EMDEs because of severe job and income losses among lower-income population groups (see [25, 35]. Several papers in the Indian context studied income inequality during COVID-19 [3, 5, 11, 15, 22, 23, 29, 33, 40], among others. These studies suggest COVID-19 has led to increased income inequality and has deteriorating impacts. The author agrees to the same but also establishes in this chapter that inequality in India decreased between January 2021–July 2021.

Similar arguments can be found in Deaton [9], a significant exception in this regard. Deaton [9] suggests that inequality may have decreased across nations during the epidemic. Another exception is Scheidel [37] who contends that historically, epidemics have decreased inequality by disproportionately affecting the wealthy. The author puts forward similar arguments in the Indian context and the paper in spirit belongs to this strand of the existing literature. It needs to be made very clear that the author's goal in illustrating how inequality decreased during the pandemic is not to downplay the difficulties faced by India's most vulnerable citizens.

The rest of the chapter is organized as follows. The following section discusses the data sources and the methodology in Sect. 2. Section 3 puts forward the results and the discussions thereof. Finally, the paper ends with a conclusion.

18.2 Objectives

Against this background, the main objective of this paper is to contribute to our understanding of the trends in income inequality in the Indian context during the COVID-19 pandemic and the implications thereof by analysing data from the CMIE's Consumer Pyramids Households Survey, corresponding to the first wave ranging from February 2020–December 2020, the Delta wave period spanning from January 2021 to July 2021 and the OMICRON wave period ranging from November 2021–February 2022.

18.3 Data and Methodology

18.3.1 Data

The income module of the Consumer Pyramids Household Survey (CPHS), conducted by the Centre for Monitoring Indian Economy (CMIE), is the main source of data used in the paper. The data on India's population comes from Census (2011),[1] Worldometer database[2] and Statista.[3]

CPHS covers practically the whole of India and stratified sampling is made use of to guarantee representativeness down to a substate level. Every family is surveyed by the CPHS every four months, and selection is staggered so that each month a representative 25% of all households are chosen. Every time a survey is conducted, CPHS updates its household register and asks questions about the entire family as well as each participant. Each of the past four months' worth of income and consumption are inquired about. Income is, thus, obtained at both the individual (individual wage income) and the household level (income for the entire household). This paper reports the results in terms of seasonally adjusted per capita real household incomes.[4] The whole idea of making the seasonal adjustments[5] is to consider the monthly differences in the pattern of income patterns, particularly in rural areas.

It needs to be noted as to why the CPHS data source is being used by the author. Every five years, starting from 1972 to 1973 and continuing till 2011–12, the National Sample Survey Organisation (NSSO), released national consumer expenditure surveys. Concerns regarding 'data quality' led to the withholding of the survey's results for 2017–18 [12]. This vacuum has been somewhat filled since 2014 by the CPHS conducted by the CMIE.

However, several scholars have questioned how representative the sample frame is, particularly in addressing the severely poor [39]. Due to this, debates about changes in the pattern of income inequality in India over the past ten years tend to stir up some controversy.

18.3.2 Methodology

We estimate income losses during the lockdown months (i.e., February 2020 – February 2022) and the subsequent recovery in the post-lockdown period (February

[1] https://censusindia.gov.in/census.website/data/census-tables.

[2] https://www.worldometers.info/world-population/india-population/.

[3] https://www.statista.com/statistics/263766/total-population-of-india/.

[4] To separate the impact of pandemic on household income, certain observed and unobserved household characteristics, basically the fixed factors which do not vary over time are controlled for. These include, certain seasonal factors, occupation, caste among others.

[5] Thus, the variable of interest becomes the monthly per-capita household income in constant terms.

2022). India experienced three waves of COVID cases during this period of pandemic. The first wave ranges from February 2020–December 2020, the Delta wave period corresponds to spans January 2021–July 2021 and the OMICRON wave period ranging from November 2021–February 2022. The calculation of the Generalized Entropy measure entailed a lot of complicated stuff. The data availability became a serious constraint.

According to Mussard [31], 'the Generalized Entropy (GE) Index derived from information theory has been proposed as a measure of income inequality in a population satisfying all the five desired properties, viz., *mean independence, population size independence, symmetry, Pigou-Dalton transfer sensitivity and decomposability*'.

The formula for GE(2) is given by,

$$GE(2) = \frac{1}{2N}\sum_{i=1}^{N}\left[\left(\frac{y_i}{\bar{y}}\right)^2 - 1\right]$$

where, N is the number of cases (e.g., households or families), y_i is the income for case i and, $\alpha = 2$ is the weight assigned to the distances between incomes at different parts of the income distribution.

The formal definition of GE(2) as reported necessitates an estimate of a ratio between the income of the ith class and the average income. But unfortunately, this data is not available, so the author has slightly kind of modified the GE(2) index and instead of that ratio this paper takes into account the ratio of 1st decile income to 5th decile income and the ratio of 5th decile income to 9th decile income. Here, 5th decile kind of acts as the mean decile. Decile groups are defined in each month separately, on the basis of incomes in that particular month.[6] This idea is drawn from the author's earlier work, Mukherjee and Karmakar [27].

Given the definition of the Generalized Entropy measure, the purpose of taking the weight equal to 2 comes from the fact that for lower values of weights, a measure from the GE class is sensitive to the lower end of the distribution. As this paper deals with countries that are mostly developing in nature, the focus remains more on the lower tail of the distribution and as a result, $\alpha = 2$ is taken into consideration."

18.4 Results and Discussion

On an average, the bottom 20% of rural households in April 2020 did not earn any income due to the lockdown (Fig. 18.1). After seven months—in October 2020, the average income of the bottom decile was 15%–20% lower than the bottom decile's average income in February 2020. As can be seen in Fig. 20.1, the difference in

[6] The author does not continuously track the same group of individuals because decile groups are dynamically established. Because household earnings fluctuate from month to month, the composition of households within any decile will shift.

the average incomes between February and December 20,202 was the largest for the 8th and the 9th decile, and this difference became smaller for the higher deciles. Surprisingly, for the 10th decile, the fall was not so much as compared to the February 2020 levels as the 10th decile represents the poorest of the poor.

The average income of the top decile dropped to a much lesser extent initially, sudden fall around October–November 2020 but the recovery from the decline was very slow. The average income for the top decile in April 2020, was 20%–25% lower than the top decile's average income in February 2020. However, the gap was reduced to 11.5% in February 2022. And note the estimates after controlling for household features[1]. As argued by Gururaja and Ranjitha [21], the kind of work may be a factor in the top decile's slower recovery. Those who work as permanent salaried employees are more likely to reside in homes in the top decile. Finding new jobs with the same pay if they lose their current ones can be challenging. Moreover, Fig. 20.1 clearly shows that the situation is better in terms of a lesser fall in the per-capita seasonally adjusted real income levels in the second phase, i.e., (January 2021–July 2021) and third phase, i.e., (November 2021–February 2022).

In line with the findings from Fig. 18.1, the paper reports the GE (2) values for the periods under consideration in Table 18.1 as follows. It needs to be noted here that the values reported are the geometric means of the monthly data corresponding to the three periods, as already mentioned.

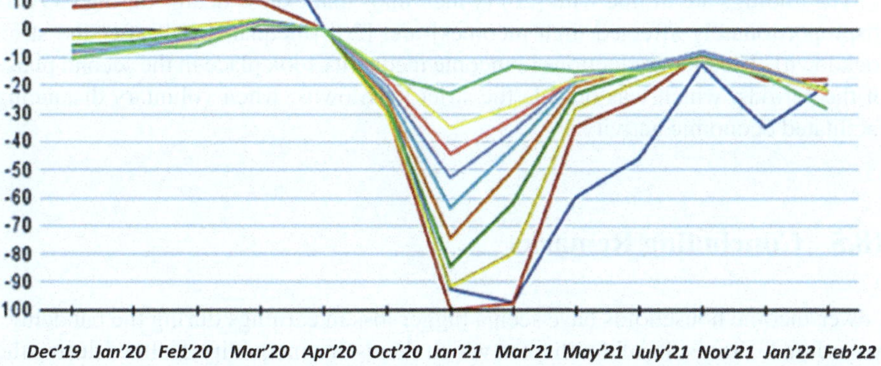

Fig. 18.1 Impact of COVID-19 on proportionate change in monthly incomes grouped by income deciles. *Notes* The y axis represents the proportionate change in seasonally adjusted per capita real household income across decile from the baseline of February 2020. *Source* Computed by the author

Table 18.1 Computation of generalized entropy (GE) measure of inequality for India

Period	GE(2) Index values#
February 2020–December 2020	0.408
January 2021–July 2021	0.323
November 2021–February 2022	0.333

#: Geometric mean of monthly values
Source Computed by the author

If one compares the GE(2) values corresponding to the three periods in Table 18.1 it is clear that between January 2021–July 2021 inequality fell corresponding to the period February 2020–December 2020. The fall from the February 2020 baseline per-capita seasonally adjusted real income for the top decile is the maximum and perhaps one of the reasons contributing to a fall in inequality. The performance of the lower-level deciles is particularly remarkable for India—as the gap with February 2020 levels was reducing and for the top decile it was increasing in the second phase—thus, contributing to a fall in inequality (see Fig. 20.1). Though inequality increased between November 2021 and February 2022, the percentage change was minimal. The success of the lower decile is particularly impressive considering that India, unlike the US, did not experience a significant amount of income transfers as fiscal stimulus. Government transfers increased throughout the COVID-19 period, but their absolute value was still low compared to household income [20]. Thus, one of the reasons contributing to the increase in inequality during the first phase under consideration. There is a rich literature that income transfers targeted to poor and vulnerable workers have worked well. In Brazil, transfers helped reduce both poverty and inequality in Brazil between May and September 2020 [16]. Similar claims have been made about five European countries: France, Germany, Italy, Spain, and Sweden [7].

The findings are in line with [26] [which finds that excess deaths during COVID disproportionately affected high incomes] and [20] [inequality fell after the strict lockdown]. The main reductions in income inequality took place in the second phase of the periods, which was outside the strict lockdowns, when voluntary distancing facilitated economic activity.

18.5 Concluding Remarks

Lower-income households have seen a bigger loss in earnings during the pandemic, according to the results of the chapter, which shows that inequality declined during the crisis. The relative income of individuals from top-two deciles households fell during and remained more depressed after the lockdown compared to incomes of those from lower the bottom-two deciles. It is also important to remember that incomes were already declining before the COVID-19 shock hit the Indian economy, presumably because of 2019's recession.

Our work has important caveats. First, the paper does not show that the pandemic caused a decline in income inequality. It has been shown that inequality declined during the pandemic, particularly, in the period between January 2021 and July 2021. Second, the paper does not compare the inequality levels with those of the pre-pandemic era. The comparison has been facilitated within the pandemic era divided into three periods as discussed. Third, because the top 5% or 1% of earners appear to be outpacing even the rest of the first decile, a large portion of the literature on inequality concentrates on them. However, it needs to be understood that 0.1% in the 1st decile is undoubtedly not covered by CPHS [20]. It is obvious that those people will reply to the CPHS. Some serious efforts have to go in if a researcher plans to compare CPHS to related government datasets [13]. Fourth, the paper works only with inequality, its trend, analysis of the same. The associated macroeconomic factors like poverty, employment, growth, among others is not under the purview of this chapter.

Interestingly, the findings in the paper are in contrast with the US where higher income persons saw smaller reductions in income lower income persons [6]. This was partly the result of better access to remote work [1]. The findings thus emphasize on the significance of taking technical advancements into account when estimating the frequency of such economic shocks across nations. In this regard, comparing India's position in BRICS or in G20, and also separately with some other developed countries like UK, EU, Japan among others, will add another dimension to the research. As already mentioned, the author's goal in illustrating how inequality decreased during the pandemic is not to downplay the difficulties faced by India's most vulnerable citizens. The author, simply, tries to portray how in different phases of the pandemic income inequality increased or decreased. And does not comment on whether inequality will rise when the pandemic ends. As future research work, it would be worth exploring the trends in income inequality for the periods under consideration across rural and urban groups vis-à-vis the pre-pandemic levels. Trends in inequality, pre-pandemic and post-pandemic, can be carried out once the pandemic ends officially and remains as another future research agenda.

As the world is still trying to come to terms with the impact of the pandemic, the author believes that the research offers crucial evidence that will be used to develop and carry out policy measures that will support households and ensure a minimum subsistence level of income in these turbulent times. This is a result of the crisis's lasting impacts. In view of this, during the pandemic period, noted economists like Prof. Abhijit Banerjee, Prof. Kaushik Basu, Prof. Raghuram Rajan among others emphasized on the importance of direct cash transfer (DCT) (consistent with the concept of universal basic income) to the bottom half of the population (see Varshney et al. [39]. DCTs do not pose a threat to the wealthy minority, rather, as argued by Naikade [32], '.......they help the poor majority improve their standard of life, which in turn improves the socio-political and economic climate of the country and benefits everyone, including the wealthy minority'. As a result, everyone in society benefits from the DCT. By addressing structural disparities now, we can make our society more egalitarian and crisis-resilient in the future. This will prevent women, low-skilled workers, and urban informal sector workers from falling further behind when India fully recovers.

References

1. Adams-Prassl A, Boneva T, Golin M, Rauh C (2020) Inequality in the impact of the coronavirus shock: Evidence from real time surveys. J Public Econ 189:104245
2. Banerjee A, Piketty T (2005) Top indian incomes, 1922–2000. World Bank Econ Rev 19(1):1–20
3. Chakrabarty M, Mukherjee S (2022) Impact of COVID-19 on convergence in Indian districts. Indian Growth Dev Rev 15(2/3):198–209
4. Chancel L, Piketty T (2019) Indian Income Inequality, 1922–2015: From British Raj to Billionaire Raj? Rev Income Wealth 65:S33–S62
5. Chaudhary M, Sodani PR, Das S (2020) Effect of COVID-19 on economy in India: Some reflections for policy and programme. J Health Manag 22(2):169–180
6. Chetty R, Friedman JN, Hendren N, Stepner M (2020) The economic impacts of COVID-19: Evidence from a new public database built using private sector data (No. w27431). National Bureau of Economic Research. Retrieved from https://www.nber.org/system /files/working_papers /w27431/w27431.pdf
7. Clark AE, d'Ambrosio C, Lepinteur A (2021) The fall in income inequality during COVID-19 in four European countries. J Econ Inequal 19:489–507
8. Crossley TF, Fisher P, Low H (2021) The heterogeneous and regressive consequences of COVID-19: Evidence from high quality panel data. J Public Econ 193:104334
9. Deaton A (2021) COVID-19 and Global Income Inequality. LSE Public Policy Rev 1(4):1. https://doi.org/10.31389/lseppr.26
10. Demena BA, Floridi A, Wagner N (2021) The short-term impact of COVID-19 on labour market outcomes: Comparative systematic evidence. In E. Papyrakis (Ed.), *Covid-19 and International Development*. Cham: Springer International Publishing
11. Deshpande A (2020) The COVID-19 Pandemic and Gendered Division of Paid and Unpaid Work: Evidence from India (No. 13815). Institute of Labor Economics (IZA).
12. Dhingra S, Ghatak M (2022) India: the economic impact of COVID-19. CentrePiece—The magazine for economic performance, 619, Centre for Economic Performance, LSE
13. Dreze J, Somanchi A (2021) View: New barometer of India's economy fails to reflect deprivations of poor households. The Economic Times June 21 (June 21). Retrieved from https://economictimes.indiatimes.com/opinion/et-commentary/view-the-new-barometer-of-indias-economy-fails-to-reflect-the-deprivations-of-poor-households/articleshow/8369 6115.cms
14. Egger D, Miguel E, Warren SS, Shenoy A, Collins E, Karlan D, Parkerson D, Mobarak AM, Fink G, Udry C, Walker M, Haushofer J, Larreboure M, Athey S, Lopez-Pena P, Benhachmi S, Humphreys M, Lowe L, Meriggi NF, Wabwire A, Davis CA, Pape UJ, Graff T, Voors M, Nekesa C, Vernot C (2021) Falling living standards during the covid-19 crisis: Quantitative evidence from nine developing countries. Sci Adv 7(6):eabe0997
15. Estupinan X, Sharma M (2020) Job and wage losses in informal sector due to the COVID-19 lockdown measures in India. Available at SSRN 3680379
16. Ferreira FH (2021) Inequality in the time of COVID-19. Finan Develop 58(2):20–23
17. Fisher J, Johnson D, Latner JP, Smeeding T, Thompson J (2016) Inequality and mobility using income, consumption, and wealth for the same individuals. RSF: Russell Sage Foundation J Soc Sci 2(6):44–58
18. Ghatak, M., Raghavan, R., & Xu, L. (2023). *Trends in economic inequality in India.* Retrieved from https://www.theindiaforum.in/economy/trends-economic-inequality-india on 25.4.23

19. Ghose AK (2020) The pandemic, lockdown and employment. Indian J Labour Econ 63:67–71
20. Gupta A, Malani A, Woda B (2021) Inequality in india declined during covid (No. w29597). National Bureau of Economic Research. Retrieved from https://www.nber.org/system/ files/ working_papers/ w29597/w29597.pdf
21. Gururaja BL, Ranjitha N (2022) Socio-economic impact of COVID-19 on the informal sector in India. Contemp Soc Sci 17(2):173–190
22. Jha P, Kumar M (2020) Labour in India and the COVID-19 Pandemic. Indian Econ J 68(3):417–437
23. Jurzik E, Nair MM, Pouokam N, Saadi-Sedik T, Tan A, Yakadina IV (2020) COVID-19 and inequality in Asia: Breaking the vicious cycle. IMF Working Paper No. 2020/217, Available at SSRN: https://ssrn.com/abstract=3744684
24. Kalar B, Primc K, Kump N (2023) Differences in COVID-19 policies and income distribution: a cross-country comparison. Sustainability 15(6):4916
25. Mahler DG, Yonzan N, Lakner C (2022) The impact of COVID-19 on global inequality and poverty. Retrieved from https://openknowledge.worldbank.org/bitstream/handle/109 86/ 38114/IDU01d94e70603dc804f990b6130751d75dccb52.pdf?sequence=1
26. Malani A, Ramachandran S (2021) Using household rosters from survey data to estimate all-cause mortality during covid in India (No. w29192). National Bureau of Economic Research. Retrieved from https://www.nber.org/system/files/working_papers/w29192/w2 9192.pdf
27. Mukherjee S, Karmakar AK (2019) A Tri-Variate Nexus of Microfinance-Growth-Inequality: The South-Asian Experience. In: Das RC (ed) Handbook of Research on Microfinancial Impacts on Women Empowerment, Poverty, and Inequality. IGI Global, USA, pp 247–265
28. Miguel E, Mobarak AM (2022) The economics of the COVID-19 pandemic in poor countries. Annu Rev Econ 14:253–285
29. Miyamura S (2021) Turbulence ahead: labour and struggles in times of the Covid-19 pandemic in India. Can J Dev Stud/Rev Can D'Études Développement 42(1–2):165–177
30. Murshed SM (2022) Consequences of the Covid-19 Pandemic Pandemics for Economic Inequality Inequalities. In: Papyrakis E (ed) Covid-19 and international development. Springer International Publishing, Cham, pp 59–70
31. Mussard S, Seyte F, Terraza M (2003) Decomposition of Gini and the generalized entropy inequality measures. Econ Bull 4(7):1–6
32. Naikade K (2018) Direct cash transfer to resolve the crisis of income inequality. Art Human Open Acc J 2(3):138–142
33. Nanda S (2020) Inequalities and COVID-19. In: Michael Ryan J (Ed.). *COVID-19* (pp. 109–123). Routledge, London
34. Narayan A, Cojocaru A, Agrawal S, Bundervoet T, Davalos M, Garcia N, Yonzan N (2022) COVID-19 and Economic Inequality. Retrieved from https://openknowledgeworldbank.org/ server/api/core/bitstreams/45203b02-eb1f-5b00-ae4c-0a0817788150/content.
35. Ray D, Subramanian S, Vandewalle L (2021) India's lockdown. In Rajib Bhattacharyya, Ananya Ghosh Dastidar and Soumyen Sikdar (Eds.) The COVID-19 Pandemic, India, and the World (pp. 64–74). Routledge, India
36. Romanello M (2021) Covid-19 and the informal sector. In: Papyrakis E (Ed.), Covid-19 and International Development. Cham: Springer International Publishing
37. Scheidel W (2018) The Great Leveler. Princeton University Press, Princeton
38. Somanchi A (2021) Missing the Poor, Big Time: A Critical Assessment of the Consumer Pyramids Household Survey (No. qmce9). Center for Open Science
39. Varshney D, Kumar A, Mishra AK, Rashid S, Joshi PK (2021) India's COVID-19 social assistance package and its impact on the agriculture sector. Agric Syst 189:103049
40. Vijayan P (2020) Challenges in the Midst of the COVID-19 pandemic. Econ Polit Weekly 55(24):11–13
41. Yang L (2020) What's New about Income Inequality Data in Asia?. World Inequality Lab, Issue Brief, 2020–08. Retrieved from https://wid.world/document/whats-new-about-income-inequality-data-in-asia/

Chapter 19
An Exploratory Analysis of Personal Finance in the Context of COVID-19

Deyanira Bernal-Domínguez and José G. Vargas-Hernández

19.1 Introduction

The present investigation arises from the need to know how spending is being oriented in the families of Culiacán, Sinaloa, Mexico, in the current macroeconomic context under the COVID-19 pandemic, which is not positive. The annual percentage variation in the first quarter 2020 in the United Mexican States was −1.28% and in Sinaloa it was −0.67%. Likewise, the quarterly indicator of state economic activity, base 2013, for Sinaloa is the percentage variation compared to the previous quarter of −0.2% and the percentage variation compared to the same quarter of the previous year is of −0.9%. Then, Mexico had the worst drop in the Gross Domestic Product in the second quarter of 2020, at −18.9% compared to the quarter of the previous year, comprising a drop in secondary activities of −26%, tertiary 15.6% and primary −0.3%, this, according to data published by the National Institute of Statistics and Geography [15–17].

In relation to the economic effects of COVID-19, based on the survey on the expectations of specialists in private sector economics in June 2020 published by the Bank of Mexico, annual GDP growth is expected by 2020 be −8.8. % and for 2021 of 2.80%. Regarding the behavior of household income and expenditure published in 2018 in the National Survey of Household Income and Expenditure (NIEGH) [14], of the INEGI, they show that in Mexico the average quarterly current income per household is higher than the expenditure quarterly average current, being 49,610 pesos and 31,913 pesos respectively.

Likewise, in Sinaloa, the income is 55,474 pesos and the expense is 32,643. In addition, according to data from the NIEGH in Mexico as well as in Sinaloa, where

D. Bernal-Domínguez
Faculty of Accounting and Management, Autonomous University of Sinaloa, Culiacán, Mexico

J. G. Vargas-Hernández (✉)
Instituto Tecnológico Mario Molina Unidad Zapopan, Zapopan, Mexico
e-mail: jvargas2006@gmail.com

R. Bhattacharyya et al. (eds.), *COVID-19 Pandemic and Global Inequality*,
https://doi.org/10.1007/978-981-99-4405-7_19

the most is spent on food, beverages, and tobacco, followed by transportation, acquisition, maintenance, accessories, and services for vehicles, communications, later education services, educational articles, entertainment items, and other entertainment expenses. The item of expenditure that is spent the least is on health.

Thus, the objective of this research is to identify types of personal expenses in households located in Culiacán, Sinaloa, Mexico as of July 15, 2020.

19.2 Literature Review

Finance is defined as the art and science of managing scarce financial resources, by individuals or legal entities with the objective of making decisions about income generation and application of cash expenses; and the percentage of expenses with respect to their income, the percentage of savings, and investment, framed these in the principle of maximization of wealth. Likewise, the purpose of personal finances is to achieve the well-being of the individual and for companies, it is the generation of profits, how they are applied in the same business or if they are distributed among the partners. Finance management is mainly directed to the analysis and control of cash flows, considering the inflows and outflows of money, to generate solvency and face credit obligations and acquire assets to meet established goals.

The purpose of personal finances is to analyze weekly, biweekly, or monthly consumption habits that allow establishing an action plan on these habits according to the priorities that are been set up. This is achieved with a "budget that determines how much you have and how much you can spend and save while maintaining balance" [21, p. 7]. Personal finances are also known as family finances, that is, it deals with the way in which money is earned to acquire their assets, how they save and interact in the financial system. The purpose is to support families to achieve financial security, some contextual issues are financial education, ability, and well-being [7]. For Chiodi [5] in 2020, he asserts that what can be more controlled in personal finances are the outflows of money or expenses, compared to the inflows of cash. He recommends that each spending decision be taken long enough to evaluate.

An analysis of the state of the art on personal finance was carried out by López-García in 2016. The main finding was that the most relevant topic is the budget, this is the basis of adequate personal financial management. This tool makes it possible to determine the financial situation at each time, plan and manage the strategies to achieve compliance, and define the control and evaluation mechanisms.

It is worth mentioning that Figueroa-Delgado [9] also proposes that a budget be made of all income and monthly expenses, so as not to spend more than necessary. First, it is necessary to identify where the income comes from and what it is spent on. Usually, the income in a family is wages, pension or retirement payments, interest or dividends, and others. Expenses can be fixed or variable expenses. The former can be rent, mortgage, taxes, insurance, childcare, elderly care, car payments, loans. Variable expenses for example are savings, utilities, food, transportation, gasoline, car maintenance, education, personal expenses, and entertainment (p. 137).

Likewise, personal financial planning for Rojas-López et al. [22], deals with a dynamic process of activities oriented to action plans to satisfy the currently and future needs of the individual. Its components are asset and investment management, indebtedness, cash income and expenses, commodities and cash management, risk management and insurance, tax and retirement, and succession. The budget consists of listing the income and expenses in a period, allowing to have control of expenses, identify potential problems before their occurrence and that they become unmanageable, adequately plan the future, and thus be able to achieve personal goals of short, medium, and long term. All this is achieved with a budget of expenses lower than income and a rational management of debts, which allows to live with greater flexibility and peace of mind. Although savings are not really an expense, they play a central role in budgeting [11].

A key aspect is to have control of expenses, which can be divided into mandatory and unnecessary. The first corresponds to those necessary to be able to lead a normal life, among which are the payment of the house (mortgage or rent), food, public services, transport, social security, and cleaning supplies. The latter are related to whims and cravings, which, although we should not completely avoid them if it is necessary to have control over them, cited by Villada et al. [23, p. 44]. Thus, the financial statement on cash flow is another that can be applied in personal finance. A cash flow is the variation and cash equivalent, which results in the changes between increases and decreases in operating, investment, and financing activities [8, p. 74]. It should be noted that this cash flow applied in organizations can be transferred to a family, for example, the variations are the increases and decreases of investments or assets such as houses, land, cars, as well as financing or debts acquired for these investments.

In relation to operational activities, they are weekly, biweekly, or monthly expenses in relation to food, clothing, security, gasoline, water services, electricity, telephone, among others. Some other relevant personal finance topics according to Zapata-Lambraño [24] are, first of all, thinking about personal goals that involve the management of financial resources, defining savings objectives, not falling into misleading or flashy offers, education and financial advice are essential, when making a financial decision think it over carefully, keep the money in a safe place until you know what will be done, future forecasts, do not make emotional panic purchases, define goals and meet them, do not be influenced by anyone outside on financial decisions, manage the cash on a budget, don't lend money, don't buy brands, and take responsibility for all financial decisions.

The topic of personal finance is underdeveloped in academia and therefore in scientific research. However, there are a variety of blogs and applications that can be useful when making decisions, among them, for example, they are published in CONDUSEF (National Council of Users of financial services) in the case of Mexico. Likewise, an investigation was carried out by Hoffmann and Otteby [13], in 2017, who found that the use of blogs could be a positive alternative to financial education for advice on personal finances and efficient decision-making.

Finally, it should be mentioned that in relation to how to make decisions in pandemic contexts such as the current one, Amat [2], affirms in his work that the measures when in a crisis, is to rescue people, companies, and sectors most affected and vulnerable, recognize the strengths of the staff and above all efficiently manage the cash flow and profit margin; This has an impact on economic reactivation and job creation.

19.3 Materials and Methods

The study presented is exploratory, on how they decided on their personal finances in this context of the COVID-19 pandemic. A survey was applied using Google forms, shared through social networks with the contacts of the person in charge of this study, and it was addressed to heads of household from June 29 to July 15, 2020. The instrument consisted of 48 research variables that were related to some elements of personal finances assumed as family expenses. It is presented in Table 19.1 the questions that were applied with the number of the respective variable.

The survey items compiled an exploratory study on personal finance elements exposed by Figueroa-Delgado in 2009, who classifies a matrix of expenses as urgent, which can be important and not important; as well as non-urgent, in the same way, important and not important. It should be mentioned that items with non-urgent and non-important aspects of expenses were not made, which are, for example: expensive clothes, expensive housing, luxurious cars, since it was not considered relevant to know if the respondents made these types of expenses in this lockdown. Now, based on some of these expenses raised by the cited author, some variables and their respective items are observed (Table 19.2). These were presented with frequency tables in the results section.

On the size of the sample, the total of the statistical sample was calculated based on the total of households in the city of Culiacán, Sinaloa, Mexico, being $N = 244{,}754$ to solve the statistical formula in the Decision Analyst STATS 2.0 software. The total of the statistical sample is of 384 households (Fig. 19.1).

The reliability of the instrument was calculated using Cronbach's Alpha, in SPSS 24.0. 488 surveys were processed. The result was 0.676, (see Table 19.3), this result is considered as a moderate evaluation attitude, according to Robinson et al. [20]. Likewise, Hair et al. [12], consider that a Cronbach's alpha "can drop to 0.6 in exploratory research" (pp. 105–106), which justifies the alpha 0.676, since this research is exploratory.

19.4 Results

The way of making decisions about personal finances is framed on the principle of doing more with less, under this gaze the scarce resources in a home or in an organization are managed. It is observed from Table 19.4 that 67.8% of the respondents

Table 19.1 Variables and items of the survey

V	Items	V	Ítems
	Sex	v24	Have you paid your car insurance in a timely manner?
	Age	v25	Do you think the government is doing what is necessary to face this health crisis?
v1	Do you budget for expenses in your home?	v26	During confinement at home, did you, or your spouse, require medical services?
v2	Is the expense budget according to your income?	v27	Have you had the need to contract a new loan in a banking institution?
v3	Do you think you spend more than you earn per month?	v28	Have you had the need to take out a new loan at a pawn shop?
v4	Do you maintain or keep a fund of money for household expenses contingencies?	v29	Have you bought any computers or accessories during home confinement?
v5	After this confinement experience, do you think that from now on you would consider saving money for a contingency fund?	v30	Have you bought any cell phones or accessories during home confinement?
v6	Do you have a retirement and retirement savings fund?	v31	Did you buy medicines as a reserve during the quarantine?
v7	Have you reduced your personal care expenses?	v32	Did you buy food as a reserve during the quarantine?
v8	Have you increased cleaning and hygiene expenses at home?	v33	Have you paid for your water, electricity, and gas services, in a timely manner during the quarantine?
v9	Have you ever needed to use your bank credit card more often?	v34	Have you paid for television, landline, and cell phone services, in a timely manner during the quarantine?
v10	Have you bought non-essential products recently?	v35	Have you taken advantage of vacation package deals to travel soon?
v11	Do your children study in private schools or colleges?	v36	Have you purchased non-essential products and/or services online?
v12	Have you complied with the tuition payment in a timely manner during confinement?	v37	Do you work from home?
v13	Do you currently pay a credit for the purchase of a car for personal use?	v38	How often do you buy food at restaurants?
v14	If the previous question is yes, have you been behind in payments?	v39	Do you usually buy your food at the supermarket?
v15	Have you been busy delaying the maintenance service for your car due to lack of money during this period of confinement?	v40	What time do you go to the supermarket?

(continued)

Table 19.1 (continued)

V	Items	V	Ítems
v16	Have you negotiated with the banking institutions about any grace period support to pay your credit cards or commercial loans?	v41	What day of the week do you go to the supermarket?
v17	Have you covered the monthly payments of your credits in a timely manner?	v42	Do you make the purchase in the supermarket by attending a list of necessary items at home that you previously make? That is, do you carry your shopping list?
v18	The house where you live is: own, rented, or loaned?	v43	According to your buying habits, how do you make your decisions?
v19	Do you pay a mortgage on your house?	v44	Do you buy all your food at the supermarket (Walmart, Ley, Soriana, others)?
v20	Have you had trouble paying the amount of your mortgage or rent in the last three months?	v45	Do you buy your meat and dairy at local butchers?
v21	Have you purchased any major medical insurance during this stay-at-home period?	v46	Do you buy vegetables and fruits, in greengrocers at the market or in small stores?
v22	Before quarantine, did you have any insurance for major medical expenses?	v47	What kind of medicines have you bought?
v23	Have you paid your insurance for major medical expenses in a timely manner?	V48	Do you consider that your family can save?

Source Prepared by the authors

Table 19.2 Research variables and item number variables items data: sex and age

Variables	Items
Data: sex and age	
General considerations	v1, v2, v3, v25, v37, v42, v48
Important and urgent expenses: Housing, rent or mortgage, utilities, food, tuition, health	v8, v11, v12, v18, v19, v20, v26, v31, v32, v33, v34, v39, v40, v41, v43, v44, v45, v46, v47
Important and non-urgent expenses: Emergency funds, Savings for future situations, Insurance, Retirement, and retirement fund	v4, v5, v6, v21, v22, v23, v24, v35
Unimportant and urgent expenses: excessive expenses in technology, and communications, consumption of credit card, high expenses in personal care, non-essential expense	v7, v9, v10, v13, v14, v15, v16, v17, v27, v28, v29, v30, v36, v38

Source Prepared by the authors, based on Figueroa-Delgado [9]

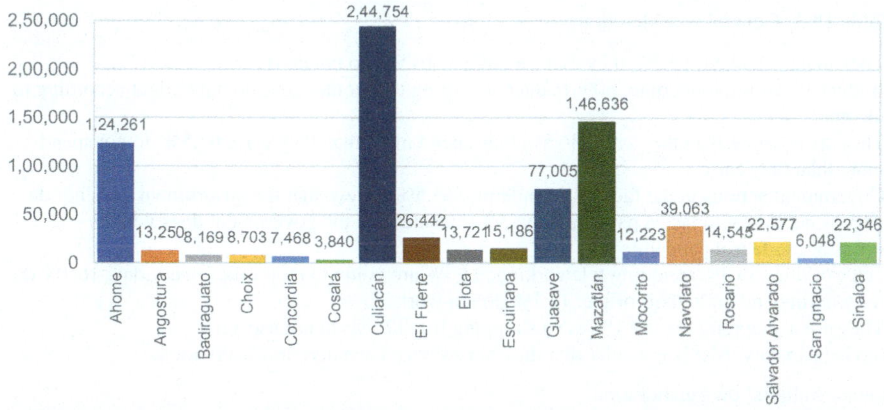

Fig. 19.1 Number of households in the different municipalities of the State of Sinaloa. *Source* INEGI. Tabulated from the Intercensal Survey (2015) retrieved from (https://www.inegi.org.mx/programas/intercensal/2015/default.html)

Table 19.3 Calculation of Cronbach's Alpha (Calculus of Alfa de Cronbach)

Statistics of reliability	
Alfa de Cronbach	Number of elements
0.676	48

Source Authors' own elaboration

are men; the age of those who responded to the form is 34.9% of those between 40 and 50 years old, as well as 30% of those over 50 years of age.

It is observed in Table 19.5 in which the general considerations are grouped that teleworking from home is present in the sample studied since 56.3% are working from home in this context of a pandemic. In relation to the fact that if they consider that the government is doing what is pertinent to address the health contingency, it is observed that 63.5% of those surveyed do not believe that the government will do what is concerned to face it. Likewise, the results of the survey show that 80% make a budget according to their income, 63.5% do not spend more than they earn, 87.1% make a purchase planning through a list and 61.8% can save. There are coincidences with the proposals of Figueroa-Delgado [9], Gitman and Zutter [10], López-García [19] and Rodríguez-Raga [21], who argue about the importance of keeping a budget and planning personal expenses according to income.

Table 19.4 Description of the respondents

	Between 20 and 30 years	Between 30 and 40 years	Between 40 and 50 years	More than 50 years	Male sex	Female sex
Age/sex	13.3%	21.8%	34.9%	30%	67.8%	32.2%

Source Prepared by the authors

Table 19.5 General considerations

They make a budget: 83.5% they make a budget; 16.5% do not do it
Budget according to income: 80% budget according to income; 20% do not budget according to income
They spend more than they earn: 36.5% they spend more than they earn; 63.5% do not spend more than they earn
Government actions in the face of a pandemic: 63.5% believe that the government does not do what is necessary to face a pandemic; 36.5% consider that the government does what is necessary to face a pandemic
Teleworking: 56.3% are doing teleworking; 13.5% are going to their office every day; 16.1% do teleworking and go to their office; 14.1% do not work
They use a shopping list: 87.1% use a shopping list; 12.9% do not use a list
Saving capacity: 61.8% consider that they have saving capacity; 38.2% do not have

Source Authors' own elaboration

Important and urgent personal expenses are rent or housing fees; public services, administration; market, schools, health, and gasoline (Figueroa-Delgado, 2009, p. 138). In this exploratory study, some questions were applied in the survey to learn about this type of expenditure in households located in Culiacán, Sinaloa, Mexico. As can be seen in Table 19.6, 83.5% of household spending decision-makers have their own house, have paid the public water, electricity, and gas services on time, and have covered the payment of telephone and television, cleaning and hygiene expenses have also increased. In this context of a pandemic, it is shown that only 7.8% of those surveyed have made purchases via the internet.

The food shopping preference is also 71.2% made in butchers and 74.5% in local greengrocers. Only 21.8% buy the cheapest; 64.7% did buy reserve food during the analyzed period. In addition, 9.4% have had problems with paying tuition; Lastly, 46.5% have bought a reserve of medicines and 73.9% did not require medical services.

The important and non-urgent expenses in the classification matrix of expenses exposed by Figueroa-Delgado, (2009), are: "pension savings, basis for home purchase, emergency fund, automobile savings, insurance, leisure savings and others (holidays) and taxes" (p.138).

It is observed from Table 19.7 that the respondents affirm in relation to this type of expenses in this pandemic context, that 55.3% have a contingency fund, and 93.5% would consider having one in the future. However, 93.5% of the respondents did not consider it urgent to have insurance for major medical expenses during the analysis period. Finally, 96.5% have not been interested in taking advantage of offers to travel in the future.

Finally, in this analysis of frequencies of the applied Google form, according to the classification matrix of non-important and urgent expenses, such as excessive expenses in technology and communications, credit card consumption, high expenses in personal care [9, p. 138], Table 19.8 shows that, regarding personal care expenses, 71.2% have decreased this type of expenses during this pandemic context. Regarding that, if they have borrowed more in this time with the use of credit cards, it is observed

Table 19.6 Important and urgent expenses

Housing, rent or mortgage
Increase in cleaning and hygiene expenses: 83.5% has increased; 16.5% has not increased
Own house, rented or loaned: 83.5% have their own house; 10.2% rented 6.3%; house loaned
Pay a mortgage: 32.4% pay a mortgage 46.3%; do not pay a mortgage; 21.4% does not apply
Public services
Paid on time for water, electricity, and gas: 88.6% did pay on time; 11.4% did not pay on time
Paid on time for television, landline, and cell phone: 84.5% did pay; 15.5% did not pay
Food
Bought reserve food: 64.7% did buy; 35.3% did not buy
Shopping at the supermarket: 77.1% go to the supermarket; 7.8% asked for it online; 13.3% go directly and ask for it online; 1.8% I do not go to the supermarket
Time that goes to the supermarket; 52.2% during the morning; 14.9% noon; 32.9% from 4 in the afternoon onwards
Day to go to the supermarket: 18% from Monday to Wednesday; 5.7% Thursday to Friday; 19.8% Saturday and Sunday; 50.4% don't have a day to go; 6.1% always ask at home
Shopping habits: 21.8% buy the cheapest; 19.4% buy quality regardless of price; 17.6% buy brands 46.1% all the above
You buy everything in the supermarket: 30.4% yes, they buy everything in the supermarket; 54.7% almost everything; 14.9% do not buy everything in the supermarket
Purchases in butchers: 71.2% do buy in butchers; 28.8% do not buy in butchers
Purchases in greengrocers: 74.5% do buy in greengrocers 25.5%; do not buy in greengrocers
Tuition
Your children study in schools: 31.8% yes; 47.3% no; 21% does not apply
Complied with the tuition payment: 34.7% yes; 9.4% no; 55.9% does not apply
Health
Required medical services: 9.4% in public hospitals; 13.5% in private hospitals; 3.1% both; 73.9% did not require medical services
Bought medicines by reserve: 46.5% did buy reserve medicine; 53.5% did not buy
Types of medicines bought: 13.3% patent; 20.2% generic; 47.5% the previous two; 19% have not bought medicines

Source Prepared by the authors

Table 19.7 Important and non-urgent expenses

Emergency funds
Accounts with a contingency fund: 55.3% yes; 44.7% do not have a contingency fund
Would you consider a contingency fund in the future? 93.5% yes; 6.5% no
Savings for future situations
You have taken advantage of offers to travel in the future: 3.5% yes; 96.5%; have not taken advantage
Insurance
Have you purchased major medical insurance? 6.5% yes; 93.5% no
You already had insurance for major medical expenses: 24.5% yes; 75.5% no
You have paid the medical expenses insurance on time: 25.7% yes; 8% no; 66.3% does not apply

Source Prepared by the authors

Table 19.8 Unimportant and urgent expenses

Excessive spending on technology and communications
You pay credit for car: 28.4% yes; 71.6% no; If yes, have you fallen behind in credit: 8.2% yes; 26.3% no; 65.5% does not apply
You have delayed car maintenance: 25.9% yes; 50.8% no; 23.3% does not apply
Have you bought a computer or accessories? 19.8% yes; 80.2% no
Have you bought a cell phone or accessories: 19.4% yes; 80.6% no
Credit card consumption
Have you used your card more during this pandemic? 37.6% yes; 62.4% no
You requested a grace period for your credits: 19% yes; 58% no; 22.9% does not apply
You have paid your credit on time: 59.6% yes; 17.8% no; 22.5% does not apply
You have had problems in the payment of the mortgage in this confinement: 10.2% yes; 41.8% no; 48% does not apply
You have needed new credit: 7.1%; 92.9% no
You have taken out credit at a pawn shop: 5.7% yes; 94.3% no
Have you reduced your personal care expenses? 71.2% yes; 28.8% no
Non-essential expenses
You have bought non-essential products 37.1% yes; 62.4% no
You have purchased non-essential products online 20.8% yes by Amazon; 21.8% by Mercado Libre; 0.2% yes by eBay; 14.9% yes through the company's website; 59.8% no
Frequency of purchase in restaurants
1% daily; 8.2% no more than 3 times a week; 26.3% only on weekends; 7.5% every fortnight; 44.1% occasionally; 12.9% did not buy

Source Prepared by the authors

that 62.4% have not done so. They have not required 58% to request a grace period to pay their debts, nor have they had 59.6% problems paying their credit on time. Similarly, 92.9% have not needed new loans either in banks or 94.3% in pawn shops.

The people who keep control of family expenses in the surveyed households, 62.4% have not bought non-essential products, neither have 59.8% of those consulted via the internet. Similarly, the frequency of buying food in restaurants is occasionally 44.1%.

19.5 Discussion

The methodology used was exploratory, to identify the types of personal expenses in the homes located in Culiacán Rosales, Sinaloa, Mexico as of July 15, 2020, from the theory of personal finance; For this, 488 surveys were applied electronically through Google form shared on social networks, the research instrument consisted of 48 items applied to the heads of the family as of June 29. Derived from the context of the pandemic, the surveyed families have directed their personal expenses, increasing products for cleaning and hygiene in the home, reducing personal care expenses and purchases of non-essential products, as well as the acquisition of food for reservation. They also develop budgets and can save.

Important and urgent expenses were covered in the first place according to the classification given by Figueroa-Delgado [9], from mortgage expenses, rent, payment of public services, food, tuition, and health. They agree with the cited author, in relation to the purchase of insurance and contingency funds, most of those surveyed consider them important, but not urgent. But not so important and urgent expenses, since most of the respondents have not considered excessive expenses of technology and communications, credit card consumption, high expenses in personal care, and non-essential expenses, for example, 82.8% have not acquired new cell phones or accessories, have not borrowed more, and 62.4% have not bought non-essential products.

19.6 Conclusions

The people surveyed who oversee making decisions about types of family expenses report that derived from the context of the pandemic, they have now considered having savings for contingency funds. They maintain that they develop budgets to control their finances. There are important coincidences with what was stated by Aguilar [1] and Cardona [4], since they advise those who see their income diminished due to the pandemic, make financial plans, and prioritize expenses on food, prescription drugs, transportation to move food and medicines, try to save, not go into debt, and negotiate with credit institutions in case of debt. Spend in a measured way and only what is mandatory. For those who do not have a change in their income, that is, who receive their salaries regardless of the situation, they recommend not suspending their obligations, likewise, creating and strengthening their emergency fund.

Some research affirms that digital life begins in this context COVID-19 and that it will come to stay, however, in the families analyzed they still do not make digital purchases to a greater extent. Finally, it is worth mentioning that some future research is aimed at improving the design of the applied research instrument, for which it is recommended to calculate the factor analysis and reduce factors or items. Likewise, include data on professional profiles and levels of financial education in the information collection, since López-Salido [18] observes that 63% of the Americans surveyed with a university level have done work from home and have been less affected in their finances personal in the current context. Another future topic is to carry out an analysis of the importance and urgency of certain expenses such as insurance for major medical expenses in times of uncertainty. Finally, develop the financial education line to identify investment alternatives for family savings [3].

References

1. Aguilar Pacas G (2020) Finanzas en familia y Coronavirus (COVID-19). Realidad Empresarial 9:51. https://doi.org/10.5377/reuca.v0i9.10070

2. Amat O (2020) La botella medio llena. Profit Editorial, España
3. Banxico (2020) Encuesta sobre las expectativas de los especialistas en economía del sector privado. Recuperado de https://www.banxico.org.mx/publicaciones-y-prensa/encuestas-sobre-las-expectativas-de-los-especialis/encuestas-expectativas-del-se.html
4. Cardona JF (2020) Finanzas personales. Recuperado de https://www.youtube.com/watch?v=Jddhe_15OIQ
5. Chiodi A (2020) Compás financiero personal. Descubre las finanzas desde lo básico e intuitivo hasta su sorprendente lado humano y pon los números a tu favor. Edición Kindle
6. CONDUSEF, Conduguía, Finanzas Personales. Recuperado de https://www.condusef.gob.mx/documentos/299734_Conduguia_finanzas_personales_y_familiares2018.pdf
7. Dew JP (2016) Family finances. In: Shehan CL (ed) Encyclopedia of family studies. https://doi.org/10.1002/9781119085621.wbefs038
8. Duque Sánchez A (2015) Estado de flujos de efectivo: aplicación de razonamientos algebraicos y de la NIC 7. Cuadernos De Contabilidad, 16(40). https://doi.org/10.11144/Javeriana.cc16-40.efea
9. Figueroa Delgado LO (2009) Las finanzas personales. Revista EAN. Núm.65, pp 123–144
10. Gitman LJ, Zutter C (2016) Principios de administración financiera (décimo cuarta edición. ed). Pearson, México
11. Guthrie CP, Nicholls CM (2015) The personal budget project: a practical introduction to financial literacy. J Acc Educ Elsevier 33(2):138–163
12. Hair JF, Anderson RF, Tatham RL, Black WC (2008) Análisis Multivariante. Editorial Pearson Prentice Hall, España
13. Hoffmann A, Otteby K (2017) Personal finance blogs: helpful tool for consumers with low financial literacy or preaching to the choir? Int J Consum Stud 42(2):241–254. https://doi.org/10.1111/ijcs.12412
14. NIEGH (2018) Encuesta Nacional de Ingresos y Gastos en los Hogares. Recuperado de https://www.inegi.org.mx/contenidos/programas/NIEGH/nc/2018/doc/NIEGH2018_ns_presentacion_resultados.pdf
15. INEGI (2020) Estimación oportuna del PIB trimestral. Recuperado de https://www.inegi.org.mx/temas/pibo/
16. INEGI (2020) México en cifras. Recuperado de https://www.inegi.org.mx/app/areasgeograficas/
17. INEGI (2020) Sistema de Cuentas Nacionales de México. Recuperado de https://www.inegi.org.mx/temas/itaee/
18. López Salido D (2020) Tribuna invitada. Confinamiento, mercado laboral y finanzas familiares. En Felgueroso F, De la Fuente A, Boscá JE, Doménech R, Ferri J, Rodríguez D, Costa i Font J, García Pérez JI, Jiménez S, Viola A, Federación de Estudios de Economía Aplicada. Aspectos económicos de la crisis del COVID-19: Boletín de seguimiento no. 2. FEDEA, España, pp 4–8
19. López García JC (2016) Las finanzas personales, un concepto que va más allá de su estructura. Estado del arte periodo 2006–2016 en Pereira, EAFIT. Tesis Digitales. Universidad EAFTI Facultad de Ciencias Administrativas, Programa de Maestría en Administración, MBA. Disponible en https://repository.eafit.edu.co/bitstream/handle/10784/11784/LopezGarcia_JuanCarlos_2017.pdf?sequence=2
20. Robinson JP, Shaver PR, Wrightsman LS (1991) Criteria for scale selection and evaluation. In: Measures of personality and social psychological attitudes, p 13
21. Rodríguez-Raga S (2017) Finanzas personales, su mejor plan de vida. Universidad de los Andes, Facultad de Administración: Ediciones Uniandes, Bogotá
22. Rojas-López MD, Maya-Fernández LM, Valencia ME (2017) Definición de un modelo para la planeación financiera personal aplicado al caso colombiano. Revista Ingenierías Universidad de Medellín 16(31):155–171. https://doi.org/10.22395/rium.v16n31a8

23. Villada F, López-Lezama JM, Muñoz-Galeano N (2018) Análisis de la Relación entre Rentabilidad y Riesgo en la Planeación de las Finanzas Personales. Formación universitaria 11(6):41–52.https://doi.org/10.4067/S0718-50062018000600041
24. Zapata Lambraño GC (2020) Manual de finanzas personales. Tesis Digitales. Universidad Cooperativa de Colombia Facultad de Ciencias Económicas, Administrativas y afines programa administración de empresas. Medellín. Disponible en http://hdl.handle.net/20.500.12494/18393

Chapter 20
Different Socioeconomic Groups' Psychological Reactions to the COVID-19 Lockdown: A Cross-Sectional Study

Ananya Jyoti Gogoi, Ujjal Protim Dutta, and Chandana Sarmah

20.1 Introduction

It has been over 3 years since COVID-19 (2019-nCoV) was announced as a public health emergency of international concern (PHEIC) by the WHO. COVID-19, which had first emerged as a group of mysterious pneumonia cases in Wuhan, Hubei Province, China had brought the entire world to a sudden standstill [31, 59]. It had affected various regions throughout the world including the US, UK, India, Brazil, and Europe [25]. To limit the spread of the disease people were initially required to quarantine themselves when exposed [25]. Lockdown, a type of non-pharmacological intervention (NPI's) for social/physical distancing was implemented to prevent the spread of disease from one person to another [10]. Based on studies, it was indicated that lockdown, in combination with various other measures including the closure of educational institutes, restrictions on travel, and social/physical distancing could reduce the spread of infection and thus in turn reduce mortality [37].

Lockdown, though helpful in the confinement of infection, results in disruption in the daily lives of the people and thus has an unintended psychological impact. Implementation of social/physical distancing measures that are unproportionate could lead to the failure to meet the public health outcome of the population which might in turn lead to severe outcomes related to psychological well-being [1]. Psychological distress arising from lockdown may trigger feelings of depression and anxiety. Such psychological distress may present itself differently among different sections of society. The negative impact of COVID-19 and lockdown on emotional/psychological health have been found in several studies [1]. The director

A. J. Gogoi · C. Sarmah
Department of Anthropology, Gauhati University, Guwahati, Assam, India

U. P. Dutta (✉)
Department of Economics, Rangia College, Rangia, Assam, India
e-mail: ujjaldtt06@gmail.com

R. Bhattacharyya et al. (eds.), *COVID-19 Pandemic and Global Inequality*,
https://doi.org/10.1007/978-981-99-4405-7_20

general of WHO emphasized striking a balance between the protection of health, and minimization of economic and social disruption while respecting human rights [55]. Significant differences have been found in the psychological outcome of COVID-19 and the subsequent social/physical distancing measures among different sections of the population [46].

20.2 Objective

The present study tries to examine the Phycological responses of various socioeconomic groups to the COVID-19 Lockdown. To meet this objective, the chapter is structured as follows. The review of the literature is in Sect. 20.3. Information about the data collecting and analysis technique is provided in Sect. 20.4. The results of the analysis are shown in Sect. 20.5. The study's conclusions and policy recommendations are presented in Sect. 20.6.

20.3 Literature Review

20.3.1 Gender Disparity in the Psychological Impact of COVID-19 Lockdown

Although both men and women are affected equally by the COVID-19 pandemic, numerous studies have revealed that it had a distinctive impact on women, especially on their psychological well-being. A person's response to stress is found to differ based on gender; females due to several biological determinants are found to be more prone to psychological issues including anxiety and depressive disorders [52]. It has been reported that hormones and biological makeup have a role in determining the susceptibility to mental health issues including anxiety and depressive disorders which are found to be higher among females [15].

Retrospective Health Impact Assessment suggests that lockdown policies have generated inequities that have led to psychological distress, especially among women [5]. Restrictive measures taken to curb the spread of infection have led to an increase in the incidence of Gender Based Violence (GBV) [17]. It was predicted by the United Nations Population Fund (UNPF) that GBV would increase at the rate of 15 million new cases with every three-month extension of lockdown [4]. Access to social support for women, both formal as well as informal was disrupted because of the ongoing restrictive measures [17]. In one of the progress reports during COVID-19 president of South Africa stated that every three hours one woman in South Africa lost her life to GBV [19].

In a study conducted among the general population of Poland, most of the population was found to suffer from various symptoms of psychological disorders [36]. It has been reported that COVID-19 had increased the existing social and gender inequalities and women were found to be at a greater risk of intimate partner violence due to various stay-at-home measures [56]. Even though different forms of Intimate Partner Violence (IPV) were present even before lockdown, implementation of lockdown has increased in the severity and forms of such violence which included physical, psychological, economic as well as sexual violence [17]. Reports of IPV included threats of eviction from home, disruption of financial independence, or disputes regarding custody of children [17]. Most of the cases reported during the lockdown period were new cases of IPV [16].

In addition to this, women's access to health services especially those related to reproductive health was likely impacted due to the various restrictive measures [11]. Pregnant women throughout the world reported various psychological issues including stress and anxiety [41]. Pregnant women had to face various problems including exposure to the virus specially during checkup which was mandatory during pregnancy and fear of poisoning due to overuse of various sanitizing agents [41]. It has been recommended that in places where possible, provision of home birth services be provided to maintain the wellbeing of the mother and the newborn child [41].

20.3.2 Age Disparity in the Psychological Impact of COVID-19 Lockdown

20.3.2.1 Old-Aged Population

During the initial outbreak of the disease people who were older and had pre-existing diseases were declared to be at a greater risk. Thus, these were designated as a vulnerable group. Special measures need to be taken to protect these sections of society from both physical and psychological issues [56]. In a study conducted in China, 23.6% of the elderly population was found to suffer from various symptoms of depression. The impact of COVID-19 and the lockdown on the daily activities of these people might further worsen their symptoms [30]. Access to proper mental health care is one of the most important challenges faced by elderly individuals, especially during the lockdown. With the suspension of the public transportation system during the lockdown, distance mental health support was initiated [32]. However, as this section of the population had limited access or was not well-versed in modern technology, access to psychological care was difficult [30]. During the Severe Acute Respiratory Syndrome (SARS) outbreak in 2003 suicide rates among the elderly were found to increase [7]. Thus, psychological support, especially for vulnerable population groups is just as important as taking steps to curb the spread of disease during a pandemic.

Access to health care and essential services among the aged population was also affected by their economic vulnerability [35]. It has been reported that due to physical distancing measures, older individuals were found to be predisposed to various other disorders including CVD, neurocognitive and autoimmune diseases [25]. ITC has been found to play a positive role in helping older adults keep in touch with their loved ones thus helping them cope with loneliness and maintain their psychological well-being [3].

20.3.2.2 Young Children and Students

The pandemic and consequent lockdown also had an impact on the emotional well-being and development of young children. Children due to their economic vulnerability depend on their guardians for support [45]. Among children during COVID-19 lockdown has resulted in some psychological issues including clinginess, lack of attention, irritability, etc. [24]. Clinginess and a sense of fear were found to be more among young children of the age group 3–6 years old compared to children of the age group 6–18 years old [44]. Sleep disturbance and nightmares, changes in appetite, separation anxiety, and lack of attention were some of the issues found to be prevalent among children of all age groups [24].

The temporary shutdown of educational institutes had a detrimental impact on children's education as well as physical health which in turn had an impact on the mothers' mental health [48]. Over 1.5 billion young students' education was negatively impacted [28]. The socioeconomic gap concerning education attainment was found to increase with the introduction of online/remote learning where children from low socioeconomic status were negatively impacted [22].

Another vulnerable group among young children is the ones with special education needs who were found to be at high risk [28]. Parents are advised to create a routine to help such children deal with issues such as anxiety stemming from uncertainty [28]. Also, among children with preexisting psychological issues, daily routines in school help in coping and structuring their behavior [28]. Among children with previous mental health issues, such restrictive measures were especially detrimental as they led to the worsening of their condition and decreased access to proper support [28]. For children suffering from symptoms of depression, school routines play a big role in helping them go through their day-to-day activities. With the closure of the school, such routine got disrupted which has led to the relapsing of some of their symptoms [28]. Economic distress caused due to COVID-19 has also increased the incidence of abuse among children [28]. In a study conducted in the Hubei province of China, reports of domestic violence have been found to increase threefold during the lockdown [28].

20.3.3 The Occupational Disparity in the Psychological Impact of COVID-19 Lockdown

During the peak, COVID-19 outbreak, healthcare workers were the first to get exposed at the front line [13]. Exposed to situations with a high risk of infection, inadequate protection from contamination in addition to other stressors including overwork, workplace insecurity, and discrimination were found to put healthcare workers under tremendous pressure [26]. In addition to the increased workload and risk of infection associated with it, scarcity of resources also posed a major issue. Healthcare workers had to make difficult discissions regarding the allocation of resources and treatment plans. As the interaction of healthcare workers with the patients was done mostly in PPE, a communication gap was created which further hindered the situation [8]. Studies have revealed that doctors and nurses suffered from higher levels of various mental health issues including depression, anxiety, and insomnia compared to non-medical healthcare workers [20, 58].

Another section of the population that was severely impacted by the initial spread of COVID-19 and the consequent lockdown was the migrant workers. In March 2020, when a complete lockdown was imposed in India, workers who had migrated to different parts of the country from their native states had to face great difficulty. Such workers usually live together in shared shelters. During major socio-economic disruptions such as COVID-19 this section of society has to face major psychological stress due to livelihood uncertainty, restriction in movement and separation from family, discrimination, etc. [2].

20.3.4 The Socio-economic Disparity in the Psychological Impact of COVID-19 Lockdown

Studies have suggested that there is an undeniable link between socioeconomic factors and psychological well-being where lower socioeconomic status was found to harm mental health. Low education level, low-income level, and unemployment were found to be associated with an increase in the prevalence of various psychological issues including depression, anxiety, stress, and PTSD [42, 54, 57].

Quality of sleep is an important factor affecting physical as well as mental health. In a study conducted in Wuhan, China individuals with a lower education level were found to be suffering from sleep disorders [18]. Lack of adequate information (especially among individuals with a lower level of education) about the disease and its mode of transmission led to a sense of worry which could in turn harm sleep [18]. The way of coping in adverse situations is influenced by a person's education level. An individual's ability to comply with the various COVID-19 protocols and a general understanding of the situation is positively associated with his/her education. Thus during COVID-19, individuals with higher education levels could develop a better-coping mechanism and also reach out for support if/when needed [18].

Lower socioeconomic status is linked with poorer health [23]. Unstable income and financial instability were found to be major stressors. Individuals' sense of well-being along with life satisfaction was found to be affected directly by a reduction in income [47]. As individuals from lower socio-economic status generally have lower savings, disruption in their source of income could lead to food insecurity [23]. Participants of the lower-than-average income group were found to suffer from poor mental health [21, 29, 34, 38]. On the other hand, stable family income was found to be associated with better emotional well-being [6].

Among the homeless population, restrictive measures could harm their mental health. Most of the people belonging to this vulnerable group live in settings that are easy ground for virus transmission and have limited access to healthcare. Also, some of the restrictive measures taken up for the general population might not be feasible for this group of vulnerable population due to their living setting. Prevalence of various chronic mental health illnesses as well as substance use issues are found to be higher among them. Thus during COVID-19, their exposure to the virus could result in a negative impact on their physical as well as mental health [27, 50]. Provision of proper health care and shelter to a such vulnerable population while taking into consideration their rights, especially during such times must be addressed [27, 53].

20.3.5 The Role of Government

Various interventions for mental health issues have been in use even before the outbreak of COVID-19. This includes mental health programs such as Mental Health Gap Action Program, which is promoted by the World Health Organization (WHO) [39]. This program works for the promotion of mental health and the prevention of various mental health issues. Interventions such as training for relaxation, ICT-based intervention strategy, and guided crisis help were found to be significantly effective in improving mental health problems [12]. The Ministry of Health and Family Welfare, Government of India has also issued several guidelines for mental health care [33]. A toll-free helpline number was issued by the MOHFW-GOI for "Behavioural Health." Various resources for coping strategies for mental health issues during the pandemic were also put up [33].

MANAS (Multilingual Mental Health and Normalcy Augmentation System Application) was endorsed by PM-STIAC (Prime Minister's Science, Technology, and Innovation Advisory Council) for the promotion of the well-being of the population within the age group 15–35 years [9].

However, the COVID-19 outbreak has highlighted the gap in the reach of various mental health services and the general population. Thus, more such action-oriented models fully integrating the various mental health issues addressed specifically to various at-risk population groups must be put into action. Different health professionals, community-level health workers, teachers, policymakers, and managers of various workplaces, NGOs, etc. must work together to counter this issue that has now taken the form of a hidden pandemic. Efforts must be made for the development of new infrastructure for institutions for mental healing while continuing to expand the existing ones [43]. As Rangaswamy et al. has pointed out, the health sector must be paid utmost attention, and having a strong public health sector both at the primary care and district level is very important. Also, attention must be given to the proper funding of the public healthcare system which as Rangaswamy et al. has rightly pointed out is "chronically underfunded" [40].

20.4 Materials and Methods

20.4.1 Data

The study conducted a cross-sectional survey by using an anonymous online questionnaire for the collection of data. It has chosen residents of Assam who are 19 years of age or older and have lived there during the lockdown period (Reviewer's comment 2). Exponential Non-Discriminative snowball sampling, which is a type of non-probability sampling method was used for the recruitment of participants. Through this method, a sample is acquired by encouraging participants to recruit additional participants. Thus, each participant recruits additional multiple participants. Google Forms was used to create the survey, and Facebook Messenger and WhatsApp conversation were used to distribute it. The survey's willing participants were urged to spread the word about it. There were 480 total responses to the questionnaires. 437 legitimate replies in all were examined. 91.04% of responses were considered valid. The IAEC at Gauhati University gave its approval to the study (Ref: IAEC/Per/2020-20/PP-IAEC/2020-20/55).

The questionnaire used included three main sections. (1) Demographic data. (2) Mental health status. (3) Perception of the lockdown and daily activities during this period. Everyone who participated provided their informed consent. Demographic information included gender, age, education, occupation, the total number of residents, residential location, and monthly family income. The Depression, Anxiety, and Stress Scale (DASS-21) was used to evaluate mental health status. It is a reliable and valid tool for evaluating the mental health of a population.

20.4.2 Methods

The present chapter has employed logistic regression model to examine the relationship between COVID-19 lockdown and its psychological impact among different socio-economic groups in Assam.

The model employed in this chapter is specified as

$$P_i = P(Y_i = 1) = F(Z_i) = \frac{1}{1 + e^{-Z_i}} \quad (20.1)$$

where,

P_i is the probability of Y_i=1,

$F(Z_i)$ is the CDF of the cumulative logistic function,

$Z_i = \alpha + \beta X_i$ is a predictor variable.

Now,

$$1 - P_i = \frac{1}{1 + e^{-Z_i}} [\text{since} P_i + (1 - P_i) = 1]$$

and

$$\frac{P_i}{1 - P_i} = \frac{1 + e^{Z_i}}{1 + e^{-Z_i}} = e^{Z_i}$$

So,

$$ln\left(\frac{P_i}{1 - P_i}\right) = Z_i = \alpha + \beta_1 X_{1i} + \beta_2 X_{2i} + \cdots + \beta_k X_{ki} \quad (20.2)$$

Here $\frac{P_i}{1-P_i}$ is the odds-ratio in favor of the event occurring and $ln\left(\frac{P_i}{1-P_i}\right)$ is the log odds-ratio.

In Eq. (20.2), Z_i is the linear function of a set of explanatory variables.

The marginal effect of change in X_i on P_i can be calculated in the following manner.

$$\frac{dP_i}{dZ_i} = \frac{d}{dZ_i}\left[\frac{1}{1 + e^{-Z_i}}\right] = \frac{e^{-Z_i}}{(1 + e^{-Z_i})^2}$$

After getting the value of $\frac{dP_i}{dZ_i}$ the marginal effect of change in ith predictor variables (X_i) on P_i can be calculated as follows

$$\frac{dP_i}{dZ_i} = \frac{dP_i}{dZ_i} \cdot \frac{dZ_i}{dX_i} = \frac{e^{-\alpha-\beta\overline{X_i}}}{(1 + e^{-\alpha-\beta\overline{X_i}})^2} \cdot \beta_i. \quad (20.3)$$

In the above equation $\frac{dP_i}{dZ_i}$ indicates change in P_i as a result of a 1-point change in X_i.

20.5 Results and Discussion

43 of the 480 survey replies were deemed incorrect because they were submitted by people who were underage, did not reside in Assam, or had mental health conditions that had already been documented. As a result, 437 valid responses with a response rate of 91.04% from 20 Assam districts were included in the study.

According to the survey, light depression affected 11.6% of women and 12.8% of men, moderate depression affected 11.6% of women and 8.2% of men, and severe depression affected 3.3% of women and 2.0% of men. There were 5.8% female and 1% male respondents in the depression subscale's extremely severe group. Similar to this, the anxiety subscale found that 6.2% of females and 4.1% of males fell into the mild category, 11.6% of females and 8.2% of males fell into the moderate category, 3.7% of females and 3.1% of males fell into the severe category, and 4.6% of females and 3.1% of males fell into the extremely severe category. In the light group of the stress subscale, there were 5.4% females and 2% males, 8.3% females and 3.1% males, and 3.7% females and 1% males. Finally, 0.8% female and 0.5% male were in category extremely severe in stress subscale (Table 20.1).

The outcomes of logistic regression were shown in Table 20.2. The calculated coefficients, standard errors, *Z*-statistics, related *p*-values, and 95% confidence interval for the coefficient are all displayed in the output table. The DASS-21 depression and anxiety subscale scores were shown to be substantially correlated with gender and age. To determine the direction of change of the dependent variable, it is crucial to know the signs of the estimated coefficients. The coefficients of gender and age are statistically significant at 5% level of significance. Hence, the likelihood of getting depression increases with age. Access to proper mental health care is one of the most important challenges faced by elderly individuals, especially during the lockdown. According to Liu et al. [32], with the suspension of the public transportation system during the lockdown, distance mental health support was initiated.

We find that model converged very quickly. The log-likelihood (−251.132) can be used in comparisons of nested models. Also, it is noted that the likelihood ratio chi^2 of 20.88 with a *p*-value of 0.03 implies that our model as a whole fit significantly. The output table displays the estimated coefficients, the standard errors, the *Z*-statistics, and associated *p*-value.

The results of the marginal effects of the covariates at mean are shown in Table 20.3. The variable gender among the covariates used in estimating the model has the highest impact on whether a person suffers from depression. Women are more likely to suffer from depression then men. A person's response to stress is found to differ based on gender; females due to several biological determinants are found to be more prone to psychological issues including anxiety and depressive disorders [52]. It has been reported that hormones and biological makeup have a role in determining the susceptibility to mental health issues including anxiety and depressive disorders which are found to be higher among females [15].

Table 20.1 Socio-demographic variables and Mental Health Status of the studied population

		Female		Male	
		Number	%	Number	%
1.1 *Socio-demographic variables*					
Age group	19–25	120	49.8	61	31.1
	26–35	59	24.5	66	33.7
	36–45	18	7.5	26	13.3
	>45	44	18.3	43	21.9
Highest education	Up to class 12	20	8.3	20	10.2
	Graduate	77	32.0	95	48.5
	Post graduate and above	144	59.8	81	41.3
Occupation	Student	93	38.6	33	16.8
	Employed	130	53.9	147	75.0
	Un-employed	18	7.5	16	8.2
Household size	<5	163	67.6	128	65.3
	>5	78	32.4	68	34.7
Monthly family income	<10,000	25	10.4	23	11.7
	11,000–50,000	83	34.4	73	37.2
	51,000–1,00,000	65	27.0	49	25.0
	>1,00,000	68	28.2	51	26.0
1.2 *Mental health status*					
Depression	Normal	163	67.6	149	76.0
	Mild	28	11.6	25	12.8
	Moderate to Extremely Severe	50	20.7	22	11.2
Anxiety	Normal	178	73.9	160	81.6
	Mild	15	6.2	8	4.1
	Moderate to Extremely Severe	48	19.9	28	14.3
Stress	Normal	197	81.7	183	93.4
	Mild	13	5.4	4	2.0
	Moderate to Extremely Severe	31	12.9	9	4.6

Source Authors

20.6 Conclusion

Psychological issues have increased exponentially during the twenty-first century with depression predicted to be the number one leading cause of disease burden globally by the year 2030 [51]. A holistic understanding of the indirect impact of lockdown on various aspects of the life of the population reveals that during public health emergencies such as COVID-19, special attention is needed to be given to vulnerable sections of society.

Table 20.2 Results of logistic regression

Variables	Coefficient	Standard error	Z-statistics	Probability
Gender (women)	0.4289	0.2381	1.80	0.072
Age (26–35)	−1.212	0.2999	−0.40	0.686
Age (36–45)	−0.944	0.4327	−0.22	0.827
Age (46 and above)	−0.8430	0.3935	−2.14	0.032
Education (Graduate)	−0.953	0.3843	−0.25	0.804
Higher education	−0.4440	−0.3986	−1.11	0.265
Occupation (Employed)	−1.487	0.3017	−0.49	0.662
Occupation (Unemployed)	0.1002	0.4168	0.24	0.810
Monthly income (5000–10,000)	−0.5210	0.3566	−1.46	0.144
Monthly income (11,000–50,000)	−0.5491	0.3831	−1.43	0.152
Monthly income 51,000–100,000)	−0.3127	0.3871	−0.81	0.419
Log likelihood	−251.132			
LR-statistics	20.88			

Source Authors own calculations

Table 20.3 Results of Marginal Effect

Variables	dy/dx	Standard error	Z-Statistics	Probability
Gender (Women)	0.0845	0.0461	1.83	0.067
Age (26–35)	−0.0257	0.0636	−0.41	0.685
Age (36–45)	−0.0201	0.0915	−0.22	0.826
Age (46 and above)	−0.1512	0.0653	−2.32	0.021
Education (Graduate)	−0.0207	0.0845	−0.25	0.806
Higher education	−0.0901	0.0854	−1.05	0.292
Occupation (Employed)	−0.0298	0.0611	−0.49	0.626
Occupation (Unemployed)	0.0211	0.0888	0.24	0.812
Monthly income (5000–10,000)	−0.1104	0.0791	−1.40	0.163
Monthly income (11,000–50,000)	−0.1157	0.0834	−1.39	0.165
Monthly income 51,000–100,000)	−0.0689	0.0868	−0.79	0.427

Source Authors own calculations

Taking the situation's relevance into account, this chapter is an attempt to examine the Phycological responses of various socioeconomic groups of Assam to the COVID-19 Lockdown. To fulfill the objective, the study has used a logistic regression model in addition to descriptive statistics. The DASS-21 depression and anxiety subscale scores were shown to be substantially correlated with gender and age. The current study reveals that depression, anxiety, and stress are common among the Assamese community under study. Compared to the results of the 2016 National Mental Health Survey of India, it was found to be quite high. Therefore, effective mental health experts' assistance is required to assist the public in coping with the COVID-19 epidemic and other similar crises.

Care must be taken to make sure that all sections of society have equal access to healthcare services. Special care must also be taken to provide mental health support, especially to vulnerable groups through telecommunication. This can be done by the creation of an intervention and a crisis management model to deal with psychological issues arising during such tough times [49]. Proper screening to identify high-risk groups of psychological comorbidities must be done and an integrated plan targeting such groups must be made which can be put into action during other such public health emergency settings. This can in turn help to find a balance between measures to stop the spread of infection while minimizing indirect harm [14].

References

1. Aymerich-Franch L (2023) COVID-19 lockdown: impact on emotional well-being and relationship to habit and routine modifications. J Leis Res 54(2):180–195. https://doi.org/10.1080/00222216.2022.2136987
2. Babu SA (2023) 5th World congress on disaster management, vol III. Taylor & Francis
3. Bakshi T, Bhattacharyya A (2021) Socially distanced or socially connected? Well-being through ICT usage among the Indian elderly during COVID-19. Millennial Asia 12(2):190–208. https://doi.org/10.1177/0976399621989910
4. Bellizzi S, Nivoli A, Lorettu L, Ronzoni AR (2020) Human rights during the COVID-19 pandemic: the issue of female genital mutilations. Public Health 185:53–54. https://doi.org/10.1016/j.puhe.2020.05.037
5. Brucki BM, Bagade T, Majeed T (2023) A health impact assessment of gender inequities associated with psychological distress during COVID19 in Australia's most locked down state—Victoria. BMC Public Health 23(1):233. https://doi.org/10.1186/s12889-022-14356-6
6. Cao W, Fang Z, Hou G, Han M, Xu X, Dong J, Zheng J (2020) The psychological impact of the COVID-19 epidemic on college students in China. Psychiatry Res 287:112934. https://doi.org/10.1016/j.psychres.2020.112934
7. Cheung YT, Chau PH, Yip PSF (2008) A revisit on older adults suicides and Severe Acute Respiratory Syndrome (SARS) epidemic in Hong Kong. Int J Geriatr Psychiatry 23(12):1231–1238. https://doi.org/10.1002/gps.2056
8. Christian MD, Devereaux AV, Dichter JR, Rubinson L, Kissoon N, Task Force for Mass Critical Care (2014) Introduction and executive summary: Care of the critically ill and injured during pandemics and disasters: CHEST consensus statement. Chest 146(4 Suppl):8S-34S. https://doi.org/10.1378/chest.14-0732
9. Community Mental-Health Digital platform MANAS launched by the Principal Scientific Adviser (n.d.) https://pib.gov.in/pib.gov.in/Pressreleaseshare.aspx?PRID=1711860. Accessed 19 Apr 2023

10. Coronavirus disease (COVID-19): Herd immunity, lockdowns and COVID-19 (n.d.) https://www.who.int/news-room/questions-and-answers/item/herd-immunity-lockdowns-and-covid-19. Accessed 26 Feb 2023
11. COVID-19: A Gender Lens (n.d.) United Nations population fund. https://www.unfpa.org/resources/covid-19-gender-lens. Accessed 1 Mar 2023
12. Damiano RF, Di Santi T, Beach S, Pan PM, Lucchetti AL, Smith FA, Forlenza OV, Fricchione GL, Miguel EC, Lucchetti G (2021) Mental health interventions following COVID-19 and other coronavirus infections: a systematic review of current recommendations and meta-analysis of randomized controlled trials. Revista Brasileira De Psiquiatria (Sao Paulo, Brazil: 1999) 43(6):665–678. https://doi.org/10.1590/1516-4446-2020-1582
13. Du J, Mayer G, Hummel S, Oetjen N, Gronewold N, Zafar A, Schultz J-H (2020) Mental health burden in different professions during the final stage of the COVID-19 lockdown in China: cross-sectional survey study. J Med Internet Res 22(12):e24240. https://doi.org/10.2196/24240
14. Dubey S, Biswas P, Ghosh R, Chatterjee S, Dubey MJ, Chatterjee S, Lahiri D, Lavie CJ (2020) Psychosocial impact of COVID-19. Diabetes Metab Syndr 14(5):779–788. https://doi.org/10.1016/j.dsx.2020.05.035
15. Elhai JD, Yang H, McKay D, Asmundson GJG (2020) COVID-19 anxiety symptoms associated with problematic smartphone use severity in Chinese adults. J Affect Disord 274:576–582. https://doi.org/10.1016/j.jad.2020.05.080
16. Eze C, Okafor N, Emmanuel EI, Iloka C, Eze C, Okafor N, Emmanuel EI, Iloka C (2023) Effects of Covid-19 pandemic on women's mental health: a critical review of literature. IntechOpen. https://doi.org/10.5772/intechopen.109109
17. Fawole OI, Okedare OO, Reed E (2021) Home was not a safe haven: women's experiences of intimate partner violence during the COVID-19 lockdown in Nigeria. BMC Women's Health 21(1):32. https://doi.org/10.1186/s12905-021-01177-9
18. Fu W, Wang C, Zou L, Guo Y, Lu Z, Yan S, Mao J (2020) Psychological health, sleep quality, and coping styles to stress facing the COVID-19 in Wuhan, China. Transl Psychiatry 10(1) Article 1. https://doi.org/10.1038/s41398-020-00913-3
19. Gender Based Violence in Nigeria During COVID 19 Crisis_The Shadow Pandemic.pdf (n.d.) https://nigeria.un.org/sites/default/files/2020-05/Gender%20Based%20Violence%20in%20Nigeria%20During%20COVID%2019%20Crisis_The%20Shadow%20Pandemic.pdf. Accessed 3 Mar 2023
20. Hall H (2020) The effect of the COVID-19 pandemic on healthcare workers' mental health. JAAPA 33(7):45. https://doi.org/10.1097/01.JAA.0000669772.78848.8c
21. Horesh D, Kapel Lev-Ari R, Hasson-Ohayon I (2020) Risk factors for psychological distress during the COVID-19 pandemic in Israel: loneliness, age, gender, and health status play an important role. Br J Health Psychol 25(4):925–933. https://doi.org/10.1111/bjhp.12455
22. Huber SG, Helm C (2020) COVID-19 and schooling: evaluation, assessment and accountability in times of crises—reacting quickly to explore key issues for policy, practice and research with the school barometer. Educ Assess Eval Acc 32(2):237–270. https://doi.org/10.1007/s11092-020-09322-y
23. Jay J, Bor J, Nsoesie EO, Lipson SK, Jones DK, Galea S, Raifman J (2020) Neighbourhood income and physical distancing during the COVID-19 pandemic in the United States. Nature Hum Behav 4(12), Article 12. https://doi.org/10.1038/s41562-020-00998-2
24. Jiao WY, Wang LN, Liu J, Fang SF, Jiao FY, Pettoello-Mantovani M, Somekh E (2020) Behavioral and emotional disorders in children during the COVID-19 epidemic. J Pediatr 221:264-266.e1. https://doi.org/10.1016/j.jpeds.2020.03.013
25. Jones K, Mallon S, Schnitzler K (2023) A scoping review of the psychological and emotional impact of the COVID-19 pandemic on children and young people. Illn Crisis Loss 31(1):175–199. https://doi.org/10.1177/10541373211047191
26. Kang L, Li Y, Hu S, Chen M, Yang C, Yang BX, Wang Y, Hu J, Lai J, Ma X, Chen J, Guan L, Wang G, Ma H, Liu Z (2020) The mental health of medical workers in Wuhan, China dealing with the 2019 novel coronavirus. Lancet Psychiatry 7(3):e14. https://doi.org/10.1016/S2215-0366(20)30047-X

27. Kirby T (2020) Efforts escalate to protect homeless people from COVID-19 in UK. Lancet Respir Med 8(5):447–449. https://doi.org/10.1016/S2213-2600(20)30160-0
28. Lee J (2020) Mental health effects of school closures during COVID-19. Lancet Child Adolesc Health 4(6):421. https://doi.org/10.1016/S2352-4642(20)30109-7
29. Lei L, Huang X, Zhang S, Yang J, Yang L, Xu M (2020) Comparison of prevalence and associated factors of anxiety and depression among people affected by versus people unaffected by quarantine during the COVID-19 epidemic in Southwestern China. Med Sci Monit 26. https://doi.org/10.12659/MSM.924609
30. Li D, Zhang D, Shao J, Qi X, Tian L (2014) A meta-analysis of the prevalence of depressive symptoms in Chinese older adults. Arch Gerontol Geriatr 58(1):1–9. https://doi.org/10.1016/j.archger.2013.07.016
31. Listings of WHO's response to COVID-19 (n.d.) https://www.who.int/news/item/29-06-2020-covidtimeline. Accessed 26 Feb 2023
32. Liu S, Yang L, Zhang C, Xiang Y-T, Liu Z, Hu S, Zhang B (2020) Online mental health services in China during the COVID-19 outbreak. Lancet Psychiatry 7(4):e17–e18. https://doi.org/10.1016/S2215-0366(20)30077-8
33. MoHFW | Home (n.d.) https://www.mohfw.gov.in/. Accessed 19 Apr 2023
34. Naser AY, Dahmash EZ, Al-Rousan R, Alwafi H, Alrawashdeh HM, Ghoul I, Abidine A, Bokhary MA, AL-Hadithi HT, Ali D, Abuthawabeh R, Abdelwahab GM, Alhartani YJ, Muhaisen HA, Dagash A (2020) Mental health status of the general population, healthcare professionals, and university students during 2019 coronavirus disease outbreak in Jordan: a cross-sectional study (p. 2020.04.09.20056374). medRxiv. https://doi.org/10.1101/2020.04.09.20056374
35. Older Europeans' experience of unmet health care during the COVID-19 pandemic (first wave) | BMC Health Services Research | Full Text (n.d.) https://bmchealthservres.biomedcentral.com/articles/10.1186/s12913-022-07563-9. Accessed 3 Mar 2023
36. Paczkowska A, Nowakowska E, Michalska J, Ficner H, Tyrchniewicz J, Szymański A, Wańkowicz K, Namyślak K, Gala A, Sulimiera Michalak S, Bryl W, Michalak M (2023) Impact of the COVID-19 pandemic and lockdown on mental health among the general population in Poland and on the availability of psychological support. Psychol Health Med 28(1):179–188. https://doi.org/10.1080/13548506.2022.2061719
37. Pan A, Liu L, Wang C, Guo H, Hao X, Wang Q, Huang J, He N, Yu H, Lin X, Wei S, Wu T (2020) Association of public health interventions with the epidemiology of the COVID-19 outbreak in Wuhan, China. JAMA 323(19):1915–1923. https://doi.org/10.1001/jama.2020.6130
38. Ping W, Zheng J, Niu X, Guo C, Zhang J, Yang H, Shi Y (2020) Evaluation of health-related quality of life using EQ-5D in China during the COVID-19 pandemic. PLoS One 15(6):e0234850. https://doi.org/10.1371/journal.pone.0234850
39. Prevention (n.d.) https://www.who.int/teams/mental-health-and-substance-use/treatment-care/mental-health-gap-action-programme/evidence-centre. Accessed 19 Apr 2023
40. Rangaswamy T, Grover S, Tyagi V, Bhan A (2022) How did the mental health care system in India respond to COVID 19 pandemic? Schizophrenia Bull Open 3(1):sgac043. https://doi.org/10.1093/schizbullopen/sgac043
41. Rashidi Fakari F, Simbar M (2020) Coronavirus pandemic and worries during pregnancy; a letter to editor. Arch Acad Emerg Med 8(1):e21
42. Rodríguez-Fernández P, González-Santos J, Santamaría-Peláez M, Soto-Cámara R, Sánchez-González E, González-Bernal JJ (2021) Psychological effects of home confinement and social distancing derived from COVID-19 in the general population—a systematic review. Int J Environ Res Public Health 18(12):6528. https://doi.org/10.3390/ijerph18126528
43. Sagar R, Singh S (2022) National tele-mental health program in India: a step towards mental health care for all? Indian J Psychiatry 64(2):117–119. https://doi.org/10.4103/indianjpsychiatry.indianjpsychiatry_145_22
44. Singh S, Roy D, Sinha K, Parveen S, Sharma G, Joshi G (2020) Impact of COVID-19 and lockdown on mental health of children and adolescents: a narrative review with recommendations. Psychiatry Res 293:113429. https://doi.org/10.1016/j.psychres.2020.113429

45. Skinner D, Tsheko N, Mtero-Munyati S, Segwabe M, Chibatamoto P, Mfecane S, Chandiwana B, Nkomo N, Tlou S, Chitiyo G (2006) Towards a definition of orphaned and vulnerable children. AIDS Behav 10(6):619–626. https://doi.org/10.1007/s10461-006-9086-6
46. Sojli E, Tham WW, Bryant R, McAleer M (2021) COVID-19 restrictions and age-specific mental health—U.S. probability-based panel evidence. Transl Psychiatry 11(1). Article 1. https://doi.org/10.1038/s41398-021-01537-x
47. Sugawara D, Masuyama A, Kubo T (2022) Socioeconomic impacts of the COVID-19 lockdown on the mental health and life satisfaction of the Japanese population. Int J Ment Heal Addict 20(3):1560–1574. https://doi.org/10.1007/s11469-020-00461-3
48. Takaku R, Yokoyama I (2021) What the COVID-19 school closure left in its wake: evidence from a regression discontinuity analysis in Japan. J Public Econ 195:104364. https://doi.org/10.1016/j.jpubeco.2020.104364
49. The Role of Telehealth in Reducing the Mental Health Burden from COVID-19 | Telemedicine and e-Health (n.d.) https://www.liebertpub.com/doi/10.1089/tmj.2020.0068. Accessed 5 mar 2023
50. Tsai J, Wilson M (2020) COVID-19: a potential public health problem for homeless populations. Lancet Public Health 5(4):e186–e187. https://doi.org/10.1016/S2468-2667(20)30053-0
51. Tucci V, Moukaddam N (2017) We are the hollow men: the worldwide epidemic of mental illness, psychiatric and behavioral emergencies, and its impact on patients and providers. J Emerg Trauma Shock 10(1):4. https://doi.org/10.4103/0974-2700.199517
52. Verma R, Balhara YPS, Gupta CS (2011) Gender differences in stress response: role of developmental and biological determinants. Ind Psychiatry J 20(1):4–10. https://doi.org/10.4103/0972-6748.98407
53. Vince G (2020) The world's largest refugee camp prepares for covid-19. BMJ 368:m1205. https://doi.org/10.1136/bmj.m1205
54. Wang Y, Kala MP, Jafar TH (2020) Factors associated with psychological distress during the coronavirus disease 2019 (COVID-19) pandemic on the predominantly general population: a systematic review and meta-analysis. PLoS One 15(12):e0244630. https://doi.org/10.1371/journal.pone.0244630
55. WHO Director-General's opening remarks at the media briefing on COVID-19—11 March 2020 (n.d.) https://www.who.int/director-general/speeches/detail/who-director-general-s-opening-remarks-at-the-media-briefing-on-covid-19---11-march-2020. Accessed 28 Feb 2023
56. WHO-2019-nCoV-SRH-Rights-2020.1-eng.pdf (n.d.) https://apps.who.int/iris/bitstream/handle/10665/331811/WHO-2019-nCoV-SRH-Rights-2020.1-eng.pdf. Accessed 28 Feb 2023
57. Xiong J, Lipsitz O, Nasri F, Lui LMW, Gill H, Phan L, Chen-Li D, Iacobucci M, Ho R, Majeed A, McIntyre RS (2020) Impact of COVID-19 pandemic on mental health in the general population: a systematic review. J Affect Disord 277:55–64. https://doi.org/10.1016/j.jad.2020.08.001
58. Zhang W, Wang K, Yin L, Zhao W, Xue Q, Peng M, Min B, Tian Q, Leng H, Du J, Chang H, Yang Y, Li W, Shangguan F, Yan T, Dong H, Han Y, Wang Y, Cosci F, Wang H (2020) Mental health and psychosocial problems of medical health workers during the COVID-19 epidemic in China. Psychother Psychosom 89(4):242–250. https://doi.org/10.1159/000507639
59. Zhang Y, Ma ZF (2020) Impact of the COVID-19 pandemic on mental health and quality of life among local residents in Liaoning Province, China: a cross-sectional study. Int J Environ Res Public Health 17(7):2381. https://doi.org/10.3390/ijerph17072381

The manufacturer's authorised representative in the EU is Springer Nature Customer Service Centre GmbH, Europaplatz 3, 69115 Heidelberg, Germany. If you have any concerns regarding our products, please contact ProductSafety@springernature.com

Printed and bound by CPI Group (UK) Ltd, Croydon, CR0 4YY
30/09/2026
02225319-0013